GUIDE TO PHILOSOPHY

GUIDE TO PHILOSOPHY

by

C. E. M. JOAD

Head of the Department of Philosophy and
Psychology, Birkbeck College
University of London

LONDON
VICTOR GOLLANCZ LTD
1953

First published January 1936
Second impression January 1936
Third impression February 1936
Fourth impression April 1936
Fifth impression January 1937
Sixth impression February 1938
Seventh impression December 1939
Eighth impression January 1941
Ninth impression October 1941
Tenth impression September 1942
Eleventh impression June 1943
Twelfth impression October 1944
Thirteenth impression January 1946
Fourteenth impression September 1946
Fifteenth impression May 1948
Sixteenth impression May 1953

PRINTED IN GREAT BRITAIN BY PURNELL AND SONS, LTD. (T.U.)
PAULTON (SOMERSET) AND LONDON

CONTENTS

* It is suggested that the chapters marked with an asterisk
should be omitted in a first reading.

* It is suggested that the chapters marked with an asterisk
should be omitted in a first reading

* It is suggested that the chapters marked with an asterisk should be omitted in a first reading.

INTRODUCTION

IT IS USUAL to introduce a book on philosophy intended for the general reader with some account of the subject matter of philosophy, the nature of its results and the methods which it pursues. The reader is told that he will not be made free of any definite and agreed body of knowledge ; he is warned that philosophers frequently do not even discuss the same questions and that, when they do, it is only to give diametrically opposite answers ; and he is informed that he will be asked to take part not in a steady and ordered advance from speculation to knowledge but in a series of marches and counter-marches, in the course of which he will traverse and retraverse the same territory in the company of travellers whose concern seems less to arrive at a goal than to obliterate the footsteps of their predecessors. It is conceivable that, if the book is of the lighter sort, he may be regaled at this point with a gibe about blind men searching in dark rooms for non-existent black cats. Nevertheless, and in spite of these drawbacks, it will be clearly intimated to him that the value of philosophy is, indeed, very great, although it happens to be rather difficult to say what it is.

I propose to forgo this kind of Introduction, partly because I have already written elsewhere[1] of the value and methods of philosophy, but also because I propose to pay my readers the compliment of assuming that those who have decided to embark upon the reading of a book of these dimensions have already made up their own minds as to the value, at any rate for them, of the task they have taken in hand.

Nevertheless, although I have judged a general disquisition upon the nature, scope and methods of philosophy to be superfluous, I owe my readers a few pages of introduction in explanation of the nature, scope and methods

[1] See my *Return to Philosophy*, Chapters VII and IX.

of this book. I want, in a word, to say what I have tried to do and how I have tried to do it.

I have not sought to cover the whole field of philosophy; I have not tried to bring in all the philosophers—not even all the great philosophers—and I have not dealt fully with the work of any single philosopher. My object has been to provide a general survey of the main field of philosophy; to introduce in the course of the survey the chief problems that philosophers discuss, to show why they discuss them and to give some illustrations of the methods by which their discussions are pursued. In carrying out this undertaking, I have sought to observe two conditions; the first, that no philosophical theory should be included which was not intrinsically important and interesting on its own account; the second, that no philosophical theory should be included which was not capable of being made intelligible to the educated layman who, possessing no previous acquaintance with philosophy, was yet prepared to accord his best attention to the subject and his best patience to its expositor.

The first condition needs no defence; the second requires a few words of explanation. Philosophy is an exceedingly difficult subject and cannot with the best will in the world be made into an easy one. For one thing, the understanding of philosophy is frequently found to entail some knowledge of a number of other subjects. Physics and theology, history and biology, aesthetics and literature—all these are intermittent grist to the philosopher's mill, and he who would follow its grindings must have at least a nodding acquaintance with them. For another, it is exceedingly abstract. There are many, and they are not by any means the most stupid of our species, who will always find philosophy largely unintelligible. The twists and turns of the speculative reason, the hair-splitting distinctions, the abstractness of the thinking, the remoteness of the conclusions reached from the interests of ordinary life, the absence of agreed results—all these cannot but seem to many at best a monument of energy misplaced, at worst an irritating perversion of the powers and faculties of the human mind.

But there are others who, by nature addicted to philosophising, are nevertheless, kept at arm's length by the habits of philosophers. A natural taste for speculation has too often been repelled by the difficulty and obscurity of professional speculators. In my view some part of this difficulty and obscurity is unnecessary. In Chapter XX I have ventured to make a distinction between two kinds of obscurity—obscurity of expression and the expression of obscurity. The latter, I point out, is pardonable and, perhaps, inevitable. There is no necessary reason—at least I know of none—why the universe should be readily comprehensible by a twentieth-century mind, or why persons of average capacity should be enabled easily to grasp the thoughts of the profoundest intelligences that life has yet succeeded in evolving. The human mind, after all, has only just got under way. It is very little that we know about the universe, and, as we are beginning to realise, the more we enlarge the area of the known, the more also we enlarge its area of contact with the unknown. And the unknown is also the obscure. . . . But obscurity of expression is simply bad craftsmanship. A philosopher should, like anybody else, study to make himself understood, and, if his failure is due to slovenly writing or to inadequate mastery of the arts of exposition, no profundity or originality of thought will excuse him from censure.

Writing primarily for the intelligent layman, I have taken special pains to be intelligible. I have, for example, endeavoured never to introduce a technical term without first explaining the precise sense in which it is being used. I have reduced footnotes to a minimum. In particular, I have omitted all footnotes containing chapter and page references to the quotations from the works of philosophers which appear in the text, and have limited such references to the pages of this book. To make up for this, I have appended at the end of each chapter what will, I hope, prove a useful bibliography, containing a short list of the books which can be most fruitfully consulted by those who wish to follow up the various subjects raised in the chapter.

It is, however, in determining the general plan and arrangement of the book that the insistence upon clarity of exposition has exercised the most decisive influence. Rejecting the chronological method, I have tried to follow what appeared to me to be the logical divisions of the subject, basing my arrangement of chapters upon relevances of thought rather than upon the personalities of thinkers, and allocating different groups of related topics to different chapters. The general arrangement is broadly as follows. I have begun with the problems which constitute part of what is known as epistemology or theory of knowledge. What sort of knowledge do we have of the external world ? How far can the claims of sense experience to reveal a world like that which we normally suppose ourselves to inhabit be substantiated ? If the knowledge yielded by sense experience seems dubious, what other kinds of knowledge have we ? Can reasoning give us knowledge ? If so, what are the conditions which reasoning must satisfy, if it is to do so ?

I then pass to Part II, which I have entitled Critical Metaphysics. In this part commonsense conceptions such as those of substance, change, mechanism, purpose, cause and the Self are subjected to critical examination. They are found to give a poor account of themselves—so poor, as to render it unlikely that the world to which they are normally supposed to belong and in which common sense supposes them to be valid, is the real world.

This brings us to the distinction between the world as it really is and the world as it appears, the celebrated distinction between Appearance and Reality. If the world as it appears to common sense is not the world as it really is, how is the real world to be conceived ? In the last and longest part of the book, entitled Constructive Metaphysics, I have outlined some of the answers supplied by the great philosophers to this question. Apart altogether from the question of their truth, the philosophical systems of Plato, Kant and Hegel are among the most notable productions of the human mind, and those who wish to know what great men have thought and said memorably about the universe and man's place in it may find the reading of these chapters a not unhelpful introduction to the works of these philosophers. At the end of this part, I have endeavoured, in chapters dealing with Materialism, Dialectical and Scientific, and the philosophies of Bergson and Whitehead, to give some account of the problems that bulk largely in contemporary discussion, notably those set for philosophy by the developments of modern science.

In the course of carrying out this plan I have endeavoured to say something about most of the questions which are commonly raised in philosophical discussion. There are, however, some absentees, which I have been compelled to omit owing to my inability to deal with them in a manner which would satisfy the condition of clarity of exposition I have set myself to observe. In the first two parts of the book the issues raised are treated on merits, and the views of particular philosophers are introduced only when they happen to be peculiarly relevant to the problem under discussion. Thus Hume's criticism of the notion of cause is given in the chapter on *Causation*, and Aristotle's doctrine of Form and Matter is presented in the chapter on *Substance and its Qualities*. In these two parts I have proceeded on the assumption that the themes of philosophy are more important than the philosophers who propounded them and the dates at which they were propounded, and the thought of particular philosophers is introduced, therefore, only in order to illustrate the themes. On coming to the systems of the great philosophers in Part III, I have not as a general rule criticised the views expounded. In some instances, however, for example in the case of Aristotle's criticism of Plato's theory of Ideas and the criticism which modern Realism has brought against the idealist account of perception, the criticism is not less historically important than the theory criticised. In others, for example in the case of the pragmatists' criticism of the Hegelian Absolute and the theory of truth which it entails, the criticism forms the starting-point of a new school. In special cases of this kind I have included the criticisms along with the views criticised. I have, however, usually abstained from criticisms of my own; usually, but not always—a point which brings me to the question of bias.

My concern being to expound the views of others, I have sought, so far as possible, to suppress my own. The attempt has, I think, been in the main successful. But it is not humanly possible always to maintain a complete impartiality where one's own views are concerned, and I am conscious that there are one or two places where it has broken down. In the treatment of the theory of Subsistent Objects in Chapter XI and in the development of Plato's theory of Ideas in relation to the philosophy of aesthetics, my own philosophical opinions have insisted on intruding themselves and views have been expressed which, I fear, own little better authority than that of the author. Bias, if inevitable in philosophy, is less harmful when avowed, and I have done my best to make amends for these lapses by giving the reader due warning when the passages in question are about to occur.

In pursuance of the same policy, I had better make avowal here and now of such philosophical beliefs as I hold. My general predilections are in favour of some form of Realism and Pluralism. I am not, that is to say, an idealist who believes that mind or thought is the only reality, and I do not think that the arguments which philosophers have advanced in favour of supposing that the universe is in some important sense a whole or unity are convincing. I am not, however, a materialist, since I hold that mind is a real and unique factor in the universe. Mind and matter are, I am inclined to hold, both distinct and irreducible reals, and I should be disposed to extend the bounds of reality to include elements of value such as are envisaged by Plato's theory of Ideas. My general philosophical views have, in fact, been more influenced by Plato than by any other philosopher. Among the moderns, the earlier philosophical writings of Bertrand Russell have chiefly influenced me.

Every philosophy is open to the charge of giving more

information about the philosopher than about the universe. I do not myself believe this charge to be a true one, but no philosopher would wish to deny that an element of the personal, of personal hopes and wishes, personal temperament and training, personal disposition and desire, is inevitably embedded in every philosophy. Nor can it be entirely excluded from an exposition which seeks to confine itself to giving an account of the philosophies of others. Some bias, then, there is bound to be ; I am sorry for it, but I cannot help it.

I said at the outset that I did not propose to defend the pursuit of philosophising or to give reasons why philosophy should be studied. One expression of opinion, however, I propose to permit myself. The attraction of philosophy consists, I think, very largely in its catholicity. The philosopher seeks to comprehend the universe as a whole, not, like the physicist or the biologist, a special department of it, but the whole mass of data to which the moral intuitions of the ordinary man, the religious consciousness of the saint, the aesthetic enjoyment of the artist, and the history of the human race, no less than the discoveries of the physicist and the biologist, contribute. The disadvantage of such a form of enquiry is the lack of established results. Philosophy has no agreed body of knowledge to offer, and many will be inclined to be impatient with its inconclusiveness.

Many, but not all ; for some, the very inconclusiveness of philosophy is its attraction. It is not knowledge but the quest for it which they find exciting, and there would seem to them to be something trite and obvious about a universe which permitted itself to be wholly known. It is pleasant to keep alive the sense of wonder by contemplating the richness and the strangeness of the world ; it is no less pleasant to contemplate the varieties of men's minds. Just as it takes all sorts of men to make a world, so does it take all sorts of minds to make the truth about the world. In the present age, when applied science has done much to rob the visible world of mystery and wonder, and forms of government have ironed out the variety of men's minds and frowned upon the exercise of the free intelligence, philosophy has a special value. In the pursuit of philosophy the human mind swings free. Untrammelled by limitations of subject matter, unaffected by the temporal and the particular, it recognises no laws save those which govern its own reasoning. This disinterested activity of the freely functioning mind is a good, among the greatest that human beings can enjoy. It is natural to feel curious about the universe in which we find ourselves, and the effort to satisfy our curiosity, even if it can never be wholly successful, is never wholly void of satisfaction. As the English philosopher F. H. Bradley has said, metaphysics may be " the finding of bad reasons for what we believe upon instinct ; but to find these reasons is no less an instinct." In the last resort, then, the reason for the study of philosophy is the satisfaction which it brings. If this book succeeds in communicating to its readers some part of the satisfaction which philosophy has given to its writer, it will not have been written in vain.

In spite of my determination to be at all costs simple and clear, I fear that some of the ensuing pages will provide rather stiff reading for those who are approaching philosophy for the first time. I have accordingly placed an asterisk against the more difficult chapters, and would suggest that they should be omitted on a first reading.

———

My thanks are due to the following for kindly reading through various chapters in manuscript, and for making valuable suggestions which I have adopted : Professor L. S. Stebbing (Chapter V), Mr. H. B. Acton (Chapters XIV and XV), Mr. H. W. Durant (Chapter XVII) and Miss Dorothy Emmet (Chapter XX). Dr. A. C. Ewing has also helped me with some of the earlier part of the book. The above are, however, in no sense responsible for any of the views expressed.

I have also to thank the Oxford University Press for permission to reprint in Chapters XVI and XIX certain passages which have already appeared in my *Introduction to Modern Philosophy*.

C. E. M. JOAD

Hampstead, *August 1935*.

GUIDE TO PHILOSOPHY

PART I
THEORY OF KNOWLEDGE

CHAPTER I : WHAT DO WE KNOW OF THE OUTSIDE WORLD?

1. The Problem Stated

Introductory. It is not easy to decide how to begin a book on philosophy. Philosophical problems are closely bound up with one another ; so closely, that some philosophers think that a completely satisfactory solution of any one of them would entail the solution of them all. Whether this is so we cannot tell, since it is extremely unlikely that a completely satisfactory solution of any one of them will be reached by the human mind in the present state of its development. It is, however, true that most philosophical questions are found sooner or later to raise the same problems. In philosophy all roads lead if not to the same Rome, at least into the same maze, so that it is a matter of not very great moment which you choose at the outset of your journey.

But the fact that there is no very good reason for choosing one rather than another makes it very difficult to choose any, as the logical ass of the philosopher Buridan[1] (1300-1350), placed between two equally large and equally succulent bundles of hay, is said to have starved because of an inability to discover any reason why he should proceed in the direction of one rather than of the other.

On reflection I have decided to begin with the problem of sense perception ; not because it is any easier or any nearer to solution than any other philosophical problem, but because it entails a consideration of issues which people

[1] Actually the illustration of the ass does not appear anywhere in Buridan's writings. It is, however, always associated with him. A similar image appears in Dante's *Paradiso*, and the conceit seems to have been a popular one in the Middle Ages.

can explore for themselves : can, and to some extent do, since, of all philosophical conclusions, the conclusion that the outside world is not really " there " or is not really " real " is most familiar to, and most frequently derided by, the non-philosophical. But whether people deride it, dismiss it, or embrace it for the controversial discomfiture of their friends, they are at least familiar with it.

Commonsense View of External World.

The problem may be stated fairly simply in the form of a number of questions. What kind of information do our sense organs give us about the external world? Is it reliable information? If it is, what is the nature of the objects about which we receive it? Of what sort of things, in other words, is the external world composed? Common sense answers these questions without much hesitation on the following lines. (1) The external world, it declares, consists of substances which possess qualities ; for example, of wood which is hard or soft, of metal which is yellow or silver. (2) These substances we perceive in the form of physical objects such as chairs and tables, gold rings and silver shillings—unless we happen to be scientists, when we perceive what are, presumably, more fundamental substances such as chemical compounds and molecules of which the ordinary substances are composed, and should perceive, if our instruments were delicate enough, which they are not, substances more fundamental still such as atoms and electrons. (3) Physical objects are " out there " in the world and are revealed to us by our senses exactly as they are. In particular, they are not dependent for their existence upon our perception of them. When our sense organs, eyes, ears or noses, are brought into suitable spatial relations with them, then we are said to know them. But common sense would hold that that which actually *knows* is not itself a sense organ, but is the mind or consciousness. The sense organs, it would be said, are the channels by which knowledge of physical objects is conveyed to the mind.

Now each one of the above propositions is denied by many

philosophers, and, although it is by no means clear what propositions ought to be substituted for them, it is reasonably certain that, in the form in which I have just stated them, none of them is true. The first proposition, that the world consists of substances possessing qualities, will be considered in Chapter VI. The consideration of the second and the third which are largely interdependent brings us to the problem of sense perception. In the present chapter we shall be mainly concerned with the third proposition, which asserts that the physical objects which we perceive are " out there " in the world, and are in no sense dependent upon our perception of them for their existence. Most philosophers have held that they are not " out there " in the world in any ordinary sense, and many have come to the conclusion that they are in some sense dependent for their existence upon the mind or minds which perceive them. Other philosophers, while maintaining that *something* exists in the world outside ourselves which is not dependent upon our minds for its existence, have, nevertheless, adduced good reasons for denying that this " something " is in the least like the physical objects with which, if the common-sense account of the matter is to be believed, we are in contact. They have, that is to say, denied the second of the three propositions asserted above. With the reasons for this latter denial we shall be concerned in the second chapter.

What do our Senses Reveal ?   Let us call the objects of which, common sense would say, our senses make us aware sensible objects. What do our senses tell us about them ? At first sight it seems that they tell us a great deal ; but on reflection we find that much of the information which our senses seem to give us relates not to what is going on outside ourselves, but to what is going on inside ourselves, not to sensible objects, but to our own experiences.

Let us suppose that I press my tongue against my teeth and ask the question : " What is it that I experience or am aware of ? " At first sight the answer would appear to be :

"I am aware of my teeth." But is this answer really correct? Is not what I *really* experience a feeling in my tongue—a feeling caused perhaps by the contact between tongue and teeth, but a feeling nevertheless, and since it *is* a feeling, something that is mental? Suppose now, that I press my fingers against the table, is what I experience the table? Again, the obvious answer proves on examination to be doubtful. The *immediate* object of my experience, that of which I am directly aware, is, many would say, a sensation in my fingers, a sensation of smoothness, hardness, and coolness.

Let us take a further example. If I stand two feet away from the fire, I experience heat, and common sense tells me that this heat is a property of the fire. If, however, I move nearer to the fire, the heat increases in intensity, until it becomes pain. Now, the pain is clearly in me and not in the fire ; since, then, the pain is only a more intense degree of the heat, the inference is that the heat also was a sensation of mine, and not a property of the fire. The leg of a cheese mite is so small that, except with the aid of a microscope, we cannot see it. Are we, then, to suppose that the cheese mite cannot see its own leg? This seems unlikely. We must infer, then, that the apparent size of the cheese mite's leg varies according to the nature of the mind perceiving it— that the leg, in fact, has one apparent size for the cheese mite and another for ourselves. But the leg cannot have two different sizes at the same time. Has it, then, any *real* size at all? May it not rather be the case that size is not an intrinsic[1] quality of the object seen, a quality possessed by it in its own right, but is relative to and dependent upon the nature of the perceiver's mind.

The Case of the Steeple.　　Let us consider the case of size in a little more detail. I am, we will suppose, looking at a church steeple. Its height appears to vary according to the distance from which I view it. It appears, for example, to have one height from a distance of half a mile, another

---

[1] For a definition of " intrinsic " see below, p. 52.

from a distance of a hundred yards, and another from a distance of five yards, while, if I stand right underneath it, I am unable to estimate its height at all. There are thus a number of different heights which the steeple *appears* to have. How am I to tell which one of them is or represents its *real* height? The commonsense answer would probably be, by applying a measuring rod or tape-measure or whatever apparatus is normally used for measuring steeples, and noting the reading on the apparatus in question. Let us suppose that the reading on the piece of apparatus—we will call it a tape-measure—is 150 feet. Then we shall say that 150 feet is the *real* height of the steeple. But will this answer bear investigation? For practical purposes no doubt it will; but for philosophical ones it will not.

In the first place, we have admitted that the steeple *appears* to have different heights to different observers situated at different distances. What we want to know is, which one of these different appearances really *is* its height. Now, 150 feet is one of these heights, the height, namely, which it appears to have to a tape-measure extended to the whole of its very considerable length along the outside of the steeple. But why should the tape-measure be accorded the title of a privileged observer, and why should the position immediately contiguous to the outside wall be regarded as a privileged position, so that we are entitled to say that *to an observer occupying that position alone* is the *real* height revealed?

Secondly, what sort of information does a reading of 150 feet really give us? We want to know what is the real height of the steeple and we are informed that it is 150 feet. But what is 150 feet? It is a mathematical expression, a name that we give to certain sorts of height, for example to the height possessed by the steeple. Thus, when we want to know what is the real height of the steeple we are told that it is 150 feet, and when we want to know what 150 feet is, we find that it is the sort of height which the steeple, and whatever other things happen to be exactly as tall as the steeple are said to possess. Our information, in fact, is purely circular.

Thirdly, what account are we to give of the tape-measure itself? We have cited a number of illustrations above to suggest that the qualities apparently possessed by sensible objects do not belong to them in actual fact, but are either qualities of our own experience or, since our experience of them varies, are at any rate dependent upon and determined by our experience. But if this is so, we have no right to assume that a tape-measure is exempt from the conclusions suggested by the previous analysis, that it *really* owns in its own right the qualities that it appears to own, and that in particular it has a length which *really* is its length. If we may assume without question these facts about the tape-measure, there would be no need to raise questions about the height of the steeple. But whatever reasons there are for doubting whether the steeple *really* has a height are equally good reasons for doubting whether the tape-measure *really* has a length. We cannot in short establish the *real* height of the steeple by reference to the *real* length of the tape-measure, for it is precisely the meaning of the words " real height " and " real length " that is in doubt.

The Shape of the Penny.   As with height so with shape. Let us consider as an example the shape of a penny. Common sense supposes the shape to be circular, but from almost any point of view from which the penny is looked at, the penny appears, as we quickly find out when we try to draw it, to be elliptical, the ellipses which we perceive varying in degrees of fatness and thinness according to the angle of vision from which we view the penny. From two positions only does the penny appear to be circular, and these, namely, the position vertically above and the position vertically below the penny, are rather peculiar positions which are comparatively rarely occupied by the human eye.

If the shape of the penny normally appears to be elliptical, why do we call it circular? It is not easy to say.

In the first instance, perhaps, because of the prevalence of a general belief to the effect that it *is* circular, a belief so widespread and deep-seated that anyone who questioned it outside a philosophical discussion would be regarded as imperfectly sane. But how did this general belief arise ? On what is it based ? Probably it rests at bottom upon the fact that the penny conforms in respect of many of its attributes to the definition of a circle. There is, for example, a point on its surface such that all lines drawn from that point to the circumference are of equal length : its circumference again is equal to $2\pi r$, its area to πr^2. But, if we take our stand on this definition, similar difficulties arise to those which we considered in the case of the steeple. What we want to know is the nature of the shape to which these mathematical properties belong ? If we answer that it is a *circular* shape the question arises, does a penny have it ? Unfortunately the penny as usually seen does not. Nor does the penny as touched ; to feel a penny is not to feel a circular shape but either a flat surface or, if a finger is crooked round its edge, a curving line of metal. Hence, to touch and to sight the penny does not normally *appear* to be circular. But to what, then, does it *appear* to be circular ? Presumably to a pair of compasses. But why should its appearance to a pair of compasses, or if the expression be preferred, the reaction of a pair of compasses to it, be presumed to acquaint us with its *real* shape, in some sense in which its appearance to eyes and fingers does not acquaint us with its real shape ? Why in fact are the compasses privileged " observers " ? Moreover, what are we to say of the properties of the pair of compasses ? Can we, when the existence of physical objects possessing properties in their own right is in question, steal the answer to the question in the case of the compasses in order not to beg it in the case of the penny ?

As it is with texture and temperature, as with size and shape, so is it with most, if not all, of the qualities which apparently belong to objects in the external world. In regard to most, if not to all, of these apparent qualities we can truly say that in the last resort they turn out to be relative to ourselves. We have only, for example, to raise the temperatures of our bodies a few degrees, and the world will look different. Still more obviously will it feel different. Yet there is no reason why that world alone should be privileged to be considered real which is perceived by a normal, Nordic adult possessing a body which is heated to a temperature of 98·4 degrees.

Implications of Modern Science.   The force of these considerations, in so far as they purport to show the relativity to the perceiver of the qualities apparently existing in the external world, is considerably strengthened by the information which science in general and the sciences of physics and physiology in particular have obtained in regard to the machinery of perception. Before, however, we indicate the bearing of the conclusions of modern science upon the problems under consideration, it is necessary to guard ourselves against misinterpretation by the introduction of a word of warning.

In the first place, the whole question of the relation between science and philosophy is controversial, and many philosophers would maintain that no results reached by science do have or can have any bearing upon philosophical problems.

In the second place, the philosophers whose line of thought I have during the course of the foregoing illustrations been mainly following and with whose general conclusion, namely, that the objects revealed to us in perception are in some sense dependent upon the mind of the perceiver, we are in this chapter mainly concerned, did not introduce scientific considerations into their arguments, or did so only to a very small extent. The philosophers in question (who are sometimes known as subjective idealists) are Locke (1632-1704), Berkeley (1685-1753) and Hume (1711-1776)[1] who lived in the seventeenth and eighteenth

_____
[1] The conclusions of their philosophies are indicated in greater detail below (see Chapter II, pp. 39-55).

centuries when the sciences of physics and physiology were comparatively immature, and as a general rule they developed their arguments without reference to such results as these sciences had achieved.

In the third place, it is doubtful whether, even if they had been fully conversant with the conclusions of twentieth century scientists, these philosophers would have been able consistently to use them in support of their general position. At least we are entitled to hope that they would have been too clear headed to have made what would in effect have been a serious elementary blunder. The reason for this doubt will be stated in its proper place,[1] after the positions which these philosophers maintained have been summarised.

So much having been said by way of qualification and reservation, I propose to enumerate certain considerations afforded by the conclusions of modern science which tend to reinforce the view that the qualities of the objects which we know in sense experience do not belong to them in their own right, but depend in a large measure upon conditions prevailing in the perceiver. Hitherto it has been with the part played by the perceiver's mind that we have been chiefly concerned. We are now under the direction of science to emphasise rather the influence of the perceiver's body in determining what we perceive.

The Physiologist's Account of the Machinery of Perception.

Let us suppose that I am looking at a star, Sirius say, on a dark night. If physics is to be believed, light waves which started to travel from Sirius many years ago reach (after a specified time which astronomers calculate) the earth, impinge upon my retinas and cause me to say that I am seeing Sirius. Now the Sirius about which they convey information to me is the Sirius which existed at the time when they started. This Sirius, may, however, no longer exist ; it may have disappeared in the interval. To say that one can see what no longer exists is absurd.

[1] See Chapter II, pp. 58, 59.

It follows that, whatever it is that I am seeing, it is not Sirius. What, in fact, I do see is a yellow patch of a particular size, shape and intensity. I infer that this yellow patch had an origin (with which it is connected by a continuous chain of physical events) several years ago and many million miles away. But this inference may be mistaken ; the origin of the yellow patch, which I call a star, may be a blow on the nose, or a lamp hanging on the mast of a ship.

Nor is this the only inference involved. It is true that I *think* I am seeing a yellow patch, but am I really justified in holding this belief ? So far as physics and physiology are concerned, all that I am entitled to say is that my optic nerve is being stimulated in a certain way, as a result of which certain events are being caused in my brain. Am I really justified in saying any more than this ?

In a celebrated example Bertrand Russell cites the case of a physiologist examining the brain of his patient. The physiologist undoubtedly believes himself to be looking at the brain of another person ; yet, Russell points out, if physiology is correct in what it asserts, the *cause* of his seeing must be something which is happening in his own. Russell's account of the process is as follows : " Light waves travel from the brain that is being observed to the eye of the physiologist, at which they only arrive after an interval of time, which is finite though short. The physiologist sees what he is observing only after the light waves have reached his eye ; therefore the event which constitutes his seeing comes at the end of a series of events which travel from the observed brain into the brain of the physiologist. We cannot, without a preposterous kind of discontinuity, suppose that the physiologist's percept, which comes at the end of this series, is anywhere else but in the physiologist's head." When we reflect that, during the period of time which is occupied by the occurrence of the series of events which precede the physiologist's seeing, the patient's brain may have gone out of existence, the difficulty of supposing that the physiologist is really looking at a brain outside his own becomes very great.

Touch and Smell.

Perception by touch makes the matter even plainer. Let us consider in a little more detail the case of a person who presses his fingers against the table. I am doing it now, as I write. Ordinarily I should say that there was contact between two material substances, my fingers and the table. Modern physics, however, lends no countenance to this view. What happens according to the physicist is that electrical repulsion is developed between the atoms composing the finger and those composing the table. The harder I press the table, the stronger are the electrical forces which repel my finger. These electrical forces set up in the nerve endings at the tip of my finger a current which reaches my brain, as the result of which I experience the sensation of touching the table. In fact, however, I am not in contact with any object outside my body and, if appropriate parts of my nervous system are suitably stimulated, I shall experience the same sensation of touching the table, although there is no table to touch. What is more, I can experience what appears to be a sensation of a pin prick in the non-existent finger of a hand which has been amputated, provided that the nerve terminals in my arm are suitably manipulated.

As with sight and touch, so with smell. I doubt very much whether even common sense assumes that the smell of a body is something which really belongs to it. Most people would probably agree that a thing's smell is at least not *in the same place* as that which is occupied by the thing. It is, they would say, something which the thing gives off —most people, I imagine, think of smell as a sort of gas composed of molecules—and it is only when the gas reaches the place where one's nostrils are and the molecules of which it is composed stimulate the sensitive tissues inside the nostrils, that certain nervous impulses are despatched to the brain, as a result of which we have the

Bp

sensation of smelling.[1] But the connection of this " something," the smell which is smelt, with the object which is
thought to have originated it remains vague. Similarly
with sound ! Waves travel through the atmosphere and
impinge on the ear drums. Complex events take place in
the outer, middle and inner ears. In the inner ear, for
example, there is a shell-like bony receptacle, the cochlea,
filled with fluid. When the vibrations of the bones and
membranes in the middle ear reach the cochlea, the fluid is
agitated. The agitation of the fluid imparts a swaying
motion to certain long, hair-like threads, the cilia ranged
along the inside of the cochlea. The swaying cilia send
neural impulses to the brain, as a result of which we hear
a sound. But if we were to ask where or what is the sound
that is heard, it is extremely difficult to answer.

Eddington's Idealist Conclusion.   The teaching of
physics and physiology with regard to the machinery of
perception seems to point to the conclusion that what
we actually know, when we have sensory experience, are
not the movements of matter, but certain events in ourselves
connected with or produced by these movements ; not
objects external to ourselves, but the effects of the impact
of light rays, gases, atmospheric waves and other forms of
energy proceeding from these objects upon our bodies.

The following quotation from Sir Arthur Eddington's
book *Science and the Unseen World* clearly indicates how
large a part of what we know of the external world is conceded by a modern physicist—and in this respect, at least,
Eddington's views are in no sense unrepresentative—to be
inferred by our minds, instead of being directly perceived
by our senses.

" Consider," says Sir Arthur Eddington, " how our supposed acquaintance with a lump of matter is attained.
Some influence emanating from it plays on the extremity

[1] In fact, odorous substances must be dissolved in the moisture which
covers the nasal mucous membrane, before they can evoke the sensation
of smell.

of a nerve starting a series of physical and chemical changes which are propagated along the nerve to a brain cell ; there a mystery happens, and an image or sensation arises in the mind which cannot purport to resemble the stimulus which excites it. Everything known about the material world must in one way or another have been inferred from these stimuli transmitted along the nerves. . . . The mind as a central receiving station reads the dots and dashes of the incoming nerve-signals. By frequent repetition of their call-signals the various transmitting stations of the outside world become familiar. We begin to feel quite a homely acquaintance with 2LO and 5XX. But a broadcasting station is not *like* its call-signal ; there is no commensurability in their natures. So, too, the chairs and tables around us which broadcast to us incessantly those signals which affect our sight and touch cannot in their nature be like unto the signals or to the sensations which the signals awake at the end of their journey. . . . It is an astonishing feat of deciphering that we should have been able to infer an orderly scheme of natural knowledge from such indirect communication."

From these considerations Sir Arthur Eddington proceeds to derive conclusions which, as the reader will see in the next chapter, are almost indistinguishable from those of idealist philosophers. Having stressed the roundabout and inferential character of our knowledge of the external world, he proceeds to contrast it with the directness and immediacy of our knowledge of ourselves.

" Clearly," he continues, " there is one kind of knowledge which cannot pass through such channels, namely, knowledge of the intrinsic nature of that which lies at the far end of the lines of communication."

This is not an inferred knowledge of outside things from the messages which they send us over the telephone lines of nervous communication ; it is knowledge of something as it is in itself. And this something as it is in itself, the one thing we know directly as it really is, turns out to be mental ; it is a mind. " Mind," Sir Arthur Eddington concludes,

" is the first and most direct thing in our experience ; all else is remote inference." We have, he adds, an acquaintance with the " mental and spiritual nature of ourselves, known in our minds by an intimate contact transcending the methods of physics."

Significance of Conclusions derived from Science.

I do not wish to suggest that the above conclusion is necessarily true. As we shall see below,[1] any philosophy which asserts, as the subjective idealists did, that the objects which we know in perception are existent in or even dependent upon the mind of the perceiver is precluded from making use of any of the considerations upon which the scientist's conclusions are based. I have introduced the scientific account of perception at this stage because my present purpose is to accumulate considerations, from whatever source they may be derived, which militate against the commonsense view that the external world is composed of physical objects possessing qualities in their own right, which by a sort of divine revelation are presented to the mind exactly as they are. Whether we emphasise the part played by the mind in the process of perception or by the body and the sense organs, it seems almost impossible to resist the view that the qualities of the world we perceive depend very largely upon ourselves. For how otherwise, it may be asked, are we to explain the fact of differing perceptions of the same thing. If X sees a delphinium blue, and Y, who is colour-blind, sees it green, it is very difficult to suppose that the delphinium is both green and blue at the same time. On the other hand there seems no good ground for affirming that it *really* is blue because it is blue to normal vision, and that its appearance to the colour-blind man is not, therefore, its *real* appearance, merely because the colour-blind man is in a minority. The plain implication seems to be that the difference between the apparent colours is due to a difference in the physiological machineries of the two perceivers. Moreover, if we place santonin in

[1] See Chapter II, p. 58.

our eyes, we see everything yellow. Since we cannot suppose that the alteration in our visual apparatus has produced a corresponding alteration in the world outside us, we can only conclude that the appearance of yellowness is the result of a peculiar condition of our visual organs. But, if this is true in regard to yellowness, there is no reason why it should not be true in regard to all the colours which we normally believe ourselves to perceive in the outside world.

———

RUSSELL, BERTRAND   The Problems of Philosophy   *Home University Library*.
   Chapters I–IV contain a clear elementary account of the problem of perception.

WISDOM, JOHN   Problems of Mind and Matter, Part II.
   Short and clear, but more difficult.

MOORE, G. E.   Philosophical Studies.
   May be consulted in connection with all the problems raised in this and the next two chapters. It is likely to become a classic, but is considerably more difficult than the books mentioned above.

A summary of the relevant information with regard to the machinery of perception obtained by the sciences will be found in Bertrand Russell's *An Outline of Philosophy*, Part II, and in my *Guide to Modern Thought*, Chapter IV.

CHAPTER II: WHAT DO WE KNOW OF THE OUTSIDE WORLD?

2. The Answer of Subjective Idealism

General Conclusion of Subjective Idealism. The philosophers who maintain that the qualities of the world which we perceive by means of our senses are dependent on the *mind* of the perceiver are known as subjective idealists. The form in which this conclusion is usually stated is that what we know, and in the long run all that we know, is our own mental states which the subjective idealists called " ideas." Thus the quality of warmth that I perceive in the fire, the quality of squareness I perceive in the chess-board would both be described by these philosophers as ideas in my mind. Their reasons for this conclusion were based very largely upon the considerations which we advanced in the first chapter to show the dependence of the qualities which we perceive in things upon states of the perceiver's consciousness. But they do not to any substantial extent make use of the *additional* arguments derived from the scientific account of the machinery of perception which seek to show the dependence of what we perceive upon states of our *bodies*, and it never occurred to them to say that *what* we perceive is analysable into events happening inside our bodies. Nor could it ; for the general conclusion of their line of thought was, as I have just said, that everything that we perceive reveals itself on analysis to be combinations of ideas in our own minds. Now, if this conclusion is true, our bodies and sense organs will also be our ideas in our own minds. I shall return to this point later.

Locke's Theory of Perception. Let us first briefly consider the historical development of the thought of the three philosophers, Locke, Berkeley, and Hume, which culminated in this conclusion. Locke (1632-1704) set out with the avowed intention of analysing human experience —what, he wanted to know, are the contents of our minds when we think—and of determining the limits of human knowledge—how much, he asked, can we know of the world outside us ? Broadly speaking his conclusion was that the mind thinks about its own ideas. By " idea " Locke meant " whatever is the object of the understanding, when a man thinks " or " whatever it is which the mind can be employed about in thinking." The ideas are of various kinds. For example, there are ideas of sensation which are supplied to us by our sense organs, and ideas of reflection, that is to say, ideas of the operations which the mind performs when it manipulates the ideas of sensa-tion, for example, in remembering, comparing, imagining and so forth. The ideas of sensation are the raw materials of all experience. The ideas of reflection constitute our consciousness of the operations which the mind performs upon the raw materials supplied by sensation.

The ideas of sensation are those chiefly relevant to our present enquiry. These, as has just been said, are the objects of the mind when it thinks. How they come to be in the mind Locke does not explain, but his general view is that they are the appearances or representations of outside things. Thus when a hot thing is brought into contact with the skin, and the resulting stimulus is transmitted to the brain, the occurrence in the brain produces in the mind the idea of heat—not, be it noted, of the hot thing, but of its heat. If the hot thing happened also to be red, and we saw it, there would be also produced in the mind the idea of redness. The idea of heat thus represents the temperature of a hot body, the idea of redness its colour, and these ideas are what the mind knows.

Thus the world of ideas constitutes a body of representa-tions of the qualities of real things. It is this world of ideas which the mind knows, and not the world of real things.

Primary and Secondary Qualities.   Primary qualities are those with which mathematicians and geometers are chiefly concerned, for example, extension in space, number, motion and solidity. These, Locke thought, do in fact belong to things in the external world, his reason for this view being that, whatever you do to things, they will still insist on exhibiting these qualities. Melt butter, for example, or burn wood ; their colours will change, but some shape, some degree of solidity, some weight and mass they will still possess. Secondary qualities, on the other hand, not only change with varying circumstances, but in certain circumstances vanish altogether. In other words, colour, taste and smell, which are examples of secondary qualities, may be possessed by things or they may not. For example, if there is no light, things will no longer possess the quality of being coloured. Secondary qualities, moreover, change as conditions in the perceiver change. If, for example, I have a cold, I shall not be able to smell.

Secondary qualities do not, then, really belong to bodies, and they are not, therefore, " out there " in the world. They are, said Locke, simply the " powers " which bodies possess of producing effects in us ; whether the effects will or will not be produced depends upon conditions prevailing in us.

Locke's Substance.   In addition to the primary qualities which bodies possess in their own right, Locke held that they also possess a substance. We do not, however, experience substance. Substance is one of the ideas of the mind, belonging to the class of what Locke called complex ideas. We find a number of ideas of simple qualities continuously going together. Accordingly, says Locke, we combine these ideas, give them a single name, and then proceed to invoke the notion of some support or substratum for the qualities in the thing which produced the simple ideas in us. This notion of " some support " is what Locke calls " Substance." An Indian philosopher declared that the world was supported by an elephant, the elephant by a tortoise, and the tortoise by he knew not what. Locke makes no difficulty about admitting that his substance is like the support of the Indian philosopher's tortoise. It is an obscure idea of some support, " we know not what " and " it is the same everywhere." Substance, then, in Locke's philosophy, is a something not itself experienced which lies at the base of, and supports the simple ideas of, heat, taste, colour, shape, extension and so forth, which are experienced, and which, because they are continuously found to go together, we regard as constituting a single thing.

Statement of Representationalism.

We are now in a position to sum up Locke's theory of perception. The theory is known as " Representationalism " because it asserts that we know not external things, but the representations, or copies, of external things in our own minds. These representations, or copies, are Locke's simple ideas. The external world consists of things which possess only primary qualities such as size, motion, number and extension, that is, occupancy of space. These things impinge upon our sense organs and cause representations or images of themselves to appear in consciousness. It is these representations or images, and not the external objects that produce them that the mind knows. But the representations, unlike the objects, are enriched by the mind with secondary qualities such as temperature and colour. The mind then proceeds to project the secondary qualities with which it has enriched the representations into the external world, supposing the objects to possess those characteristics which it has itself engendered. The mind is thus conceived after the model of a dark cabinet containing a brightly lit screen which is illuminated by the light of consciousness. Upon this screen our senses throw the images, or representations, of external things, and it is these that the mind knows, at the same time investing them with secondary qualities. The following quotation, a celebrated passage from Professor Whitehead's *Science and the Modern World*, admirably sums up Locke's view : " Thus the bodies are perceived as with qualities which in reality do not belong to them, qualities which in fact are purely the offspring of the mind. Thus nature gets credit which should in truth be reserved for ourselves : the rose for its scent : the nightingale for his song : and the sun for his radiance. The poets are entirely mistaken. They should address their lyrics to themselves, and should turn them into odes of self-congratulation on the excellency of the human mind. Nature is a dull affair, soundless, scentless, colourless ; merely the hurrying of material, endlessly, meaninglessly." Thus what, according to Locke, is really out there in the world is a kind of featureless stuff called " substance " which, though it is without qualities, serves as a substratum, or foundation, for the primary qualities which inhere in it.

Berkeley's Criticism and Development. Locke's is a very confused account of perception and in the light of the considerations advanced in the last chapter, the reader will have no difficulty in picking holes in it. It represents, it is obvious, a half-way house rather than a completed journey. Either it goes too far, or it does not go far enough. Berkeley (1685-1753), Locke's successor, had little difficulty in showing that it did not go far enough. Locke had posited an external world which exists independently of perception, and which contains substance and the primary qualities inhering in substance. Berkeley departs from Locke in two particulars ; he abolishes the distinction between primary and secondary qualities, and he eliminates substance.

Let us take each point separately. So far as the qualities are concerned, the distinction between primary and secondary qualities is clearly arbitrary. Any arguments which show that a secondary quality, heat, for example, is an idea in the mind of the perceiver apply also to size, or solidity, or motion. When we were engaged in showing that the qualities of the alleged external object were not really properties owned by the object, but were dependent upon the mind of the perceiver, we did not find it necessary to make any exceptions. The height of the steeple and the size of the cheese mite's leg were revealed on analysis as properties relative to and dependent upon the perceiver, just as evidently as the heat of the fire.

The arguments for the elimination of substance belong to a different discussion, or rather to two different discussions, the discussion of abstract ideas and the discussion of the relation of substance to its qualities which will occupy us in later chapters.[1] But the introduction of an unknown substance is, it is obvious, only a particular example of a general weakness in Locke's position.

The theory of Representationalism entails the presence of three separate factors in the process of perception. There is the knowing mind (M), the ideas which the mind knows (I), and the external world of objects (O) which are the causes of the ideas. (O) impinges upon the sense organs with the result that images are thrown upon the screen of consciousness and are there known as ideas (I). When the ideas in our minds agree with or correspond with reality, then, Locke would say, we have knowledge.

A moment's reflection shows this position to be untenable, for, if we do not know reality directly, how can we possibly know whether our ideas agree with it or not? A simple analogy will make this plain. Let us suppose that we were to see a number of reflections of a man's face in a number of different mirrors, but never saw the face itself. Let us suppose further that the mirrors reflected the face in different ways, some showing it dark, some light, some pink, some yellow, some emphasising the hollows, others throwing up salient features into high relief, some giving a slightly concave, others a slightly convex effect. (Anybody who has looked at himself in the glass will recognise how different in point of pleasingness are the representations of himself with which different mirrors confront him.) Then let us suppose that we were asked which of these images, reflected

---

[1] See, for the discussion of abstract ideas, Chapter X, pp. 260–262 and of substance and its qualities, Chapter VI, pp. 160–164.

in the different mirrors, was the one which represented the man's face as it *really was*. We should find it impossible to say, since, never having seen the original, we should have nothing with which to compare the reflections. Locke's representationalist view of knowledge is exposed to precisely this difficulty.

Nor, as Berkeley saw, is this the end of the trouble. For what grounds has Locke for postulating an external reality at all? If (M) always knows (I) and never knows (O), (M) cannot know anything about (O)? Any endeavour to obtain knowledge of (O) would, on Locke's analysis, turn out to yield only a more extended knowledge of (I's). (O's) in fact are only an inference from (I's). But if we do not know (O's), we cannot know anything about (O's); we cannot, therefore, know that they have the property of being like (I's), or of being able to cause (I's). What we know are (I's) and, so far as our experience goes, the world may consist entirely of them. Why, then, should we go out of our way to postulate the existence of something which we do not know and never can know, and which, moreover, is totally unlike the only things we ever do know or can know, namely, the ideas—for is not this something supposed to be material while they, the ideas, are mental? —simply in order to be the cause of the ideas which we do know. There is in fact no need, says Berkeley, to postulate external objects at all. The world may very well consist of minds and their ideas and, so far as our experience goes, we never succeed in discovering anything else. The argument which eliminates the external objects which are supposed to be the causes of ideas, also eliminates Locke's substance in which the qualities of the external objects are supposed to inhere.

Berkeley's Arguments. In this way the development of Locke's position for which Berkeley is responsible consists mainly in the elimination of external objects and of substance. Berkeley, however, accepts Locke's position, in so far as it asserts that what we know are our ideas and that these are ideas of simple qualities, for example, or roughness and sweetness, squareness and whiteness, and not of physical things like lumps of sugar. Berkeley has excelled all other philosophers in respect of the force and appropriateness of the arguments which he adduces against the commonsense view that perception brings us into contact with a world of objects which exists independently of our perceiving them. The reader who wishes to make acquaintance with these arguments is recommended to read the "Three Dialogues between Hylas and Philonous"[1] in which the contentions of Hylas, the believer in matter, are one by one demolished with ruthless logic by Philonous, the lover of mind. The following quotation will serve to show their quality :

"*Phil.* Is it your opinion, the very figure and extension which you perceive by sense, exist in the outward object or material substance ?

"*Hyl.* It is.

"*Phil.* Have all other animals as good grounds to think the same of the figure and extension which they see and feel ?

"*Hyl.* Without doubt, if they have any thought at all.

"*Phil.* Answer me, Hylas. Think you the senses were bestowed upon all animals for their preservation and well-being in life ? or were they given to men alone for this end ?

"*Hyl.* I make no question but they have the same use in all other animals.

"*Phil.* If so, is it not necessary they should be enabled by them to perceive their own limbs, and those bodies which are capable of harming them ?

"*Hyl.* Certainly.

"*Phil.* A mite therefore must be supposed to see his own

[1] They will be found at the end of the volume in the Everyman Library entitled : *Theory of Vision and Other Writings*, by Bishop Berkeley.

foot, and things equal or even less than it, as bodies of some considerable dimension ; though at the same time they appear to you scarce discernible, or at best as so many visible points.

" *Hyl.* I cannot deny it.

" *Phil.* And to creatures less than the mite they will seem yet larger.

" *Hyl.* They will.

" *Phil.* Insomuch that what you can hardly discern, will to another extremely minute animal appear as some huge mountain.

" *Hyl.* All this I grant.

" *Phil.* Can one and the same thing be at the same time in itself of different dimensions ?

" *Hyl.* That were absurd to imagine.

" *Phil.* But from what you have laid down it follows, that both the extension by you perceived, and that perceived by the mite itself, as likewise all those perceived by lesser animals, are each of them the true extension of the mite's foot, that is to say, by your own principles you are led into an absurdity.

" *Hyl.* There seems to be some difficulty in the point.

" *Phil.* Again, have you not acknowledged that no real inherent property of any object can be changed, without some change in the thing itself ?

" *Hyl.* I have.

" *Phil.* But as we approach to or recede from an object the visible extension varies, being at one distance ten or a hundred times greater than at another. Doth it not therefore follow from hence likewise, that it is not really inherent in the object ?

" *Hyl.* I am at a loss what to think.

" *Phil.* Your judgement will soon be determined, if you will venture to think as freely concerning this quality, as you have done concerning the rest. Was it not admitted as a good argument, that neither heat nor cold was in the water, because it seemed warm to one hand, and cold to the other ?

" *Hyl.* It was.

" *Phil.* Is it not the very same reasoning to conclude there is no extension or figure in an object, because to one eye it shall seem little, smooth and round, when at the same time it appears to the other, great, uneven, and angular ?

" *Hyl.* The very same. But does this latter fact ever happen ?

" *Phil.* You may at any time make the experiment, by looking with one eye bare, and with the other through a microscope.

" *Hyl.* I know not how to maintain it, and yet I am loath to give up *extension*, I see so many odd consequences following upon such a concession.

" *Phil.* Odd, say you ? After the concessions already made, I hope you will stick at nothing for its oddness. But on the other hand should it not seem very odd, if the general reasoning which includes all other sensible qualities did not also include extension ? If it be allowed that no idea nor anything like an idea can exist in an unperceiving substance, then surely it follows, that no figure or mode of extension, which we can either perceive or imagine, or have any idea of, can be really inherent in matter ; not to mention the peculiar difficulty there must be, in conceiving a material substance,[1] prior to and distinct from extension, to be the *substratum* of extension. Be the sensible quality what it will, figure, or sound, or colour ; it seems alike impossible it should subsist in that which doth not perceive it."

Berkeley's Conclusions.

Berkeley's philosophy issues in two main positions. The first (A) is to the effect that, since all the qualities which we perceive in things are dependent

[1] Berkeley is thinking of Locke's Substance.

on our minds, and since the brute, featureless substance conceived by Locke as a support for the qualities is a myth, therefore things can only exist in so far as they are known or perceived by minds. To exist, in other words, is to be an idea in some mind or, as the Latin tag asserts, the " *esse*," that is to say, " the being " of things, is their " *percipi*," that is, " their being perceived." Hence Berkeley's famous conclusion, one of the most celebrated in philosophy : " Some truths there are so near and obvious that a man need only open his eyes to see them. Such I take this important one to be, viz. that all the choir of heaven and furniture of the earth, in a word all those bodies which compose the mighty frame of the world, have not any subsistence without a mind—that their *being* is to be *perceived* or *known*."

The other conclusion which has historically attracted less attention, but whose effect upon subsequent philosophy has been equally far reaching, is (B) that the ideas in our minds into which our knowledge of the external world resolves itself are ideas of simple qualities. Our so-called sensory knowledge, Berkeley maintains, is always of our own ideas, and these ideas are ideas of qualities and not of things. Admittedly, we believe ourselves to possess a number of separate ideas of a single substantial thing. We believe, that is to say, that our ideas of sweetness, of roughness, of squareness and of whiteness are all ideas of *the same lump of sugar*. But, Berkeley points out, " That which I see is only variety of light and colours. That which I feel is hard or soft, hot or cold, rough or smooth. What similitude, what connection have those ideas with these ? Or how is it possible that anyone should see reason to give one and the same name to combinations of ideas so very different, before he had experienced their co-existence." " If," then, Berkeley concludes, " we take a close and accurate view of the matter, it must be acknowledged that we never see and feel one and the same object. That which is seen is one thing, and that which is felt is another." It is only as a result of an unconscious inference, Berkeley would say, that we come to assume that our visible and tangible ideas are ideas of the same object.

When I enter a room and say, " That object which I see is a table " the mental processes which, according to Berkeley, have occurred in my mind are roughly as follows : I first have a visual experience, which Berkeley would call the " visible idea," of a shining, black, oval surface. I then infer, on the basis of past experience, that, if I take a certain number of steps in the direction of this shining, black, oval surface which is occupying my field of vision, and put out my hands, I shall have another experience, an experience this time of a hard, cool something. I shall have, in other words, what Berkeley calls a " tangible idea " ; and because the visible idea of the shining, black, oval surface has been frequently found in the past to be associated with the tangible idea of hardness and coolness, I infer that they are ideas of the same thing, and conclude that a single physical object which is both black, and shining and oval, and hard and cool is the source of my ideas. But if we eliminate Locke's Substance, and accept Berkeley's view that whatever exists is dependent on a mind, the conclusion cannot be justified.

It is important to keep in mind these two general positions of Berkeley. The position, first (A), that whatever is known is an idea in the mind that knows it with the corollary that only minds and ideas in minds exist, and the position, secondly (B), that our ideas are not of physical objects such as tables, but of sensible qualities such as heat, hardness, blackness, squareness and so forth.

In What Sense do Physical Things Exist?   The question is often asked whether, if Berkeley is right, we can have any assurance of the existence of physical things when we are not perceiving them. If, for example, I go out of my room, are we justified, on Berkeley's premises, in supposing that the empty room goes out of existence and comes into existence again when I re-enter it ? Berkeley repudiates this suggestion. All that he has shown is that to exist is to be an idea in, or to be dependent upon, a mind. But the mind in question need not necessarily be mine ; it may be God's. According to Berkeley the ideas we know do, in fact, exist independently of *our* knowledge, since they continue to exist as ideas in the mind of God. It is on these lines that he seeks to distinguish between perception and imagination. The things I perceive come into my mind whether I want them there or not ; the things I imagine can be summoned and dismissed at will. Why the difference ? Because, says Berkeley, the things I perceive, which are ideas in my mind, are also ideas in God's mind which He passes into mine, but the things I imagine exist only in my mind and go out of existence, therefore, when I am not imagining them. The whole of what we call the external world continues, therefore, to exist on Berkeley's theory even when we cease to perceive it, because God's perception sustains it. It is, however, clear that, unless we are prepared to follow Berkeley in introducing God to give independent reality to a world whose existence, apart from knowledge, has been destroyed, we are reduced to the position that the only things which exist are our own mental states.

Hume's Position.   This is, in effect, the position reached by David Hume (1711–1776). Accepting the psychology of Locke and Berkeley according to which (1) the objects of so-called sensory knowledge are our own ideas, and (2) all our knowledge is derived from our ideas, agreeing also with Berkeley in dismissing Locke's notion of substance in which primary qualities are supposed to inhere, he develops the subjective idealist position to its logical conclusion. For example, his theory of perception dispenses with the concept of God whose knowledge, in Berkeley's philosophy, sustains my ideas when I am not thinking of them. In this he is obviously right. For, if we are thoroughgoing in our acceptance of the view that all our knowledge is derived from the simple ideas obtained in sense experience, we must admit that we have no *sense* experience of God. We cannot, then, invoke His existence to sustain the world when we are not perceiving it. There is, therefore, Hume broadly concludes, no reason to believe in the existence of anything other than what we are immediately perceiving.

Impressions and Ideas.   Following Locke and Berkeley, Hume apparently takes it for granted that what we perceive are our own mental states. These Hume divides into two classes. There are " impressions," which are mainly yielded by what we should normally call sense experience (passions and emotions are also called " impressions "), and " ideas." Hume makes this distinction in the first paragraph of his *Treatise of Human Nature*. The passage is celebrated, and is worth quoting :

" All the perceptions of the human mind resolve themselves into two distinct kinds, which I shall call *impressions* and *ideas*. The difference betwixt these consists in the degrees of force and liveliness, with which they strike upon the mind, and make their way into our thought or consciousness. Those perceptions which enter with most force and violence, we may name *impressions* ; and, under this name, I comprehend all our sensations, passions, and emotions, as they make their first appearance in the soul. By *ideas*, I mean the faint images of these in thinking and reasoning ; such as, for instance, are all the perceptions excited by the present discourse, excepting only those which arise from the sight and touch, and excepting the immediate pleasure or uneasiness it may occasion. I believe it will not be very necessary to employ many words in explaining this distinction. Every one of himself will readily perceive the difference betwixt feeling and thinking. The common degrees of these are easily distinguished ; though it is not impossible but, in particular instances, they may very nearly approach to each other. Thus in sleep, in a fever, in madness, or in any very violent emotions of soul, our ideas may approach to our impressions : as, on the other hand, it sometimes happens, that our impressions are so faint and low, that we cannot distinguish them from our ideas. But, notwithstanding this near resemblance in a few instances, they are in general so very different, that no one can make a scruple to rank them under distinct heads, and assign to each a peculiar name to mark the difference."

It will be observed that Hume distinguishes between the "impressions" and the "ideas" by reference not to their relations to other things, those things, for example, which cause them, but to their intrinsic qualities. An "intrinsic quality" is a quality which a thing possesses in its own right independently of its relations to any other thing, or to all other things.[1] It is, in short, that quality which it possesses in virtue of the fact that it is itself, so that, lacking it, it could not be itself. Thus that it should have weight and that it should be yellow are intrinsic qualities of gold ; but it is not an intrinsic quality of gold that it should be more valuable than silver, or that it should depreciate in terms of sterling.

How Ideas are Distinguished from Impressions.

Now the usual way of distinguishing "impressions" from "ideas" —we should to-day call them respectively "sensations" and "images"—would be by reference not to their intrinsic qualities, but to their relations to other things. A sensation, we should say, has a cause in the external world and it is a sensation of that which causes it. Thus, when I sit by the fire, we should hold that my sensations are *caused by* the warmth of the fire and that they are sensations *of* the warmth that causes them. Images, whatever their ultimate causes may be, are not caused in the first instance by contact with external things. If, for example, I now have an image of St. Paul's Cathedral, it is not, we should say, necessary that St. Paul's should be present to my senses, in order to cause the image. Not only may the object of the image be absent, but, most people would agree, the image need not have an object at all. For example, I can have an image of two lamp-posts when I am drunk, although there is in fact only one. I can also have an image of my study with

[1] Some philosophers have held that there are no "intrinsic qualities" in this sense. See Chapter XV, pp. 413–415.

the desk at the other end. In fact I can, if I choose, live for a time in an "imaginary" world, the contents of which have no counterparts in the actual world, and, if I become a lunatic, I may never leave my imaginary world at all. Thus the ordinary method of distinguishing images from sensations is not in terms of their intrinsic qualities, but by reference to the outside world. Sensations, we should say, have an external reference to that which causes them ; images need not have. But Hume, asserting that our knowledge is only of our own mental states, is clear sighted enough to realise that he is not entitled to distinguish between mental states by reference to external things : for, if we do not have any direct knowledge of an external world of things, we are not justified in referring to them in order to enable us to distinguish between our mental states. In other words, Hume is careful to avoid the mistake of Locke's Representationalism.

Inadequacy of Hume's Criterion.

Deprived of the criterion of external reference, he has to fall back upon a criterion of *intrinsic* difference, and finds it in " degree of liveliness." It is not a satisfactory criterion and, as Hume himself admits, breaks down in extreme cases in which images have as great a degree of liveliness and violence as sensations. To cite an instance given by Bertrand Russell, Macbeth speaks of

> *that suggestion*
> *Whose horrid image doth unfix my hair*
> *And make my seated heart knock at my ribs,*
> *Against the use of nature.*

It is difficult to imagine a sensation having a more violent effect than the image of Macbeth's dagger.

In the last resort, then, there is no satisfactory distinction between the mental contents which, in Hume's view, constitute our knowledge. Our experiences, he has told us, are of our own mental states. Some, which are more violent than others, we call impressions and believe to have an external cause ; but we do not know the external cause.

So far, then, Hume endorses the first of Berkeley's two main positions, the one we have called (A).

Association of Ideas.

Hume also endorses the second Berkeleyan position (B). Our impressions and ideas are, he holds, fragmentary and isolated. They are not connected, when they come into the mind, and the mind, which he conceives to be passive and not active, does not itself connect them. " All our distinct perceptions are distinct existences," says Hume, and, he goes on, " the mind never perceives any real connection among distinct existences." How, then, it may be asked, do we contrive to think at all, since thinking obviously implies that there is *some* sort of connection between our ideas—a connection in virtue of which we can form *chains* of reasoning ? Because, says Hume, some of our impressions habitually go together. For example, impressions of sweetness, squareness, roughness and whiteness go together and as a result we think of sugar. But about this " going together " there is nothing necessary. Hume speaks of " some bond of union . . . some associating quality, by which one idea naturally introduces another." But the uniting principle is no more than " a gentle force, which commonly," not universally, " prevails " ; it is not an *active associating* by the mind. All that we can say is that some impressions tend naturally to occur in clusters, and as a result we form the idea of a physical thing. But at any moment the prevailing form of clustering may cease and be succeeded by a different one. The mind being completely passive is helpless in the matter, and has no control over the clusterings which are responsible for our ideas of what we call the world of things.

The conclusions of this doctrine, which is known as " The Association of Ideas," are momentous. Among them is the denial of the so-called necessity of the law of cause and effect—this too for Hume is a mere " determination of the mind," a particular instance of the association of certain ideas, that of the cause and that of the effect which are found habitually to go together—and a denial of the unity of the Self. These conclusions will be described in some detail in later chapters.[1] For the present, I am concerned to emphasise Hume's endorsement of the second Berkeleyan principle (B), namely, that what we know in sensation are not impressions of physical things, but impressions of isolated qualities ; not, that is to say, ideas of lumps of sugar, but impressions of roughnesses, hardnesses, sweetnesses and whitenesses.

Effect of Hume's Analysis of the Self.

A word may be added on the bearing of Hume's analysis of the Self (to be considered in detail in a later chapter)[2] on the theme of the present discussion. Broadly, the effect of this analysis is to eliminate the Self and to replace it by a succession of psychological states, those, namely, which would normally be said to belong to the Self. Hume does not deny that there is a stream of consciousness which consists of such psychological events as moods, fears, hopes, wishes, thoughts, ideas and sensations. What he does deny is that there is anything else. There is, that is to say, for Hume no unifying, continuing Self which *has* the moods, fears the fears, hopes the hopes, wishes the wishes, thinks the thoughts, and experiences the ideas and sensations.

What follows ? Let us revert for a moment to the three entities postulated in Locke's theory of perception (see above, p. 43) : (M) the knowing mind, (I) the ideas which are known, and (O) the objects which cause the ideas. Berkeley, as we have seen, eliminates (O), or rather he replaces (O) by the mind of God. As, however, we have pointed out, the assumption of God's mind is inconsistent with the premise that all our knowledge comes through sense experience, and Hume refuses to have recourse to Berkeley's device for sustaining the existence of the world when we are not perceiving it. Hume, then, finally eliminates (O). But he also, by virtue of his analysis of the Self, eliminates (M), the knowing mind, leaving only (I).

[1] See Chapters VIII and IX, pp. 207–211 and 229–232.
[2] See Chapter IX.

The ideas for Hume are known. They are, that is to say, conscious ideas, but there is no mind or Self to know the ideas which is other than and additional to the ideas which are known. My world, so far as there is or can be knowledge of it, resolves itself, therefore, into a succession of known ideas which are not ideas of anything and are only by courtesy called " mine."

Solipsism. This, the logical development of the theory of Subjective Idealism or Mentalism, is usually known as Solipsism. Solipsism may be described as the view that, since all our knowledge is of our own mental states, nothing which is other than our own mental states can be known to exist. Now there is no ground for asserting the existence of something that cannot be known. Therefore, my mental states, for all I know to the contrary, constitute the universe. Whether anything in addition to them exists I cannot tell, since being completely enclosed within the circle of my own ideas, eternally incarcerated in the prison-house of my own experience, I cannot penetrate beyond its walls.

There is, so far as I know, no reason to think that this conclusion is true. Nevertheless, it is exceedingly difficult to refute, so difficult that many hold it to be logically irrefutable.[1] It is, however, a perfectly logical conclusion of the line of development which starts with Locke, who uses the apparent relativity to the perceiver's mind of the qualities we perceive in things, as a ground to justify the deduction that what the perceiver perceives is somehow *in* his mind. If, then, we are to attempt to escape from Solipsism, it is upon this deduction that we must concentrate our attention. An outline of some of the attempts which philosophers have made will be given in the next chapter.

Relevance of Modern Physics. There is one point to be disposed of before we conclude this one. I have had

[1] Even if it cannot be refuted, it certainly cannot be proved. See, in this connection, the argument in Chapter III, pp. 70–73.

occasion, at various stages in the development of the preceding arguments, to make use of considerations derived from the scientific account of the machinery of perception. The fact that an interval of time must elapse before light rays travelling from an object reach the retina of the eye suggests, for example, that it cannot really be the object that we are seeing, since it may have gone out of existence during the interval. Again, the fact that I am only aware of the stimuli received by my sense organs after certain events have taken place in the nervous system and in the brain, suggesting, as it does, that it is the events in my brain which are the cause of my becoming aware, has led some thinkers to the conclusion that, so far as my knowledge of the external world is concerned, I am completely enclosed within the circle not of my own ideas, but of my own neural and cerebral reactions. These considerations certainly tend to strengthen the doubts which the idealists have suggested as to the validity of the commonsense theory of perception, and it was for this reason that they were introduced. Moreover, it is obvious that, if anything even remotely approximating to the physicist's current account of the world is true, the world as it really is must be very different from that which, in ordinary experience, we believe ourselves to perceive. Physics analyses material objects into arrangements of atoms and electrons which are divested of most of the qualities which we believe ourselves to perceive in the objects. The fundamental constituents of matter are, according to the physicist, neither coloured, noisy, hard nor sweet. They lack texture, shape—even, on the most modern views, exact position in space.[1] Yet, if it be true that colourless, tasteless, textureless atoms constitute the reality of external things, whence, we are bound to ask, do the colours, tastes, hardnesses, and the rest of the qualities that we experience come from? It is difficult to resist the conclusion that they are supplied by our own consciousness. Thus by virtue of its destruction

[1] See Chapter XI, pp. 313–316 and 320–322, for a development of this point of view.

of the commonsense world, physics tends to give support to idealist conclusions.[1]

Nevertheless, Physics plays no Part in Subjective Idealism.

Whether these considerations which are derived from modern physics do or do not justifiably bear the idealist construction which some scientists place upon them, they cannot, it is obvious, be invoked by the supporters of Subjective Idealism. They may, or they may not, be arguments in favour of *physiological* Solipsism, that is to say, the view that the world we know is limited by, and confined to, events taking place in our own bodies ; but they can have no bearing on *psychological* Solipsism, that is to say, the view that the world we know is limited by, and confined to, events taking place in our own consciousness.

And they cannot for the following reasons : If Subjective Idealism is true, there are no material things in the world, or, if there are such things, they cannot be known. Now objects are material things ; so are light rays, waves in the atmosphere, sense organs, nerves, neural messages, brains and living cells. If, therefore, Subjective Idealism is true, these things are only ideas in the physicist's mind. If, then, they are taken to be physical things, they are illusions. Now science certainly takes these things to be both real and physical, and it is by taking them as real and as physical, and using them as cogs in the very elaborate perceptual machinery which physics and physiology describe, that it reaches the conclusions at which we have already glanced.

Hence, although it may in fact be the case that we only know events taking place in our bodies and brains (although how, if we do, we can also know light rays, atoms, electrons and the other inhabitants of the physicist's world by means of which the conclusion that we only know body and brain events is built up, is not clear), we cannot invoke this conclusion or the reasons for it in support of Subjective

[1] See Chapter XI, pp. 313–316 and 320–322, for a development of this point of view.

Idealism. Moreover, we must not, if we wish to argue for Idealism, begin by taking as real the physical, neural and cerebral machinery postulated by physics and physiology which, if we accept the conclusions of Subjective Idealism, is not physical. The point has a certain contemporary importance because some scientists are to-day asserting that the researches of modern physics support the conclusions of Idealism.[1] A moment's reflection shows that, if Subjective Idealism is meant, the claim is unfounded. Indeed, it is nonsensical. For if Subjective Idealism is correct in what it asserts, the physicist's world, no less than the methods by which he explores it, consists of ideas in minds. But if this is so, no conclusions at which he arrives by assuming matter to be real can possibly be true. In other words, if everything is an idea in somebody's mind, the world of physics is also an idea in somebody's mind. This is not, of course, a conclusion of physics ; but it is a postulate of Idealism. Is the postulate true ? To this question we must now turn.

The philosophers Locke, Berkeley and Hume should be read for a development of the lines of argument followed in this chapter. The relevant books are :

LOCKE   Essay Concerning Human Understanding.

BERKELEY   A Treatise Concerning the Principles of Human Knowledge.

Three Dialogues between Hylas and Philonous.

HUME   A Treatise of Human Nature.

Both Berkeley and Hume may be obtained in volumes in the Everyman Edition. Each volume has an Introduction by A. D. Lindsay. All these three philosophers are comparatively easy reading. The best commentary is *Locke, Berkeley and Hume*, by C. R. Morris.

[1] See Chapter XI for an account of the philosophical bearings of modern physics.

*CHAPTER III : WHAT DO WE KNOW OF THE OUTSIDE WORLD?

3. The Realist Answer

Introductory : Origins of Realism. The position reached at the end of the last chapter is not one which many philosophers would now maintain. The reasons for rejecting it fall into two rather different categories. In the first place, there are many philosophers who, while maintaining that whatever exists must be minds or thoughts, or at least of the same nature as minds or thoughts, deny that to exist is to be an idea or a thought in the mind of a particular person. Arguments were, for example, adduced by Kant to show that whatever can be known includes some mental elements, but that these elements are general and common to all human minds and not particular events in particular minds. Again, Hegel sought to show that the universe is a universe of thought and that whatever exists is an aspect of thought. The things which mind knows are on this view, equally with the mind that knows them, particular expressions or aspects of thought. The views of Kant and Hegel will be described in later chapters[1] ; they are usually known as Objective Idealism to distinguish them from the Subjective Idealism of Berkeley which, as we have seen, maintains that the meaning of the expression " a physical thing exists " is that certain ideas occur in, or are dependent upon, the mind of some *particular person* or " subject." In so far as philosophers have followed what is known as the idealist tradition—and most philosophers since Kant have

[1] See Chapters XIV and XV.

maintained some one or other of the many forms of Idealism —they have adopted the Objective Idealism of Kant or of Hegel rather than the Subjective Idealism of Berkeley.

The nineteenth century was dominated by the philosophy of Hegel. The early years of the twentieth century, however, witnessed a reaction against the whole idealist mode of thought. This reaction began in England with the publication of a celebrated article by Professor G. E. Moore, entitled *The Refutation of Idealism,* which first appeared in 1903, in which he pointed out certain fallacies in the arguments which Berkeley adduced in support of the conclusion that " to be " is the same thing as " to be perceived," that, in other words, " being " and " being perceived " are synonymous terms. Moore's original paper was succeeded by a number of others in which the whole problem of perception was subjected to an acute critical analysis, the results of which made it extremely difficult to maintain the idealist position that what is perceived is necessarily dependent for its existence upon some mind. Professor Moore's views attracted a number of adherents both in this country and in the United States, with the result that there grew up what for a time ranked as a definite school of philosophical thought, the school of Modern Realism. Prominent among English realists are Professor G. E. Moore, Bertrand Russell,[1] Professor C. D. Broad and Professor John Laird, while, among the Americans, Professors Holt, Montague and Perry, who collaborated in the production of a

[1] Perhaps in the case of Moore and Russell, the most celebrated of contemporary English philosophers, I should say " were " rather than " are." Bertrand Russell's views have undergone a number of changes, and it is doubtful whether he would now be prepared to call himself a realist. Moore's thought has been increasingly influenced by the school of philosophical analysts (see Introduction to Part III, pp. 253–257), and it is possible, indeed it is probable, that he would now dismiss as meaningless many of the questions which have formed the subject of controversy between realists and idealists in the past. His present view seems to be that the proposition " physical objects exist " is certainly true, but that, when we say anything about them, what we mean is always analysable into propositions about human sense data actual or possible. The reader who wishes to acquaint himself with these latest views is recommended to consult A. C. Ewing's *Idealism,* Chapter VII.

co-operative philosophical work known as *The New Realism*, first published in 1912, are regarded as leading exponents of realist views.

Forms of Realism.

For a time modern realists maintained a fair show of agreement in regard to a number of important philosophical problems. They all, for example, agreed that what was directly known in sensory experience was in no sense dependent upon the mind of the knower : they all, that is to say, concurred in rejecting Idealism. But when attention came to be concentrated upon the problem of what precisely *was* known in perception, the question began increasingly to be discussed whether, although the qualities of what was known were independent of the mind, they might not be dependent upon the body of the knower, and especially upon his brain, nerves and sense organs. With the raising of this question important differences in realist theory began to appear. Some realists, whom we may conveniently denominate commonsense realists, maintained that what was perceived was a physical object, even if this object was only perceived partially and in some cases delusively ; others took the view that what was perceived was not a physical object at all, but what they termed a sensum or a sense datum.[1] The sensum or sense datum had, it was obvious, an important relation to the physical object, but it turned out to be very difficult to say what that relation was. Moreover, the sense datum was usually regarded as being dependent for some of its qualities upon the brain or sense organs of the perceiver. These differences have now gone so far that it is very doubtful whether a school of Realism—if the expression " school " is interpreted in its usual sense to denote a number of independent thinkers who, nevertheless, maintain in common a set of important and distinctive conclusions—can with justice be said any longer to exist. Nor, unfortunately, in spite of the prepossession in favour of common sense upon which their

---

[1] An example of a sense datum is a patch of colour or a rap of sound A more detailed account is given later (see pp. 91, 92).

protest against the apparent extravagances of some idealist theories was based, can it be said that realists have succeeded in maintaining a view of the external world which approximates at all closely to that of the ordinary man.

Difficulties of Summary.

The differences which have appeared in realist thought, especially of recent years, make it difficult to summarise ; for we have not to present the thought of a single school, but the views of a variety of thinkers, any selection from which is bound to appear somewhat arbitrary. A convenient framework for treatment is, however, afforded by the two main conclusions reached by Berkeley's philosophy, the conclusions, namely, that to exist is to be either a mind or an idea in some mind—that is to say, only minds and ideas in minds exist—and the conclusion that our ideas are of simple separate sense qualities, of whiteness, sweetness, hardness and so forth, and not of physical things. The first conclusion is one that all realists would deny, and we shall begin with a consideration of some of the reasons for this denial. The second a number of realists would accept, with the reservation that for " ideas of simple separate sense qualities " we must read " sense data characterised by simple separate sense qualities," such sense data or sensa, as they are sometimes called, being neither ideas in minds nor physical objects, but particular physical happenings such as patches of colour and raps of sound. From the refutation of Idealism we shall proceed to give instances of some of the arguments which realists have advanced in favour of this second conclusion, and try to show how, in consequence of the difficulties which were encountered in the endeavour to maintain what may be called Commonsense Realism, the sense data type of Realism, which embodies the second of Berkeley's conclusions, has come largely to supersede it.

I. THE REFUTATION OF IDEALISM

It will be convenient to divide the arguments which realists have brought against the Subjective Idealism of Berkeley into two categories—the logical arguments and the psychological. The division is not a clear-cut one, but it will serve a useful purpose in showing how the conclusion that what is known in sense experience does not depend upon the mind of the knower may be reached by two rather different routes. Most of the arguments which follow, but especially those in the first category, appear in one form or another in the works of Professor G. E. Moore, who, as mentioned above, was one of the first philosophers in England effectively to challenge the prevalent philosophy of Idealism.

A. Logical Arguments

I propose to give these some prominence, as they are typical of a certain kind of philosophical thinking of which Professor Moore is a master. The object of this type of thinking is to show that a particular position which is being critically considered can be shown, when adequately analysed, either to involve itself in self-contradiction or to be based upon some premise which is quite obviously false. It is, however, advisable to warn those readers who are making their first acquaintance with philosophy that the significance of these purely logical arguments is not always easy to grasp, and that, even when grasped, many will find them singularly unconvincing. Nor is it only those who are unfamiliar with philosophical modes of thought who profess themselves to be unconvinced by this type of argument, even when they are unable to detect mistakes in the actual arguments used or to find appropriate answers to them. What is at issue here is, I suspect, largely a question of temperament and outlook. There will always be those to whom considerations whose force is of a purely logical order will seem barren and unconvincing, but the existence of such an attitude does not necessarily impair the force of logical argument.

1. A HIDDEN INFINITE REGRESS. Let us consider the Berkeleyan position that a thing's existence consists in its being perceived, that its *esse*, to use the Latin tag in terms of which this position is usually conveyed, is *percipi*. If a thing exists, it is real. To be real, then, if Berkeley is right, is the same thing as to be perceived—that is to say, the same thing as to be the object of a perception. What sort of perception, a real one or an unreal one ? Obviously a real one, since to say that the definition of a real thing is " a thing which is the object of an unreal perception " is nonsense. In order, then, that a thing may be real, it must, on Berkeley's view, be an object of a real perception. What is a real perception ? According to the Berkeleyan definition of reality, it is one which is the object of a perception. This second perception, of which the real perception is the object, we will call perception$_2$. Is perception$_2$ real or not ? Obviously it is real. In what, then, does the reality of perception$_2$ consist ? If the Berkeleyan position is correct, it consists in being the object of a perception. This we will call perception$_3$. Our formula now runs : A thing is real in so far as it is the object of a perception, which is real in so far as it is the object of a perception$_2$, which is real in so far as it is the object of a perception$_3$, and so on indefinitely. The Berkeleyan definition of reality involves, therefore, what is known as an infinite regress. This does not mean that the definition is necessarily false ; but it certainly constitutes a powerful objection to it. Moreover, there does not seem any reason to suppose that Berkeley ever suspected anything of the kind.

2. FAULTY ARGUMENT FROM PREMISE TO CONCLUSION. The subjective idealist position has been accused by realists of basing a false conclusion on a true proposition. The true proposition is, " It is impossible to discover anything that is not known," since it becomes known by the mere process of being discovered. From this proposition

CP

it follows that it is impossible to discover with certainty what characteristics things possess when they are not known. The idealist then proceeds falsely to conclude, " Things have no characteristics when they are not known ; therefore, the characteristic of being known is that which constitutes their existence : therefore, things only exist when they are known."

But the idealist conclusion does not in fact follow. The only conclusion which can validly be based upon the proposition quoted above is that " All known things are known." This is a truism, and in so far as the idealist argument asserts more than this, in so far, in fact, as it draws the conclusion which it does draw, it achieves this result by tacking on to this truism a falsity, this falsity being " All things are known." But from the fact that we cannot always or even usually tell what characteristics things possess when they are not known, it does not follow that all things are, therefore, known. Nor does it seem to be always the case that we cannot tell what characteristics things possess when they are not known. We can assert, for example, of a number that is so large that it has never been thought of, the following characteristic—" The number in question possesses the characteristic of being half of an even number."

3. What Precisely Is "In" The Mind ? Let us now look a little more closely into the process known as perceiving. What, exactly, does it involve ? The following answer to this question is based very largely upon the analysis originally suggested by Professor G. E. Moore.

It is clear that whenever I have any kind of experience, whether I am dreaming, thinking, having hallucinations, or merely perceiving, something is dreamt, thought, hallu-cinated, or perceived, and that my mind has *some* relation to this something. Let us concentrate upon the case in which the something is perceived—that is to say, is taken to be a something in the external world which is present to my senses. As I am reserving for later consideration the question of what precisely this something is, I will call it for the present non-committally X. Now X, the subjective idealists contend, is an idea which is in the mind, and the question with which we are immediately concerned is whether this contention is correct. We may begin by noticing that the relation of the mind to X is one which varies. For example, the experience of seeing or hearing X is quite obviously different from the experience of remembering or imagining it. The fire that I remember when I am cold does not warm, the meals that I lovingly imagine when I am hungry do not feed me. In other words, the causal effect of remembered and imagined things is different from the causal effect of perceived things. Now it is clear that the mind has *some* relation to the things which it imagines and remembers, since otherwise it could not make judgements about them. It seems to follow that the relation which the mind has to the things that it perceives is different from its relation to the things that it imagines and remembers ; what is more, it is probably a unique relation. Let us call this relation, the relation of directly apprehending. When, then, I perceive X, we will say that I directly apprehend X, or that there is in my mind a direct apprehension of X.

The above analysis enables the realist to point out what seems to be a serious confusion underlying the idealist position. For, in the first place, if X is in my mind as well as the direct apprehension of it, there would be no difference between the experience of seeing X and that of remembering or imagining it, for in each case X, whether perceived, remembered or imagined, would be in my mind and, since nobody has suggested that a thing can be *in* the mind in more than one way, X would, presumably, be in my mind in the same way ; yet, as we have seen, there is a clear difference. It seems to follow that my mind's relation to X when I directly apprehend it, must be different from its relation to X when I remember or imagine it. But this would not be possible if X were always and in each case in my mind, and in my mind in the

same way. Secondly, when I say that X " is experienced,"
the phrase certainly seems at first sight to suggest that X
is a part of my experience, or, as the idealists put it, is
" in " the mind which is experiencing. But do we mean
any more by these expressions than that the direct apprehension of X is a part of my experience, or is in my mind ?
If we mean more than this, if we mean that *X also* is a part
of my experience or is in my mind, in what sense is it "a
part of" and in what sense is it " in " ? There seem to be
two possibilities. First, that X is " in " my mind in precisely the same sense as that in which the direct apprehension of X is " in " my mind. Secondly, that it is
" in " my mind in some entirely new sense. If it is " in "
my mind in precisely the same sense as my act of directly
apprehending it, then it will have to my act of directly
apprehending it the same relation as one of my acts of
direct apprehension has to another. The relation of X to my
apprehension of it, that is to say, will be of the same kind as
the relation of my apprehension of X to my apprehension
of Y, or, to take a concrete example, the inkpot on my desk
will have the same kind of relation to my apprehension of it
as my apprehension of it has to my apprehension of the
chair. As to this, the only possible comment seems to be
that it quite obviously has not. If an objector cannot see
that it has not, there seems to be no way of convincing him.

But if, recognising that it has not, we insist that X is
" in " my mind in some other sense, the question arises,
what can that sense be ? It is a sense which is open to
introspection, and we ought, therefore, to be able to
define or at least to describe it. Yet nobody has ever succeeded in doing this. The conclusion suggested is that in
no sense at all is X in the mind.

4. CONTINUITY OF X. But even if X is not in my
mind, it is still possible that it exists only when a mind is
perceiving it ; it is still possible, that is to say, that, even
if the being of things does not consist in their being perceived, they do only exist when they are in fact being

perceived. Even if we cannot prove that Berkeley, in so far as he holds this latter view, is wrong, there seems to be no reason for supposing that he is right. Let us suppose that X is the fire at which I am looking. It has recently, we will further suppose, been replenished with coal and is blazing. I go out of the room for an hour and return to find that the fire has burnt low. Now the subjective idealist hypothesis requires us to suppose, first, that the fire went out of existence when I left the room ; secondly, that it came into existence again when I re-entered it, but that, when it did so, it had an altered appearance, the altered appearance being precisely such as it would have exhibited, if it had been burning all the time I was out of the room. As I have just remarked, this hypothesis cannot be disproved ; but it seems, to say the least of it, extremely unlikely.

Again, let us suppose that I am looking at the desk at which I am writing ; that I then get up, turn my back to it, walk round it, and look at it again from the other side, so that I obtain a different view of it. If Subjective Idealism is correct, we are required to suppose that the desk went out of existence when I turned my back, and that another desk in due course came into existence exhibiting certain recognisable marks of similarity with the first desk, but exhibiting also a different aspect, this different aspect being precisely such as the original desk would have exhibited, if it had been in existence all the time I was walking round it in order to look at it from the opposite side. Now although we cannot prove that the fire and the desk continued to exist during the intervals when they were not being perceived, the hypothesis that they did continue is certainly the simplest way of accounting for the facts. Moreover, as Hume would say, we have a strong propensity to believe it.

What are the arguments against the hypothesis ? There is, first, the argument, based upon the scientist's account of the machinery of perception, which seeks to show that the properties of that which is perceived depend to a large extent upon the condition of the nervous system. But if the distinction made above between the act of apprehension and the object apprehended is scrupulously observed, it will be seen that this dependence, while it may be true of the former, is not necessarily true of the latter. Nothing, that is to say, which happens in and to my nervous system can, if the distinction is valid, possibly affect X, upon which my act of apprehension is directed.

Secondly, it is said that since I can perceive a tulip to be blue which a colour-blind man perceives to be green, and since the same tulip cannot be both blue and green at the same time, it follows that we cannot both be perceiving the same tulip. Now it is certainly true that this consideration does make it difficult to hold that the object of the act of apprehension, which I have been calling non-committally X, is a physical object, namely, a tulip, and that this tulip is the object which both the colour-blind man and I directly apprehend. This difficulty constitutes one of the reasons why many realists, as we shall see below, while admitting that X is independent of the mind, deny that it is a physical object : and, if they are right, it may very well be the case that the X which I perceive is different from the X which the colour-blind man perceives. But it does not necessarily follow that his X is dependent on his mind or is in his mind, or that my X is dependent upon or is in mine, nor does this consideration afford any ground for thinking that it is.

5. THE ARGUMENT AGAINST SOLIPSISM—Berkeley's position, as we have seen from the brief account of its logical development in the second chapter, reduces itself to Solipsism—that is to say, to the view that my mental states are the only things that I can possibly know, and that I have no reason, therefore, for supposing that anything except myself and my own mental states exists in the universe. This position is often described as one which is strictly irrefutable, although there may be no reason for thinking it to be true. Whether it is irrefutable or not, I do not know ; but it is easy to show that there cannot be any reason for holding it.

According to Berkeley's contention, when I have a sensation of seeing something, that which I see no less than
my act of seeing it, the object of my act of apprehension
no less than the act itself, is in my mind. It is, that is to say,
a part of my experience. A term which is often used in
philosophy to describe what we mean by " is a part of "
or " in," when we say that so-and-so " is a part of " experience or is " in " consciousness, is the term " content."
Berkeley's position may, then, be described by saying that
what common sense would call the object of an experience
is its content or is a part of its content: it is, that is to say,
quite literally an event or a series of events in the biography of the person experiencing. Now Berkeley and
Hume took, as we shall see in the next chapter,[1] what is
known as an empirical view of knowledge. They believed,
that is to say, that all knowledge is derived from sense
experience, and that what was discovered to be true of
sensation and of the relation of a sensation to its object
was, therefore, also true of thought and of the relation of
thought to its object. Moreover, all, or at any rate most, of
those philosophers who have taken idealist views, however
widely they may have differed from Berkeley and Hume
on other matters, have agreed with them on this one ;
they have agreed, that is to say, that the relation of a sensation to its object is of the same kind as the relation of
any type of experience to its object, and of the same kind,
therefore, as the relation of thought to its object.

Now we have seen that, if Subjective Idealism is right,
the object of a sensation is the content or part of the content of the sensation. Therefore the object of a thought is
the content or is part of the content of the thought. Hence
when an idealist philosopher thinks about other people,
what he is thinking about—that is to say, the other people
who are the objects of his thought—is, if his philosophy
is correct, a part of the content of his thought, is, that is to
say, a phase of his own biography. His thought, therefore,
turns out to be thought *about* nothing, since whatever would

[1] See Chapter IV, pp. 111-113.

normally be called the *object* of the thought is found on analysis to pass over into its content and to reveal itself as *part* of the thought. If, therefore, Subjective Idealism is true, we can never be conscious of anything other than ourselves, since anything which might normally have been supposed to be " other " will, in virtue of the fact that it is part of the content of our consciousness, reveal itself as a part of ourselves. It follows that a man can never know anything but the content of his own consciousness. This sounds at first sight like an argument for the solipsist conclusion. But is it? For if a man can only know the content of his own consciousness, he cannot know anything other than his own consciousness. Therefore he cannot know any arguments for Solipsism. And, if it be said that this fact is one which itself constitutes an argument for Solipsism, he cannot know that it does, since to have such knowledge would be to know something other than himself. Hence, if there are any arguments for Solipsism, we cannot, if Subjective Idealism is true, know them or know *that* they are arguments for Solipsism. We can only know the contents of our own consciousness. To put this conclusion in another way, we may say that in order to know that a thought is true, we must know that it refers to or applies to something other than itself. But if we can only know the content of our own thought, we cannot know that it does do this. Therefore we cannot know that any thought is true ; therefore we cannot know that Solipsism is true, and we cannot know that there are any arguments for it.

Physiological Solipsism. It is perhaps worth pointing out at this stage that a similar argument may be used to stultify, if not to refute, the physiological Solipsism which is some-times thought to be entailed by the scientific account of perception. This account may, as we saw in the first chapter,[1] be invoked in support of the conclusion that the only things that we can know are events occurring in our bodies and brains. For physics and physiology show that these events are the *proximate causes* of everything that we

[1] See Chapter I, pp. 31-34.

know, and there is, therefore, a sense in which they may be said to condition and to determine what we know. How does the argument which we have just advanced bear upon this conclusion ? The conclusion is that whenever I know something, the consciousness which *is* my knowledge is the determined effect of events in my body and brain which it reflects. What, therefore, this knowledge testifies is that my body and brain are in a certain condition. Can it testify anything else ? Clearly it cannot ; because, even if it were to be maintained that there must be in the external world certain objects which by stimulating my sense organs cause these events in my body and brain, I cannot know that this is the case, since any such knowledge, if I were to make the attempt to obtain it, would involve the occurrence of more events in my body and brain of which it would be the determined effect, and would, therefore, be evidence not that there was an outside world in contact with my sense organs, but that a further set of events was occurring in my body and brain. I cannot, then, on this view, know anything external to myself ; I cannot, therefore, know that things external to myself are the cause of those events in the body and brain which are said to be the causes of my knowledge, since this knowledge, if I were to have it, would be knowledge of a fact external to myself. But if this is so, I cannot know that all the mental events which are my perceptions are caused by events in my body and brain ; nor can I know any of the arguments for believing that they are so caused.

This conclusion has considerable importance in connection with the conclusions of Scientific Materialism, according to which consciousness is a function of or emanation from the brain, all events in the mind being determined by prior events in the brain. I shall, therefore, have occasion to refer to it again in the chapter which deals with Scientific Materialism.[1]

Positive Conclusions : Awareness and its Objects.

What follows ? That whether we are experiencing

[1] See Chapter XVII, pp. 534-537.

through our five senses or whether we are using our minds, whether we are perceiving or whether we are thinking, our acts of consciousness are always in contact with something other than ourselves. The objects of our perceiving and of our thinking are, in fact, never the same as, or part of, the acts of perceiving or thinking them. It is, Professor Moore concludes, a characteristic at once common and peculiar to all mental acts that they should be aware of something other than themselves. To say of an act that it is mental is, indeed, to say of it that it is an awareness of something other than itself. This conclusion entails the corollary that the " something other," of which there is awareness, is unaffected by the mind's awareness of it. As experienced, in other words, it is precisely what it would be, if it were not being experienced.

The conclusion is reinforced by its application to the case of self-consciousness. That I can not only be aware of the table, but be aware that I am aware of it, nobody would wish to deny, and this awareness of my own awareness which constitutes the essence of self-consciousness is commonly regarded as a distinct and recognisable kind of experience. Let us denote my awareness of the table by the letter (A) and my awareness of my awareness of the table by the letter (B). Now if the conclusion reached above is valid, the relation in self-consciousness of my awareness (B) to its object, which is my awareness (A) of the table, is the same as the relation of my awareness (A) to the table. Now we can be conscious without being self-conscious ; in other words, awareness (A) of the table can exist without awareness (B) to be aware of it. Awareness (A) is, therefore, not affected by being the object of awareness (B). Now there is no reason to suppose—none at any rate has been adduced—that the relation of the mind to its object in the case of self-consciousness is not the same as the relation of the mind to its object in ordinary consciousness. The conclusion seems to be that the object of awareness in the case of ordinary consciousness is not affected by the awareness of it.

B. Psychological Arguments

1. ATOMISTIC PSYCHOLOGY. The above arguments are, realists hold, reinforced by a consideration of the psychological processes involved in perception. The Subjective Idealism of Berkeley and Hume is based upon what has come to be known as the atomistic psychology. This is the view that our experience comes to us in little separate bits, " between which," as Hume says, " the mind never perceives any real connection," and that whatever else there may come to be in the mind is the result of the putting together of the little bits. These little bits are what Berkeley called " ideas." An " idea," therefore, is the ultimate unit of experience ; it is conceived as the atom of thought, just as the atom was once conceived as the ultimate unit of matter.

Now many philosophers would deny altogether that our experience comes to us in this way. They would, that is to say, deny that it is atomistic. They would affirm, on the contrary, that experience is connected and continuous and that the connections between the bits are just as much there to begin with as the bits. William James, for example, contended that our experience comes to us initially in the form of a continuous stream, the connecting links between one part of our experience and another being themselves indistinguishable parts of what we experience ; " the relations that connect experience," he wrote, " must themselves be experienced relations, and any kind of relation experienced must be accounted as ' real ' as anything else in the system."[1]

Kant, again, insisted upon the fact that our experience is given to us not as a mosaic of little bits, but as a connected whole, the connections being contributed by the mind. These views will be described in later chapters.[2] For the present it is sufficient to point out that the psychological foundation for the whole subjective idealist way of thinking, namely, that consciousness consists of a series of distinct,

[1] For William James's theory of perception see Chapter XVI, pp. 450, 451.
[2] For Kant's theory of perception, see Chapter XIV, pp. 378–384.

separate unitary experiences, the ideas, can be challenged, and, in the opinion of most philosophers, successfully challenged.

2. USE OF THE WORD " IDEA." The above criticism is applied with particular force to the idealist's use of the word " idea." The " ideas " of Locke, Berkeley and Hume fulfil a double function. They constitute both the mind's experience and that upon which the mind's experience is directed. They are, that is to say, both the units of our thinking and that which is in front of the mind when it thinks. To use a technical expression, they are both the subjects and the objects of our thinking. Now this double use of the word " idea " conceals a certain hidden premise, the premise that there is no real distinction between the mind and its objects, and this premise begs the very question at issue. Indeed, it does more ; it not only begs the question but steals the answer, by suggesting that the same idea can fulfil both rôles, can function in both capacities. " Ideas," the subjective idealists say, are in the mind. So they are, if by idea is meant the thinking of, or, as we have called it, the direct apprehension of things—that is to say, the active side of our experience. So they are not, if by idea is meant the thing thought about or directly apprehended, the object of experience. The following passage from Bertrand Russell's book *The Problems of Philosophy* clearly reveals this ambiguity in the use of the word " idea," which, realists affirm, lies at the basis of the subjective idealist account of perception. " We think," says Russell, " of an idea as essentially something *in* somebody's mind, and thus when we are told that a tree consists entirely of ideas, it is natural to suppose that, if so, the tree must be entirely in minds. But the notion of being ' in ' the mind is ambiguous. We speak of bearing a person in mind, not meaning that the person is in our minds, but that a thought of him is in our minds. When a man says that some business he had to arrange went clean out of his mind, he does not mean to imply that the business

itself was ever in his mind, but only that a thought of the business was formerly in his mind, but afterwards ceased to be in his mind. And so when Berkeley says that the tree must be in our minds if we can know it, all that he really has a right to say is that a thought of the tree must be in our minds. To argue that the tree itself must be in our minds is like arguing that a person whom we bear in mind is himself in our minds."

Logical Formulation of Preceding Objection. Let us proceed to a logical formulation of the objection which has just been generally stated. The idealist argument may be stated in the form of three propositions.

(1) Ideas are incapable of existing apart from a mind.
(2) Things, in so far as they are perceived or known, are certainly ideas.
(3) Therefore things are incapable of existing apart from a mind.

Any apparent validity which this argument possesses depends upon precisely that ambiguity in the use of the word " idea " which has been pointed out. In the first proposition, the word " idea " is used to denote the act of perceiving. In the second, it denotes the object of the act, that is, what is perceived. But as the logical arguments against Idealism summarised in (A) above show, the object of an act of thought can never be the same as the act of thought of which it is an object. Therefore " idea ", in the first proposition cannot mean the same as " idea " in the second. But if it does not mean the same, then the third proposition does not follow from the first and the second.

3. THE INDESCRIBABILITY OF SENSATIONS. It is worth while pausing for a moment to consider how this apparently simple confusion between idea and object came to be made. Nobody, with a reasonably clear mind, let alone a competent philosopher, could, one is at first sight tempted to think, be guilty of it. But the matter is not quite

so simple as this contemptuous disposal of the idealists would seem to imply. Let us for the sake of clarity follow Professor Moore, from whom the ensuing exposition is taken, and substitute the word " sensation " for " idea." What, then, is the correct analysis of the experience which I call " my sensation of blue " ? I will begin by comparing it with an analogous but different sensation, which I call " my sensation of green." It is obvious, in the first place, that there is something in common between the two sensations, namely, that which makes them both mine. This common element is my consciousness. There is also an element which is different, since the sensation of blue is a perceptibly different experience from the sensation of green. This something different we will call non-committally (since we are not here arguing in defence of the realist position, but only trying to show how the confusion between idea and its object may have arisen) the object. We may say, then, that the object of the first sensation, " my sensation of blue," is different from the object of the second sensation, " my sensation of green."

Now prima facie it would certainly seem that to say " the sensation of blue exists " is different from saying " blue exists," and different also from saying " the sensation of blue exists *and* blue exists." But, if the subjective idealists are right, all these expressions mean precisely the same thing, since, for them, blue cannot exist apart from the sensation of it ; indeed, it *is* the sensation of it. Our question, then, is why is it that the two things, the sensation and the object of it, have been treated as if they were one and the same thing ?

(*a*) First, Professor Moore suggests, because of the deficiencies of language. Language, he points out, offers us no means of referring to objects such as " blue," " green " or " sweet," except by calling them sensations.[1] We cannot, that is to say, easily refer to them as being what they in fact are, namely, *objects of sensations*. Let us

[1] Most realist philosophers would now call them sense data. See pp. 91, 92 below.

consider the expression "my sensation of blue." I am now going to try to say something about "the blue" without introducing a reference to the fact that I am experiencing it. I find that I cannot, and because I cannot, because I have no means of referring to blue except in terms of my sensation of it, it is easy for me to fall into the mistake of assuming that blue *is* my sensation of it. Thus, because of the deficiencies of language, we find that we are in practice frequently forced to talk of things in terms of our sensations of them. Habitually we use expressions which ignore the difference between the two elements, the sensation and the object, which we distinguish above and concentrate attention solely on the first—that is to say, on the sensation.

(*b*) When, however, we resort to introspection, and, looking into our experience, try to say exactly how the sensation of blue appears to us, it is equally difficult not to make the opposite mistake, the mistake, namely, of ignoring the sensation and concentrating upon the object. That which is denoted by the term "blue" is easy enough to distinguish; but the other element, which is the sensation of blue, is exceedingly difficult to track down.

We saw above, that what the sensation of blue has in common with the sensation of green is the element of consciousness. But can we actually detect this element when we introspect our experience? Unfortunately we cannot, and the fact that we cannot is often invoked by materialists[1] as evidence for the view that there is no such thing as consciousness regarded as a distinct and separate element in our make-up. To quote Professor Moore: "That which makes the sensation of blue a mental fact seems to escape us: it seems, if I may use a metaphor, to be transparent—we look through it and see nothing but the blue." And because we are unable to track down and fix, as it were, for our inspection this element of consciousness in contradistinction to the object upon which the consciousness is directed, we have a tendency to ignore it and to

[1] See Chapter XVIII, pp. 510–513.

think that it is nothing apart from its object. Because of these two reasons, which are in a sense opposite reasons, we are apt to ignore either the one element in perception, the experiencing, or the other, the object experienced, running the object and the experience, as it were, together, and tending to think of them as if they were one and the same. Hence the ambiguous use of the word " idea " to denote both the act of experiencing and the object experienced.

4. The Right Analysis of Perceptual Experience. If we reject the idealist identification of sensation and object, what is the true analysis of the experience, which I describe by the expression " my sensation of blue " ? A sensation, say the realists, is simply the name we give to a recognisable kind of experience, namely, the kind of experience that we have when we are knowing an object external to ourselves, what we call a sensation being simply our way of perceiving or experiencing that object. The relation which a mind has to an object when it perceives or experiences the object is a unique relation. It is a relation which is common to all mental acts, but it is peculiar to them in the sense that it is only minds which are capable of entering into it.

Now Locke and Berkeley certainly held that some things could exist of which they were unaware in the sense that they were not, when they knew that these things existed, actually experiencing them. Locke, for example, believed in the existence of Substance, Berkeley in that of other minds and of God's mind. We can, then, they would agree, be aware of some things, namely minds, which are *not* parts of our experience in the sense that they can only exist when we are experiencing them. Hume, although actually believing in the outside world, thought that this belief was philosophically unjustifiable. He could, that is to say, see no method whereby reason could disprove the view that everything that exists is a part of our experience. But, once we have admitted that *some* things can exist which are not parts of our experience, the chief ground for Hume's scepticism in regard to reason disappears. If, then, it is the case with regard to our consciousness of some things, namely, other minds, that that of which we are conscious is not part of our experience, why, it may be asked, should it not be the case with regard to our consciousness of other things, for example, our consciousness of blue, that the blue is not part of our experience ? And if it *is* the case, then it will follow that to have a sensation of blue is to be aware of something which is not part of the experience of the mind which is aware of it.

The general conclusion of these psychological arguments is broadly the same as the conclusion of the logical arguments. All consciousness by its very nature is related to something other than itself, namely, the object of consciousness. This relation to something other is common and peculiar to all conscious acts, and is such that the object of a conscious act can never be a part of the conscious act that knows it. We can now proceed to a statement of some realist theories of perception, which, starting from the conclusion just reached as an axiom, attack the problem from the new standpoint which its assumption affords.

II.   COMMONSENSE REALISM

Development of Realism.   Let us assume that we feel ourselves to be justified, in the light of the above arguments, in rejecting the first of the two Berkeleyan positions that to exist is to be an idea in some mind, or, at least, to be dependent upon some mind. We have still to examine the second, that our ideas are not ideas of physical things but are ideas of simple sense qualities, such as blue, sweet, hard and cool ; or, to translate into the terms which our rejection of the first proposition necessitates, that the objects of our acts of direct apprehension are not chairs and tables, but are sense data characterised by particular sense qualities, such as the qualities blue and sweet, hard and cool.

Many realists, as I hinted at the outset, are to-day

prepared to accept the second of the two Berkeleyan positions, with the modification just stated. What we have, then, now to consider are the reasons which have influenced their acceptance. One of these reasons is the difficulty of maintaining the position known as Naïve or Commonsense Realism, which seeks to maintain that sensory experience is a process in which the mind makes direct contact with physical objects such as chairs and tables, even if it never perceives the *whole* of any one such object. This is, in fact, the position which many realists did at one time maintain, and a statement of it will prepare the way for the more advanced form of Realism, which the difficulties of Commonsense Realism were thought to entail.

Perception as a Two-Term Process.   Commonsense Realism starts from the axiom, established in the first part of this chapter, that in sensory experience the knowing mind always makes contact with something other than itself. Whereas Representationalism[1] conceives of perception as a three-term process in which the mind knows ideas which are produced in it by the world of external objects, and, by reason of its inability to show any ground for retaining an external world which cannot be known, finds itself unable to avoid a reduction to Subjective Idealism, Realism insists that, if we are to avoid this reduction, it is essential to begin by regarding perception as common sense regards it, that is to say, as a two-term process in which something other than the mind is directly revealed to the mind. " That there cannot be an act of knowing without something to know, or, more generally, that there cannot be an act of judging, even an act of apprehending, at all, without something to judge, something to apprehend, is one of the most self-evident propositions yielded by a quite elementary conception of these processes." The quotation is from the Austrian philosopher, Meinong (1853–1916), one of the earliest of the modern realists.

---

[1] See Chapter II, pp. 41, 42.

That most sensations are primarily caused by and result from the excitation of the nervous system, that is to say, from the impact upon the sense organs of external stimuli, no realist would wish to deny. What is denied is that this excitation of the nervous system is *what* we are aware of in perception, or that in any significant sense it determines what we are aware of in perception. The excitation of the nervous system is, it would be held, a matter of machinery only. It constitutes the method by which we become aware of stimuli ; it is not the stimuli of which we become aware. A simple analogy may help to elucidate the point. If I put a penny in an automatic chocolate-machine, the penny acts as a stimulus which excites certain machinery inside the machine, the result being a chocolate. But nobody would dream of confusing the penny with the excitation of the machinery and nobody would dream of confusing the excitation of the machinery with the chocolate. Similarly, when we want to know what it is that in the first instance *causes* us to perceive and what it is *that* we perceive, physical and physiological considerations relating to wave motions, retinal changes, neural currents, cerebral disturbances and so forth are irrelevant. These things are, no doubt, parts of the machinery which must function before the application of a stimulus to the sense organs results in a perception ; but they do not throw any light upon the question, " What is it that we perceive ? " The problem of perception is in part the problem of the nature of the original stimulus, and in part the problem of the nature of the act of perceiving it. It is not a problem of the method by which that stimulus is conveyed to the brain.

Meinong's Theory of Perception.

Insisting as they do that perception is a two-term process, the supporters of Commonsense Realism are concerned to maintain that the stimulus which is the original cause of an act of perception and the object of the act are one and the same. The physical object, in fact, possesses a two-fold relation to the act of perceiving. It both stimulates the act and forms its object. What, in fact, on Meinong's view, happens when we perceive is briefly as follows : An object which is placed in appropriate juxtaposition to any one of the sensory organs produces a stimulation of those organs which in turn excites the nervous system. The disturbance in the nervous system is conveyed to the brain, where it stimulates an act of consciousness. This consciousness, as Meinong puts it, is " directed upon something," the something being the physical object from which the stimulation of the senses initially proceeded. Thus the physical object is both the cause of an act of awareness taking place and the object of the act.

Now this act of awareness, which is an event taking place in the consciousness of the perceiver, is not bare and featureless. On the contrary, it exhibits differentiating features, whereby one act of awareness may be distinguished from another. Thus the act of awareness of red is different from the act of awareness of green. This does not mean that the act of awareness of red is a composite mental state made up of two elements, awareness and red. On the contrary, it is an indivisible whole which cannot, like a material whole, be divided into separate component elements or parts. As a whole, however, it is qualitatively different from any other mental act, such as the awareness of green. This indivisible whole, namely, the awareness of red, can never, it is insisted, " be the object of the act of which it is the content,"[1] the object of the act in question being a red object. It is along these lines that those who retain the commonsense notion that it *really is* the same external object that two men are perceiving, endeavour to explain how one man's perception of the object may be palpably different from another's.

But does the explanation so far given take adequately into account the problems raised in the first chapter ? Does it, for example, really make provision for the fact upon which subjective idealists lay stress, the fact, namely,

[1] See p. 71 above for the technical use of the word " content." The quotation is from a paper by Professor Dawes Hicks.

of the different perceptions which different people clearly do have of what would normally be called the same thing ? Can it really be the case that, when I see a blue carnation and a colour-blind man sees a green one, our acts of direct apprehension, whose contents are in these cases so manifestly different, are directed upon the same external thing ?

The Importance of Mental Activity in Perception.

Only, Commonsense Realism would reply, if we are prepared to amplify the above account by making provision for the activity of the mind. For the mind, it is strongly emphasised, is not passive in perception, but active. Let us consider in a little more detail what forms this activity of the mind takes. There are two main ones :

(1) It discriminates and selects from the presented environment.

(2) It goes out beyond it and adds to it.

As regards (1), the process of discrimination accounts for the different way in which the same object appears to different perceivers.

To take an instance given by Professor Dawes Hicks, it is obvious that a red rose, which we will call R, will appear in different ways to an artist, a botanist, and a colour-blind person. These different appearances we will call r_1, r_2, and r_3. Now these different appearances are brought into being by reason of the fact that we make discriminations in the whole which is presented, and emphasise certain features at the expense of others.

Thus r_1 will contain only a certain percentage of all the attributes of the presented rose R, and r_2 will contain a different percentage ; r_1 and r_2 become, therefore, that part of the presented whole R which is actually perceived ; the percentage of attributes perceived forms the content apprehended, and this content apprehended is other than the complete content, that is the sum total of all the qualities of the physical object from which we have made our selection. This does not mean that r_1, r_2, and r_3 exist independently of being perceived. R exists independently of the act of perception, but r1, r2, and r3 are selections from R, which are only called into being by that act. Thus we never sense reality completely, but are always directly in touch with a selected part of it.

The way in which we make this discrimination or selection depends upon our general mental make up. As a rule, we select, as the psychologist would say, according to systems which interest the perceiver. Differences of mind, of bodily equipment and, above all, of interest will condition the kind of r which we shall carve out from the whole R.

Thus differences of discrimination dependent upon differences in direction of attention account for what are sometimes called the different appearances which the same object exhibits to different persons.

Element of Judgement in Perception. As regards (2), it would seem that the capacity which mind possesses of going out beyond the actual data which are given to it, is brought into play in practically all acts of perception.

That portion of reality with which our senses actually acquaint us in perception is small : " Psychologists have made us aware," says Bertrand Russell, " that much of what at first sight seems to be given is really inferred." Thus, when we think we see a table, we may in reality see directly only two legs and the surface of one horizontal plank of wood, without actually perceiving the place where they join. We do not see the other two legs, and we do not see the underside of the table, but from the incomplete portion which we do see we construct the whole table.

It is the business of the mind, on this view, to go beyond these fragmentary appearances apprehended by the senses, and to piece them together so that a complete physical object emerges as the result. We get a discontinuous and fragmentary view of reality in all perception, but by selecting from the given whole those aspects that interest us, and at the same time synthesising and piecing together the aspects selected, we manufacture for ourselves that which forms the content of our consciousness. This content is not other than the content of reality, but is a selection from it, a selection which, it may be, has been arranged differently in the process of being selected.

In this sense, it is said, all perception involves an element of judgement. There is, in fact, no such thing as a pure awareness of something which is outside ourselves. In all perception we go beyond what we actually perceive, and it is this activity of " going out beyond " that provides an opportunity for the operation of judgement. Thus when we are aware of a patch of red colour, a noise of crackling and a sensation of warmth, we *judge* that these sensations together indicate a fire, and we say that we *perceive* a fire. In fact, however, if by *perception* we mean direct sensory apprehension, we *perceive* nothing of the sort.

Now, it is the intrusion of this element of judgement in perception which, while enabling us to synthesise the fragmentary appearances which we have discriminated in physical objects, enables us also to synthesise them in such a way as to construct what are in effect *different* physical objects, that is to say, physical objects which are not really " there." It is this construction of physical objects which are not really " there " which accounts for the fact of error.

The Difficulty raised by Erroneous Perception.

The difficulty of accounting for error[1] is one which besets any attempt to give an account of perception on realist lines. If we accord to the mind, as some idealists do, the capacity of being able to construct, whether in whole or in part, the objects which it perceives, engendering them, as it were, out of the stuff of its own consciousness, or contributing parts of them out of the stuff of its own consciousness, the fact that it may make mistakes, constructing what is not there, or contributing elements which own no counterpart in reality, offers no particular difficulty. Admittedly, we should not on this basis be able to maintain,

[1] See Chapter XVI, p. 435, for an account of the theory of truth and error which Commonsense Realism entails.

as in common sense we certainly wish to maintain, that the perceptions of a mind were accurate, or that its ideas were true, in so far as they squared with or truly represented external facts, since there would be no means of directly knowing the external facts by reference to which the accuracy of the perceptions or the truth of the ideas could be established and their falsity detected. But idealist theories, as we shall see in a later chapter,[1] provide their own criterion of truth and error which fits naturally into the general system of idealist thought. If, however, we take the realist standpoint, and hold that the function of the mind in perception is that not of construction but of exploration, that its activity is not that of a creator projecting from within itself ideas which it then proceeds to know, but which are in no sense there until it knows them, but rather of a searchlight illuminating the world upon which it is directed, how, the question inevitably arises, can it illuminate what is not there? How, in fact, account for erroneous perception?

Only, it may be answered, by crediting the mind in perception with some active function, which it may perform wrongly. It may perform this function when, in going out beyond what is actually given in perception in the manner described above, it puts together various fragmentary data into a completed object which is not warranted by the data, or which is warranted nine times out of ten, and is lacking in the tenth.

The peculiar feature of error seems to be that appearances which are taken by mind to indicate a certain kind of physical object, act as cheats, and actually signify a different object.

This is seen most clearly in cases where the appearances of things are deliberately made to act as cheats, as for instance for the purpose of deceiving the mind of an opponent in a game. Thus at tennis the flight of the ball is commonly taken by the receiver to afford an indication of the way in which it will bounce. The mind, in fact,

[1] See Chapter XVI, pp. 438, 439.

constructs in advance the bounce of the ball from the data afforded by its flight. Presently, however, the server, by imparting a screw to the ball, causes the same apparent flight to produce a *different* result, and the mind, accordingly, falls into error through just this activity of going out beyond the appearances afforded by what is given to it, and making a false construction from them.

Summary. The above constitutes a brief account of the arguments of the Commonsense Realism, which endeavours to maintain the two positions that the external world consists of physical objects, and that sensory experience is a process which directly reveals them to the mind of the person having the experience. The number of philosophers who can be found to maintain these positions to-day is not large. We have, then, now to consider the reasons which have led many contemporary philosophers to abandon this attempt to uphold the naïve presumptions of common sense ; these are also the reasons which have contributed to the adoption of the more advanced form of Realism which affirms that sense data and not physical objects are the immediate objects of our acts of direct apprehension.

III. THE THEORY OF SENSE DATA

How Much of the Object is Perceived ? Let us begin by considering what is entailed by the supposition we have just been making, that in perception the mind goes out beyond the fragmentary data with which our senses supply us and pieces them together to form physical objects. What is it that is supposed, on this view, to happen in a particular case, the case in which I am said to be perceiving a table ? Let us consider this case in a little more detail than we have hitherto done. If I look at a table from a normal position, what actually lies within my field of vision is a couple of legs, a ledge under the top, part of the surface of the top, the rim of the surface, and possibly a glimpse of the under side. Yet, in practical life I assume that I am seeing, and certainly make statements as if I saw, the whole table. The whole table, then, on this view, is in part perceived and in part a mental construction, the mind going out beyond the data actually presented to it, and supplying the remainder from its memory of the tables it has seen in the past, and its past observation of their conformation and behaviour. Thus the core of the total perception of the table, being given as it were from without, is *actually* perceived ; the rest is supplied by the mind which automatically invests the core with the accretions of memory and association. In other words, the fragment actually seen *hints at* or *is representative of* the whole, and the mind, which notes the representation, is quick to take the hint and to fill in from its own resources the content which is represented.

The Physical Object As an Unknown Substance.　The account at first sight seems sufficiently straightforward, but two difficulties are latent in it. First, it is admitted that the table which, as I say, I perceive is a composite table. Part of it, we are asked to believe, is actually given to my senses ; part is supplied by my mind. But can I distinguish the one part from the other ? I cannot. I cannot, then, affirm with any degree of certainty of any part that it *is* given to my senses from outside, that, in other words, it is *not* supplied by my own mind. But, if I cannot, I can find no answer to make to the idealist who tells me that it is all *supplied* by or is in my own mind. In the second place, if, as is admitted, there is a difference between the fragmentary data which I directly apprehend in sense experience and the physical object to which they are said to belong, what sort of knowledge do I have of the physical object ? Do I know it by means of my senses ? Presumably not, not, at any rate, all of it. However hard I may try, I shall only succeed in directly apprehending more fragmentary data ; I shall never succeed in attaining to a direct sensory experience of the whole physical object itself.

　　What right, then, it may be asked, have I to postulate

such an entity at all? Have not the conclusions of Common-sense Realism reduced themselves to a position not very different from that of Representationalism, a position, that is to say, which, requires us to postulate in addition to what is actually apprehended, namely, the fragmentary data revealed to our senses, something which underlies the data apprehended and to which they are supposed to belong? And is not this something very like Locke's Substance, in that it is not itself something that is directly known but something that is inferred? The position, in fact, may be expressed by means of the three-term formula which we used to describe Representationalism. There is the mind that knows (M), the fragmentary data that are known (D), and the physical object (O) which is supposed to cause the data or to which the data are supposed to belong. Now M always knows D and never knows O. What right has it, then, to postulate O, in addition to D, to be the cause of D? For if M does not know O, it cannot know that O causes D or that D belongs to O.

The Definition of Sense Data.

The importance of these questions and the far-reaching character of the criticisms that they raise will be realised, if we consider more closely the nature of these so-called fragmentary data which, most realists now maintain, are the objects of our acts of direct apprehension. So far we have spoken of them as if they were what at first sight they seem to be—that is to say, parts of physical objects. We have spoken, that is to say, as if, although admittedly we do not see the whole of the table, what we do see is recognisably the legs and the top of the table. But is this true? Do we see the whole even of the legs, or the whole even of the top? Most realists would maintain that we do not, that the immediate objects of our acts of direct apprehension are in fact not legs and tops of tables but what we have been calling sense data, and that the assumption which we have hitherto made that these sense data are recognisable parts of physical objects begs a very important question.

What do those who take this view mean by sense data ? The following is a celebrated definition given by Bertrand Russell : " Let us," he says, " give the name of ' sense data ' to the things that are immediately known in sensation : such things as colours, sounds, smells, hardnesses, roughnesses and so on. We shall give the name ' sensation ' to the experience of being immediately aware of these things. Thus, whenever we see a colour, we have a sensation *of* the colour, but the colour itself is a sense datum, not a sensation."

Sense data, in fact, are like the simple ideas of sense qualities which we have already met with in the theories of Locke and Berkeley, with the difference that, instead of being in the mind like the simple ideas, they are external to the mind and are the objects of its acts of direct apprehension (which Russell calls " sensations ") of which they are independent. We are, that is to say, now affirming in its realist form Berkeley's second conclusion, namely, that our sensory experience is not of physical objects, but is of the simple sense qualities which would normally be said to belong to physical objects.

Now it can, I think, be clearly shown that the entities with which our senses make us acquainted when we have experience of the external world, are not, as common sense assumes, physical objects but are sense data. In support of this contention I propose to cite a number of considerations, most of which are adapted from Professor Broad's book *The Mind and its Place in Nature*.

Sense Data not Identical with Physical Objects.

(1) If I am looking at a bell, nobody would maintain that what I see is, or is identical with, the whole of the surface of the bell. For example, the bell has an inside as well as an outside ; yet what I see is a coloured patch of indefinite boundaries, which, although it may be part of the outside, is certainly not part of the inside. Therefore what I see is not identical with the whole surface of the physical object.

(2) The bell, considered as a physical object, is extended not only in space but in time ; it has a past and a future, and the length of its history from the time of casting to that of demolition is in theory measurable. What I see is a single, comparatively short event. It may be true that the short contemporary event which is the object of my seeing is also a contemporary slice of the history of the bell, but it is certainly not identical with the whole stretch of the history of the bell, which extends backward into the past and forward into the future.

(3) A bell is more than a coloured surface, and the surface itself has qualities other than that of colour ; it is, for example, also hard and cold. What I see when I look at the bell has colour but is neither hard nor cold. Therefore, what I see is not identical with the surface of the bell.

(4) What I touch, when I touch the bell, is both hard and cold but is not coloured. The surface of the bell is coloured. Therefore what I touch is not identical with the surface of the bell. It is also different from what I see when, as I say, I look at the bell. The conclusion is that neither in visual nor in tactile experience is what I directly apprehend by means of my senses the *whole* surface of the bell.

(5) Let us suppose that I place a half-crown and a florin in positions in which the half-crown is considerably farther away from me than is the florin. Then the shining elliptical patch which I shall see in the place in which the half-crown is will be smaller than the shining elliptical patch which I shall see in the place in which the florin is. But the half-crown is larger than the florin ; also both are circular. Therefore the patches which I see cannot be identical with the surfaces of the half-crown and the florin.

(6) I can be the victim of what are commonly called hallucinations. A hallucination is a state of mind in which I believe myself to see things which would in common parlance be said not to be " there." A similar state of mind attends intoxication ; the drunkard sees what he calls pink rats in circumstances in which no person who is not drunk sees them, and in which consequently there would

be common agreement among all sober persons that the pink rats were not " there."

Accepting this argument at its face value, assuming, that is to say, that the drunkard's experience is, as we say, delusive, in the sense that there really are no pink rats " there," then we are justified in saying that, whatever it is that the drunkard perceives—and he certainly does perceive something—it is not identical with a physical object, since in this case no such object exists.

Direct Apprehension is not of Objects but of Sense Data. The above are some of the considerations which make it difficult to suppose that what we are aware of when we have direct experience by means of our senses of the external world is, or is identical with, a so-called physical object. So far as the sense of smell is concerned, this conclusion, as I have noted in the first chapter, is recognised by common sense ; there is, that is to say, a general consensus of opinion to the effect that *what* I am actually aware of when I smell a flower is not identical with the flower itself, is not even part of the flower. A similar concession might be made in respect of the sense of hearing ; it might, that is to say, be conceded that *what* I hear is not a physical object, such as a trumpet or violin—although common sense is in such an inextricable muddle with regard to the question of what precisely it is that is the object of my direct apprehension when, as I say, I listen to something, that it is difficult to say what view it takes—but it is not, so far as I can see, generally conceded in respect of the objects of the senses of touch, taste and sight.

On the strength, however, of the considerations adduced above, it seems difficult to deny that the entity which I directly apprehend when, as I say, I see something, is not *identical* with the physical object which I should normally be said to be seeing, and that the data which I directly apprehend when, as I say, I touch something, are not *identical* with the physical objects which I should normally be said to touch or taste. We may summarise the conclusion of the above arguments as follows: the coloured, round, green patch which I directly apprehend when I look at an apple is not identical with the apple; the sharp angular ridge which I directly apprehend when I run my hand along the edge of the table is not identical with the table; and the sweet-tasting " something " (the language is without an appropriate word for the immediate objects of our taste experience) which I directly apprehend when I put a lump of sugar into my mouth is not identical with the lump of sugar. Nevertheless it seems clear that sense data do stand in some very important relation to physical objects, since otherwise I should not be led to say that I see or taste the latter, when in fact I only directly apprehend the former.

What, then, is the nature of this relation?

Relation between Datum and Object.   It is very difficult to say. There are two possible relations which immediately suggest themselves. The first, that the sense datum is a part of, or a part of the surface of, the physical object. The second that the physical object is, in some sense, a cause of the datum. To each suggestion there are grave objections which have been pointed out by Professor Moore. Let us consider them in turn.

The Datum not Part of the Surface of the Object.   (a) Let us suppose a case in which the surface of an " object " would normally be said not to have changed. Then, if we focus our vision upon a certain part of what would normally be called the surface, the object which we do in fact directly apprehend does perceptibly change according to the position from which and the conditions under which we look at the part. If we look at the alleged part from a greater distance, that which we actually see is different from what it is, if we look at the part from a smaller distance; different, if we look at the part obliquely, from what it is, if we look at the part from a position vertically above it; different, if we look at the part after santonin has been put into our eyes, from what it is, if we look at the part when our eyes are in a normal condition. Most noticeably of all, the object which we feel, when we touch the part, is quite different from the object which we see, when we look at the part.

Thus the object which we directly apprehend perceptibly changes according to the changes in our position and changes in the state of our visual organs. The object seen is also perceptibly different from the object touched. Yet we have assumed a case in which the surface of the physical object does not change. If the whole surface of the physical object does not change, no part of it can change. Therefore the object of our direct apprehension is not identical with a part of the surface of the physical object ; the sense datum, in other words, is not a part of the surface of the object.

(b) If two people with different eyesight, or two people standing at different distances, focus their vision on what would normally be called the same part of the surface of the object, they will each directly apprehend a different sense datum. Since the sense data are different, they cannot both be identical with the same part of the surface of the object. It is of course just possible that one of them may be in fact identical with the part in question and the other not, but there is absolutely no reason to suppose that this is the case ; there is no reason, that is to say, to suppose that, of the infinite number of positions from which the object can be viewed, one and one only is privileged in the sense that from it and from it alone the sense datum which is directly apprehended is identical with a part of the surface of the object. Moreover, even if it were the case, it would be quite impossible to say which of all the possible positions the privileged position was. It would seem, then, that we cannot know of any sense datum that it is, or is identical with, a part of the surface of the object, and that it is practically certain that no sense datum is, or is identical with, a part of the surface.

But if this is so, the Commonsense Realism described above, which entails the assumption that what is directly apprehended in sense experience is a part of an actual physical object, even if it is never the whole of it, would seem to be untenable. Indeed, if the sense datum is not a part of the physical object, it seems highly doubtful whether we can ever be said to have *sensory experience* of physical objects at all.

The Object not the Cause of the Datum.

Let us now consider the suggestion that the physical object is in some sense the cause of the datum. Here again there seem to be two serious objections. (*a*) The first is a restatement of the objection that we have already urged against any form of Representationalism.

If we always perceive the sense datum and never perceive the object, and if the object is a constituent of the physical world, all our knowledge of the object, such as it is, will be dependent upon our perception of a number of sense data. We shall have, in other words, no *direct* knowledge of the object. Having no *direct* knowledge of the object, we cannot know any of its properties (except in so far as we may be said to know them indirectly by directly apprehending the sense data). Now the property of being able to cause a sense datum is not a property of the object which we know through directly apprehending sense data. Therefore since we cannot know the alleged property of the object by any other method, we do not know that the object has the property of being able to cause the sense data. In other words, the knowledge that the object is the cause of the sense data would involve just that direct acquaintance with the object, an acquaintance which is independent of and obtained otherwise than through the sense data, which, on the view we are considering, we do not possess. Hence, if the object is the cause of the sense data, we cannot know that it is.

(*b*) The suggestion that the object is the cause of the sense data is open to the further difficulty that it presupposes that a sense datum has one cause and one cause only, and that this cause is the object. This is certainly not the case.

Dp

Sense data have a number of different causes, some of which, as we saw in the first chapter, are certainly bound up with the state of my sense organs and nervous system at the moment when I apprehend them. Thus, to take a simple example, if I put santonin into my eyes the colour of the sense data I shall see is different from the colour of the sense data I see with normal vision. Others of the causes are bound up with conditions external to myself which are, nevertheless, not part of or dependent upon the object. For example, the sense data I see vary according to the state of the atmosphere, the quality and intensity of the light in which I look at them, and the direction from which the light strikes my retinas. Now there does not seem to be any good ground for asserting in regard to the object that it is *the* cause of the sense data in some sense in which these factors, and many others which have not been mentioned, but which indubitably determine the properties of the sense data, are not their causes.

Apprehension of Sense Data in the Absence of Objects.

It is of course conceivable that the object *may* play some part in causing the sense data, but if it does, it is quite impossible to assess the relative parts played by the causative influences of the object and of these other factors respectively, or to say which of the properties that the sense data perceptibly exhibit are due to the object and which to the other factors. Hence the view that the object is, in fact, a cause of the sense data must remain a belief for which, in the nature of things, there cannot be any evidence, since it will never be possible to affirm of any of the properties of the sense data, for which the causative influence of the object is invoked, that they are in fact due to the object and not to one or other of the other factors. In point of fact there are cases, such as that of the drunkard's perception of pink rats, in which it would be commonly said that there is no object at all. Nevertheless, in these cases sense data are certainly apprehended. If, then, the common view is correct, we must suppose that the other factors, to some of which I have referred, are in such cases exclusively responsible for the occurrence of the sense data.

Nor, I imagine, would anybody wish to deny that the causation of the sense data of which a man is aware when drunk must be ascribed largely to the influence of factors operating within the drunkard's own body. Yet there is no *intrinsic*[1] difference between my perception of pink rats when drunk and my perception of a postage stamp when sober. So far as introspection is concerned, they are on all fours : in each case I believe myself to be receiving information about an independently existing, physical object. It is, indeed, characteristic of the state of drunkenness that the drunkard is convinced that he is receiving such information. If, then, it is possible for the conviction to be mistaken in one case, it is at least theoretically possible that it is mistaken in all cases. Hence, so far as my immediate sensory experience is concerned, it affords me no grounds for postulating a physical object to constitute even a partial cause of my sense data. It is to precisely this somewhat unsatisfactory negative conclusion that a number of philosophers have come.

Possible Conclusions.

We have now entered the realm of contemporary controversy, and it is not possible to point to any *positive* conclusions which most or even many philosophers would agree to have been established by the preceding arguments. It is, indeed, largely because of its inability to arrive at any satisfactory account of the relation between sense data and physical objects that the school of modern Realism, which began by maintaining a more or less coherent body of agreed doctrine, has to all intents and purposes broken up, so that to-day Realism consists of little more than the divergent views of a number of individual thinkers. Broadly speaking, however, there are three main lines of advance from the position which we have just reached.

[1] That is to say, no recognisable difference in the experiences involved in having the perceptions considered in and by themselves. (See p. 52).

1. RUSSELL'S ELIMINATION OF THE PHYSICAL OBJECT. First, there is the view at which we have just glanced, which, accepting the logic of the foregoing analysis, insists that the notion of the physical object must be abandoned as a myth. This, in fact, is the position which Bertrand Russell has been disposed to adopt in his later books,[1] with the reservation that he calls the physical object not a myth but a logical construction. The arguments by which this position is reached are technical; nor is the conclusion in which they issue very easy to understand. Let us, however, start from the premise that different sets of sense data are presented to different people. These appearances are necessarily always different, since owing to its association with a body, each mind looks out upon the world from a standpoint peculiar to itself. It follows that, in Russell's words, the " world seen by one mind contains no place in common with that seen by another, for places can only be constituted by the things in and around them." We may suppose, however, that " in spite of the differences between the different worlds, each exists entire exactly as it is perceived, and might be exactly as it is, even if it were not perceived." There are, therefore, an infinite number of such worlds, as many, in fact, as there are places from which a view of the world can be obtained ; whether any of these places is occupied by a mind or not, there will be a special and peculiar view of the world from that place. Hence aspects of the world exist from all possible points of view, although no observer need necessarily be perceiving them from those points of view. It follows that each aspect of the universe which is presented to a different place is independent of mind in respect of its existence, and an external reality is, therefore, established which is not mind-dependent.

Every observer, then, gets a different view of the world which Russell calls a perspective, and this perspective will be occupied by sets of sense data which are peculiar to itself, which are, that is to say, different from those situated

[1] In *Our Knowledge of the External World, An Outline of Philosophy,* and *The Analysis of Matter.*

in every other perspective. Now my view of the world from one place, or, in other words, my perspective, will be exceedingly like the view I obtain from a place situated a couple of inches to the right of it, although no two sense data appearing in the two perspectives will be absolutely identical. Hence, I can establish a correlation between the two sets of similar sense data which appear in the two neighbouring perspectives, a correlation which is taken in ordinary life to justify me in asserting that they are produced by, or that they belong to, the same object.

The object itself, however, is, on this view, simply the sum total of all the sense data which would be presented by the object, if there were in fact an object, at all possible points of observation. This conclusion may be put in Russell's own words :

" Given an object, in one perspective, form the system of all the objects correlated with it " (by means of similarity) " in all the perspectives ; that system may be identified with the momentary commonsense ' thing.' Thus, an aspect of a ' thing ' is a member of the system of aspects which *is* the thing at the moment." But the aspect is not the thing : the aspect—that is to say, that which is immediately experienced—is a set of sense data, and the thing, which is the system of all the different sense data which appear in all possible perspectives, is a logical construction and not a real existent.

2. KNOWLEDGE BY ACQUAINTANCE AND KNOWLEDGE BY DESCRIPTION. Let us suppose, however, that we try to retain the notion of the physical object. What sort of knowledge do we have of it ? It is plain that, if we know anything about it, such knowledge can only be reached *via* the sense data—that is to say, the data of colour, shape, texture, temperature and so on which we normally associate with it. But, for the reasons already given, we are not entitled to say that these sense data *are* the object.

In an early work entitled *The Problems of Philosophy*, whose publication constituted one of the starting-points of modern

Realism, Bertrand Russell makes a celebrated distinction between two sorts of knowledge, called respectively " knowledge by acquaintance " and " knowledge by description." We have knowledge by acquaintance of those entities which we directly apprehend by means of our senses—that is to say, of sense data. But in some sense we also, Bertrand Russell affirms, know physical objects. In what sense ? Russell answers that we know them " by description." We *describe* the object by means of the sense data which we know by acquaintance. We also feel ourselves to be justified in holding some such general proposition as that the sense data in question are caused by or belong to a certain physical object. Hence our knowledge of the object involves a knowledge of truths. It involves, that is to say, a knowledge of the truth of some proposition which asserts that the sense data we know by acquaintance belong to and are caused by a physical object and by only one physical object.

What, then, we are really knowing when we know a physical object is, to quote Bertrand Russell, " a description, and we know that there is just one object to which this description applies, though the object itself is not directly known to us. In such a case, we say that our knowledge of the object is knowledge by description."

But how can we know truths ? We can know truths, Russell holds, only in so far as we can know by acquaintance certain entities whose nature is essentially different from that of sense data. These entities are usually known by philosophers under the name of universals. The nature of universals will be considered at some length in a later chapter.[1] For the present it is sufficient to say that they are denoted by general terms such as " whiteness," " justice," " humanity," by relations such as " to the north of " or " bigger than," and by verbs and prepositions. Of these universals Russell holds—or rather he held at the time when *The Problems of Philosophy* was written—we have knowledge by acquaintance.

[1] See Chapter X, pp. 259, 260.

Now the knowledge of physical objects, being an example of knowledge by description, always, as we have seen, involves some knowledge of truths—that is to say, of the truth of some particular proposition. But we can only know truths, or, more precisely, we can only know that a particular proposition is true, when we know the constituent parts of the proposition by acquaintance. Now, every proposition contains one or more universal. It follows that knowledge of physical objects is, if this view of Bertrand Russell's is correct, dependent both upon the existence of universals and upon our ability directly to know them by acquaintance. In the writer's view any realist theory which denies a direct *sensory* knowledge of physical objects must concede a direct acquaintance with universals. It is doubtful, however, whether many realists would agree to this.

3. THE RETENTION OF THE PHYSICAL OBJECT AS AN UNDERLYING SUBSTANCE. The above theory is not exposed to any very obvious logical objection, and, provided that we are prepared to accept the existence of universals and to agree that we know them by acquaintance, it may be offered as a reasonable solution of the problems we have been considering. Is there, however, no more direct method of establishing the existence of physical objects, and of establishing also the fact that we know them ? In so far as an act of faith may be termed a direct method, there is.

But in the last resort, it is nothing less than an act of faith that is involved. It is, however, one which, according to many competent philosophers, it is reasonable to make. Among these philosophers is Professor Broad.

What, he asks, are the outstanding presumptions that we make about physical objects ? First, they are presumed to be more permanent than the sense data we directly apprehend, which apparently come into and go out of existence, as the position of our bodies changes. Secondly, they are presumed to be public, that is to say, to be common to many observers ; and they are presumed, thirdly, to be extended in space and to have a bounded surface which determines their shape and size. Now for all these three presumptions there are, Professor Broad thinks, reasonably good grounds. For the first, there is the ground which we have already noted, that, if I leave my room when the fire is burning red and come back in an hour's time and find that it has burnt grey, the changed appearance which I observe is consistent with the view that the fire has been in existence, but has been slowly burning away all the time I have been out of the room. Moreover, it is exceedingly difficult to account for on any other basis.

The main ground for the second presumption is the correlation between the experiences of a number of observers.

The Correlation between the Appearances of the Penny. Consider the case in which a number of observers are looking at the top of a penny. Then each of the following statements will be true.

(*a*) They are all looking in a direction such that, if they were to move in that direction, they would all meet in the same place.

(*b*) All the observers have in the middle of their visual fields patches of some shape of brown, and all the patches possess shapes which are projections of a circle.

(*c*) All the observers would be aware of certain describable tactile sense data, if they were to walk up to the place at which their lines of vision intersect.

The reasonable inference from these considerations is that the correlated experiences of the various observers depend upon two factors ; that one factor, namely, the sense data factor, varies as the positions of the observers vary, but that the other remains constant in spite of the variations. It is to this other that we give the name " the penny."

In favour of the third presumption is the fact that our visual sense data occupy space and are spatially related to each other. They also vary according to the laws of perspective, as we move our heads and bodies. Now these facts are most easily accounted for on the assumption that there are physical objects, that included among physical objects are our own bodies, and that our bodies and the physical objects in question are extended in space and are spatially related to each other. In other words, in order to account for the spatial character of the visual sense data we apprehend, it is reasonable to assume that they are in some way produced by physical objects which are also spatial. Nor does any other hypothesis account equally well for the fact of the spatial correlations of our sense data.

Return to Locke's View. The above argument from spatial correlation does not apply to such qualities as taste and temperature. Indeed, it may well be the case that the conditions which determine what tastes, smells, and temperatures our sense data will have are events which are taking place wholly within the observer's body. The conclusion of this third line of development from the analysis of what we directly apprehend in terms of sense data is, therefore, not unlike Locke's.[1] It may be summarised as follows. The external world contains physical objects possessing primary qualities which exist independently of us. These, when brought into the appropriate spatial relations with the physical objects, which are living human bodies, produce sense data which we directly apprehend by means of our senses. These sense data are partly caused in respect of *all* their qualities, and wholly caused in respect of some of their *secondary* qualities, by conditions prevailing in the bodies of those who experience them. They do not, therefore, exist except when the experiencer's body is present.

This is, it must be admitted, not a very satisfactory conclusion. But it does have the merit of enabling us both to retain physical objects and to meet most of the objections which have been urged against their retention. This is undoubtedly a merit, since everybody believes, or at any rate acts as if he believes, in the existence of physical

[1] See Chapter II, pp. 41, 42.

objects. This belief has, therefore, a high degree of initial probability. If this initially highly probable belief can be supported by reasonably convincing considerations, we should be showing an undue degree of scepticism in refusing to adopt it. Those who, like Professor Broad, adopt the conclusion which we have just outlined (development 3) are inclined to take the view that the considerations just enumerated are reasonably convincing. It must, however, be admitted that on this third view we do not directly apprehend physical objects by means of our senses, and in this respect the view does violence to commonsense beliefs. If, however, this is a disadvantage, it is one which, as the reader will shortly find, it shares with almost every philosophical view that has been propounded.

The number of books on modern Realism is very large. The most important are :

MOORE, G. E.   Philosophical Studies.
BROAD, C. D.   The Mind and Its Place in Nature.
    See especially Section B for a statement of the sense data theory.
HOLT, E. B., AND OTHERS   The New Realism.
DRAKE, D. AND OTHERS   Essays in Critical Realism.
LAIRD, JOHN   A Study in Realism.

These are all fairly difficult. Much the best non-technical treatment of perception from the realist standpoint is contained in Bertrand Russell's volume in the Home University Series entitled *The Problems of Philosophy*. *Idealism*, by A. C. Ewing, contains a comprehensive survey of the various arguments which have been urged against Idealism.

CHAPTER IV : WHAT ARE THE ORIGINS AND NATURE OF OUR KNOWLEDGE?

Rationalism and Empiricism

Does Sense Experience provide us with all our Knowledge?
In the preceding chapters we have discussed the problems suggested by a consideration of the nature of sense experience. Whatever view we take with regard to the controversial issues involved, it seems, to say the least of it, unlikely that sense experience gives us *knowledge*, or, more precisely (assuming that we are prepared to dignify with the name of knowledge the seeing of a particular red patch, or the feeling of a particular rough surface, into which on examination sense experience seems to resolve itself), it does not give us knowledge of a world in the least like that which in everyday life we believe ourselves to inhabit. What the external physical world is like we may not know, but it is at least fairly certain that it is a very different affair from the collection of solid objects extended in space which common sense affirms. But, if the view of the world for which the commonsense interpretation of our everyday experience is responsible turns out to be faulty, have we any other means of obtaining knowledge about the external world, which will represent it to us more truly? Can we, for example, obtain knowledge by speculating, by reasoning, or even by some intuitive faculty such as that which the artist or the mystic is commonly supposed to possess? Mathematics, for example, certainly seems to give us definite knowledge—nobody, so far as I know, has ever successfully challenged the view that seven times seven make forty-nine—and this knowledge is, it is obvious, not obtained by means of our senses. We are here brought face

to face with some of the most important questions in philosophy, the questions, namely, of how we obtain our knowledge and of how we can know that it is valid. It is to these questions that we must now turn.

Rationalist Contentions.   Philosophy provides us roughly with two main historical answers to the question of how we obtain knowledge. The first is that knowledge is in fact obtained entirely in and through sense experience. This answer we have already by implication examined in the preceding chapters. The second answer, that it is obtained by our reasons, we shall now consider. This second answer has usually been given by philosophers known as rationalists, who have argued that the mind is provided initially with a number of ready-made principles or faculties, and that in order to obtain knowledge it only needs to reason in accordance with these principles and to use these faculties. Just as a mathematician sitting in his study could, provided he reasoned well enough, deduce the whole of mathematics from one or two fundamental axioms by sheer process of reasoning, so, the rationalists taught, the philosopher, provided he was a good enough philosopher, could discover the truth about the universe by the same methods. Hence a rationalist philosopher was one who took the view that reason itself, unaided by observation, can provide us with philosophical knowledge, which is also true knowledge. Such knowledge is generally called *a priori*.

Now, if the universe were like a mathematical problem, the claim put forward by the philosophical rationalists on behalf of reason could be sustained. But unfortunately the realm of what exists is different from the realm of mathematics ; it contains the sort of facts with which mathematicians concern themselves, and, in so far as it does so, may legitimately be explored by pure reason ; but it contains other facts as well.

Necessity and Contingency.   The sort of facts with which mathematicians concern themselves are usually known as necessary. These may be defined, as Leibnitz defines them, as facts[1] which we know in such a way that the certainty of our knowledge is not increased by repetition. They are also, he points out, such that their opposite is not possible or conceivable. Leibnitz considered that the existence of this sort of fact entailed the existence of God, since the necessity of necessary facts is only explicable on the assumption that they are being thought of by God. For this reason he calls God's understanding " the region of necessary truths." We shall presently suggest grounds for rejecting proofs of God's existence based on this type of reasoning.

An example of a necessary fact is that the three interior angles of a triangle are equal to two right angles. This fact is necessary, because it follows necessarily from the definition of a Euclidean triangle ; because a triangle is what it is, this is necessarily a fact about it. Another illustration of a necessary fact is that, if A is greater than B and B than C, then A is greater than C; another, that three and two make five. Facts of this kind can be discovered by process of reasoning. They are also facts which we cannot conceive, in any kind of world we choose to imagine, to be different. I can conceive worlds which contain things of an entirely different kind from the contents of this one, but, however different they might be, I cannot conceive three of them and two of them making six.

Leibnitz's Views : The Principle of Sufficient Reason.

Rationalists were inclined to regard all facts as necessary. Thus Leibnitz makes use of a principle, which he calls the principle of sufficient reason, to show that everything in the universe must be just as it is. He defines the principle as that " in virtue of which we believe that no fact can be real or existing and no statement true, unless it has a sufficient reason why it should be thus and not otherwise." Leibnitz deduced this principle from the existence of God.

[1] Leibnitz, for reasons which do not concern us here, generally speaks of " truths," not of " facts." What we should call a necessary fact was for him a truth which was being thought by some mind.

Everything that existed was, he held, a centre of spiritual experience and activity which he called a monad, and every monad was, he maintained, a thought in the mind of God : " God," he says, " regards all aspects of the universe in all possible manners," and " the result of each view of the universe as seen from a different position is a substance." Since God's thinking must be the best that is possible, it follows that everything in the world must necessarily be as it is, since it too must be the best that is possible. Leibnitz was not always consistent in this view since he maintained that the acts of those monads which were rational souls, that is to say, the acts of human beings were not necessary, but free. He also believed that there were in the universe contingent facts, and invoked the principle of sufficient reason to postulate a first cause, that is God, to prevent the series of contingent facts continuing indefinitely : " Thus," he says, " it is necessary that the sufficient reason which has no more need of another reason should be found outside the series of contingent things in a substance which is the cause of the contingent things— that is, in a necessary being carrying in itself the reason of its existence ; otherwise there would still be no sufficient reason at which one could end. Now this last reason of things is called God."

Now the freedom of the rational monads and the existence of contingent facts are plainly at variance with the view that everything that exists in the world must be as good as possible, and everything that happens must happen in the best possible manner. Indeed, if God exists and causes the world by thinking about it, as Leibnitz says that He does, it is difficult to see how there can be such things as contingent facts.

In fact, however, Leibnitz fails to offer any satisfactory proof of the existence of God. Referring to the argument quoted above, we may pertinently ask why he should take it for granted that the series of contingent things should end, or rather, why it should begin ; why, in fact, should there be a first cause at all ? Even if there were, it seems fairly plain that it could not perform the function for which Leibnitz invokes it. There must, he says in effect, be a first cause to originate the series of contingent things. But this cause would either be inside the series or outside it. If inside, it must be itself contingent and therefore have a cause ; if outside, it cannot be related to the series in the way in which its postulated causation of the series implies. In fact, it cannot cause the series at all. If, however, we do not accept Leibnitz's proof for the existence of God, the ground for drawing the conclusion which the proof should, if successfully established, have led him to draw (although he did not in fact draw it), namely, that all facts are necessary, disappears.

Let us, then, provisionally assume that there are contingent facts. We may define contingent facts as those which do not follow from any preceding fact ; they just happen to be what they are, and could perfectly well be imagined to be different. For example, the fact that a substance with the specific gravity of gold should be yellow is a fact which no amount of reasoning will enable us to discover, because there is nothing reasonable about it. It is also a fact which might quite conceivably be otherwise. I can, for example, imagine a substance with the specific gravity of gold being blue, just as I can imagine the moon's mean distance from the earth being 237,800 miles and not 238,800.

Contentions of Empiricists.

It was by concentrating their attention upon facts of this latter kind that a school of philosophers presently began to insist that, if a man wanted to know what the universe was like, the only way was for him to go and look, that is, broadly speaking, to adopt the method of science. To put the point in another way, we may say that, although reasoning will tell you what will follow from the fact that X exists, reasoning cannot tell you whether in fact X does exist. Observation alone can inform us of the nature of what exists. Those who have insisted that observation or sense experience is the basis of all knowledge are known as empirical philosophers or as empiricists, from the Greek word ἐμπειρία, which means experience. Empiricists, emphasising the actual brute facts of the world, the facts, that is to say, which are known in sense experience, have tended to arrive at sceptical conclusions with regard to such questions as the existence of design or purpose in the universe, or the ability of mind to function freely. That the universe is ultimately spiritual in character, or that God exists, are facts, if facts they are, which are certainly not given in sensation, and, in denying that anything could be known except through the medium of sense experience, empiricists have usually found themselves unable to admit the existence and efficacy of spiritual agencies. Thus their philosophies have been agnostic rather than theistic in tendency, and their effect has been to confirm the outlook of the scientist and the man of hard common sense. There are exceptions to this generalisation, but it is true in the main. Rationalist philosophers who have relied upon the operations of the reasoning faculty to give them knowledge about the universe have tended to arrive at conclusions which are more conformable with our aspirations, affirming that the universe is fundamentally spiritual, and is, therefore, such as we should wish to inhabit. The existence of God, for example, could, they held, be proved by reasoning, and a number of different proofs were in fact advanced. Hence, when the brute facts of experience have seemed to contradict the spiritual character of the reality which reason has affirmed, the rationalists have sought to show that the world revealed to us by our sense experience is in some sense illusory, in that it presents an appearance which belies the reality to which philosophical reasoning points. Thus Rationalism in philosophy has issued in beliefs which are directly opposed to those of the rationalists of the modern world who deny the existence of a supernatural element in the universe.

Descartes (1596–1650), Leibnitz (1646–1716), and Spinoza (1632–1677) are rationalists in the philosophical sense just indicated ; the English philosophers, Locke

(1632–1704), Berkeley (1685–1753), and Hume (1711–1776) are prominent exponents of the empirical school.

Examples of "a priori" Knowledge.

I pointed out above that, if the universe were fundamentally of the same nature as the realm of mathematics, it would be possible to discover the truth about it by the process of reasoning from self-evident premises. Descartes and Leibnitz were both eminent mathematicians, and their philosophies are accordingly markedly mathematical in character. Affirming, that is to say, that we possess incontestable knowledge independently of sense experience, they proceeded to use their reasons to deduce what the universe must be like in order to account for our having such knowledge.

The question whether we do in fact have knowledge independently of sense experience, whether, in other words, we have *a priori* knowledge, is exceedingly controversial. The most apparently convincing examples of it belong to the realms of logic and mathematics. In order that we may realise how the existence of *a priori* knowledge is possible, let us take as an example our knowledge of the fact that two and two make four. How do we come to know this fact? It is, no doubt, necessary in the first place that we should have some actual experience of concrete objects such as counters. The child learning arithmetic actually handles such objects, and is made to realise that any pair of them when combined with any other pair of them makes four. The next stage is the realisation of the truth that this fact in no way depends upon the nature of the objects counted, in order that it may be a fact; that it is, in short, a fact not only with regard to those objects which have actually been counted, but with regard to all objects of whatever kind, both those which have been counted and those which have not. No additional number of instances is, therefore, required to establish the truth of the general proposition that two and two make four, which is seen to be independent of any of the instances by which it happens to have been illustrated. Although an instance may have been necessary to draw our attention to the general proposition, adequate consideration of this one instance establishes the general proposition with complete psychological certainty.

Relation of Sense Experience to " a priori " Knowledge.

When we grasp the truth of a general mathematical proposition, our minds make a jump from the actual instances in which the truth of the proposition has been verified to the realisation of the truth of all instances both verified and unverified—that is to say, to the apprehension of the general proposition itself. Now, since the general proposition embraces instances which have not been experienced, our knowledge of it, entailing, as it does, knowledge of unexperienced instances, cannot be based entirely upon experience. Experience of instances though necessary to draw our attention to this piece of general knowledge, does not therefore constitute its sole ground, nor does our knowledge of the general proposition, once it has been obtained, depend upon the instances we have examined. One way of putting this is to say, with the philosopher Kant (1724–1804), that although all our knowledge begins with experience, it does not all spring from it, and the knowledge that does not spring from experience is what we have called *a priori*. It is knowledge which we have possessed, in some sense, all the time, but to the existence of which the instances actually experienced have been necessary to draw our attention.

In asserting that there is knowledge of this kind the rationalists were right, and the empiricists, in so far as they denied it, were wrong. Although, therefore, most modern philosophers find it impossible to agree with Descartes and the other rationalists that we do, in fact, know *a priori* many of the things which they thought we did, they agree with them that this sort of knowledge is at least possible. If we assume that there is *a priori* knowledge, then it will follow that we know many things that we shall be unable to prove ; that they should be self-evident to the intellect will be a sufficient guarantee of their truth. Thus we find Descartes saying that knowledge is given by the clear vision of the intellect. That I should clearly and distinctly conceive something in my mind is, in other words, for him a sufficient reason for regarding what I clearly and distinctly conceive as true. This assertion is highly controversial, but the questions which it raises belong more properly to the next chapter. .

Limitations of "a priori" Knowledge.

In the light of the above discussion we may, I think, safely conclude that we do in fact possess knowledge that is not derived from sense experience. But we must be careful against allowing ourselves to suppose that this knowledge is more extensive than it really is. It will help us to guard against this error, if we lay down two principles which govern and to some extent limit its scope. First, though it cannot be proved by experience, *a priori* knowledge is normally elicited by experience. It seems to be necessary, that is to say, for us to have sense experience of some things before we can have *a priori* knowledge of anything—of particular couples before we can know that two and two make four, of triangles drawn on the board before we can have knowledge of general geometrical truths. One way of stating this principle is that our psychological limitations are such that it is necessary for us to have sense experience before we can have *a priori* knowledge, though that of which we have *a priori* knowledge is other than that of which we have sense experience. In the second place, *a priori* knowledge cannot inform us of what exists in the physical world. It may, of course, be the case that the physical world is not the world that really matters, and that there is another world at once more real and more perfect than that with which our senses acquaint us, which we can know *a priori*. Many philosophers have, as we shall see, held this view, and regarded philosophy as the sustained endeavour to determine by means of *a priori* reasoning the characteristics of a real world which, they believed, underlay the world of sense experience.

Philosophy so conceived is known as Metaphysics or the study of reality, and we shall concern ourselves with it in Part III. Whatever view we may feel disposed to take with regard to the existence and nature of this so-called real world, we may, I think, safely assume that, so far as the physical world is concerned, it is by means of sense experience and not by means of *a priori* knowledge that we become acquainted with its contents.

The above is intended to serve as a brief summary of the conclusions of a discussion to which philosophers have devoted considerable attention—the controversy with regard to the existence and scope of *a priori* knowledge formed the centre of philosophical interest in the seventeenth and eighteenth centuries—and as a statement of the conclusions to which most modern philosophers would subscribe.

Without pursuing the discussion further, I propose to supplement the conclusions outlined above, to which, as I have said, most philosophers would now be prepared to subscribe, by various arguments illustrative of the limitations and achievements of *a priori* knowledge taken from the actual history of philosophy. Let us begin with its limitations.

Ontological Proofs for the Existence of God.   As I have already noted, many philosophers have held the view that we could by sheer process of reasoning deduce what the nature of the universe must be. A famous example of this type of reasoning is the ontological proof for the existence of God. This proof, which seeks to deduce the existence of God from the idea of Him, appears in a number of different forms in the works of various philosophers. The earliest statement of it appears in the works of the philosopher St. Anselm, Archbishop of Canterbury (1033–1109). Kant states St. Anselm's proof as follows: "The realest of all beings contains all reality ; and one is justified in assuming that such a being is possible. . . . But existence is included in all reality ; therefore existence belongs to the concept of a possible being. If, now, this thing does not exist, the inner possibility of it is denied, and this denial is a contradiction." This reads strangely to modern ears, and a more intelligible statement is that of Descartes. " When the mind," says Descartes, ". . . . reviews the different ideas that are in it, it discovers what is by far the chief among them—that of a Being omniscient, all-powerful, and absolutely perfect ; and it observes that in this idea there is contained not only possible and contingent existence, as in the ideas of all other things which it clearly perceives, but existence absolutely necessary and eternal. And just as because, for example, the equality of its three angles to two right angles is necessarily comprised in the idea of a triangle, the mind is firmly persuaded that the three angles of a triangle are equal to two right angles ; so, from its perceiving necessary and eternal existence to be comprised in the idea which it has of an all-perfect Being, it ought manifestly to conclude that this all-perfect Being exists."

The argument may be stated in modern terms as follows : I have an idea of perfection. If I had not, I should not know, as I certainly do know in regard to various imperfect things that they are in fact imperfect, since I should not have any standard by reference to which to convict them of imperfection. But perfection which does not exist is not really perfect, since, lacking existence, it would lack an element whose presence would, it is obvious, enhance and improve it. Therefore the idea of perfection implies the existence of the perfect thing or being which the idea postulates. Therefore perfection exists. Therefore God exists. More briefly, the idea of God is the idea of an all-perfect Being. But to perfection or completeness belong all attributes, power, goodness, knowledge, and also *existence*. Therefore God, of necessity, exists.

Kant's Criticism. This proof was sharply criticised by Kant. In so far as it appears to be plausible, its plausibility depends, as he shows, upon a confusion between *conceived* existence, that is to say, existence which is reflected upon by us, and *real* existence. The proof in fact treats conceived

existence and real existence as if they were synonymous.
But the circumstance of my conceiving of something does
not make the something real ; I can conceive of the planet
Venus as being inhabited by Jabberwocks who spend their
lives in solving quadratic equations, but my " conception "
affords no reason for supposing that the inhabitants of
Venus are in fact of this nature and do in fact engage in
this pursuit. As Kant puts it : " No doubt there is in my
purse a hundred dollars more, if I actually possess them,
than if I have the conception, that is have merely the
possibility, of them." The conclusion is that the fact that
we can and do present to ourselves the conception of an
all-perfect being does not in itself afford any guarantee of
that being's existence.

The Cosmological Proof.　　Another famous example of an
a priori proof for the existence of God, which was also
criticised by Kant, is known as the Cosmological. This proof,
which was employed by philosophers as diverse as Descartes,
Berkeley, Leibnitz, and even Hobbes (1588–1679), and is
frequently invoked by theological apologists in our own
time, is stated by Leibnitz as follows : " Thus it is necessary
that the sufficient reason which has no more need of
another reason, should be found outside the series of contingent things, in a substance which is the cause of
contingent things—that is, in a necessary being carrying
in itself the reason of its existence ; otherwise there would
still be no sufficient reason at which one could end. Now this
last reason of things is called God." (And God so defined
must exist, since existent things require an existent cause.)
Kant's statement is more summary ; it is also clearer :
" If anything exists an absolutely necessary Being must
exist, . . . [for] every contingent thing must have its cause,
and this cause—if contingent—must have its cause till the
series of subordinate causes end in an absolutely necessary
cause, without which the series would have no completeness. . . . Now, at least I myself exist, therefore an absolutely necessary being exists."

The argument contains two stages : (1) Every contingent[1] fact must have a cause ; (2) everything that exists must have an ultimate cause which completely explains and accounts for the thing, but is itself uncaused. Kant accepts (1) but denies (2). Why, he asks, should not the causal series of linked events stretch back indefinitely, in which event, however far we might push our enquiries, we should never reach an ultimate and completely explanatory first cause ? Because the causal relation as we know it is universal, it does not follow that there must therefore be an ultimate cause. The view that there must is not either a corollary of or a deduction from the view that all contingent facts have causes. It is rather a contradiction of that view, since a first cause, being itself *ex hypothesi* uncaused, runs counter to our experience of universal causation.

The application of these criticisms should not be extended beyond their immediate intention, which is to expose the invalidity of " proofs " advanced by rationalist philosophers purporting to establish by *a priori* reasoning the existence of God. As a matter of fact, Kant did believe strongly in God's existence and advanced important arguments in favour of his belief. But he is anxious that the belief in God should not be based upon unsound arguments—in point of fact, Kant's own belief in God was derived rather from a consideration of the facts of human personality and the nature of moral experience, than from conclusions reached by abstract reasoning—nor did he assent to the rationalist view that it was possible by the use of the speculative *a priori* reason *alone* to establish propositions purporting to show what the ultimate nature of the universe must be. Kant's view will be described in greater detail in Chapter XIV.[2]

" A priori " Disproof from Fact of Pain and Evil.   One of the drawbacks to *a priori* arguments about the nature of the universe as a whole is that they can be invoked to support contradictory conclusions. Indeed, it is possible to

---

[1] See above, p. 111, for the meaning of " contingent."
[2] See especially pp. 397, 398.

produce reasonably good *a priori* arguments for almost any metaphysical belief that we choose to propound—for it and against. Let us take as an example the belief in question, that the universe is the creation of an omnipotent and benevolent God. The belief has to encounter at the outset the difficulty occasioned by the obvious facts of pain and evil. Of these it is clear that some account must be given. If they are real and exist by God's will, it is difficult to see how He can be benevolent. If they are real and exist in His despite, it is difficult to see how He can be omnipotent. Many theologians have accordingly declared in favour of the view that they are unreal. It is difficult to see what meaning can be given to the word " unreal " in this connection, but to avoid controversy on a side issue let us suppose that pain and evil are conceived to be unreal in some sense in which happiness and goodness are real. Now there is no doubt that I *think* that I suffer and that men do me evil. I certainly *think*, that is to say, as I go about my daily life, that pain and evil are real. If they are in fact unreal, this belief of mine is an error. Is this error real or unreal ? If it is unreal, it will not be *really* false to hold that pain and evil are real, and pain and evil will, therefore, be real. If, however, the error is real, then the universe contains real error, real, that is to say, in precisely the sense in which pain and evil were pronounced to be other than real. Now either God created this real error, or it exists in His despite. In the former event He cannot be all good, since the deliberate creation of error is not the mark of an all good being. In the latter, He cannot be all powerful.

Relevance and Intention of Above Argument.

No finality is claimed for the above argument. It is, indeed, introduced less for its own sake, than as an illustration of the ease with which the human mind which has been trained in dialectic can produce *a priori* arguments for and against any general metaphysical conclusion purporting to show what the nature of things *must* be. As a matter of historical fact most of these trains of argument have been elaborated in order to establish a theistic conclusion, human beings having exhibited a marked tendency to employ their reasons to discover grounds for supposing that their spiritual aspirations must be fulfilled ; but it is possible to prove by similar methods and the use of arguments no less apparently cogent that the theistic hypothesis is untenable. The above argument is introduced as an illustration of this possibility.

Limitations of Reason and Claims of Intuition.

Many philosophers are and always have been inclined to doubt whether questions relating to the ultimate origin, nature and purpose of the universe can be fruitfully tackled by the method of speculative reasoning. When such doubts are expressed, it is reason in the strict and narrow sense of the word that is impugned, the contention being that knowledge of the ultimate nature and purpose of things, if, indeed, such knowledge be possible in the present stage of our development, withheld from reason, is revealed to a faculty more akin to what is popularly known as intuition or insight.[1] The mystic, the saint, the good man, even the artist, are, supporters of this view maintain, more closely in touch with truth than the philosopher or the scientist. Their pursuits constitute the avenues along which the real nature of things can most readily be discerned. It is, it would be admitted, unfortunately the case that they are unable to give an account of their truth-revealing experiences, or to adduce in support of the world-view to which the experiences point, anything in the nature of what reason would be prepared to accept as evidence— unless, indeed, the beauty of picture and symphony or the appeal of disinterested goodness can be regarded in the light of evidence. (That these do in fact constitute evidence for any view of the universe whatsoever, would be widely denied.) Nevertheless, there is a sense in which the heart, and still more the spirit of man may have reasons of their own of which the reason knows nothing. The issues raised

[1] See Chapter XIX, pp. 550, 551, for an example of this contention in the philosophy of Bergson.

by the claims which are made on behalf of intuition as a faculty revelatory of the nature of reality will be further considered in Chapter XIX.

Spinoza's Philosophical Method.

The recourse to intuition for information as to the true nature of reality is, however, something of a heterodoxy in philosophy, most philosophers having maintained that the nature of things could be discovered, at least in part, by the exercise of the reasoning faculty. They have, in other words, been rationalists. Perhaps the most impressive of the attempts which have been made to establish and to demonstrate the fundamental nature of reality by pure reasoning is that of Spinoza. I do not propose to enter here upon a detailed description of his philosophy.[1] One or two examples of his mode of reasoning will, however, serve the purpose of further illustrating the character and limitations of rationalist methods in philosophy.

Spinoza's philosophy belongs to the class of metaphysical systems known as monistic (from the Greek word μόνος). He holds, that is to say, that the universe is in an important sense One, and that this One is a single whole which is a unity. He also holds that this unity is God. His system, therefore, is a pantheistic one, in that it asserts that in the last resort God is all and all is God. We are, however, here concerned not so much with Spinoza's conclusions as with his method of establishing them. This is, broadly speaking, the method adopted by Euclid to prove propositions in geometry. Spinoza's most important work is his *Ethics*, which is divided into five parts—" Of God," " Of the Nature and Origin of the Mind," " Of the Nature and Origin of the Emotions," " Of Human Bondage," and " Of Human Freedom." Each division of the *Ethics* begins, like a geometry book, with a series of definitions supplemented by a set of axioms (sometimes by a set of postulates), and followed by propositions with their proofs and corollaries.

[1] Spinoza's philosophy is a form of Monism, a doctrine which will be most conveniently considered in relation to the philosophy of Hegel, its most prominent exponent. See Chapter XVI, especially pp. 410, 411.

Spinoza in fact believed, with Descartes and Leibnitz, that the universe was sufficiently like mathematics for the truth about it to be attainable by the process of *a priori* reasoning from premises which were taken to be self-evident. Now the charge which can be, and usually is, brought against such a method, as Spinoza employed it, is that his definitions and axioms are in fact very far from being self-evident ; that on the contrary they contain or imply the very conclusions which he is setting out to establish ; and that the whole process of apparently logical proof by which Spinoza proceeds to establish these conclusions presupposes in the premises from which it starts the very beliefs which it is purporting to prove.

Spinoza's Proof of Monism.

Let us take as an example Spinoza's method of establishing the proposition that the universe is a single all-embracing unity, which is God. A number of proofs of this proposition are adduced, of which the following may be taken as typical. There is, says Spinoza, obviously something in the universe ; the universe, in other words, consists of some kind of stuff or Substance. Let us, then, define this stuff or Substance—" By Substance," he says, " I mean that which is in itself and is conceived through itself : in other words, that of which a conception can be formed independently of any other conception," and proceeds to contrast Substance so defined with what he calls a mode or modification of Substance, that is to say, any particular mind or thing which " exists in, and is conceived through, something other than itself."

The important part of this definition is contained in the expression " conceived through itself," for it is on the basis of this expression that Spinoza purports to show that the universe is one single all-inclusive whole.

Let us, he says, suppose that something exists besides Substance. Then Substance would have to be conceived as limited at least in extent by this something. The universe, in fact, would consist of Substance *plus* something, that is, of Substance limited by something. To give a complete account of Substance would, therefore, involve mentioning that which, by virtue of occupying the universe together with Substance, limited Substance. Therefore, if it is to comply with the definition and be " conceived through itself," Substance must be unlimited. By the same reasoning Substance can be shown to be uncaused, since, if there were causes other than itself to produce it, it could not be "conceived through itself." Substance, then, if it is " conceived through itself "—if, that is to say, the conception " not that other thing " is not to be tacked on to the idea of Substance—must exist single, all-inclusive, and uncaused.

Criticism of Proof.   But why, it may be asked, should it be so conceived ? The answer apparently is " because that is how we began by defining it." But why should it be so defined ? It is not clear. If Substance means simply " all that there is," it is of course the case that it must exist, that it must be " conceived through itself " and that it must be all-inclusive. " If people would consider the nature of Substance," Spinoza says, " . . . this proposition " (namely, that existence belongs to the nature of Substance) " would be a universal axiom and accounted a truism." Most certainly it would, if Substance means " all that there is " ; but in that case all that the argument will have proved is that " all that there is " exists, is " conceived through itself," and is all-inclusive ; it will have proved, that is to say, that " all that there is " exists and is " all that there is." In other words, if we assume that Substance in the original definition means simply " all that there is," then the initial definition contains within itself the conclusion. Such a conclusion is not worth proving. It is, indeed, merely a tautology—that is to say, an asserting of the same thing in two different ways ; and it is certainly not a tautology that Spinoza is concerned to prove. What he is anxious to establish is that " all that there is " has a certain character, that it is, in fact, a unity, and that this unity is God. But his argument, successful in proving a tautology, is very far from establishing this further proposition.

He proceeds as follows. He gives, first, another definition, this time of God, as " a being absolutely infinite." We have already proved that " there can be only one Substance " and that " Substance is necessarily infinite." Therefore, Spinoza concludes, Substance is God. But the conclusion does not follow. What has been shown is that Substance exists in the sense of being " all that there is." What is being assumed is that this " all that there is " is a God who is infinite. *If* there is a God who is infinite, then certainly He must be identical with Substance and, therefore, must exist. But this conclusion is not established ; it is assumed in the original definition of God. All that Spinoza has proved is that Substance, in the sense of " all that there is," exists. He has not proved that Substance, which is both a unity and also a God who possesses the particular characteristics of being good, wise and powerful, exists.

Doubt as to the Success of Methods Similar to Spinoza's.

Thus Spinoza's attempt to prove by *a priori* reasoning from premises assumed to be self-evident that the universe is of a certain kind may be held to have failed. We may, indeed, well share the modern doubt whether any attempt to demonstrate by such methods *alone* that the nature of the universe is "so and so" can succeed. At any rate it would not appear that any of the numerous attempts that have been made on these lines up to the present have been successful.

RUSSELL, BERTRAND The Problems of Philosophy. Chapters VI–VIII.
AARON, R. I. The Nature of Knowing.

Spinoza's *Ethics*, Parts I and II, published in the Everyman Edition, affords a good example of the *a priori* rationalist method in philosophy. Leibnitz's *Monadology* (also in Everyman, with an introduction by C. R. Morris) may also be read with advantage. R. Adamson's *The Development of Modern Philosophy*, Vol. I, is a standard work which contains in Part I an account of the rationalist philosophers and their methods, and in Part II an account of the empiricists.

Chapter V: LOGIC AND THE LAWS OF THOUGHT

Introductory : Function of Logic. In the last chapter I pointed out the limitations of *a priori* knowledge. We cannot, I suggested, obtain by *a priori* reasoning information as to what exists in the physical world, while it seems unlikely that the attempts which have hitherto been made to determine by exclusively *a priori* methods the characteristics of the universe as a whole have been successful in their object. I further ventured the view that it is unlikely that any subsequent attempt along these lines will succeed. In this chapter I shall be concerned rather with the achievements of *a priori* reasoning. Of what kind, I shall ask, are the things that we can know *a priori* and what kind of knowledge is it that *a priori* reasoning supplies ? The answers to these questions involve some consideration of the branch of philosophy known as Logic.

Logic has historically formed one of the main departments of philosophy. It is also sometimes treated in isolation as a separate subject of study ; when so treated it is usually known as Formal Logic. Formal Logic may be defined as the systematic investigation of the principles of valid reasoning, that is to say, of the principles upon which valid reasoning depends. Some philosophers have described Logic as the study of the " Laws of Thought " or of the " Processes of Reasoning." But not only is the expression " Laws of Thought," as we shall see later, ambiguous, but, in so far as it suggests that the laws which govern right thinking are themselves mental laws, in the sense of " mental " in which to be a " mental law " is to be a law about the workings of minds, it is definitely misleading. For, to revert to the definition just given, most logicians are now agreed that " the principles upon which valid reasoning depends " are principles of form. When, therefore, logic asks what are the conditions which our reasoning processes must satisfy, if they are to reach true conclusions, or what are the differentiating characteristics of a valid process of reasoning and what are the marks of an invalid one, the answer will be in terms of certain formal principles and conditions which, though they govern chains of reasoning which are valid, are not themselves reasoning or parts of reasoning. The workings of the mind may, indeed they must, if it functions properly, conform to these principles, but they themselves are independent of the ways in which our minds work. Formal Logic has tended of recent years to fall into disrepute. Its elements were laid down by Aristotle (385-322 B.C.) in the latter part of the fourth century B.C., and Aristotelian Logic, as it was called, completely dominated the subject until comparatively modern times. Of recent years, however, Aristotelian Logic has been subjected to serious criticism. This criticism takes two main forms. It is said, first, that, from the point of view of psychology, Aristotle's principles do not provide a true account of the way in which the mind works ; and it is said, secondly, that Formal Logic is apt to degenerate into a series of verbal exercises in which dialectical skill is regarded as more important than the attainment of truth. Both these criticisms have been urged with considerable force by a modern school of philosophers known as Pragmatists.[1] An example of the kind of criticism which Pragmatists have levelled against the traditional methods of Formal Logic will be found below.[2]

Modern or Generalised Logic.

In recent years a new type of logic has arisen which has effected what amounts to a revolution in the subject. This, which is known specifically as Modern, or sometimes as Generalised, Logic, dates from the publication, just before the war,[3] of a celebrated work entitled *Principia Mathematica*, by

[1] Some account of Pragmatism will be found in Chapter XVI, pp. 448-464.

[2] See pp. 140-142.

[3] The first volume was published in 1910, the second in 1912.

Professor Whitehead and Bertrand Russell. The publication of this work gave a new impetus to the study of logic, and occasioned a break with the Aristotelian tradition which had dominated the subject for two thousand years. The break was, however, with the Aristotelian tradition rather than with Aristotle himself. In *A Modern Introduction to Logic*, the best known text-book on the subject, Professor Stebbing is careful to point out that the views of the modern logician constitute a perfectly natural development of those of Aristotle. " Throughout the book," she says in introducing her work, " emphasis is laid upon the continuity of some of Aristotle's doctrines with those of the mathematical logicians."

The introduction of the word " mathematical " requires some explanation. While maintaining continuity of development, modern logicians have made an important departure from the traditional Aristotelian logic. Many of Aristotle's most important doctrines—for example, the doctrine that every proposition ascribes a predicate to a subject,[1] the classification of the types of propositions and the reduction of every deductive process to the syllogistic form[2]—are rejected by modern logicians. The distinctive characteristic of the modern conception of logic is its formality. Logic, that is to say, is conceived by them as a study not so much of the process of reasoning, as of the nature of form. Logic so conceived has much in common with pure mathematics ; for mathematics reveals that proofs are only completely cogent when they are completely formal. The idea of modern logic may be described as the establishment of proof in realms other than the mathematical, and it can, its exponents hold, only succeed in realising this ideal, in so far as its subject matter shares the formality of mathematics. Like mathematics, it makes considerable use of symbols. Another characteristic of modern logic is its greater degree of generalisation as compared with traditional logic. Its object is to

[1] See Chapter VI, pp. 166, 167.
[2] See below, pp. 139, 140, for an account of the Syllogism.

exhibit all processes of formal reasoning as springing from a very few fundamental principles which logic shares with mathematics. It is for this reason that it is sometimes known as Generalised Logic. Modern logic is apt to be both difficult and technical and is still in a condition of flux and growth. For these reasons I shall not attempt to deal with the subject in this book, but shall content myself with recommending the reader to *A Modern Introduction to Logic* by Professor Stebbing, which contains a comprehensive account of the subject.

Logic as an Example of A Priori Knowledge.

From what has been said the reader is entitled to conclude that the logic which has been studied during the last two thousand years—that is to say, the so-called Formal Logic which derives from Aristotle—has lost much of its traditional importance. No reasons for this conclusion have, admittedly, been given, since to give them would entail precisely that exposition of the views of modern logicians from which I have just excused myself on the score of their technicality. I can, therefore, only ask the reader to accept the fact, which I am now proposing to invoke as a ground for omitting any formal account of Aristotelian Logic. To omit modern Logic because it is immature and Aristotelian Logic because it is dead may strike the reader as somewhat disingenuous. I can only assure him that this cavalier treatment, or rather lack of treatment, does correspond to the facts of the case, and seek to defend myself by pointing out that my failure to give a formal treatment of Logic does not mean that all discussion of logical problems will be omitted. On the contrary, I am proposing to introduce some of the most important of the questions with which Logic deals as a continuation of the general discussion of *a priori* knowledge begun in the last chapter. This is a natural mode of treatment, since the knowledge whose existence Logic demonstrates forms one of the most eminent and conclusive examples of this type of knowledge.

EP

The Inductive Principle.   There are, it is obvious, some truths which we know with a feeling of as complete psychological certitude as we are capable of entertaining. We know, for example, that, if the sun rises to-morrow, then it will rise in the east. We know that, if the hands of the clock are now pointing to 10 o'clock, then, after an interval of an hour, they will, if the clock is going, be pointing to 11 o'clock. We also know certain laws of a general character which, we believe, govern the workings of nature—for example, that, if oxygen and hydrogen are associated in a certain proportion, the result will be water, that the attraction between bodies varies inversely with the square of the distance between them, and that, if water reaches a certain temperature, it will turn into steam. These laws are said to illustrate a general principle which we know as the uniformity of nature, and on reflection it will be found that most of the beliefs which we entertain with regard to the behaviour of specific things on particular occasions, as, for example, the belief that the sun will rise in the east to-morrow, and the 10 o'clock belief that the hands of the clock will be pointing to 11 in an hour's time, are based upon a belief in this principle. It is because we believe the workings of nature to be orderly and to be governed by uniform laws, that we believe that future occasions which exemplify these laws will resemble past ones. This belief in the resemblance of the future to the past, a belief which is sometimes expressed in the phrase " same cause, same effect," is obviously of the very greatest importance both to the scientist and to the practical man. Indeed, our assumption of its truth is implied in almost every action of our waking lives. If I did not believe on sitting down to breakfast that the bacon and eggs which gratified and nourished me yesterday will again gratify and nourish and not poison me this morning, I should starve.

What is the source of our knowledge of, or, if the expression be preferred, what are the grounds for our belief in, the uniformity of nature, upon which our beliefs with regard to the behaviour of particular things are in their turn founded ? The answer to this question is that the knowledge of or belief in the uniformity of nature is based upon a principle known as the Inductive Principle, which may be stated as follows : " When two things have been found to have been associated together on a large number of occasions and on no occasion has one of them been observed to occur without the other, then the occurrence of one of them on a fresh occasion makes it probable that the other will also occur. Under the same circumstances a sufficient number of cases of association[1] in the past increases the probability of a fresh association in the future, and the increase of probability continues without limit until it approaches certainty." For example, the association of water with a certain temperature has always in the past in the absence of disturbing conditions been found to result in steam, and, *given the same circumstances*, no instance has been known of the association of water and the temperature in question which has not resulted in steam. On the basis of these facts the Inductive Principle entitles us to say, that in all future cases also, water associated with a given temperature will become or result in steam. This knowledge, which the Inductive Principle affords, may be stated in the form of a general law : " When water reaches a temperature of 212 degrees Fahrenheit it becomes steam."[2] Now this law purports to describe the behaviour of all water, not only of the water which has reached the temperature in question and been observed to turn into steam, but of water which reaches the temperature in question but does not happen to have been observed : not only of all the water that has existed in the past and is now existing in the present, but of all

---

[1] " Association " means statistical association—that is to say, association in actual fact. It does not mean mental association—that is, the associating together of instances by us in our minds. The importance of this distinction is brought out by the discussion in pp. 144–150.

[2] I am omitting for the sake of simplicity the complication introduced by the fact that at high altitudes, where the air pressure is less, water turns into steam at a lower temperature.

water which may or will exist in the future. It makes, in short, a statement about the behaviour of all water, everywhere and at any time, which is associated with the requisite temperature. In so doing, it outruns experience. Experience can verify the law in regard to those instances which have been examined, but it can throw no light upon those which have not. Experience, moreover, can have nothing to say about the future. Yet, most people would agree, we do have knowledge of this general law governing the behaviour of water, and we do believe very strongly that it will apply to the behaviour of water in the future ; and we have this knowledge and entertain this belief because we know, or think we know, that the Principle of Induction is true. How, then, do we come to know this ? Not, as we have seen, as a result of experience, since the Principle of Induction, by reason of its very generality, applies to things which we have not experienced. Thus the Principle itself cannot be proved by experience.

A Priori Knowledge Presupposed in the Organisation of Sense Experience.

Moreover, the Principle of Induction, or some similar principle, both underlies sense experience and is implied by it. This fact has an important bearing upon the controversy between the empiricists and the rationalists from which the present discussion originated. That we have knowledge which has not been obtained by sense experience is, I submit, in the light of the preceding discussion, reasonably certain, and on this point, then, the rationalists were in the right. But must not such knowledge be presupposed in order to account for our having sense experience at all ? The answer depends upon what we mean by sense experience. It also depends on the view we take with regard to the nature of sense perception, which was discussed in the first three chapters. Let us suppose, however, that we provisionally adopt the view that the entities which we directly apprehend in sense experience are not chairs and tables but are the patches of colour and raps of sound which we have called sense data.[1] Even if we do have direct sensory contact with physical objects, it is at any rate clear that we do not experience with our senses *the whole* of what is called a physical object. What, then, on this assumption is implied by the common view that we do in fact have sensory experience of chairs and tables ? Clearly some general principle which, if made explicit, might be stated somewhat as follows : " The laws of perspective entitle me to infer that this patch of colour which I am now seeing and that patch of colour which I should see, if I were to move my head two inches to the right, belong to, or are caused by, the same table." Or, again : " This brown oblong shape that I now see and the four cylindrical brown shapes that I should see, if I were to crawl on the ground, are both of them parts of the same object, namely a table." How, then, do I know this principle ? Because past experience has taught me that patches of this sort and shapes of this sort do really belong to or are really caused by the same physical object, a table, and on the basis of this past experience I proceed to infer that they do so belong or that they are so caused on this occasion also. And the point of the illustration is that, unless we are prepared to adopt a very simple and commonsense view of the process of perception—and such a view is almost certainly untenable—certain general principles such as the Principle of Induction must be assumed to be true, in order that we can account for the fact that we believe ourselves in ordinary life to have sensory experience of chairs and tables, when in point of fact we directly apprehend with our senses something quite different. Thus the experience which we believe ourselves to have of the commonsense world of objects involves the Principle of Induction, and presupposes, therefore, our knowledge of the validity of the principle. What we call sense experience, in short, presupposes the use of *a priori* principles to organise the fragmentary data which are given to us in sensation. Yet these principles sense experience neither

[1] See Chapter III, pp. 91, 92.

suggests nor confirms. But if we cannot prove the Principle of Induction by experience, can we prove it by any other method—for example, by reason ? Unfortunately we cannot.

Principle of Inference. The fact that we cannot, will appear, if we proceed to consider certain other general principles which we certainly know and which we very constantly use. Let us suppose that two men are discussing whether a certain road will take them to their destination, X. "You will agree," says one of them, " that, if we can get to Y, we shall be well on the way to X." "Yes, that is so," replies the other. "Well, then," the first continues, " this road goes to Y because it says so on the signpost. Therefore it will take us on our way to X." This would be regarded as a perfectly reasonable argument, and as constituting a valid ground for taking the road going to Y. Yet, it is obvious, a definite jump is involved in the reasoning, a jump which is indicated by the word " therefore." Because so and so is known to be the case (namely, that Y is on the road to X) and something else is also known to be the case (that this is the road to Y), " therefore," we infer, something else is the case (this is the road to take), and this something else which we infer, and which we should call our conclusion, constitutes a piece of new knowledge. It tells us something that we did not know before. How, then, do we come by this knowledge ? In virtue of a principle which is sometimes known as the Principle of Deduction or Inference, which may be stated as follows : " Suppose we know that, if proposition A is true, then proposition B will be true. Suppose further that we know that proposition A is true. Then it will be the case that proposition B is true." Thus our principle states that whatever is implied by a true proposition is true. It is, that is to say, a principle about implication and what it tells us is about some of the conditions in which one thing truly implies another. Now whenever in the course of an argument or a chain of reasoning we use expressions like " therefore," " it follows that," " hence," " thus," " the conclusion is," " we may infer," we are making use of this principle. We are saying in effect that, if we start from two premises ([1] The road which goes to Y is also the road which will take us to X, and [2] This is the road to Y) both of which are true and are known to be true, then we may draw a conclusion (This is the road to take), which is other than the premises and is also true. How is the principle, the Principle of Inference, in virtue of which we reach this conclusion which is both new and true, itself known ?

Principle of Inference not known by Experience.   Not, it is obvious, by experience, for the kind of knowledge that the principle gives us, the knowledge, for example, that by following this road we shall reach X, is knowledge about something which we have not yet experienced, but expect to experience in the future by reason of our belief in the principle. Moreover, the Principle of Inference, like the Inductive Principle, is of universal application. The things to which propositions A and B refer need not be things that we have experienced ; they need not even be things that exist. Nevertheless, we know that the Principle of Inference will hold in respect of propositions about them. More surprising still is the fact that it is not even necessary to know the propositions themselves or to know that they are true, in order to reach conclusions by applying the principle. What, in its most generalised form, the Principle of Inference asserts is : " If there is a Proposition A and if we know that it is true, and if, further, we know that, if the Proposition A is true, then another Proposition, namely B, will be true, *then* we shall also know that Proposition B *is* true." This statement, be it noted, does not contain any affirmation to the effect that there *is* a Proposition A, that it *has been asserted*, or that it *is true*. In other words, we are making statements not so much about propositions as about the relations which in certain circumstances would hold between them, if there were propositions. We are talking, in fact, not about that which does exist, but about that which might in certain circumstances exist ; not about what is true, but about what would be true, if something else were true.

Nor proved by Reason.   But equally the Principle of Inference cannot be proved by reason, since any proof which might be attempted would have to assume its truth. We are dealing, it will be remembered, with a principle which entitles us to say " because this, therefore that," or " this follows from that," that is to say, with a principle which enables us to advance from one step in a chain of reasoning to another. Now this principle could, presumably, only be proved by means of a chain of reasoning ; but in order that such a chain of reasoning could be established, the truth of the principle would have to be assumed. We must, in fact, assume the principle to be true before we can prove anything at all. Therefore we should have to assume the principle to be true before we could prove the principle. The point is so important that I venture to restate it in another form. Let us suppose that I am asked by a sceptic to prove the truth of what appears to me to be an obviously true proposition. I embark upon a connected chain of argument, the conclusion of which appears to me clearly to demonstrate the truth of the proposition. To my surprise the sceptic remains unconvinced. " That," he says, " does not prove what you want to prove, for the simple reason that it is not in fact a proof at all. You cannot prove anything like that." A question, it is obvious, is being raised as to what constitutes a proof. Since the sceptic will not accept my chain of reasoning as a proof, what will he accept ? After reflection I suggest a certain set of conditions, which we will call X, such that if this set of conditions is satisfied, then a proof will have been established. X, in short, is proposed by me as a formula for proof. " But how," persists the sceptic, " do you know that this formula actually does constitute a proof? Personally, I doubt it. Can you convince me ? " I am now faced with the necessity of proving to the sceptic that my suggested formula for proof really is a formula, that, if the set of conditions comprised by the formula is satisfied, then there has been a proof. But this obviously I cannot do. What I am being asked to do is to establish that X is a formula for proof; but if X really is a formula for proof, in order to prove anything I shall have to proceed by showing that the formula X applies. Therefore to prove that X is a formula for proof, I shall have first to assume that X is a formula for proof. If it were not, I could not prove anything at all. The same conclusion emerges, namely, that the validity of the ultimate laws of reasoning and demonstration cannot be proved by reasoning, for the sufficient reason that they must be assumed in all reasoning.

Aristotle on the First Principles of Science.

The establishment of this conclusion was one of the great contributions made by Aristotle to philosophy. He pointed out that all the special sciences—physics and chemistry, biology, zoology and geometry—start from certain postulates and axioms. In the case of one of these sciences, namely, geometry, the postulates and axioms are explicitly stated. Given the postulates and axioms, the science proceeds by observation and reasoning to demonstrate certain conclusions which follow from them. By means of these conclusions, a body of information is gradually built up which constitutes the knowledge proper to the science in question. Thus the method of science is the method of demonstration. Science observes, deduces and infers, and proceeds as a result to demonstrate the conclusions which constitute what we call scientific knowledge. But there are two things which it does not demonstrate. First, it does not demonstrate its initial postulates. It assumes them. Physics, for example, does not demonstrate that there is a physical universe and that we can observe it. It assumes or postulates a physical universe lying out there in space, and it assumes further that it is revealed to the mind of the physicist. Secondly, it does not demonstrate that the laws in accordance with which it infers, deduces and demonstrates are true. It assumes them, and assumes, therefore, that, if it reasons correctly in accordance with these laws, it will reach valid conclusions which constitute true knowledge. But, if science does not establish its initial postulates or the validity of the principles which it assumes, when it proceeds to draw conclusions from the postulates, by what method are they established ?

Aristotle's answer is by Logic, for which his term was Analytics. It is the function of Logic to study the methods common to all the sciences with a view to establishing the premises or postulates from which each science starts, and the laws of reasoning of which each science makes use. One of the functions of Logic, then, as Aristotle conceived it, is to examine the postulates and the methods of the sciences. In so far as it succeeds in determining what these should be, the conclusions at which it arrives will constitute the premises or starting-points of the sciences. In this sense the sciences begin where Logic leaves off.

Some of the postulates which the sciences assume could, Aristotle held, be satisfactorily established by reasoning. But what of those general principles of reasoning of which the logician, in common with the scientist, makes use, and whose validity he assumes ? Could Logic establish these ? Aristotle came to the conclusion that it could not, since the logician can only establish any conclusion by the method of reasoning, and his reasoning must, as we have seen, assume the validity of certain principles such as those of induction and inference before it can occur at all. The logician cannot, therefore, establish by reasoning the principles of which all reasoning must make use. How, then, does he know them ? Aristotle's view, broadly, was that he intuitively perceives them, not of course by the senses, but by the mind. They were, he held, revealed to a faculty which he called " nous," an untranslatable word meaning the intuitive intellect whose apprehension carries with it a conviction of the truth of that which it apprehends. Science Aristotle termed "demonstrated knowledge"; it is, that is to say, the knowledge that certain truths follow from simpler truths. But since we must start somewhere, the simplest truths of all will not themselves be capable of being demonstrated, since, if they were, there would be still simpler truths from which they could be shown to follow, in which event the truths in question would not have been the simplest. These simplest truths, then, are intuitively apprehended by the knowing mind, and among them are the principles of reasoning, such as the Principle of Induction and the Principle of Inference or Deduction. Here, then, is what we have called *a priori* knowledge appearing in a new guise as the knowledge of those principles of reasoning or laws of thought, upon the assumption of the truth of which the attainment of all other knowledge depends.

The Syllogism.

For many years it was thought that there was a kind of structure or pattern, such that all thinking which, on the basis of something that was known, proceeded by reasoning to establish something that was not known, must conform to this pattern. The pattern is as follows. It begins with an assertion of a general character, known as the major premise—e.g. " All men are mortal." It proceeds to make an independent assertion of a particular character, known as the minor premise—e.g. " Socrates is a man." On the basis of these two assertions, the mind, it is said, is enabled to draw a conclusion : " Therefore Socrates is mortal." This pattern is known as the Syllogism.

It was claimed that conclusions reached by the Syllogism satisfied three conditions ; they were true, necessitated, and new. Aristotle, in fact, defines the Syllogism as " a discourse wherein certain things (viz. the premises) being admitted, something else, different from what has been admitted, follows of necessity because the admissions are what they are." Whenever by means of thinking we reach conclusions which are true and necessitated and new, then, according to the traditional Logic, the thinking in question can be shown to fall within the syllogistic framework.

Throughout the history of philosophy the Syllogism has

been subjected to criticism. In modern times, this criticism has been urged most strongly by the school of philosophers known as Pragmatists.[1] The gist of their criticism is that thinking does not in fact proceed by the syllogistic method at all, or, rather, that in so far as it does so, it must of necessity be valueless. By saying that syllogistic thinking is valueless, the Pragmatist means that it cannot give us new knowledge which is also true knowledge. All thinking, he points out, is undertaken with a purpose. We think because we want to know something, and this something must be new, since, if we knew it already, there would be no point in thinking in order to ascertain it. Also we must have some assurance that the conclusions to which our thinking has led us are true, since, if they are not, we shall be afraid to act upon the basis of the conclusions we have reached.

The object of thinking, then, is to reach conclusions which are both new and true. Do the conclusions reached by the syllogistic method conform to these two conditions? The Pragmatist answers that they do not. The Syllogism, he asserts, contains a fundamental flaw, which is that the conclusion which it purports to prove must be assumed before its premises can be truly stated. The Syllogism, therefore, sets out to establish that which, if it is to be *proved*, must be assumed to have been already known.

Criticism of the Syllogism.   Let us consider, for example, the Syllogism : " All men are mortal. Socrates is a man. Therefore Socrates is mortal." If the major premise, " All men are mortal," is interpreted as making a statement about all those men who have ever in actual fact lived, it is false, because it leaves out of account men such as Elijah, Tithonus, the Struldbrugs and the Wandering Jew, who have never died. It will, no doubt, be said that these cases are mythical. But how can we know that they are? Only by examining severally all the cases of men who are alleged to have lived upon the earth and pronouncing in respect of some of them, that is to say, in respect of Elijah,

[1] See Chapter XVI, pp. 448-464, for an account of Pragmatism.

Tithonus and the others, that they are mythical. But in the course of this examination we shall have come across the case of Socrates and noted that he did in fact exist, but died, before being in a position to assert our major premise. Thus the conclusion must have been already known before the major premise could have been truly stated.

Let us suppose, however, that we decide that Elijah, Tithonus and the rest are not in fact mythical, but are cases of men who have miraculously evaded death. What, then, happens to our major premise? We can only save it if we decide to exclude these persons from the class of " men." On what ground? On the ground that they did not die. But if this is a ground for exclusion, mortality will become at once the distinguishing characteristic and the essential definition of mankind. An assertion about any-body to the effect that he is a man will include, therefore, the assertion that he is mortal. Hence to say of Socrates that he is a man is to say at the same time that he is mortal, and the conclusion is included in the statement of the minor premise.

Finally, it might be denied that the major premise is a statement about all those men who have in fact lived, in which event every alleged instance of a man would have had to be examined in turn and his mortality established before it could be stated. The effect of the major premise, it might be said, is to state a " law of nature," a law which affirms a universal connection between manhood and mortality. But this suggestion does not avail to save the Syllogism, for the question inevitably arises, " Is the case under discussion, that of Socrates, one to which the law of nature applies? Is it, in fact, a case in point? " If we assume that it is, if, that is to say, we assume that Socrates is a person to whom the alleged law of nature applies, we shall be assuming the very point to be proved, whereas if we are in a position to *know* that Socrates' is a case in point, we shall know already what the Syllogism purports to prove. The dilemma then remains. Either the conclusion is not proved, or, if it is, it is not new. And the inference ?

That it is not by the route of the Syllogism that our thinking proceeds when it leads us to new conclusions which are also true.

The Laws of Thought. It cannot be said that any definite scheme or pattern of thought has been successful in replacing the Syllogism as a description of the process by means of which we think. It seems unlikely, indeed, that thinking proceeds in accordance with any cut and dried pattern of the syllogistic type. There are, as we have seen, certain general principles, such as the principles of inference and of induction, which are involved in all, or at any rate in most, thinking, and these principles must be assumed to be true before thinking can occur. For historical reasons, three of these principles have been given special prominence and called the " Laws of Thought." They are as follows : (1) *the Law of Identity*—" Whatever is, is," (2) *the Law of Contradiction*—" Nothing can both be and not be," and (3) *the Law of Excluded Middle*—" Everything must either be or not be." These principles are undoubtedly true, and they are intuitively perceived. But there is no reason why we should regard them as being more fundamental than those to which attention has already been called. In fact the denomination of them as *the* Laws of Thought has had an unfortunate effect upon the history of philosophy.

In the first place, the suggestion that there is a determinate number of self-evident principles which are involved in thinking tends to obscure the fact that *all* thinking must proceed by means of self-evident stages. If we employ the somewhat ambiguous word " intuition " to denote that faculty of the mind which immediately perceives certain propositions to be true, but is unable to give reasons why what it perceives to be true should be true, we may say that every chain of reasoning consists of a series of linked intuitions.

Reasoning as a Series of Jumps. Reasoning, as we have already pointed out, involves a series of steps. " *Because* of this," we say, " *therefore* that." Or, more simply, " This *follows from* that." A definite jump on the part of the mind from the knowledge of " this " to the knowledge of " that " is, it is clear, involved. Let us suppose that somebody questions the validity of this jump : " I do not agree that this follows from that," he says. How are we to convince him except by endeavouring to fill in the gap over which the mind has jumped between " this " and " that " with intermediate stages of reasoning, in the hope that his mind, moving over these stages as a man will use stepping-stones to cross a stream, will the more easily make the transition from " this " to " that." Now, however near together we place these stages, there will always be room between any two of them for other stages, and these other stages may be infinite in number. For either the space between the two stages is completely filled up or it is not. If it is not, then further stages can be inserted *ad infinitum*. If it is, it will not be necessary for the mind to jump from one stage to another; there will be no transition, therefore, from one thing which is known to another thing which is not, and the primary object of all thinking, which is to arrive at something new, will not have been fulfilled.

In this way it can be seen that every chain of reasoning, however close, involves jumps on the part of the mind from step to step. But the jump from one step to another is not one which reasoning can justify, since any chain of reasoning by means of which the justification was attempted would itself involve such jumps. Hence if the validity of the jumping process on the part of the mind is questioned, all that we can say is that the various stages in the chain of reasoning are plainly seen to follow one from another. That one *necessitates* another is, as we should say, self-evident, but we cannot prove that it does so. The process known as reasoning involves, therefore, a constant use of the principle of self-evidence, since it can adduce nothing in support of its inference that step B follows from step A except its conviction that it self-evidently appears to do so. Hence it seems arbitrary to single out three laws as constituting the foundational element of self-evidence which is involved in all thinking, when in fact they only illustrate a principle which is being continuously invoked.

Laws of Things and Laws of Thought.   In the second place, the expression "Laws of Thought" conveys the suggestion that such principles as the Law of Contradiction are only descriptions of the way in which we think. That they are descriptions of thinking nobody would wish to deny, but the significance of the word "only" in this connection is considerable. For its implication is that they are *not* descriptions of the way in which things behave. It is easy to see why these principles should have come to be called Laws of Thought, since it is by means of thought rather than of sense experience that they have been formulated. It is not by using one of my five senses that I come to realise that "nothing can both be and not be," but by using my reason.

Moreover, whatever it is, whether thought or things, that the Laws in fact describe, *the knowledge of* the Laws is certainly thought. In other words, the awareness on the part of my mind of the truth of the Law of Contradiction is definitely a thought in my mind, even if the Law of Contradiction of which I am aware is not itself a description of the way in which my mind works.

The fact that knowledge of the Law is certainly thought has led to a confusion between thought and its objects similar to that which we encountered when examining the use of the word "idea."[1] As a result of this confusion, because a thought is necessarily in a mind, there has been a tendency to say that its object must also be in the mind which thinks the thought. Yet although the considerations just mentioned enable us to see why these laws came to be called Laws of Thought, there cannot, I think, be any reasonable doubt that we do intend them to apply to the behaviour of things. There cannot, that is to say, be any reasonable doubt that when we assert that a tree cannot both be and not be a beech tree, or that three things and two

[1] See above, Chapter III, pp. 76, 77.

things make five things, we are purporting to make assertions not about the nature of our minds but about the nature of things. We do not, that is to say, mean to assert : " Our minds are so constituted that they cannot think of trees both being and not being beech trees ; so constituted, that they cannot think of three things and two things making anything but five things, although to minds differently constituted such thoughts might quite well be possible and, indeed, necessary " ; we do mean to assert : " This world is such that the trees which are in it cannot both be and not be beech trees, nor, indeed, could they be in any other world ; and the nature of numbers is such that three things and two things will make five things both in this world and in all possible worlds." This, I say, is certainly what we mean to assert, and in my view it is precisely this that we do assert. The contrary view that the Laws of Thought are descriptions of the way in which the mind works is not, I should say, the view which would normally occur to us. It was not, most of us would say, anything of this kind that we were intending to assert when we asseverated our belief in the Law of Contradiction. Indeed, it was only as a result of philosophical speculation that people were ever led to raise the question whether, when we thought we were talking about the behaviour of things, we were really only talking about the workings of our own minds. Nevertheless, in the light of the foregoing, it should be clear that any argu-ments of which such speculation might make use would, like all processes of reasoning, themselves involve the use of the Principle of Induction and the Law of Contradic-tion, and would entail therefore a belief that this Principle and this Law applied to things other than the workings of the mind of the speculator, for example, in the case in ques-tion, to the arguments employed in the chain of philo-sophical reasoning which sought to deny precisely this.

It is, nevertheless, the case that many philosophers have taken a different view, and it is important to consider the reasons which influenced them. It is undoubtedly true, they would say, that the Laws of Thought purport to apply to the behaviour of things. Moreover, they do seem to describe the workings of the world we know. Yet the fact that they do is something of a puzzle.

Mathematics as Independent of Experience.   Consider, for example, the case of mathematics. There seems to be good historical evidence for the view that it was not merely by manipulating and counting physical things that the human mind discovered the laws of mathematics. Some sensory experience was no doubt, as we have seen,[1] necessary to stimulate mathematical thought. Some counting of particular objects there must have been, before the mind leapt to the comprehension of the general truths of addition and multiplication. But there seems to be no reason to suppose that *every* step in the discovery of mathematics was either suggested by experience, verified by experience, or felt to require experimental verification. Mathematics is pre-eminently the sphere in which the mind swings free and, reasoning abstractly in accordance with its own laws, discovers the truths that regulate the complex relations of numbers and symbols. The binomial theorem and the differential calculus, can no doubt be used to predict the behaviour of physical things, and in the physical sciences their application has been found very fruitful. But it was by letting their reasons operate freely in their studies, not by observing nature or experimenting in laboratories that Newton and Leibnitz discovered them. Indeed, we all of us can and do perform feats of mathematical reasoning which owe nothing to experience. I do not, for example, know who the inhabitants of London will be in a hundred years' time, but I do know that any two of them and any other two of them will make four. I can even make statements which I know to be true about numbers that I have never thought of and that nobody else has ever thought of. For example, I can truly assert of a number which is so large that nobody has ever thought of it that twice that number will be an

1 See above, pp. 113, 114.

even number ; or again, since all the numbers whose products are less than a hundred are known to me, it follows that of any two numbers which I do not know I can truly assert that their products will be more than a hundred. Thus many mathematical statements outrun experience, and some seem even to outrun the possibility of experience, at any rate upon this planet. It cannot, then, have been by sense experience, that is to say, by the method of observing the behaviour of things, that men discovered them.

Yet although mathematical laws were not derived from the observation of things, things are nevertheless observed to obey them. Hence arises the following puzzle. Mathematics is a product of the mind's *a priori* reasoning in accordance with self-evident principles from self-evident premises ; it owes little or nothing to experience. Yet when we come to experience the world, we find that it obeys the very laws which our reasoning has derived from the study of abstract principles. Now this is a very surprising fact. To show how surprising, Sir James Jeans makes use of an analogy, in which he likens the laws of mathematics to the rules of the game of chess, which mankind has invented for itself—" And now," he says, " it emerges that the shadow play which we describe as the fall of an apple to the ground, the ebb and flow of the tides, the motion of electrons in the atom, are produced by actors who seem very conversant with these purely mathematical concepts—with our rules of our game of chess which we formulated long before we discovered that the shadows on the wall " (i.e. physical things) " were also playing chess."

Explanations of Applicability of Mathematics.

The fact is no doubt on first reflection sufficiently surprising. Yet it is not difficult to think of explanations for it.

Whatever process is responsible for the ordering of the world is, we might say, responsible also for the ordering of our minds. Since, then, our minds and the world own a common origin, it is only to be expected that they should operate according to common laws. Thus Sir James Jeans considers that the facts to which attention has been drawn afford evidence for the view that the universe was created by a mathematically minded deity, who stamped the laws of mathematics upon the human mind no less than upon the physical world. It is for this reason that we recognise in the physical world the mathematical hall-mark which is also incorporated in the texture of our own minds.

But it is not necessary to subscribe to this particular hypothesis in order to conclude that the fact of common laws of working points to a common origin. We may say, for example, that the operations of our minds are determined by the characteristics of our brains ; proceed to point out that the brain is a part of a living organism, and clinch the argument by the admitted fact that living organisms have evolved in an environment which has imposed its characteristics upon them, as a mould will stamp its impress upon the fluid material submitted to it. Our brains, on this hypothesis, function in a manner which reflects the operations of the physical world, and the mental counter-part of this cerebral functioning is our apprehension of the laws of logic and mathematics. Whether we can accept this view or not will largely depend on the attitude we adopt to the philosophy of Materialism.[1]

Or again, we may begin by defining mind as that which, by its very nature, knows or is directly aware of entities which are neither physical nor mental, but which are nevertheless real, such as numbers. Just as our senses are usually held to discern and give us information about the nature and workings of the *physical* world, so, on this view, our minds discern and give us information about a non-physical mathematical world. What we call "thinking" is the exploring and mapping of its structure. The resultant map is what we know as mathematics. This explanation would in its turn depend for its acceptance upon a certain view of the nature of the universe. This is the view known

[1] For an account of the materialistic philosophy upon which this view depends, see Chapter XVIII.

as Conceptual Realism, which is prepared to accord to entities such as numbers a real existence which is independent both of knowing minds and of the physical world.[1]

The Kantian View.

Another explanation, which has on the whole been adopted by most philosophers, is that things in the physical world behave in accordance with the requirements of the *a priori* reason because they are in a large measure the products of that reason : or, more precisely, even if they themselves exist in their own right, the laws governing their behaviour are those which our minds have prescribed to them. On this view, the laws of things and the laws of thought are the same, for the sufficient reason that things, so far as their general characteristics are concerned, are the creatures of thought. When, on this view, we say that a tree cannot both be and not be a beech, we are in the first instance making a statement about the nature of thought. But since trees, or rather those characteristics of trees in virtue of which in common with all other objects they exemplify the Law of Contradiction, are themselves creatures of thought, we are also making a statement about the behaviour of things. This in essence is the explanation offered by Kant. Everything, Kant taught, that we experience must have the characteristics which our *a priori* knowledge affirms of it, for the reason that these characteristics are imposed upon it by our minds, as a condition of their knowing it. This line of thought will be developed in a later chapter, in which Kant's philosophy will be considered in detail.[2] It is largely because of the importance of this philosophy and the influence which it has exerted on subsequent thought, that there has been a general tendency on the part of philosophers to regard the Laws of Thought as being primarily descriptions of the workings of our minds and only secondarily descriptions of the behaviour of things.

[1] For an account of Conceptual Realism, see Chapter X, pp. 266, 267.
[2] See Chapter XIV.

Implications of Kantian Theory.   If it is true, this view of thought and of the relation of thought to things has momentous consequences which it is worth while pausing for a moment to consider. If thinking about things is in essence a process whereby we contribute to them the mind's characteristics and prescribe to them the mind's laws, then the more we think, the more we shall misrepresent reality. Every physical thing that I know is of a certain quantity, possesses a certain quality, is the cause of one thing and the effect of another, and obeys the laws of physics. It seems to me to be necessary that it should be of this character and behave in this way. I cannot in fact think of it as being or behaving otherwise. Yet, if Kant is right, this so-called necessity is a necessity only to my thought. There is no reason to suppose that the thing itself is or behaves in the least like this. It is merely in order that I may be able to think about it, that I must represent it to myself as so being and behaving. Thinking, then, is like looking at reality through distorting spectacles. The harder we look, the more we shall distort it.

If to think about the real is to misrepresent it, have we, the question inevitably presents itself, any other method of making contact with reality ? It is almost inevitable that the philosophies which take this view of the functions of thought should be found to concede to some other faculty a superiority over thought as a means of making contact with reality. Thus Kant believes that it is in moral experience that we obtain an insight into the real nature of things ; and Bergson, who, on different grounds, shares Kant's scepticism as to the ability of the ratiocinative reason to give us truth, praises a faculty which he terms intuition.

These views will receive further consideration in the Part dealing with Constructive Metaphysics.[1] It is sufficient for my present purpose to emphasise the pessimistic conclusion as to the present capacities and future

[1] See Chapter XIV for Kant's and Chapter XIX for Bergson's Philosophy.

performances of human reason, which this solution of the problem of the relation between the laws of thought and the behaviour of things entails. If it be true that to think is of necessity to misrepresent what is thought about, philosophy, in so far as it is regarded as the attempt to understand the universe as a whole, is a gigantic conspiracy of error, and philosophers would be well advised to cease speculating and cultivate the religious ecstasy of the saint, the musical inspiration of the composer, or the instinctive behaviour of the insect. By continuing to reason they would appear to be engaged in the disinterested dissemination of error.

Recapitulation. This chapter has been a lengthy one and has covered a good deal of ground. Beginning with a consideration of Logic, it has led us into the territory of Metaphysics, thus affording a good example of the tendency of philosophical questions to ramify into one another which I emphasised in the first chapter. It is notoriously difficult to isolate philosophical topics, so difficult that, wherever you start in philosophy, you are reasonably certain to come sooner or later within sight of the same perennial problems.

It may be worth while, before proceeding to the more metaphysical section of this book, to survey the ground which has been covered in the last two chapters. We have been engaged in considering the nature and validity of knowledge, of knowledge, that is to say, as distinct from sense experience. The questions raised belong more specifically to what is known as Epistemology. Does our knowledge spring from, and is it all limited by, sense experience, as the empiricists asserted, or does it outrun sense experience, as the rationalists believed? Do we, in fact, possess *a priori* knowledge, or do we not?

We saw, first, that such knowledge does in fact exist, and that, although sense experience may be and usually is necessary to elicit it, the knowledge itself is strictly independent of sense experience. We then turned to the question of the character and extent of this knowledge, which led us into the sphere of what is known as Logic. The chief examples of *a priori* knowledge are, we saw, afforded by the principles of mathematics and the laws of reasoning. These laws and principles cannot, however, in the last resort be demonstrated, since they are assumed in all demonstration. The laws of reasoning, in short, cannot themselves be established by reasoning ; they must be intuitively perceived to be true. Principles such as those of Inference and Induction are in fact so perceived and are regarded as self-evident. These Principles are invoked in the processes and activities of everyday life no less than in the operations of abstract thought. In particular, they are employed in the organisation and arrangement of the chaotic data of sense experience. On this point also the rationalists appear to have been in the right as against the empiricists, since the employment of *a priori* principles, which the rationalists stressed, appears to be a condition of our enjoying an ordered sensory experience instead of a chaos of sensory impressions. We then proceeded to consider the question whether the laws of Logic could be regarded as applying to the behaviour of things, or were only descriptions of the workings of the mind. Arguments were given in favour of the former view, but the importance of the latter, as entailed, for example, by the philosophy of Kant, was stressed. The implications of this latter view bring us to the threshold of metaphysics, which we must now cross.

JOSEPH, H. W. B.   An Introduction to Logic.
WOLF, A.   A Text Book of Logic.

L. S. Stebbing's *A Modern Introduction to Logic* is a textbook dealing with the Modern or Generalised Logic which has grown up during the last fifty years. F. C. S. Schiller's *Formal Logic* represents the pragmatist standpoint.

PART II
CRITICAL METAPHYSICS

CHAPTER VI: THE PROBLEM OF SUBSTANCE AND ITS QUALITIES: THEORY OF JUDGEMENT

I. INTRODUCTORY

Appearance and Reality. Our consideration of the problems of Epistemology has resulted in the establishment of two main conclusions. First, there are many reasons for supposing that sense experience, as ordinarily interpreted, tells us very little about the world as it really is : sense experience, it appears, is subjective and relative. Moreover, it requires, and, whether it is aware of it or not constantly receives, active interpretation from the mind so that there is little ground for supposing that the world of physical objects extended in space with which sense experience is supposed to acquaint us, really exists in the way in which common sense assumes. No doubt it exists in a sense, but it is highly doubtful whether it is independent of our observation of or thought about it.

In the second place, it seems probable that we possess ways of knowing the world other than that of sense experience, and that, in particular, we have that kind of knowledge to which we have given the name of *a priori*. This conclusion will hold good even if the world which we know *a priori* is one which, as Kant believed,[1] is largely the product of our own knowledge. Proceeding on the basis of this second conclusion, we must now consider what is the nature of the reality whose existence philosophers have believed that they were able to establish by the methods of *a priori* reasoning. The conceptions which they

[1] See Chapter XIV.

have formed of it are many and diverse. But they all possess in common the characteristic of being different from the world revealed to commonsense experience and explored by science. This commonsense world, many philosophers have maintained, is an appearance only, an appearance of a reality that underlies it. While the world of appearance is largely relative to the knower, and owes its apparent characteristics to the operation of his brain and sense organs, his mental peculiarities, and even his wishes, and is thus different for each observer, the world of reality which underlies it is independent of us, and, in so far as we are able to discern its characteristics at all, we are entitled to assert that they are the same for all. In so far, then, as two observers or thinkers make different reports about the nature of this *reality*, one of them will be right and the other wrong, or both of them will be wrong. They cannot both be right in the way in which two so-called observers of the world of sense experience can both be right. Moreover, since it is by thinking or reason, supplemented in the view of some thinkers by intuition[1] that we obtain knowledge of reality, a view of reality which is false will be due to faulty reasoning. The study of reality in contradistinction to the commonsense world of appearance is usually known as Metaphysics.

Metaphysical Systems Unlikely to be True.

I have hinted at the possibility that where metaphysical systems differ, both may be wrong. This, I would here venture to suggest, is almost certainly the case, since it seems to be exceedingly unlikely that the truth about the universe as a whole has yet been discovered by any human mind. How unlikely, may be inferred from a brief reference to certain time facts. The whole past of life from its earliest beginnings upon the earth is broadly reckoned at about 1,200,000,000 years.[2] The past of human life, giving all

[1] For the claims of intuition to know reality, see Chapter XIX, pp. 549–551.

[2] The estimate is exceedingly rough ; it may be incorrect by hundreds of millions of years.

doubtfully human species the benefit of the doubt, is estimated roughly at about 1,000,000 ; of human civilisation, on the most generous interpretation of the word " civilisation," at about 3,000. Let us scale these figures down to make them manageable. If we reckon the whole past of life upon the earth at a hundred years, the whole past of human life is reduced to one month, and of human civilisation to just over two hours. Let us now consider the future. It is estimated that the time during which the earth will remain habitable—the time, that is to say, during which the heat of the sun will be sufficient to maintain life upon the earth—is about twelve hundred thousand million years, or a thousand times as long as the whole past history of life. Scaling down, we reach the result that a time scale which reckons the past of human civilisation at something over two hours gives man a future of about a hundred thousand years. As Sir James Jeans, who is using a different time scale, puts it : " As a being destined to live for three score years and ten, humanity although it has been born in a house seventy years old is itself only three days old. But in only the last few minutes has it become conscious. . . ." It seems unlikely, to say the least of it, that the truth about the universe has been discovered in these few minutes. If, indeed, only a small part of the truth about the universe has been revealed to the human mind in the three thousand years of its thinking history, one cannot help wondering how our descendants will occupy their no doubt infinitely more powerful intelligences during the twelve hundred thousand million years of man's future. From the point of view of these descendants, we can only hope that it is unlikely that the metaphysicians of the past and present have discovered any large measure of truth about reality. This hope is almost certainly justified ; and, even if most systems of metaphysics are not, in the words of a contemporary philosopher, adequately described as " variations on the theme of cosmic lying," it would be unwise to accept any metaphysical account of the universe as embodying absolute truth. This pessimistic view as to the achievement and prospects of metaphysics should not discourage prospective metaphysicians. No man with a tincture of philosophy will, indeed, be induced to abandon his efforts to probe the nature of reality by the reflection that he is unlikely to be successful. In any event, since reality as conceived by most philosophers is that which, being independent of *human* thought, is the same for all thinkers, reality really *is* there, waiting to be dis-covered in a sense in which the world of appearance, being to some extent dependent upon and relative to the observer, is not. This distinction is frequently described by the assertion that reality is objective[1] whereas appearance is subjective.[1]

Aristotle on Metaphysics.   The classification of meta-physics as a separate branch of study is due to Aristotle, whose term for it was " First Philosophy." This he defined as a "science which considers What Is simply in its character of Being, and the properties which it has as such." Two points may be noticed in connection with this definition. There is, first, the significance of the words " simply " and " as such." There are, it is obvious, many different ways in which things can exist, or, as Aristotle would say, many different modes of being. There are substances—gold and clay ; organisms—men and earwigs ; all these are things : qualities—sweet and blue, which are the attributes, or, to use Aristotle's word, " affections " of things : and actions—building or killing, which produce or destroy things. All these, it is obvious, in some sense are ; they exist. What, then, Aristotle wishes to know, is the character-istic which existent things of all kinds and every kind must possess in order that they may *be* ? What, in other words, are the common characteristics of being, or, since in Aristotle's view all the other forms of being derive their nature from Substance, which is the most primary of all modes of being, what are the characteristics common to all substances ?

[1] See, for an account of the meaning of these terms, Chapter XIII pp. 331–335.

Such is the significance of the phrase " Being . . . as such."
Secondly, since metaphysics is concerned with the common
characteristics of what is simply because it is, it cannot
afford to limit the scope of its interests. In this respect
it is to be distinguished from the sciences, which deliberately confine their attention to some special department
of what is—physics to the world of matter, biology to
living organisms, geology to rocks, botany to plants, and
so forth. The scope of metaphysics being unlimited, the
metaphysician will have to consider the ultimate grounds
which underlie all these special branches of study and the
assumptions on which they proceed. Physics, for example,
assumes that there is matter and proceeds to its analysis ;
biology that there is life which is distinct from matter,
and must be studied by appropriate methods peculiar
to itself. Metaphysics alone asks what is meant by matter,
what by life. Are these, it wants to know, ultimate forms
of Being and is the distinction which is commonly made
between them an ultimate distinction ? Metaphysics, in
other words, examines the presuppositions of the sciences.
Its enquiries leave off where theirs begin. From another
point of view, its enquiries begin where theirs leave off.
The meaning of the Greek word μετά is " after," and
the significance of the title *meta*physics is that it denotes
the branch of study which comes *after* physics, in the sense
that its interests begin at the point at which those of
physics stop.

From the point of view of its generality metaphysics
is like logic.[1] Indeed, for Aristotle both logic and what
we now call metaphysics were branches of " First Philosophy." But whereas logic was concerned to examine
and to justify the *methods* of the sciences, the interest of the
Aristotelian metaphysician lay rather in their subject
matter. The logician is interested in how the scientist
thinks ; the metaphysician in the general nature of that
which he thinks about.

[1] See Chapter V, pp. 138, 139.

Course of Ensuing Enquiry. Metaphysics, then, is concerned to establish the common character which everything that is must possess in order that it may be at all. It enquires into the nature of reality as such. It is with the results of the enquiries which the great philosophers have historically made that the third Part of this book will be mainly concerned.

I have noted that, while metaphysical systems may and do differ in the most bewildering fashion, they are all or almost all unanimous in denying the title of full reality to the worlds affirmed by common sense and explored by science. Our account of metaphysics will, therefore, conveniently fall into two parts. We shall, first (in Part II), examine some of the reasons which have led philosophers to deny the reality of the commonsense world. Secondly (in Part III), we shall give some account of the conceptions of reality which the great philosophers have elaborated. The object of Part II, which consists of this and the next three chapters, will be to illustrate the way in which philosophers have criticised commonsense notions. Part III will contain some examples of well-known metaphysical systems which philosophers have constructed.

II. THE NOTION OF SUBSTANCE

Commonsense View of Substance. Commonsense regards the physical world as consisting of things. These things are divided by chemistry into solids, fluids, and gases, and they have the qualities peculiar to their chemical class. Solids are hard, fluids wet, gases tenuous. They also have distinguishing qualities which are peculiar to the nature of the thing. Thus, some solids are blue, others red, some sticky, others dry, some angular, others round. Science postulates behind these different classes of things substances which are common to all of them. Thus solids and gases are composed of molecules, the differences between a solid and a gas being due to the spatial arrangement of the molecules ; in a solid the molecules are more closely packed.

The molecules are composed of elements, of which ninety-two have been distinguished, and the elements of atoms. As to the nature of the atoms, there is contemporary controversy. We may, however, safely assert that, in so far as we are able to think of them at all, we must conceive of them after the likeness of " things " possessing qualities. All attempts to conceive the atom after any other model—as consisting, for example, of charges of electricity which are charges in nothing, or as waves in a hypothetical ether—however closely such conceptions may or may not represent the facts, carry us beyond the limits of our imaginations. We can say that the atom is a charge of electricity in nothing, but, if we try to visualise what is meant, we find that the remark is strictly meaningless. The scientist, then, if we are to remain able imaginatively to follow the development of his thoughts, must still cleave to the commonsense notion of the universe as composed of things which possess qualities.

But, directly we begin to subject this conception to the scrutiny of reason, it reveals unsuspected difficulties. These difficulties, at some of which we have already glanced in another connection,[1] arise from the difficulty of conceiving the relation between a thing and its qualities. A chocolate we normally think of as being more than a mere collection of qualities—brownness, roundness, softness, sweetness, stickiness, and so forth. The chocolate is something other than the qualities, something which *has* them ; so that we are entitled to say, " *This* is the something which is both sweet and sticky." Yet what can this something be ? Certainly it is not the sum of the remaining qualities ; for the brownness is not round, and the roundness is not sweet or sticky. What, then, is it ? One is tempted to reply " It is a sort of brute substance or stuff," thus postulating a something which, itself devoid of qualities, acts as their bearer or carrier. But how, it may be asked, can there be a something which is devoid of all qualities ? And, further, since it is only in terms of their qualities that

[1] See Chapter II, pp. 47, 48.

things are known and recognised, how, if there was such a thing, could we know it ?

Aristotle on Form and Matter.   Aristotle was the first philosopher to make a specific attempt to deal with this problem, and his solution of it is exceedingly interesting. In any individual thing, he taught, we can distinguish two components—the stuff of which it consists, which may be of the same kind as the stuff of which very different things consist, and the structural law or form of arrangement of the stuff, which is peculiar to the thing in question. Thus a candlestick and vase may be made of the same metal, bronze. In what way, then, do they differ ? In respect of the fact that the former possesses the kind of structure which renders it fit for use as a candlestick, the latter the kind of structure that enables it to hold flowers rather than candles. The distinguishing structure of a thing Aristotle called its Form, the stuff of which it is made, its Matter. This is not to say that the Matter and Form of a thing are somehow combined together to make the thing, as dough and currants are combined to make a pudding. The two are indissolubly united, and were so from the first. The Form, in fact, is manifested and expressed in and through every part of the Matter. The individual thing, to state the relationship in another way, is the Matter organised in accordance with a determinate principle of structure, the Form. Matter and Form so considered are strictly correlative, what is Form at one stage being Matter at another. The Form, in other words, is the sum-total of the distinguishing characteristics of the thing at the particular stage of organisation or development which it has reached. The Form, that is to say, at the stage in question, is the *last* determination of the thing in virtue of which it has reached that stage. But at that same stage we are also entitled to think of the thing as Matter in respect of the next phase of organisation or development, which it may still have to undergo. An example may serve to illustrate Aristotle's conception.

Let us consider a statue of Venus. Its distinguishing Form is the representation of the goddess Venus. Strip this away, and there will still be a statue in the Form of a woman. The distinguishing Form is now female representation. Strip this away, and there will still be a statue, although it may no longer be possible to say whom or what the statue represents. The distinguishing Form at this stage would be the representation of the human figure. Strip this away, and we shall be left with a block of marble. The Form will now be marble and the Matter stone. Thus at every stage of the process involved in the production of a statue of Venus, a new Form is superinduced upon or developed in a Matter which is already itself a combination of Matter and Form.

Limitations and Criticism of the Theory.

But we can, it is obvious, continue the process of analysis. We can, for example, proceed to strip away the marble. The material that remains will then be any kind of stone, that is to say, it will be in terms of the formula, Matter possessing a Form which has the characteristics of being hard and cold, possessing what might be described as the Form of stoniness. Continuing the process, let us strip away this Form. What now remains ? At this point we begin to get into difficulties. Stone, after all, is a chemical compound, and is, therefore, presumably further analysable. The state of science in Aristotle's time led him to regard the so-called elements of his predecessor, Empedocles (*circa* 490–430 B.C.)—earth, air, fire and water—as the Matter of all chemical compounds, the Form being their specific law of composition. Are we not, then, entitled to push the analysis still further ? Can we not apply the formula to the elements themselves ? Aristotle thought not. The logical end of the process upon which we have been engaged is, it is obvious, the postulation of an ultimate Matter, which constitutes the stuff of all individual things, is the same throughout the universe, and is yet without any definite structure at all. This structureless or qualityless stuff would be Locke's Substance in another guise,[1] and, as such, is open to the objection which we have already brought against a featureless Substance, namely, that it is strictly inconceivable. Aristotle seeks to evade the difficulty by asserting that " pure Matter " or " prime Matter " " all alone, before a rag of Form is on " is a creation of thought, which is not to be found in the realm of actual existence. The most primitive Form in which Matter is actually found, is, he held, that of the elements. Matter, in other words, does not exist except in the structurated Form of the elements. But this will not do ; for, if there is no such thing as pure Matter, there is nothing which can receive the determination of the first Form, and the formula which Aristotle seeks to establish to explain the process of the development of things, namely, the superimposition of fresh Forms upon an already structurated Matter, breaks down at the first stage of the process. Indeed, unless we are prepared to accept the universe as a going concern initially composed of earth, water, air and fire, which we have expressly excluded from the Matter and Form formula, we shall not be in a position to apply the formula.

Idealist Corollary. For this and other reasons mcst philosophers would to-day profess themselves unable to accept the Aristotelian account of Substance. What follows ? As usual, there are a number of alternatives. Many have taken the somewhat heroic course of denying the validity of the whole concept of Thing and Qualities. The usual corollary of such a denial is some form of Idealism, since, if things with qualities are rejected as the models on which we are to conceive of reality, minds and their thoughts suggest themselves as the obvious alternatives. Hence, the criticism of the commonsense notion of Substance has historically provided an important contribution to the great stream of Idealist thought.

[1] See Chapter II, pp. 40, 41.

The Nature of Judgement. There is another way in which this criticism has strengthened Idealism. Philosophers have historically been preoccupied with the question of the nature of what is called judgement. The form in which this question has presented itself is as follows : " What precisely is it that I am affirming when I judge that so and so is in such and such a condition, or has such and such a quality ? " and "What are the conditions which must be satisfied, if my judgement is to be valid ? " Am I, for example, when judging, merely making a statement about my own thoughts and experiences, or am I making a direct affirmation about the nature and structure of the world outside me ? If the latter, if, that is to say, my mind is directly in contact with an external reality, how are we to account for the fact that I sometimes affirm what is not, that my judgement, in other words, is sometimes false? If the former, what guarantee have I for thinking that my judgement ever relates to or corresponds with reality ? Can I, in fact, on this assumption, be said ever to know reality at all ? The dilemma is a serious one. Either we are entirely enclosed within the circle of our own thoughts, and what we call judging—as, for example, when I judge that it is raining now or will rain to-morrow —is simply a process of making assertions about what is going on in our own minds, or our minds are like searchlights which can be thrown upon the outside world to give us information as to its contents. On this latter assumption, what we call judging will be a turning of the searchlight of the mind upon a particular area of the world and a reporting on what is found there. On the former assumption there is no contact with reality ; on the latter no explanation of error.

Aristotle's Theory of Judgement. The issues raised by the theory of judgement belong to the more technical side of philosophy, and a full account of their ramifications would take us outside the scope of this book. It will be sufficient for my immediate purpose to consider their bearing upon the problem of Substance with which this chapter is more particularly concerned.

The discussion of the nature of judgement has, in common with many philosophical topics, been historically dominated by Aristotle's treatment of the subject. Aristotle attributes to the question of judgement a position of cardinal importance. For the " judgement " or, as it is more frequently called to-day, the " proposition " is for him the fundamental unit of thought. It is, in other words, the form which our thoughts inevitably take, when we think anything at all. So conceived, the judgement or proposition may be defined as the statement which we make when we affirm or deny something. " It is raining now." " It did not rain yesterday." " All cream is white." " Most swans are not black." " The last Emperor of China had a moustache." These are all examples of what philosophers call judgements or propositions. They all, in other words, affirm or deny something, and they may all, therefore, be either true or false. In saying, then, that we think in terms of judgements or propositions, what Aristotle means is that, whenever we think anything at all, that which is thought is a judgement or a proposition. Now all propositions are analysed by Aristotle into two factors. There is, first, that about which something is affirmed or denied ; secondly, there is that which is affirmed or denied about it. Aristotle called the first, the Subject (S), the second, the Predicate (P). Thus when I judge that " so and so is a man," what, according to Aristotle's account, I am affirming, is the Predicate (P), Substance, of the Subject (S). When I judge that " this is white or hard," I am affirming the Predicate (P), Quality, of the Subject (S). When I say that " this is to the right of Y or to the north of Z," I am affirming of S the Predicate known as the Predicate of relation.[1]

Throughout the history of philosophy this Aristotelian view, that under all its forms and disguises the process of

[1] In Aristotelian language these particular Predicates are known as Categories.

thinking could be shown to be in essence a process of judging, and judging to be in its turn a process of affirming a Predicate of a Subject, has persisted. This theory of thinking is, it is obvious, closely allied to, indeed it is bound up with, Aristotle's metaphysical view already described, that a thing can be exhaustively analysed into two elements—its Matter and its Form. Combining the two doctrines, we may say that the Form is the sum of the Predicates ; the Matter, the Subject *of* which the Predicates are asserted. As philosophy developed, the commonsense notion of a thing as consisting of a Substance and its qualities was subjected to increasingly severe criticism. At some of the grounds for this criticism we have already glanced. Nevertheless, the Aristotelian theory of judgement as a process which affirms Predicates of a Subject persisted.

Bradley's Theory of Judgement.

But if there were no Subjects, in the commonly accepted sense of the word Subject, the sense in which *things* were Subjects, of what were the Predicates affirmed ? A celebrated theory of judgement was advanced by the English philosopher F. H. Bradley (1846–1924) primarily as an attempt to answer this question. In his book, *The Principles of Logic*, first published in 1882, Bradley advanced the view that the subject in all judgements was the same, and was nothing less than reality itself. Reality, in fact, constituted a single, unified whole such that, whatever we might believe ourselves or purport to be talking about, we were in fact talking about reality. What in fact we were doing when we made a judgement was to predicate certain ideas of reality, that is to say, to assert that reality was of such a kind as to be capable of assimilating or accommodating the ideas that we were asserting of it. "Judgement proper," according to Bradley's celebrated definition, " is the act which refers an ideal content (recognised as such) to a reality beyond the act." I cannot here describe the arguments with which Bradley supports his theory, nor the criticisms to which it has been subjected. Its interest in the present context arises from the fact of its constituting a pre-eminent illustration of the idealist corollary of the philosophical criticisms of the commonsense notion of Substance.

Monism and Objective Idealism.

The foregoing analysis provides us with two conclusions. First, the commonsense notion of a thing as being a lump of stuff with qualities attached to it is untenable. Secondly, judgement is a process which asserts a Predicate of a Subject. One corollary of the first conclusion is that there can only be one Subject, namely reality, or the universe as a whole ; one corollary of the second that, whatever we may think and say, we are in fact referring to reality as a whole. Moreover, since whatever we think and say must itself form part of reality, in thinking and speaking about reality as a whole we are adding to the reality of that about which we think and speak. Thus thought both refers to reality and adds to it ; it is both descriptive and creative. The implications of these conclusions and their corollaries constitute the foundations of the system of Objective Idealism which will be considered in a later chapter.[1] They point to, if they do not necessitate, the following Idealist implications :

1. Since the notion of a physical thing with qualities is untenable, to be real is to be like a thought rather than to be like a thing.

2. Reality is probably a single unified whole.

3. All our thoughts are in the last resort about this single unified whole, since there is nothing else which can constitute an object of thought.

4. Since in thinking about reality we add to it, thinking is constitutive of reality—that is to say, it makes reality. Hence the distinction between thinking and what is thought about, namely reality, may be expected to prove invalid.

Of these suggestions, 1 and 4 point to the idealist conclusion that the universe is fundamentally mind or thought,

[1] Chapter XV.

2 and 3 to the monist conclusion that the universe is fundamentally one or a unity. All these suggestions have actually been incorporated in systems of idealist metaphysics. They constitute, in fact, the starting-point of one of the most famous metaphysical systems, known as Monistic Idealism. Before we can proceed to a description of this system there are, however, a number of other common-sense notions, such as those of change, cause and effect, and the Self, which fall to be considered under the heading of Critical Metaphysics.

———

Taylor, A. E. Elements of Metaphysics. Chapter IV.

Aristotle's Metaphysics (*Clarendon Press*) with an introduction by W. D. Ross.

Ross, W. D. Aristotle. Chapter VI.

A comprehensive modern treatment of the problem of Substance will be found in C. D. Broad's *Examination of McTaggart's Philosophy*, Vol. I, Chapter VII. The theory of judgement referred to at the end of the chapter will be found in F. H. Bradley's *The Principles of Logic*, Vol. I, Book I.

Chapter VII: THE PROBLEM OF CHANGE: TELEOLOGY AND MECHANISM

Introducing the Problem. We commonly think of the world as consisting of changing things which somehow remain the same things throughout and in spite of the changes that happen to them, so that we can say, " *This* is the thing which yesterday was so-and-so and is to-day something else." But this conception will not stand critical examination. Strip away from a so-called changing thing all the changes which occur in and to it, as we stripped away its qualities from the chocolate,[1] and what is left? Presumably, a core of changeless stuff. But we never in fact find such a core. Everything we know, and every part of everything we know, seems to be in a continual state of change or flux. For example, it occupies at any given moment a new point in time, and is therefore older than it was at the preceding moment. But if everything is changing all the time, and changing in respect of every part of itself, in what sense can *it* be said to be the same thing which somehow persists through the changes that occur to *it*? Yet if *it* is not in some sense the same thing persisting through the changes, we are not entitled to say that *this* is the thing which was so-and-so and is now something else, and the conception of a world composed of things which change, but which, nevertheless, remain somehow the same through change, must be abandoned.

It is from considerations of this kind that philosophical theories of change arise. These are very numerous, ranging from a denial of the existence of change to the affirmation of change as the sole reality. They are, however, unanimous in rejecting the commonsense notion of the world as composed of changing things.

[1] See above, Chapter VI, p. 161.

I. CHANGE AS UNREAL

· We will begin with those which deny the reality of change. One of the earliest philosophers to attempt to prove that change was unreal was Parmenides (about 500 B.C.).

Parmenides's Position.   Parmenides was a mathematician, and to the mathematician anything which can be thought about must in some sense be, for we cannot, Parmenides pointed out, think that which is not. Now, if anything exists, it cannot, he argued, have come into being, because, if it did come into being, it must have arisen either from something or from nothing. It is impossible that it should have arisen from nothing, since there is no nothing ; it is also impossible that it should have arisen from something, that is to say, something other than what is, since there is nothing other than what is.

Again, nothing can come into being in addition to what is. For what is cannot become more than it is, except by the addition of something else. But if we start with literally everything that there is, there is nothing left that can be added to it. Moreover, as Parmenides pointed out, there is no empty space in which something other than what is could arise. Similarly, everything that is could only become less than it is by reason of some part of it becoming separated and departing somewhere else. But once again, if you start with everything that is, there is no empty space outside everything that is, whither the separated part could proceed, that has not already been comprehended within the whole of what is with which we are assumed to have started.   Finally what is, that is to say, the whole of reality, is immovable, since, if it moved, it could move only into empty space. But empty space is nothing, and there is no nothing.

The inference is that reality is a solid immovable lump, a "plenum," as it is sometimes called, that is to say, something which occupies the whole of space and is solid and continuous without distinction or division in any of its parts. This solid indivisible lump which is reality did not begin and cannot change.

Now if reality is a solid and indivisible lump, there cannot, said Parmenides, be more of it in one place than there is in another Hence, the coming into existence of particular portions of what is is impossible. It is further impossible that there should be distinction between one thing and another, since if reality is a continuous and indivisible lump, there can be no room between one part of it and another ; nor, indeed, could anything but reality itself prevent its parts from coming into contact. Hence not only is the universe a whole, not only is it homogeneous throughout, but no single part or element in it can change. There cannot, that is to say, be growth or diminution in respect of any particular quality in the universe, since the whole notion of elements and qualities, which presupposes that one part of the universe is different from another, is illusory. Coming into being and ceasing to be are, therefore, said Parmenides, mere names, and we reach the famous conclusion *ex nihilo nihil fit* (out of nothing there comes nothing). The whole line of reasoning is strongly reminiscent of Spinoza's argument for the all inclusiveness of Substance to which reference has already been made.[1]

Zeno's Arrow and Achilles and the Tortoise.

Greek philosophers were fond of maintaining paradoxical positions, and invented a variety of ingenious arguments to prove the unreality of change. Of these the most famous is that of Zeno, the philosopher of Elea (early fifth century B.C.). Consider, he said, any apparent example of change or motion, an arrow, let us say, in its flight. At any given moment of its flight, it either is where it is or it is where it isn't ; if it is where it is, it cannot be moving, since, if it were, it would not be there ; and it cannot be where it isn't. Therefore, at that particular moment it is not moving. Similar arguments apply to any other point or moment

[1] See Chapter IV, pp. 123, 124.

in the flight of the arrow ; therefore at no point or moment does it move ; therefore its apparent movement is an illusion.

The well-known paradox of Achilles and the tortoise was used to illustrate the same conclusion, namely, the illusoriness of change or motion. Achilles and the tortoise run a race—Achilles, as is proper, seeing that he is so much the faster, giving the tortoise a start. But Achilles will never catch the tortoise, since by the time that Achilles has reached the point (P1) where the tortoise was, the tortoise will have moved forward to another point (P2). By the time Achilles has reached P2, the tortoise will be at P3. By the time he is at P3, the tortoise will be at P4 and so on *ad infinitum*. Admittedly the distance between Achilles and the tortoise continually diminishes ; but, so the argument maintains, it can never be entirely abolished, since, whatever point Achilles reaches, the time which he occupies in reaching it will have enabled the tortoise to move forward to a further point.

William James used a similar argument to show that a given period of time can never elapse. Let us, he said, consider any period of time, say half an hour. Then half of it must elapse before the whole of it can elapse. Let us concentrate attention on that half of it which must first elapse ; then once again it will be true that half of it must elapse before the whole of it can. Let us concentrate attention on the $7\frac{1}{2}$ minutes which must now elapse first. Again it will be true that half of it, namely $3\frac{3}{4}$ minutes, must elapse before the whole of it can. In this way we can proceed indefinitely, gradually reducing the period of time which must " first elapse," yet never actually abolishing it. For, however small the period that remains, it will still be the case that half of it must elapse before the whole of it can elapse. Something, therefore, must *always* happen before half an hour can elapse. Therefore half an hour can never elapse.

These examples are all designed with a common purpose, namely, to show the irrationality of our ordinary conceptions of change, time and motion. The nature of change,

time and motion cannot, they suggest, be such as is ordinarily supposed, since if it was, it would not be possible
to reach such absurd conclusions by reflecting upon them.
William James's argument, it is true, was put forward
in a spirit of caricature, in order to expose the absurdities
of what he called a vicious intellectualism[1] ; but the examples of the Greek philosophers were intended as serious
criticisms of the commonsense notion of change.

Analysis of the Concept of a Changing Thing.

Now the
commonsense notion of change bases itself, as we have
seen, upon the conception of the changing thing—that is
to say, of something which both changes and remains
the same—and it is upon this particular conception that
the critical attention of philosophers has chiefly been
directed. Let us take as an illustration the case of a leaf
which is green in spring and becomes yellow in autumn.
What precisely is it that has changed ? One way of answering this question is to invoke the Aristotelian distinction
between Matter and Form described in the last chapter.[2]
A green leaf may from this point of view be described
as Matter, namely, the Matter of the leaf, upon which the
Form of greenness has been superimposed. Now the Matter
of the leaf has not changed, since if it had, the leaf would
not be the same leaf. Nor has the Form ; for the Form
of greenness cannot change into the Form of yellowness. It
can only be succeeded or replaced by it, and this, as Plato
concluded,[3] is precisely what has happened in the case
of the leaf. An unchanging immaterial Form, the Form
of yellowness, has in fact replaced another immaterial
Form, the Form of greenness, in the Matter of the leaf.
Now this account, it will be noticed, frees us from the
necessity of postulating a changing thing. For, if it be

[1] William James was a pragmatist. See Chapter XVI, pp. 448, 455,
for an account of the pragmatists' criticism of the method of abstract
reasoning, which has been the traditional method of philosophy, on
the ground of its vicious intellectualism.

[2] See Chapter VI, pp. 162, 163.

[3] See Chapter X, pp. 278–281, for an account of Plato's views.

correct, there is no *thing* that has changed. All that has happened is that one Form has substituted itself for another in an unchanging subject matter. According to this analysis, then, all cases of apparent change in things are really cases of replacement of one unchanging Form by another in the same unchanging subject matter. This conclusion, therefore, suggests that change, at any rate in the commonsense acceptance of the term which entails the notion of *things* that change, is illusory.

Spinoza's Proof of the Changelessness of the Whole.

In general, however, the arguments which philosophers have adduced to show the illusoriness of change are derived from considerations relating to the nature of the universe as a whole. If reality is a unified whole, and if this whole can be shown to be changeless, it will follow that any apparent change in the parts of reality will be *only* apparent. Subjected to examination by the critical reason, the appearance of change which things undoubtedly present, will be found, so runs the argument, to disappear.

In Chapter IV, I cited certain arguments of Spinoza's purporting to show that the universe was a single all-embracing unity, as an illustration of the way in which *a priori* reasoning has been employed to establish conclusions which are regarded as being necessary and, because necessary, therefore true.[1] Spinoza's arguments have an important bearing on the question with which we are at present concerned—that is to say, the question of the nature of change. It will be remembered that Spinoza defines Substance as that which is " conceived through itself," and proceeds to deduce that Substance must be unlimited, since, if Substance were limited, there must be something to limit it, in which event Substance could not be " conceived " solely " through itself," and would have to be conceived as " limited by that other." A similar argument could be, and has been, used to show that Substance must be unchanging. The argument begins

[1] See Chapter IV, pp. 123, 124.

by pointing out that a thing can be changed only in one or other of two ways. Either the change is effected by some external agency or it is self-originated, springing up, as it were, spontaneously within the thing. Now if Substance is all that there is, it cannot, as Parmenides pointed out, be changed by some external agency, since there can be no such agency. Nor, if Spinoza is right, can it be changed from within, since, if it were, one state of Substance would be different from another, and we should no longer be able to define Substance as that which is " conceived through itself," since it would now have to be conceived as that which is " potentially liable to become ' that other.' " The conception of the universe as liable to become a different sort of universe is in fact incompatible with the affirmation of the universe's fundamental unity, since the universe as it is and the universe as it may become are not one but two, and it is difficult to see how we are to avoid qualifying the universe as it is with the potentiality of developing into the universe as it may become. Once we concede this possibility, that the universe may become a different universe, the possibility becomes a fact about it as it now is. As Aristotle would say,[1] the universe as it may become is latent in the actuality of the universe as it is, and this latency cannot, therefore, fail to impair the unity of the universe as it is. For this reason most monistic[2] philosophers—that is to say, most of those philosophers who have affirmed that the universe is a single whole or unity—have denied the reality of change and conceived of the universe as fundamentally changeless.

Moral Argument against Change on the part of God. A further argument is derived from ethical considerations. Let us suppose that, following Spinoza, we affirm not only that the universe is an all inclusive Substance but that this Substance is identifiable with a personal spiritual God. God so conceived cannot, as Plato pointed out in the

[1] See pp. 181, 182, below.
[2] See Chapter XV for an account of Monism.

Republic, be credited with the possibility of changing. Why cannot He? Let us provisionally adopt the distinction made above between change from without and change from within. Now if God is all, we cannot suppose that change in God is effected by any external agency ; it must, therefore, be self-initiated. Now change in a person is either for the better or for the worse. There cannot be change in order to achieve that which one already is or has ; hence, if God could change for the better, it would imply that there was some good, namely, that which God could realise by changing, which, prior to the change, God lacked. But if there is some good which God lacks, then He cannot be completely perfect. On the other hand, God cannot change for the worse, since the desire for, or even the possibility of, such change on His part would argue an imperfection in God as He now is. We cannot, then, it is said, conceive of God as changing, and if we cannot, prayer, which is offered on the assumption that God can be induced to change, must be illogical. If now we adopt a monistic view of the universe and further identify the single whole or unity which our Monism affirms with God, it will follow from the moral impossibility of change on the part of God that there cannot be change on the part of reality. Since reality as a whole cannot change, any apparent change in the parts of reality must be illusory.

Argument from Time.

A further set of considerations has been derived from a consideration of the nature of time. By a variety of subtle arguments, the notion of time can be shown to be full of contradictions. The reader who wishes to acquaint himself with these arguments will find them set out at length in F. H. Bradley's celebrated work, *Appearance and Reality*. They are, however, highly technical, and unsuitable for inclusion in a book of this kind.

Many philosophers have, however, denied the objective reality of time ; they have, that is to say, denied that time is a factor in the world which is independent of human

consciousness. One of the forms taken by this denial appears
in the account of Kant's philosophy in Chapter XIV.[1]
Now, if time does not belong to the nature of things, the
universe must be changeless, since the notion of change
which entails the conception of before and after, also
entails the notion of time.

II.   CHANGE AS THE ONLY REALITY

I now turn to the arguments devoted to establishing the
contrary position, first adopted by the Greek philosopher
Heracleitus (540–475 B.C.), that change is the only reality
and that the universe is, therefore, in a state of flux, or,
more precisely, that the universe *is* a flux. These arguments
have been restated in recent years by the philosopher
Bergson (born 1859), whose celebrated work, *Creative
Evolution,* is the most sustained and convincing exposition
of the universality of change which has appeared in the
history of philosophy. The positive tenets of Bergson's
philosophy will be outlined in a later chapter.[2] I am here
concerned only with those of his arguments which are
directed against the commonsense notion of the universe
as composed of things which change.

Bergson's Arguments for the Universality of Change.
Bergson begins by considering the nature of consciousness.
We commonly think of ourselves as beings possessing a
consciousness which passes through certain well-defined
phases or states, which we know as emotions, desires,
moods, and so forth. At first sight, indeed, consciousness
appears to consist of the succession of such states, each of
which is a single and independent entity, the states being
strung together along something which is called the ego,
like beads on a necklace. But reflection shows this conception to be erroneous ; and the error consists more

[1] See Chapter XIV, p. 379.   [2] See Chapter XIX.

particularly in the fact that, when we admit that one state changes and gives way to another, we overlook the fact that it changes even while it persists. " Take," says Bergson, " the most stable of internal states, the visual perception of a motionless object. The object may remain the same, I may look at it from the same side, at the same angle, in the same light ; nevertheless, the vision I now have of it differs from that which I have just had, even if only because the one is an instant older than the other. My memory is there, which conveys something of the past into the present. My mental state, as it advances on the road of time, is continually swelling with the duration it accumulates." If this is true of the perception of external objects, it is even truer as a description of our internal states, our desires, our emotions, our willings, and so forth. The conclusion is, in Bergson's words, that " we change without ceasing, and the state itself is nothing but change." " There is," he asserts, " no feeling, no idea, no volition which is not undergoing change at every moment : if a mental state ceased to vary, its duration would cease to flow."

It follows that there is no real difference between passing from one state to another and continuing in what is called the same state. We imagine such a difference because it is only when the continual change in any one state has become sufficiently marked to arrest our attention that we do, in fact, notice it, with the result that we assert that one state has given way to another. Thus we postulate a series of successive mental states, because our attention is forced upon them in a series of successive mental acts. It is for the same reason that we tend to regard ourselves as beings in whom something endures, in spite of change. Just as we speak of separate psychological states which succeed each other, so we speak of a self which experiences changing psychological states, and this self, we say, endures. But we have no more experience of an unchanging ego than we have of an unchanging psychological state : however far we push our analysis, we never reach such an unchanging ego. There is, in fact, nothing which endures through change, because there is nothing which does not change.

Hence Bergson arrives at the truth that we ourselves are beings who endure not through change, but by change. Our own lives, as actually experienced, as the reality of which we are most directly assured, are simply change. " If," says Bergson, " our existence were composed of separate states with an impassive ego to unit them, for us there would be no duration. For an ego which does not change does not endure, and a psychic state which remains the same so long as it is not replaced by the following state, does not endure either."

Elimination of the THING which Changes.   There is thus no self which changes : there is, indeed, nothing which changes, for in asserting the existence of that which changes we are asserting the existence of something which, from the mere fact that it is subject to change, is not itself change ; there is simply change.

The truth that we are beings whose reality consists in continuous change is for Bergson the clue to the understanding of the universe itself. For the universe is shown by him to belong to the same stream of change or " becoming," as Bergson calls it (since it never actually is any one thing, but is always on the way to becoming something else), as we do ourselves. Just as we are unable to penetrate through the continuous changes of our consciousness to something stable that underlies them, so, when we consider the nature of the world around us, do we find it impossible to discover anything which passes through changes, but is itself something other than the changes which occur to it. The universe, in other words, is itself a stream of perpetual change.

The development of Bergson's metaphysical theory, which includes the assertion that intuition is the faculty by means of which reality is known, and a conception of the intellect as a faculty which misrepresents reality by cutting up the flow of change into apparently static objects, thus generating such paradoxes as that of Zeno's arrow and

Achilles and the Tortoise, will be described in a later chapter.[1]

III. ARISTOTLE'S VIEWS ON CHANGE

Aristotle on Potentiality and Actuality. We have considered arguments to show that change is unreal and also that change is the only reality. Both sets of arguments are destructive of the commonsense notion of the world as composed of things which persist through change. The question may be asked, " Can no philosopher be found to defend the commonsense notion ? " Strictly speaking the answer is that there cannot. A celebrated doctrine, the doctrine of potentiality and actuality, which originated with Aristotle may, however, be cited as affording some concession to commonsense notions, although, strictly speaking, the question which it seeks to answer is not " What is the nature of change?" but " How do things come to be what they are ? " Aristotle's doctrine is of great importance in the history of philosophy. It also completes the doctrine of Matter and Form outlined in the previous chapter, and it will be well, therefore, to give a brief account of it. Aristotle's attention was chiefly directed to the process of growth. What, he asks, is the nature of the process of change or growth which takes place when an unfinished or growing thing becomes finished or mature? He asks us to consider two seeds of two plants or two embryos of two animals at such an early stage of development that even the botanist or the zoologist may be unable to tell the difference between them. Yet it is certain, even at this stage, that one of the seeds will grow into an oak and the other into an ash, and that one of the embryos will become a mole and the other a weasel. Aristotle's way of stating this is as follows. Of the first seed, he says, " Although it is not yet *actually* an oak, nevertheless it is so *potentially* " ; that is to say, it will in due course become an oak, if it is not interfered with. Also, it is implied, by no possibility can

[1] See Chapter XIX, more especially pp. 547-556.

it become a beech. Growth, then, may be described as a process whereby something which at first possesses a tendency to grow along certain lines, or some raw material which is to be worked up into a certain condition, achieves, when it has grown or been completed, the form or the condition for which it already possessed the tendency. In other words, growth is a process by which the Form of a thing which was potential becomes actual, or, to revert to the language of the previous doctrine of Matter and Form and to combine the two, an individual thing which has reached its appropriate Form is the actuality of which the indeterminate Matter was the potentiality.

Change, then, or rather that kind of change which we know as growth, is the development of the potentiality already latent in the organism, the result being that what was potential becomes actual. Nor is the formula limited to the growth of natural organisms ; it applies equally to things which are made by hand. Thus Aristotle would say that a statue is an embodiment in actuality in stone of the Form which existed potentially as an idea in the mind of the sculptor.

The Limits of the Process of Growth. But the process of development is not, as Aristotle conceived it, unlimited. The growth of natural organisms is not an unending process in which successive material Forms, representing the maturing of ever new potential capacities, become actual. It comes to an end when the last stage is reached in the realisation of the proper Form of the thing's kind or species. The seed becomes an acorn, the acorn a sapling, the sapling an oak ; but there the process stops. Nothing is related to the oak as the oak is related to the sapling. Aristotle identifies this final stage in the case of natural organisms with that on reaching which the organism is able to exercise the power of reproducing its kind. Thus the stage of maturity is recognised as the end of the process. This conception of an "end" or "telos," as it is sometimes called, is constantly invoked in Aristotle's philosophy, and affords the clue to his conception of the motive force of change and development. The end to which things develop is thought of as pre-existing the development towards it, and it is the pull upon them exerted by the end which they are represented as seeking to realise, which causes things to change and develop. In view of the importance of this conception both in its own right and as an explanation of the fact of change, it will be desirable to consider it in rather greater detail. First, however, it will be convenient to round off the brief sketch of some of the leading notions of Aristotle's metaphysics contained in this and in the preceding chapter by an account of his doctrine of the Four Causes, which Aristotle put forward as constituting a final explanation of the present world order.

Aristotle's Doctrine of the Four Causes.

The doctrine of the Four Causes combines Aristotle's teachings on the subject of Matter and Form and Potentiality and Actuality. It is in intention an answer to the question " How does the world order come to be what it is ? "

There are, Aristotle maintained, four partial answers to this question, each of which must be included in the complete answer. In other words, the absence of any of the four factors which he proceeds to specify as the causes why things are as they are, would, he insists, have resulted in things being different.

There is, then, first, Matter or " the material cause " of the thing. There must, that is to say, be the germ from which the oak grows, the stone on which the sculptor works. Secondly, there is the law according to which the thing develops, which Aristotle calls the Form or " the formal cause." The acorn must develop in accordance with a definite tendency of growth, a tendency, that is to say, to develop in a way characteristic of oaks and not of elms ; there must be the Form or idea of the statue present in the sculptor's mind directing the activities of his chisel. Thirdly, there is the agent, whose initial impulse started the whole process, called by Aristotle the " efficient cause." The acorn did not appear from nowhere ; there must have been a parent oak to produce it, and the activity of the parent oak is, therefore, the efficient cause of the process which ends with the production of a new oak. Similarly, there must be the activity of the sculptor to chisel the stone from which the statue is to emerge. Finally, there is the result of the process which in the world of nature is implicit or potential in the whole process of development towards it, and in the sculptor's mind constitutes the conclusion of his efforts. This is known as " the final cause." The development in the acorn stops when it has become a fully matured oak, and Aristotle conceives of this achievement of maturity as constituting the goal or end which the whole process is seeking to reach. Similarly with the completed statue.

Coalescence and Opposition of the Causes.

Both in nature and in art the second or formal and the fourth or final causes tend to coalesce. In both, the guiding agency which directs the whole developing process is the Form which, initially latent or potential, becomes actualised in the realisation of the end. Thus the Form normally performs the office of both formal and final cause. In its rôle of formal cause, the Form may be conceived as that which is striving to express or to actualise itself in the process of development. In its rôle of final cause, it is the completed actuality which the process is striving to realise. Since the efficient cause is in the case of natural objects the Form already realised in different material, that is to say, the parent oak, and in the case of manufactured products, the idea in the mind of the maker which impels him to give it realisation in some material, whether paint or sound, stone or wood, we may say that the second, third and fourth causes are all of them the Form in different stages of actualisation. The basic distinction, then, is between the material cause, the primitive stuff or substance in which the development takes place, and the final cause, which is what the development is seeking to achieve. This distinction, a distinction which takes on the character of an opposition, assumes great importance in the history of philosophy, and deserves further examination.

IV. MECHANISM AND TELEOLOGY

The Two Kinds of Causation. The opposition to which I have just referred is usually expressed in modern phraseology as the opposition between Mechanism and Teleology. Each connotes a type of causation. Mechanism connotes the type of causation which is held to operate in the world of science in accordance with which every event is and must be determined by an immediately preceding event. A machine offers the most obvious example of this type of causation, since every movement in a machine is the result of some preceding movement. The spring is wound and the watch goes, the handle turned and the engine starts. Moreover, given the requisite preceding movement, the ensuing movement follows necessarily upon it, provided that the machine is in working order. Thus we are led to think of events which are mechanically caused as being determined by the events which went before them. Given the appropriate preceding event, they must, we hold, be what they are, and cannot be otherwise than they are.

Teleological causation connotes determination not by what went before, but by what lies in front, the expression " teleological " being derived from the Greek word τέλος, meaning end or goal. Thus we may think of the movements of a runner trying to outstrip his competitors in a race as being determined by his conception of the goal, the finishing post, the reaching of which is something waiting for him, as it were, in the future. Similarly the efforts of a man who is reading for an examination may be regarded as being influenced, if not determined, by the passing of the examination, which he represents to himself as something which is in front of him : as ordinary language puts it, his reading is inspired by his determination to pass the examination. Greek thought is dominated by this conception of the telos or end, and of effort and growth as inspired by the purpose of achieving it. Aristotle in particular tended, as already mentioned, to think of the end as an actually existing something, lying out there, as it were, in front of a developing thing, and determining the direction of development towards the thing's achievement of the end.

The Two Conceptions of a Thing's Nature:

The distinction between Mechanism and Teleology may be brought out by considering the two senses in either of which we may use the word " nature," when we speak of the " nature of a thing." We may mean by the expression " the nature of a thing " its initial state or condition ; its nature in fact is that which the thing began as. Adopting this point of view, we shall regard its subsequent development as being determined wholly or largely by its original nature. Or we may think of its nature as being realised only at the highest point of its development. Taking this second view, we should say that the nature of a man is not that which he possesses as an embryo, a baby, a boy, or even a youth, but is revealed only in the fullest development of all his faculties and powers, mental, spiritual and physical. Only at the limit of his development, we should say, has he realised all that he has it in him to be, and so achieved his full nature. Proceeding along these lines we may think of the " end " of maturity as determining the whole course of development towards it.

The nature of a State may be similarly treated. We may think of the nature of a State as constituted by its earliest and most primitive form, when the State was a collection of human beings banded together for purposes of aggression and defence. Or we may think of it as being realised only when the State has reached its fullest development in a perfect community. Any State which falls short of this perfect community we shall refuse to regard as completely a State, just as we shall refuse to regard a moron or a halfwit as completely a man. And, as in the case of the human being, we may proceed to think of all existing communities as striving to develop a greater degree of perfection in the endeavour to realise their true nature as perfect communities. Taking this view, we shall further be disposed to interpret the phenomena presented by all existing States as being at least in part expressions of the drive which impels an imperfectly realised State towards the full realisation of the nature of State-hood in the achievement of the perfect State.

Alternative Modes of Explanation.

These two ways of regarding the nature of a thing may be developed into two highly important modes of interpretation, representing what are in effect two alternative and opposing methods of approach to almost every outstanding philosophical problem. The first is the method of science. The scientist is, it is obvious, bound to think of the phenomena he investigates as completely caused by preceding phenomena. If he were not in a position to make this presumption in regard to the causation of events, he would be unable either to calculate or to predict.[1] Hence the scientific approach to the universe is in essence mechanistic, and mechanistic modes of thought issue in Materialism in metaphysics, Naturalism in ethics, and Agnosticism in religion.

Teleology lays emphasis on the causal efficacy of the end. Aristotle, as we have seen, was an outstanding teleologist and he shall state the doctrine in his own words. In the following quotation Aristotle's object is to distinguish telelogical causation from the allegedly inadequate mechanist causation of the scientists, that is, the Nature-philosophers.

" . . . when," he says, " we are dealing with definite and ordered products of Nature, we must not say that each *is* of a certain quality because it becomes so, but rather that they *become* so and so because they *are* so and so, for the process of Becoming or development attends upon Being and is for the sake of Being, not *vice versa*.

" The ancient Nature-philosophers, however, took the

[1] See Chapter XVIII, pp. 529–531, for a further description of his necessity of scientific method.

opposite view. The reason for this is that they did not see that the causes were numerous, but only the material and efficient and did not distinguish even these, while they made no enquiry at all into the formal and final causes.

" Everything then exists for a final cause, and all those things which are included in the definition of each animal, or which are means to an end or are ends in themselves, come into being through this cause and the rest."

Aristotle then proceeds to explain what he means by " the rest," namely, the environmental influences which bring about secondary modifications in living things, that is to say, the efficient causes.

Teleology emphasises the concept of purpose, and usually presupposes the reality of free will. Since minds alone can conceive of purposes and be influenced by consciously conceived ends, Teleology also affirms the independence of minds, has a preference for modes of explanation which presuppose the causal efficacy of minds, and is compatible with a religious attitude to the cosmos. Teleological modes of explanation may be applied with the greatest effect in those spheres in which science is weak. For example, science has proved unable to give satisfactory accounts of art, religion or morality. During periods when mechanistic modes of explanation are dominant, the tendency is either to ignore these forms of human activity or to try to explain them away. It is in precisely these spheres that teleological modes of thought have proved most applicable. In sum, idealists tend to prefer the mode of teleological, materialists of mechanical causation. A few examples may serve to illustrate these generalisations.

1. SELF-DETERMINISM. Let us begin by applying the mechanistic concept of causation to the Self. The result of this application is a doctrine which has come to be known as Self-Determinism. According to this doctrine, which appears in Aristotle's *Ethics*, we are determined, not by natural forces nor by our external environment, but by ourselves, that is by forces and tendencies operating within

us, yet often operating beyond the bounds of our consciousness. These forces and tendencies determine the strength and the nature of our conscious desires.

A man, as Aristotle says, comes to have a good character because he has continually performed good acts. But he cannot continually perform good acts, unless he is the sort of man whose nature it is to perform them; unless, that is to say, he has the good character from which the good acts necessarily spring. This character will, in its turn, proceed from and be formed by a preceding series of good acts. Retracing our steps by this method over the past history of the individual, we find that the actions which he performs at any given moment spring from, and are conditioned by, his being the sort of person that he is at the moment, and further that he is the particular sort of person that he is at that moment because of the impulses which he experiences and the tendencies which he exhibits. If, therefore, we go far enough back, we can show that the tendencies and impulses which were originally his on the first occasion on which he acted are those which really determine the whole subsequent tenor of his life. Modern theories of psycho-analysis, as we shall see in a subsequent chapter,[1] have done little more than dot the i's and cross the t's of this doctrine. They represent human beings not as drawn from in front but as pushed from behind; as motivated, that is to say, not by rational desires to achieve ends and to fulfil purposes envisaged by the imagination as desirable, but as impelled by a drive from below whose strength is derived from forces which are both incalculable and irrational.

Thus a mechanistic treatment of the Self in terms of causation by "what went before" leads to a determinist conclusion, even though the immediately determining agents may be our own psychological states.

2. TELEOLOGICAL VIEW OF THE SELF. To treat the Self teleologically is to deny that it can ever be completely

[1] See Chapter IX, pp. 238–241.

determined either by its heredity, or by its environment, or by its own past deeds. All these, the teleologist will affirm, may influence and bias the Self; but they never completely determine it. They incline its desires without necessitating them, predisposing it to follow courses which it is nevertheless free to avoid, and to shun ends which it is nevertheless free to pursue. The Christian doctrine of past wrongdoing in its relation to present temptation, declaring, as it does, that every time we went wrong in the past makes it harder for us to resist temptation in the present, but that it never makes it impossible, constitutes a good example of this attitude to the Self. As Kant would say,[1] we are always free to do our duty, and the only effect of past derelictions is to make our duty more difficult for us to do. Now all these doctrines imply that the Self is free, free at any rate to act morally in spite of the accumulated influences of heredity, environment, disposition, past habits, and the rest. Yet the freedom of the Self envisaged by teleological doctrines is not an irresponsible caprice, a freedom to act in fulfilment of whatever impulse happens to come uppermost at the moment. On the contrary, it implies the capacity to be actuated by motive and to acknowledge purpose. The man of strong will is, indeed, precisely he who has dovetailed all the separate impulses and desires of his nature in the service of some dominant purpose. Freedom of the will, say the teleologists, is not incompatible with the pursuit of ends. It is, on the contrary, most clearly exhibited in the resolute pursuit of an end in the face of obstacles to be overcome and tempting distractions to be resisted. Now it is precisely this kind of influence, the influence of a dominating end or purpose conceived of as something waiting to be achieved which we have seen to be characteristic of teleological causation.

3. CHRISTIAN DOCTRINE OF THE SOUL. To pursue this topic further would take us far beyond what is intended

[1] See Chapter XIV pp. 387–394, for an account of Kant's ethical views.

only as an illustration. Mention should, however, be made, —it is, indeed, an outstanding example of a teleological conception—of the Christian doctrine of the soul of man. Man's soul is conceived by Christianity as an essentially immaterial entity, which, temporarily associated with matter, will ultimately transcend the material connection and realise its full nature in the achievement of complete spirituality. It is an essential feature of this conception that the ultimate spiritual condition of the immortal soul should be envisaged as exerting a directive influence or pull upon it even in its present, transitional state. The exhortation to realise the highest that is in us, no less than the acknowledgement of the pull that beautiful and noble things have over us even in our present imperfect condition, implies, as it were, an advance recognition of the ultimate development of the soul in the realisation of the end which its present state imperfectly foreshadows. But teleological causation is never in the Christian doctrine regarded as being completely and finally determining. The end may be conceived as existing and exercising its pull over the soul's development towards it ; but the pull can always be resisted. The spirit can already recognise beauty ; but a man may nevertheless close his eyes to what is beautiful. The developing mind may feel the attraction of what is generous and noble ; but it is free to perform actions which are cruel and mean. The soul may be destined for Heaven ; but it may frustrate its destiny and end in Hell. In this way, while the efficacy of teleological causation is acknowledged, the element of freedom is preserved.

4. BRAIN AND MIND. The different consequences which attend the application of mechanical and teleological modes of explanation to any particular problem may be clearly seen by considering their respective bearing upon the question of the relation of body and mind, a subject which will be dealt with in greater detail in a later chapter.[1] If we regard mechanical causation as ultimate, then we shall

[1] See Chapter XVIII, pp. 498–521.

find ourselves committed to a view of the mind-body relationship which issues in Materialism.[1] Every event in the body, we shall hold, is the result of some preceding event, this preceding event being in its turn the result of an event which precedes it. We are thus committed to the following out of a chain of bodily events, of which the first link can be shown to be the body's reaction to some stimulus which reaches it from its external environment. Thus all bodily events are in the last resort traceable to the body's reactions to the application of an external stimulus. This external stimulus may be either immediate and in the present, as when my eyes blink on their sudden exposure to a bright light, or my foot jerks forward when my leg is struck just below the knee by the side of the hand, or remote and in the past, as when the present state of my liver and the bodily behaviour and temperamental aberrations which it occasions are due to the curries which over a period of thirty years I consumed as a young and middle-aged Anglo-Indian. As for events in the mind, they must, if mechanical causation is ultimate, be caused by events in the body. The mind, indeed, will be reduced to the status of an apparatus for reflecting or registering the events that occur in the body and brain, the so-called mental reflection of events in the body and the brain being what we call a conscious experience. But, since consciousness cannot register what is not there, the whole of our conscious experience is, on this view, determined by the bodily conditions which it reflects. This view was very popular in the nineteenth century and formed an integral part of the dominant philosophy of Materialism. It is still prevalent among men of science to-day, and it is not easy to refute. It is the inevitable corollary of the application of the principle of mechanical causation to the living mechanism, and, as we shall see in Chapter XVIII, it issues in complete Determinism.

The alternative view, which affirms that mental experiences are at least partially independent of bodily events,

[1] See Chapter XVIII for an account of scientific Materialism.

denies that causation proceeds always from the body as cause to the mind as effect, and insists on the contrary that some bodily phenomena can only be interpreted as effects of mental causes, as when the dread of a coming ordeal causes my face to grow pale and my teeth to chatter. This type of causation, in which the mind occupies the role of cause and the body that of effect, may, of course, still be envisaged on mechanistic lines. But when we speak of the mind's sensitiveness to a coming ordeal, we are, it is obvious, introducing a conception which is more analogous to teleological causation ; we are affirming, that is to say, the determining influence of something that lies in front. Directly, in fact, we affirm that the mind is at least partially independent of the body, we find ourselves enabled and, indeed, forced to attribute to it the capacity of being influenced by objects which are not present to the bodily senses and by events which have not yet occurred. A man sits down to his books in the evening, *because* he wants to pass a coming examination. He goes to bed early and refrains from beer and cigarettes, *because* he wants to row in a coming boat race. Now the body cannot, it is clear, be influenced by what does not yet exist. The most obvious way, therefore, of accounting for such mortifications and abstentions is in terms of teleological causation, that is to say, in terms of the domination of an at least partially free mind by a sense of purpose, namely, the purpose to achieve a goal. Thus the belief in teleological causation is bound up with a view of mind as being at least partially independent of the body, since it is only a mind so conceived which can be regarded as capable of acknowledging causative influences, other than the mechanical causation which governs the physical world.

Generalised Application of the Principles.

The scope of the two principles of interpretation which we have been considering is, it is obvious, exceedingly far-reaching. It is scarcely too much to say that every branch of human activity, every expression of the human spirit, every organic

GP

phenomenon studied by biology, every conscious event investigated by psychology, is susceptible of interpretation in terms of one or the other. Wherever we find a growing and developing thing, a living organism, a culture, a civilisation, a community, or an art form, we can either explain it from behind in terms of the origins from which it arose, or from in front in terms of the goal which it is seeking to achieve, and in each case the results of the two modes of interpretation will be found to be very different.

Let us consider in the connection the familiar rationalist criticism of religion. Normally it takes the form of revealing the origins of religion in human fear and need. Human beings feared phenomena which they did not understand, and felt a need to stand well with the powers which were assumed to be responsible for what they feared. Thus, it is said, religion began. Those who take this line are, we shall find, pleased to be able to show that the earliest forms of religion involve totemism and exogamy. The implication is then drawn that there is essentially no more in religion than totemism and exogamy now. In the light of what has been said, it is obvious that the implication entails an assumption, the assumption, namely, that mechanistic modes of causation are universal and exhaustive and may, therefore, appropriately be invoked to interpret the development of religion. But this assumption may, as we have seen, be called in question, and it may well be the case that when it is applied outside its appropriate sphere, for example, in explanation of the evolution of the religious consciousness, the results to which the concept of mechanical causation leads are misleading. To take a parallel case, mathematics may be shown to have developed from very humble beginnings ; the savage, for example, can only count on the fingers of one hand. But the fact is not usually regarded as invalidating the multiplication table.

In general, it may with truth be said that to explain a thing in terms of its origin, is not to give a *complete* account of it as it is *now*. For a *complete* account we must consider not only its origin, but its consummation ; we must, in other words, not only look backwards to the germ from which it arose, but forwards to the end which it is seeking to achieve. The present state of a growing and developing thing reflects its past, no doubt ; but it also foreshadows its future.

Let us suppose that we take, as an example of such a growing and developing thing, a youth of fifteen years old. How are we to describe his nature ? To know that he was once an embryo, and that his body still bears the traces of having been a fish is no doubt important ; but it is equally, perhaps more important, to know that he will one day be a man. We may go further and say that it is only in so far as he does one day become a man, that he realises his full nature and become fully himself. In so far as he falls short of manhood, in so far as his faculties are still immature and his body undeveloped, he has not attained the proper form of his species, and has not, therefore, realised all that he has it in him to be. The nature of a growing thing, in other words, is not exhibited at some half-way-house stage on the road to its full development ; it is exhibited at, because it is only realised in, its full development. To give a complete account of it, therefore, we must await, or at least know, that development.

The moral is that, if we wish to understand the nature of a man, we must take him in the full flood of his energies and exercise of his powers ; we must take him, in fact, at his zenith. Until he reaches it, he is not yet completely himself ; he is only trying to become himself. And since, while his nature falls short of its full development, he is only incompletely himself, it follows that a description of his nature, as it is in his immaturity, will be only incompletely a description. If it is to be complete, it must include a reference to what he is trying to become, it must, in other words, introduce the conception of teleological causation.

Comments on the Two Principles.   It is, I think, clear that the two principles whose implications we have been engaged in considering cannot both be true, or cannot, at least, be universally true. The principle of mechanical causation purports to give a *complete* account of the present state and condition of a thing in terms of its origins. A thing on this principle is what it is entirely and in every respect because its causes were what they were. It cannot, then, owe any of its characteristics to the operation of teleological causation. The principle of teleological causation does not, as usually stated, make such all-embracing claims, if only because it tends to be allied with theories that maintain the reality of free will. A human soul may be teleologically influenced by its destiny, moulded by its ideals, or dominated by its purpose. In extreme cases, when a man is, as we should say, obsessed with an idea, this domination may appear to become absolute. But it never, the believer in free will would maintain, becomes quite absolute. Thus teleological causation is rarely conceived of as being universally operative and completely explanatory. Nevertheless it is clear that, in so far as its efficacy is recognised, in so far, that is to say, as a man's conduct is conceived of as being determined by his conception of goal or end, mechanical causation is inapplicable. Assuming, then, that the obligation were to be laid upon us of choosing between them, the question would arise which of the two principles we should choose.

The choice is a difficult one, and we may well ask whether it is forced. At first sight, admittedly, it is not. It seems at first sight fairly simple to admit the efficacy of both principles, but to limit the scope of their application. Mechanical causation, we shall say, applies in one sphere, teleological in another. Nor is there any great difficulty in assigning the respective spheres. Broadly, we should say, Mechanism holds in the world of matter, Teleology in that of spirit. To put the point in another way, we may say that the spheres in which the principle of Mechanism operates are those explored by the natural sciences ; the spheres of teleology are those of art, religion and ethics. We might feel tempted to go further and delimit spheres of influence within the boundaries of a single whole, maintaining that while the body is mechanically determined, the mind or spirit is teleologically influenced ; or, again, in a picture, the chemical composition of the paints and the colours which they will exhibit when applied to a canvas are, we shall say, explicable in terms of the laws of chemistry and physics, are explicable, that is to say, in terms of the concepts of a world in which Mechanism applies ; but the significance or beauty of the picture belongs, we should add, to the world of values, and values influence the mind teleologically.[1]

Difficulty of Bifurcating the Universe.

This assignment of different realms to the two principles, entailing as it does a bifurcation of the universe, is regarded by most philosophers with disfavour. In the first place, it violates the instinctive feeling which lies at the back of most people's minds that the world is in an important sense a whole, a whole which is fundamentally also a unity. This doctrine, known philosophically as the doctrine of Monism, is, it is clear, incompatible with any such bifurcation. If it were true that mechanistic causation ruled in one part of the universe and teleological causation in another, the world would not be a unity, but would be a duality. It would contain, that is to say, or rather it would be, at least two realities of fundamentally different orders. In the second place, it is difficult to see what point of contact there could be between two realms so conceived.[2] Let us call the reality in which mechanical causation operates M, and that which acknowledges teleology T. Then does T interact with M, or does it not ? Presumably it does. T, then, has influence upon M. Is this causative influence of T upon M teleological or mechanical ? If the former, then M is admitting the influence of teleological causation and ceases to be wholly M. If the latter, then T is exerting an influence which is other than teleological and ceases to be wholly T.

[1] See Chapter XIII for a discussion of æsthetic value.
[2] This difficulty is illustrated by the discussion of the difficulties entailed by the notion of human free will, which will be found in Chapter XVIII, pp. 504-507.

Difficulty of Bifurcating the Living Organism. This difficulty presents itself nowhere with greater force than in connection with the attempt to apply both the two principles to the interpretation of the living organism. The question of the relation of the mind to the body, at which we have already glanced and which we shall consider in more detail in a later chapter,[1] is one of the most controversial and frequently discussed in contemporary philosophy. That the mind and the body interact is obvious : this interaction, furthermore, bears witness at least in part to the apparent influence of the mind upon the body. Now this influence is, presumably, in part teleological. The mind, that is to say, causes the body to behave in such a way as to further the ends which the mind conceives to be desirable, as when our bodies encase themselves in stiff white shirts and dinner jackets as a preliminary to appearing at formal receptions, where we hope to curry the favour of important and reputable persons with a view to obtaining appointments to the responsible posts that our hearts desire. Other movements of the body, however, appear to be determined mechanically. If my body and a lifeless material object of equal weight, size and density are dropped over a cliff, both will reach the bottom at the same moment and behave very similarly as a result of the impact. My body, in other words, is subject to the laws of mechanics and dynamics which cause it to fall in precisely the same way as a material object of equal weight, size and density. Are, then, the movements of my body subject to two different forms of causation, the teleological and the mechanical, and, if they are, how are we to distinguish those which bear witness to the one from those which exemplify the other ?

The activities of the mind raise a similar difficulty. Some of them, it is obvious, are dependent upon and caused by states of the body, as when a nightmare follows indigestion, and we see double as a result of intoxication. Are the activities of the mind, then, also subject to the operations of both principles ? The difficulties of supposing that they are

[1] See Chapter XVIII, pp. 498–521.

are great, especially when it is remembered that mental life as a whole is continuous and that one mental state shades into another without any perceptible break.[1]

These are some of the reasons why most philosophers profess themselves unwilling to bifurcate the universe in the way in which the admission of the efficacy of both the two principles seems to entail. The conclusion would seem to be that we must adopt one or other of the two principles, and so extend its application that the causation of all kinds of phenomena is brought within its scope. What, in fact, our discussion entails is a decision between two different modes of envisaging the universe. If we adopt the idealist mode of interpretation, which stigmatises matter as illusory, and reduces the status of the physical world to one of dependence upon mind, we shall find little difficulty in conceding universal application to the teleological principle. If, on the other hand, we adopt the philosophy of Materialism, and regard mind as not in essence different from the matter of which it is a function or emanation, we shall be prepared to accept the form of causation which apparently governs the physical world as ultimate. Thus the difference which separates the philosophies of Idealism and Materialism is fundamental. Each form of philosophy will be considered in some detail in later chapters. It is unnecessary, therefore, to pursue the discussion on which we have been engaged further on its present lines.

Criticism of the Principles.

So far we have been content to apply and to illustrate the principles of Mechanism and Teleology, and to show how they ramify through every sphere of natural happening and human activity. There are, however, certain outstanding difficulties to which each of the principles whose ramifications we have been discussing are exposed. It will be as well to complete our discussion by a brief mention of these. Mechanical causation, if treated as ultimate and universal, is exposed to the

[1] The difficulties attending this hypothesis are further developed in Chapter XVIII, pp. 504-507.

criticism that it obviously fails to account for some mental phenomena, notably those involved in moral, aesthetic and religious experience. It is not easy to believe that the good man's sense of obligation is entirely a by-product of his nervous system, and that the whole world of man's ideal aspirations is a function of the state of his body. If this were in fact the case, we should have to admit that the arguments for and the conceptions of Mechanism were only a function of the state of the mechanist's body. Unless, then, we are prepared to accept a thoroughgoing materialist account of all mental phenomena such as is outlined in Chapter XVIII,[1] we shall find ourselves unable to accept the universal application of mechanical causation. Not less important is the fact that the notion of mechanical causation is far from clear and is in the opinion of many philosophers open to grave suspicion. What precisely do we mean when we say that A causes B? It is, indeed, extraordinarily difficult to give any intelligible answer to this question, so difficult that it has been possible, as we shall see in the next chapter,[2] for philosophers to maintain with every appearance of plausibility, that *all* that we mean is that A habitually precedes B. Now if the notion of mechanical causation is ambiguous at best and untenable at worst, it cannot form an adequate principle of cosmic interpretation. Finally, as we shall try to show in criticising Materialism, if mechanical causation can be correctly invoked to explain the workings of mind, it cannot be true to say that it can. In other words, the doctrine of mechanical causation, when applied to the processes of thought, is revealed as being self-contradictory.[3]

To the doctrine of teleological causation it may be objected that it is *prima facie* inapplicable to the behaviour of physical phenomena. It seems absurd to say of the egg which is placed in a saucepan of hot water that it is striving to achieve the condition of being hard-boiled, or of the assemblage of the scattered parts of a car in a Ford factory

[1] See Chapter XVIII, pp. 510–521.   [2] See Chapter VIII, pp. 207–211 and 212–216.   [3] See Chapter XVIII, pp. 534–538.

that each, as it is fitted into its appointed place, is seeking to fulfil the end of the complete or perfected car. Even when applied to living organisms, the notion of teleological causation seems to entail the pre-existence of the end which is aimed at, in order that it may be in a position to exert the influence which, it is said, inclines, if it does not compel, the developing process in the organism which seeks to realise the end. Either the end exists, or it does not. If it does, we are committed to the notion that the oak tree which the acorn will become, which in Aristotelian language is the final cause of the acorn's development, somehow pre-exists the acorn and pre-determines the development of the acorn towards it. If it does not, in what sense can it be said to influence the development of the acorn as its final cause ?

V. RETURN TO ARISTOTLE: THE PRIME MOVER

Aristotle's Final Analysis of Change.   This difficulty, if difficulty it is, will appear most clearly, if we resume our consideration of Aristotle's doctrine of change which originally led us to undertake the discussion of Teleology and Mechanism. Aristotle, as has already been noted, is one of the most prominent exponents of the doctrine of teleological causation. His doctrine of the Four Causes finds the true source of the process of change in the realisation of the Form, which is represented as the final cause. Every natural process, in other words, has for Aristotle a last stage in which the Form which was once latent in the developing organism becomes fully realised. Let us now proceed to apply this conception to the universe itself. Two elements may be stressed.

First, in any process of change there is a changeless something, the Form ; this is present as an idea in the mind of the agent and its realisation in some material is the formal cause of the process ; there is also the matter in which the change takes place. The cause of change or motion is, therefore, something which, while not moving itself, produces by its mere presence change or movement in something else. Matter, in fact, is regarded as being sensitive to the presence of the efficient cause, and as passing through successive changes in the effort to make actual the Form whose complete realisation is the end of the process. Now Aristotle held that the processes of change and development as a result of which potential forms become actualised are eternal. The species of living creatures for him are fixed and unchanging and perpetuate themselves without end. For the universe as a whole, then, there is no culmination ; its motion is everlasting and continuous.

The Prime Mover.   What is the source of this motion ? Aristotle's answer is that it is God. God, Himself unmoved, is the efficient cause whose presence in the universe sets up a process of movement whereby potential Forms become actual. God did not create the world ; at least, He did not create the matter of which it is composed. But He is the cause of the movement in the world and of the various characteristics which, as the result of the movement, it comes to possess. This does not mean that God is Himself a part of the process of change and development which goes on in the world. He stands outside it and the fact of His presence initiates it. Moreover, God alone in Aristotle's universe is not composite. While all the products of development are composed of Form and Matter, God Himself is without Matter : He is pure Form. While all the things in the universe are products of development, God Himself has undergone no development. In Him no Form has proceeded from potentiality to actuality. Thus He is at once immaterial and changeless. He is indispensable to the world's existence, but He transcends the world.

Aristotle's Theology.   So far as God's own activity is concerned, it is purely inward ; Aristotle expressly calls it an " activity of immobility." God, in fact, has no concern for, or interest in, the world. Nor should we expect it, since the world, being imperfect, is no suitable object for the contemplation of a perfect being. God's thought, then, is directed not upon it, but upon the one and only perfect object in the universe, namely Himself. His activity, then, is one of everlasting self-contemplation. It is what Aristotle calls a " thinking of thought itself," and, he characteristically remarks, since all unimpeded activity is pleasant, and God's activity is both unimpeded and continuous, God's life is continuously pleasant.

But though God is not Himself conscious of the world, the mere fact of His presence moves the world's desire. God, in fact, is the world's good, His function in relation to the world being to arouse its appetition. God's relation to the world is not, then, either that of a creator who makes it or a shepherd who cares for it ; it is rather that of a magnet which pulls it. In this sense God may be regarded as the end or goal of the world's travailing, although He is an end or goal which must be for ever unrealised. If God were not present in the universe as an unrealised end, initiating by virtue of the world's desire for Him the process by which the potential Forms in things become actual, the world would be without change or movement. Thus Aristotle's conception of the function of God in relation to the universe is a particular example of his notion of the determination of a development by its end or goal. It is the effort of things to achieve their end, not by realising it, for they can never realise it, but by drawing ever more closely to it, which is the source of the world order, and, as I have already noted, the end is conceived as in some sense pre-existing the movement towards it. Aristotle's philosophy entails, therefore, that there is in the universe an element, stable, unchanging and, therefore, eternal, which is at once the goal and the source of change.

Not only the Aristotelian account of change, but the whole conception of teleological causation, would appear to depend upon the inclusion of this element. If we feel unable to accept it, we must dispense both with the doctrine of Potentiality and Actuality and with the doctrine of the Four Causes, with which it is inextricably bound up.

If we do accept it, we are faced once again with a Dualism, a Dualism between the changeless element in the world and the changing material which it influences, if it does not determine. This Dualism most philosophers have felt themselves unable to accept.

Recapitulation.   Our examination of the problem of change has been a lengthy one and has branched off into a number of related topics. It will, perhaps, be useful to recapitulate the main heads of our discussion. We began by pointing out that all philosophical accounts of change are destructive of the commonsense conception of a changing thing, which is conceived in some sense to remain the same through change. The commonsense notion proving untenable, the tendency of philosophers has been to assert either

(*a*) That the only reality is change, the universe being defined, as the Greek philosopher Heracleitus and later as Bergson defined it, as a flux of change, or

(*b*) That change is illusory and that reality itself is changeless. On this latter hypothesis, we shall be committed to a denial of the reality of time as an independent factor of the universe existing in its own right, and shall tend to regard it as one of the ways in which, because of the peculiarities and limitations of our minds, we are forced to regard phenomena which are themselves timeless. This is in essence the view of Kant, which will be considered in some detail in a later chapter.[1]

We next proceeded to an examination of the Aristotelian account of change as the actualisation or making explicit in matter of a form, which is originally potential or implicit. We saw that Aristotle's account implied the acceptance of the doctrine of teleological causation and the postulation of a changeless factor in the universe, Aristotle's unmoved mover or God, to be the goal or end of the process of change which we know as evolution. Unless we are prepared to accept this or some similar conception of the goal

[1] See Chapter XIV, pp. 378, 379.

or end, we shall find ourselves unable to subscribe to the Aristotelian formula.

Possible Alternatives to the Notion of the Changing Thing.

We are now in a position to apply the results of this discussion to the commonsense notion of the changing thing. Unless we adopt the second of the two views summarised above, and agree to write off change as one of the illusions of the human mind, one or other of two alternative possibilities seems to be open to us. It will be possible to hold that the universe consists of a certain finite number of changeless events, which we may conceive of as atoms or as sense data according to our preference for a scientific or a philosophical analysis. We shall say that although these units are changeless, the relations between them change, so that they are continually entering into new combinations. An analogy for this conception would be the way in which the various pieces of a puzzle can be put together to form different patterns or pictures, the difference between one pattern and another being due to the different combinations in which the same constituent pieces can be arranged. Change, then, on this view, will be due to alteration in the arrangement of fundamentally changeless units.

The alternative view would be that the universe consists of non-enduring units which are constantly coming into and going out of existence. So long as it persists, the unit, we shall say, does not change. What is normally called change will on this view be the supersession of one unit by another. Just as the only changes envisaged by the first view are those of alteration of position and arrangement, so on this second view the only changes will be those of generation and annihilation. An analogy for this second conception would be the constituents of a cinematographic film. These constituents are single static photographs ; the illusion of continuous change is produced by turning the reel, so as to cause the photographs to succeed one another very rapidly. As a result, we appear to be viewing a continuous but very slightly changing personage, smoking, let us say, a continuous but very slightly changing pipe, whereas what we are in fact observing is a very large number of separate static personages each of whom is almost exactly like the last personage, and each of whom is holding in his mouth a separate static pipe which is almost exactly like the last pipe. According to this second conception, the apparently continuous living man is an illusion in just the same sense as the cinematographic man whom we see on the pictures is an illusion ; he is, in fact, not one continuous man, but a series of successive men. As each member of the series is annihilated, another is generated in its place ; but, so long as it persists, there is no change in any member of the series. This view, that the only form of change is the sort of change which we know as generation and annihilation, receives some degree of support from the quantum theory in modern physics and has been widely entertained by modern philosophers. Whichever view we take, the commonsense notion of the changing thing disappears. The criticism of the notion of change thus forms yet another count in the philosopher's indictment of the commonsense world, and constitutes, therefore, a further ground for regarding this world not as ultimately real, but as only an appearance of some deeper reality which underlies it.

TAYLOR, A. E. Elements of Metaphysics, Chapter V.
BERGSON, H. Creative Evolution, Chapter I.
Aristotle's Metaphysics (*Clarendon Press*), with an introduction by W. D. ROSS.
ROSS, W. D. Aristotle, Chapter VI.

John Burnet's *Early Greek Philosophy*, Chapters IV and III, may be consulted for the views of Parmenides (Chapter IV) and Heracleitus (Chapter III). For a modern treatment of mechanism and teleology see C. D. Broad's *The Mind and Its Place in Nature*, Section A. Modern works interpreting evolution from a teleological point of view are Sir J. Arthur Thomson's *The System of Animate Nature* and *Purpose in Evolution*, J. C. Smut's *Holism and Evolution*, and my *Matter, Life and Value*.

*Chapter VIII : THE PROBLEM OF CAUSATION : HUME'S CRITICISM

Introductory. Scientists believe that most of the events[1] that take place in the world are subject to the law of cause and effect. Many, including all those who take materialist or determinist views, would go further and assert that all such events are caused. Common sense shares the views of science in this matter, and holds that events are connected by causal laws. If I throw a stone at a piece of glass the shivering of the pane would be ordinarily re-graded as the effect of the impact of the stone. Now when common sense says that " A causes B," what, presumably is meant, is that there is some necessary connection between the two events such that, given the event B, an earlier event A could be discovered which stood in a certain relation to B. We might describe this relation by saying :

(i) Whenever A occurred it was followed by B.
(ii) In this sequence there was something necessary. It was not, in other words, *just* a series of coincidences that whenever A happened first, B happened afterwards.

Now it is this notion of necessary relation that has been subjected to criticism by philosophers. The views of Hume (1711–1776) are particularly relevant to a discussion of this topic, since Hume's criticism of the law of cause and effect is one of the landmarks in the history of philosophy.

Hume's Criticism of Cause. The essence of the criticism can be stated very briefly. Let us suppose that one billiard ball strikes another. As a result of the impact the second

---

[1] An event may be loosely defined as a happening at a given time, e.g. a flash of lightning, a rifle shot, or a volcano eruption.

billiard ball moves. The commonsense interpretation of
what has happened is that there is a power in the moving
ball which causes the second ball to move also. Hume simply
denies this. There is, he asserts, no power in the moving ball
to make the second ball move, and the movement of the
second ball is not, therefore, the necessary result of the
impact of the first. Admittedly the movement of the second
ball has been observed repeatedly to follow the impact of
the first. It is for this reason that our minds, influenced by
this repeated conjunction of events, namely, impact followed by movement, conclude that the second event will
always follow the first, and jump to the idea of necessary
connection. All, however, that we are entitled to assert is a
repeated conjunction of events. When we postulate a law of
cause and effect, we are not, therefore, talking about something which exists and operates in the world outside us. We
are talking about " a determination of the mind "—that is
to say, a firmly rooted idea of our own founded on our
experience of the repeated conjunction of events. The
reasons given by Hume for this denial of a necessary law of
cause and effect, in virtue of which some power or force is
exerted by the cause over the effect, are broadly as follows.

Causation not given in Experience: 1. There is first, a
reason derived from experience. If we were really conscious
of one thing having power over another, we should, says
Hume, have some experience of this power. But in fact
we experience nothing of the kind. " When we look about
us towards external objects . . . we are never able, in a
single instance, to discover any power. . . . We only find
that one does actually, in fact, follow the other." Select,
says Hume in effect, any case you care to take in which one
thing is said to cause another, and examine your experience
of what is taking place as carefully as you can. You will
observe what you call the cause and then you will observe
what you call the effect. But that is all. You will not observe
anything else. In particular you will not observe any
attribute belonging to the cause which you are entitled to

call its " power " of producing the effect. Its colour, shape, weight, size—all these are observed ; but not its alleged " power to produce an effect." But do we not say that we " see " that a match produces an explosion of gunpowder ? Certainly we do ; but this is a grossly inaccurate way of speaking. What we in fact " see " is first the ignition of the match and secondly the explosion of the gunpowder. We do not see the " producing " of the one by the other. We have, then, no sensory experience of a power in the cause in virtue of which it produces the effect.

Nor established by Reason. 2. But if experience is unable to discover any such " power," can thinking show that it must exist ? Is it, in fact, a postulate of reason ? Hume answers that it is not.

(a) His first argument under this head is based upon the difference between necessary and contingent facts, to which reference has already been made.[1] A necessary fact, or a necessary relation, is defined by him as one which it is impossible to conceive of differently. One cannot, for example, conceive of the relation between 7×7 and $48 + 1$ being other than that of equality. The relation of equality between them is, therefore, a necessary relation. But the so-called relation of cause and effect is not of this kind. In fact, it is only possible to find out what so-called causes will have what so-called effects by experience. It is only by experience, for example, that we discover that a drop of acid will turn a blue fabric red ; it might just as well have turned it black. Although we have become so used to the second billiard ball moving when the first hits it that we now find it difficult to imagine any other result, when we were first brought into the world we could very well have conceived " that a hundred different events might as well follow from that cause." As a matter of historical fact, we had in the first place to go and look at the billiard balls to find out what the effect actually was. Since, then, we cannot without repeated experience find out what so-called effect a

[1] See Chapter IV, pp. 108, 109, 111.

given so-called cause will have, that cause A should have B as its effect is not a postulate of reason.

(*b*) If a cause and an effect are two different events, each must be really distinct and separate from the other. But if they are separate, there can be no necessary connection between them. "The mind," says Hume, "can never possibly find the effect in the supposed cause, by the most accurate scrutiny. . . . For the effect is totally different from the cause, and consequently can never be discovered in it. Motion in the second billiard ball is a quite distinct event from motion in the first; nor is there anything in the one to suggest the smallest hint of the other. . . . In a word . . . every effect is a distinct event from its cause. It could not, therefore, be discovered in the cause."

What Hume is here denying is the notion that there is anything in the nature of a "tie" binding the events together. If there were such a tie, he implies, they could not be separate, and, if they are not separate, then we have no right to talk of cause and effect but only of continuous process. But if there is no tie, then the cause cannot possibly exert any power over the effect.

(*c*) If the causal relation were a necessary one, it would have to occur universally and with absolute uniformity. We should, moreover, be able to know that it did, as we know, for example, that 7 × 7 will everywhere and always make 49. But have we any similar assurance with regard to the so-called causal relation ? Do we have it, for example, in regard to the operation of the causal relation in the future ? We do not. Although certain events in the past may have been always followed by certain other events, we do not know that similar events will be so followed in the future. For, says Hume, " past *experience* can be allowed to give *direct* and *certain* information of those precise objects only, and that precise period of time, which fell under its cognisance ; but why this experience should be extended to future times, and to other objects. . . . this is the main question. . . . It is impossible that any arguments from experience can prove this resemblance of the past to the future." This is not to say that the future will not probably, in fact almost certainly, resemble the past ; it is merely to point out that we can never be *quite* certain that it will. And if we cannot, then we have no assurance that the so-called law of cause and effect denotes a *necessary* relation, since, if the relation were necessary, it would hold universally.

Comment on Hume's Criticism.

I do not wish to maintain that all the above arguments prove precisely what Hume intended them to prove. The first of the arguments from reason, for example, (2a above) would not seem to disprove the so-called postulate of reason that every cause must have an effect, and every effect a cause. It merely demonstrates that experience is required to show us just what particular effect a particular cause will have. But my inability to know without experience precisely what effects will follow from what causes does not in itself prove either that the relation of cause and effect is not a necessary one, or that I am not certain of its necessity. Nevertheless, the arguments as a whole have great cumulative force. Argument 2b is particularly strong and is exceedingly difficult to refute. Indeed, it is not too much to say that the whole of the subsequent history of philosophy in this particular department of enquiry has been influenced by the necessity of either refuting Hume, or of so adjusting our view of the universe that his denial of necessary connection can be incorporated within the adjusted scheme. Moreover, Hume has a positive contribution to offer in explanation of the universal belief in the causal relation. He does not for a moment deny that we do in fact regard a certain number of the sum total of events observed by us as being causally related to each other, and he proffers an explanation of why it is that we do so. The explanation is, he says, that we have regularly observed the events in question to follow one another. All, in fact, that Hume is denying is that there is any power in things such that one of them, the " cause," can, by exerting it, produce another, the " effect." He has, then, to find some substitute for this alleged power and finds it in what he calls a " determination of the mind." This " determination " has been formed as the result of the observation of constant conjunction in the past, and is a " determination . . . to pass from one object to its usual attendant." What happens is that we observe an event A to be followed by an event B ; we then observe an event very closely resembling A, namely A_1, to be followed by an event very closely resembling B, namely B_1 ; we then observe another closely resembling event, A_2, to be followed by B , and so on, on a very large number of occasions. The effect of observing this resemblance between what has happened on numbers of different occasions—B following A, B_1 following A_1, and so on—is to produce " a determination of the mind . . . to carry our thoughts from one object to another." It is this " determination " which Hume substitutes for the commonsense notion of a " power " in external things. What we call causality, in fact, is nothing but a customary conjunction of events, a conjunction which, when it has occurred often enough, produces in the mind a determination or habit of passing from or inferring one event from the other. Hence Hume's final definition of a cause is as follows : " An object precedent and contiguous to another, and so united with it in the imagination, that the idea of the one determines the mind to form the idea of the other, and the impression of the one to form a more lively idea of the other."

Modern Statement of Hume's View.   The implications of Hume's criticism are, to say the least, startling. How much weight are we entitled to attach to it ? Let us consider the question on merits. There can, I think, be no reasonable doubt that we do in ordinary life make a distinction between *post hoc* and *propter hoc*, between the things which happen *after* this and those which happen *because of* this. Our presumption is that the meaning of the phrase " because of this " is entirely different from that of " after this," and, moreover, that we know that it is. If Hume is right, it is not different, and, if it is not different, we cannot know that it is. Let us, then, consider what we

do in fact mean by the expression " This happens *because of* this." An important school of modern philosophers, the school of Logical Positivists,[1] maintains that the only way of discovering the meaning of a proposition is to find out how its truth is verified. Let us suppose that I am ill, take medicine and subsequently become well, that this sequence of events happens on a number of occasions and that it is observed to happen not only to myself but to a number of other people. I shall in all probability be inclined to say that the medicine is the cause of my recovery. How do I verify this assertion ? Simply by observing the sequence—illness, medicine and recovery. Do I observe anything more? I do not. Therefore all that I have observed is regularity or uniformity of sequence. This sequence of events, say the logical positivists, which is what I observe, and by observation of which I verify my assertion that the medicine is the cause of my recovery is all that my assertion *means*. They would, therefore, be inclined to agree with Hume that the only thing that distinguishes a purely temporal sequence " this after that " from a causal sequence " this because of that " is the greater regularity of the latter. If A is regularly followed by B, then, if Hume is right, we may say that A is the cause of B, since " regularly followed by " and " is the cause of " mean the same thing. If it be objected that day regularly follows night, but that we do not say " night is the cause of day," the answer is that " day " and " night " are not really events at all in the sense in which science uses the word event. They are *series* of natural events for which the names day and night respectively stand, and, as soon as this series is examined, we find that it affords a very good example of what is commonly called causal connection.

It is on these lines that a short modern statement of the sort of position which Hume sought to maintain would run. The position is, as I have already remarked, of very great importance in the history of philosophy and has

[1] See Introduction to Part III, pp. 254-257, for a reference to their general views.

subsequently been developed in various ways. I propose to give one or two examples of the way in which Hume's position is capable of development, and has in fact been developed by modern philosophers.

1. ARGUMENT FROM CONTINUITY OF PHYSICAL PROCESSES

The previous chapter[1] emphasised the fact that everything in the physical world is in a state of continuous change or flux. It follows that what we have been calling an event—for example, a clap of thunder—is for a scientist a continuous process. A clap of thunder is a travelling outwards from a centre at a known velocity of waves in the atmosphere which are characterised by a certain periodicity, frequency and wave-length. When the waves reach the place at which our ear-drums are, we are said to hear the clap, and this so-called hearing of the clap would normally be regarded as another and a separate event. In fact, however, the physiological events in my outer and inner ears, and the nervous impulses that travel as a result of these events to the brain, are only later parts of the process whose earlier parts were the spreading outwards of the waves in the atmosphere.

Now if the event, namely, the clap of thunder, which turns out on analysis to be a continuous process, is to cause another event as its necessary effect, they will have to be next to each other in time, since, if there were an interval between them, something might occur during the interval to prevent the effect. We cannot suppose, at any rate so far as physical processes are concerned, that changes in the earlier part of the process which we are calling the cause can make any difference to the later part which we are calling the effect, so long as the later part of the cause process remains unchanged. Let us, for example, suppose that a man gets his feet wet, fails to change his shoes and socks, catches pneumonia and dies. The pneumonia set up by the

[1] See Chapter VII, pp. 178–180.

chill is, we should ordinarily say, the cause of death. Yet here again we are, it is obvious, considering what is in effect a continuous process. Whatever in this process precedes the wetting of the feet may be ruled out as irrelevant. So, too, may the circumstance of the wetting itself, *unless* this circumstance is followed by pneumonia. Even the pneumonia is not the proximate cause of death. Pneumonia produces congestion of the lungs, but this congestion is not effective in producing death, unless it first causes certain physiological changes which include the stopping of the heart. Even these changes are not *necessarily* the cause of death, since the patient might be shot in the heart immediately before dying and in that case the bullet would be *the* cause. Proceeding in this way we can continually shorten the process which we are calling the cause, until we have restricted it to the latest event in the causal process, which we are supposing to be the stopping of the heart. But can the event which is the stopping of the heart justly be called *the* cause of death ? Are we not equally entitled to regard it as constituting death itself—as being, that is to say, not the latest part of the cause, but the earliest part of the effect ? This question brings up the further question, what is it that actually constitutes death ? A doctor will sign a death certificate when he has noted the cessation of heart beats. But it is notorious that people have been made to live again after the heart has momentarily stopped beating. The failure of the pupil of the eye to contract when exposed to light is sometimes taken as an indication of death. But the pupils of cataleptics do not contract. A physiologist would tend to regard such occurrences as part of the overture which must be played before the spectre of death can enter from the wings.

Perhaps the most satisfactory scientific definition of death is the presence of bacterial decomposition in the vital bodily organs. But, as recent researches at the Rockefeller Institute have shown, it is now possible to maintain organs which have been separated from the body for an indefinite period in a sterilised glass chamber. Not only is decomposition indefinitely delayed but the organs can be made to function. A heart, for example, can be coupled up with a series of glass tubes and small pumps which are kept at the normal blood temperature. By pressing a button the apparatus is set in motion and the heart contained in the glass chamber is seen at once to begin to beat. This preliminary analysis seems to show that death is not an event, but a continuous series of many events. Provided the first events in this series take place, all the later events may be ruled out as irrelevant, just as we ruled out the *earlier* events of the cause series, so that our two chains of series—the causal series and the effect series—fine themselves down to two contiguous events which we may, if we like, denominate *the cause* and *the effect*. But so to denominate them is a wholly arbitrary proceeding, since between them an infinite number of other events could have been inserted, any one of which might with equal justice be termed *the cause* and *the effect*. The truth of the matter seems to be that what we are dealing with is not a series of separate events at all, but a continuous process between any two parts of which, however near together they may be placed, other parts could be inserted. Once this is realised, it will be seen that there is no ground for arbitrarily selecting two of these parts and denominating respectively *the* cause and *the* effect.

Two conclusions appear to follow. First, to speak of *a* cause and *an* effect is unjustifiably to single out two events from what is in fact a continuous series. All that we are really entitled to assert is a certain direction of change in a continuous series of events over a given period. Secondly, the notion of *the* cause, which carries with it the implication that to every effect B, there is one cause A, which is the *real* determiner of B in a sense in which no other event is the determiner of B, is illusory. There is, in short, no such thing as *the* cause. When we loosely speak of something as *the* cause, we are arbitrarily selecting a prominent event which happens to have caught our attention from among a number of other events, any of which might with equal justice have been given this description.

2. DEVELOPMENT BY PROFESSOR WHITEHEAD

The implications of Hume's denial of causation have an important bearing upon our metaphysical views, a bearing which has been emphasised in recent times by Professor Whitehead. In *Science and the Modern World* Professor Whitehead criticises the notion, unquestioningly accepted by common sense and fostered by the natural sciences, that the physical world consists of pieces of matter which are separate from one another, and each of which occupies a determinate position in space and time. According to the commonsense view every piece of matter is *at* a place *at* a time and no other piece of matter can be at that place at the same time. This commonly accepted view Professor Whitehead calls the notion of " simple location." I cannot here develop Professor Whitehead's criticism of this notion, which ranges over a wide field.[1] Part of the criticism, however, consists in emphasising the close connection between " simple location " and the commonsense view of causation, and some mention of this may properly be made here.

The two notions, causation and " simple location," are in Professor Whitehead's view bound up with each other, inasmuch as the ordinary view of causation presupposes that one event, a cause, which is separate from another event, the effect, and earlier than the effect in point of time, nevertheless produces the effect, while the commonsense concept of the physical world as consisting of separate pieces of matter existing at different times is only rendered intelligible by assuming their causal connection. If we adopt the modern scientific expression " an event " to denote a happening in or to a piece of matter at a given time, then we may say that according to the commonsense view which is also the view of the sciences, an event which is the putting of the kettle on the fire is *the* cause of the event which is the boiling of the water ; the event which is the impact of the stone is *the* cause of the event which is the

[1] Some account of Whitehead's general views and of the part played by the criticism of " simple location " in their development will be found in Chapter XX.

shivering of the pane. Further we should say that this causal connection between the separate pairs of events is a necessary one. But if the events are really separate, how, Professor Whitehead asks, can they be brought together in the way in which the holding of the causal relation between them presupposes ? The causal relation, as ordinarily conceived, may be likened to a thread, which, stretching out from the first event, tacks it on to the second. But if this were the case, an exhaustive inspection of the first event would reveal the starting point of the thread in the event. It would, therefore, reveal the first event as being causally linked on to something else and as being, therefore, not completely separate. The point of Professor Whitehead's criticism is, then, that if we reflect carefully on what the notion of causal connection involves, we cannot avoid seeing that it is not compatible with an absolute separation of events. How, again Professor Whitehead asks, if the two events are really separate, can one of them give us information about the other, which would justify us in saying of the one that it is the cause of the other ?

The World a Process, not a Collection of Events.   The commonsense notion that events are really separate in space and time is, in Professor Whitehead's view, no less fatal to induction than to causation. The principle of induction, as we have seen in a previous chapter,[1] enables us to infer one event from another. But, in order that we may infer one event from another, the one event must somehow be able to give us information about the other. " Either," says Professor Whitehead, "there is something about the immediate occasion which affords knowledge of the past and the future, or we are reduced to utter scepticism as to memory and induction," and, he would be prepared to add, as to causation.

What is the conclusion ? That if we are to take the fact of causation seriously we must give up the notion of simple location, that is, the notion that the physical universe consists of separate pieces of matter occupying different parts

[1] See Chapter V, pp. 130–132.

in space to which events happen at different moments of time. But if events are not really separately located in space and time, we shall not be able to postulate A as cause and B as effect, on the assumption that A and B are two different isolated events, and that A is really separate from B. We shall either have to substitute the conception which we have already envisaged of a continuous process between any two parts of which an infinite number of other parts could be inserted, or, alternatively, we shall have to think of the universe, as Professor Whitehead does, as an organic system in which every event pervades and interpenetrates and is in its turn pervaded and interpenetrated by every other event.[1] Whatever course we adopt, the same general conclusion emerges as before ; there is something exceedingly wrong with the ordinary notion of causation.

3 Hypothetical Illustration from the Speed of Light

I insert one further consideration, not so much because I wish to claim validity for any particular conclusion to which it may seem to point, or even because the state of affairs which it envisages is regarded as being physically possible,[2] as because it affords a good example of the disintegration of the traditional notion of causation for which modern relativity theory is responsible.

Let us suppose that an observer is situated upon a comet travelling away from the earth and is viewing events upon the earth through a telescope. He will, it is clear, only be able to see what is happening as and when light rays travelling from the earth bring to him the report or message of the events occurring there. The faster the comet travels, the longer will it take the light rays proceeding from the earth to catch up the comet and bring to the observer the report of the earth-events. Let us now suppose that the speed of the comet is equal to that of light. It seems to follow that to the observer events upon the earth will now appear

[1] See Chapter XX, pp. 572, 573, for an exposition of this view.
[2] Nothing, we are assured, in the universe as conceived by the Theory of Relativity, can travel faster than light.

to cease, since, if he begins his observation at a time which we will arbitrarily call 11 a.m., no events subsequent to those occurring at 11 a.m. will be visible, for the reason that no light rays carrying the message of these subsequent events can catch him up. The planet, then, will appear to him to be frozen into a state of immobility. Now, let us suppose that the velocity of the comet is further increased, so that it exceeds that of light. The observer will now gradually begin to catch up the light rays which, spreading out from the earth, convey the message of events earlier than those which he has already observed. He will, therefore, see the sequence of events in reverse order. If we conceive him to be permanently observing the earth from a position on the comet travelling at this velocity, he will record as causes all the events which we term effects, and as effects all those which we term causes. He will, that is, observe the steam issuing from the spout of the kettle, before the placing of the kettle upon the fire ; and the shattering of the pane of glass before the throwing of the stone. Now, there is no reason, it may be said, why the view of events upon the earth taken by the hypothetical observer on the comet should be unreal or illusory, in some sense in which the view of them revealed to the earth dweller is real and valid. All that we are entitled to say is that the point of observation occupied by the man on the comet is unusual. It follows that whether we say " A " is the cause of " B," or " B " is the cause of " A " depends upon our point of observation. The direction of causation, in other words, is relative to us. If the direction of causation is relative to an observer, are we not entitled to go further and deduce that causation is itself merely one of the ways in which our minds are forced to regard the relation between events? This, as we shall see in Chapter XIV, was in essence the view of Kant.

Implications. The implications of Hume's criticism of the law of cause and effect are, as I have already hinted, exceedingly far-reaching. In particular, they are incompatible with the existence of the world assumed by common sense and affirmed by science. If, in other words, Hume's criticism of causation can be sustained, then no one thing can ever be said to be the cause of any other ; we have no rational basis for calculation or for prediction, since both calculation and prediction assume that the same causes will in the future produce the same effects as they have done in the past, while, so far as anticipation is concerned, we have no ground for supposing that any action may not produce the most totally irrelevant and unanticipated results. There is no more reason to expect that the explosion of the gunpowder will follow the application of a lighted match than that it will follow the impact of a jet of water, no more reason to expect that the kettle will boil when it is put on the fire than when it is placed on a block of ice. If, in other words, Hume's criticism is true, then our ordinary commonsense notions of what the world is really like are hopelessly wide of the mark. As a matter of fact we do not really believe that Hume's criticism is true : he may be very hard to refute, but he is almost impossible to believe. We simply must hold that there is some ground for supposing that, if a man puts his hand into the fire, he will feel pain, which is other than and additional to our memory of the fact that contact with the fire has been regularly succeeded by pain in the past. There is, in other words, what in philosophical language is called an antinomy[1]—that is to say, an apparently irreconcilable incompatibility, between the effects of Hume's criticism of the law of causation and the commonsense notion of the way in which things happen. They cannot, it seems, both be true. To put the point in another way, the notion of causation as a law which operates in the world, as common sense conceives the world, like the commonsense notion of a changing thing and the commonsense notion of Substance and its qualities will not bear critical examination. Thus, the conclusion to which we have already been driven in previous chapters, namely, that the world as it appears to common sense cannot be the world as it really is, is strengthened and confirmed.

[1] See p. 407 for a fuller definition.

Either, then, we must give up the notion of causation, or else we must give up the commonsense world. Our belief in causation is unshakable. We are convinced that there is such a thing in spite of all the arguments that may be brought against it. Very well, then, most philosophers would argue, we must give up the commonsense world. In other words, since a world of separate objects and events linked together by an alleged causal relation seems unable to withstand the results of careful examination, and since the world as it really is must be intelligible, the world as it really is must be other than the world as it appears. Having reached this conclusion, we are faced with the task of defining the world as it really is in such a way as to eliminate the antinomy.

Alternative Possibilities;   We can say, for example, that the world does not in fact consist of a collection of objects arranged in space, or of a succession of separate events; that it is in reality a continuous flux without distinction or separation, and that the division of it into objects and events joined by a causal relation is the misleading work of the intellect. This is the line taken by some modern philosophers such as William James and subsequently Bergson, who conceived of the intellect as a sort of surgeon's knife which operated upon and cut up the living body of reality's homogeneous flow.[1] Or we may say, following Kant, who deliberately set himself to devise a way of meeting and answering Hume's criticism, that causation is a mental mould or framework into which our experiences must of necessity fit. In the very act of knowing the outside world, Kant taught, the mind imposes this framework upon what it knows.[2] Events as they really are are not causally related ; but that our experience of them should be so related is a condition of our having experience at all. Or we may adopt a whole-hearted idealist view, maintaining that the existence of physical objects is a delusion, and that whatever exists is in some sense a mind or an event in a mind.[3] There

[1] See Chapters XVI, pp. 450, 451, and XIX, pp. 551–553.
[2] See Chapter XIV, pp. 379, 380.   [3] See Chapter II, p. 48.

will then be no need to invoke a law such as that of cause and effect to govern the relations between physical things which, on this assumption, do not exist. Or we can, with Hegel[1] repudiate the Pluralism which sees the world as a collection of many different things, and insist that the results of philosophical reasoning reveal it as a unified whole in which all differences are resolved and distinctions transcended. Hegel's universe outflanks the causation difficulty, just as Bergson's outflanks it, for if things are not really separate from one another, there will be no need to invoke a law of causation to link them. In the light of the above, it will be seen how seriously philosophers have regarded Hume's criticism of causation. It has, indeed, proved a veritable challenge to metaphysicians. Stimulated by the need to answer Hume, philosophers have sought to construct metaphysical systems which would either silence his criticisms with a convincing answer or so revise the universe as to exhibit their irrelevancy. Some of these systems we shall outline in succeeding chapters.

Causation and Modern Science: Nineteenth Century Materialism:

There is one further matter about which something must be said before we leave the implications of Hume's theory of causation. Some metaphysical views, notably Materialism, base themselves upon physical causation as an ultimate cosmic fact. The arguments, for example, against free will, at some of which we glanced in the previous chapter, presuppose that when we say that one thing is caused by another, as for example, that our wills are caused by our motives or that mind events are caused by cerebral events, we mean something and that we know what we mean. Modern philosophical thought is increasingly hostile to this facile acceptance of causation as something which is simple, ultimate and intelligible and is, as a result, unsympathetic to materialist views of the universe and determinist interpretations of human psychology. It is common knowledge that the materialist

[1] See Chapter XV, pp 410, 411 and 413-415.

scheme of the universe sponsored by the nineteenth century
sciences has to-day been largely abandoned. I propose to
give an outline of this scheme in a later chapter and to
indicate at the same time. some of the criticisms which
philosophers have brought against it.[1] But it is pertinent to
stress here the importance of the part, which modern criticism of the concept of causation has played in leading to
its supersession. The nineteenth century universe was conceived after the model of the works of a gigantic clock.
Every event in it was determined by a preceding event,
and nothing, therefore, could be other than it was. In such
a world causation was conceived to be ultimate and universal. Moreover, the type of causation affirmed was the
mechanical causation which governs the workings of
machines, and not the teleological causation which is
appropriate to the activities of a mind.[2] Mechanical causation being universal, life and mind had, by some means, to
be brought within its scope. Life must be shown to be an
emanation from matter, which at a certain point of its
purely physical development has incidentally acquired the
attribute of " livingness " ; mind must be exhibited as a
function of the brain. The extension of the mechanist
hypothesis to include life and mind was recognised to be a
matter of some difficulty because of the apparently radical
differences between material phenomena on the one hand,
and psychical phenomena on the other. For, the question
inevitably presents itself, is not an act of conscious knowledge a happening of a different order from the movements
of a number of atoms, so different that by no possibility
could the movement of atoms become or generate the act
of knowledge ? To common sense it would certainly appear
that it is. But, so long as the belief in the efficacy of causation in the physical world persisted, it was at least worth
while to try and bring everything that occurred in the
universe within its scope.

[1] See Chapter XVIII, especially pp. 534–539.

[2] See above, Chapter VII, pp. 185–187, for a discussion of the
difference between these two types of causation.

Twentieth Century Physics.   But to-day this belief is for various reasons being abandoned by physicists themselves. Modern scientists are, indeed, disposed to be increasingly critical of the whole conception of physical laws, in so far as the expression "physical law " is taken to mean, as it has been taken to mean in the past, a sort of compulsive framework which governs the occurrence of phenomena, such that all possible events must accommodate themselves within the framework. Most physical laws, for example, involve the notion of action from a distance. Let us suppose that a body X is attracted by a body Y. How is the attraction to be explained ? It used to be thought that some mysterious force started from Y, stretched over the space intervening between it and X, and then made contact with X. In the Newtonian system bodies which were under the action of no forces moved in straight lines with uniform velocity. When bodies did not move in this way, their change of motion was ascribed to a " force." To-day this conception has been given up. Twentieth century physics bids us conceive of the cause of the movements of X solely in terms of happenings in the *immediate vicinity* of X. So-called effects in X would not now be ascribed to some force emanating from an object Y separated from X by a distance in space and an interval in time, but to what is immediately contiguous to X in space-time. A quotation from Bertrand Russell's *The ABC of Relativity* may perhaps make this clearer. He first takes as an illustrative instance the case of a tiger let loose in a Bank Holiday crowd. Everybody in the crowd would move, and a person who could see the people and not the tiger would infer that there was something repulsive causing everybody to move away from a certain centre. Actually, however, they move because of something which is happening in and to them, and not merely because of the presence of the tiger in their vicinity. They move, that is to say, because they can see and hear the tiger, this seeing and hearing being due to the fact that waves of light and sound reach their eyes and ears. " Let us now," continues Bertrand Russell, " apply similar

HP

considerations to the sun's gravitation. The ' force ' exerted by the sun only differs from that exerted by the tiger in being attractive instead of repulsive. Instead of acting through waves of light or sound, the sun acquires its apparent power through the fact that there are modifications of space-time all round the sun. Like the noise of the tiger, they are more intense near their source ; as we travel away they grow less and less. To say that the sun ' causes ' these modifications of space-time is to add nothing to our knowledge. What we know is that the modifications proceed according to a certain rule, and that they are grouped symmetrically about the sun as centre. The language of cause and effect adds only a number of quite irrelevant imaginings, connected with will, muscular tension, and such matters. What we can more or less ascertain is merely the formula according to which space-time is modified by the presence of gravitating matter. More correctly : we can ascertain what kind of space-time *is* the presence of gravitating matter. When space-time is not accurately Euclidean in a certain region, but has a non-Euclidean character which grows more and more marked as we approach a certain centre, and when, further, the departure from Euclid obeys a certain law, we describe this state of affairs briefly by saying that there is gravitating matter at the centre. But this is only a compendious account of what we know. What we know is about the places where the gravitating matter is *not*, not about the place where it is. *The language of cause and effect (of which 'force' is a particular case) is thus merely a convenient shorthand for certain purposes ; it does not represent anything that is genuinely to be found in the physical world.*" (My italics.)

The Law of Cause and Effect as a Special Case.

It will be seen from the above that the modern suspicion of the law of cause and effect is only a special case of a more general suspicion, the suspicion with which modern physics now regards the whole conception of force operating from a distance. In so far as X is not immediately contiguous to Y, it does not, modern physics would assert, produce effects in

Y, and it does not, because the conception of action at a
distance is illusory.

What has taken the place of the physical laws of which
the law of cause and effect was the most familiar example ?
We are offered one or other of two alternative conceptions.
So-called physical laws are, we are told, statements of statistical averages, recording the behaviour not of individual
phenomena, but of vast numbers of phenomena ; alternatively, they are projections on the part of the mind of the
physicist, who imposes the patterns of his own thinking
upon the world which he believes himself to explore. The
first alternative does not here concern us. The second is in
essence the view of Kant.

Transition to Idealism.   Upon a world of disorderly
happenings the investigating mind imposes, Kant held, its
own principles of order. Modern physicists have slightly
varied Kant's view by suggesting that from a world of disorderly happenings the mind selects for its investigation
only those which fit into its ready-made categories. Thus
the mathematical theory of relativity reduces the external
world to a structure of featureless point-events. The mind,
faced with this world of evanescent point-events, notices
that some of the point-events fall into patterns or arrangements. These patterns it selects as being of special interest.
Or, alternatively, upon the shifting flux of point-events it
imposes its patterns. Whichever concept we choose, the
mind so selects or imposes, because it happens to be that
kind of mind. Given creatures with different minds—
Martians, for example, or dogs—different patterns would be
selected or imposed, and a different world would result.
For the physical objects of every-day life are, on this view,
simply the result of the way in which the mind orders and
works up the comparatively featureless raw material which
is all that mathematical physics is prepared to postulate in
the external world. Thus, to increase our knowledge of the
world, is in effect to learn more about the principles of
order which we ourselves have put into the world. As Sir

Arthur Eddington puts it, " all through the physical world runs an unknown content which must really be the stuff of our own consciousness." We have found that " where science has progressed the furthest, the mind has but regained from nature that which the mind has put into nature." Thus the scientist is a man who fares through the uttermost confines of reality to discover himself. " The footprint on the sands of time," as Eddington poetically put it, is our own. It is not without reason that Kant,[1] is acclaimed by modern physicists as the philosopher whose views of the universe are most in harmony with the world picture of modern physics.

Two conclusions emerge.

1. The modern scientific criticism of the law of cause and effect, a criticism to which it is exposed in common with all physical laws which involve the conception of action from a distance, makes the philosophy of Materialism extremely difficult to hold, since the efficacy and intelligibility of mechanical causation was the foundation stone of that philosophy.

2. The tendency to regard the law as an ordering principle of the human intellect suggests an idealist view of the universe, and is so interpreted by many modern physicists. Hence the conclusion by Sir James Jeans of his Presidential Address to the British Association in September, 1934 : " Little is left of the forbidding Materialism of the Victorian scientists : modern physics is moving in the direction of philosophical Idealism."

HUME. A Treatise of Human Nature (*Edition in Everyman*), Part III.
LAIRD, JOHN. Hume's Philosophy of Human Nature, Chapter IV.
MOORE, G. E. Philosophical Studies, Chapter IV.

C. D. Broad's *Examination of McTaggart's Philosophy*, Vol. I, Chapter XIII, contains a comprehensive discussion of the subject of causation. Bertrand Russell's *The ABC of Relativity* (Chapters XII and XIII) contains an untechnical account of the considerations which have led to the abolition of the conception of force in modern physics.

[1] See Chapter XIV, pp. 362, 363.

CHAPTER IX: THE PROBLEM OF THE SELF: FREEDOM AND DETERMINISM

Commonsense View of the Self. I propose to conclude this survey of philosophical criticisms of commonsense notions by a chapter on the Self. It is convenient to insert this chapter here for two reasons. First, the destructive criticism of the commonsense conception of the Self originates, like that of the notion of cause, with Hume. Secondly, it is a criticism of fundamentally the same order. Just as the criticism of cause denies the existence of a nexus or tie binding events and asserts only a succession of events, so the criticism of the Self denies a nexus or tie between ideas and experiences and asserts only a succession of ideas and experiences.

The commonsense conception of the Self, like the commonsense conception of a piece of matter, presupposes the existence of a something which endures through change. The Self is conceived of as something which remains relatively permanent, even, on some views identical, in and through the changing flux of ideas and experiences which constitute its conscious life. Thus a man working at his desk at 10 a.m. is considered by common sense to be justified in saying, " I am the person who an hour ago was having breakfast," the word " I " being intended to denote an entity which remains unchanged, or relatively unchanged in spite of the difference between its present experiences and its experiences of an hour ago.

The Self is also commonly conceived, as Locke's Substance was conceived,[1] as a kind of support or substratum. As Substance supports qualities, so the Self supports experiences. It is the unifying foundation in which experiences inhere, the psychological backbone, as it were, to which they are

[1] See Chapter II, pp. 40, 41

attached. And, inevitably, the criticism follows the same lines as the criticism of Substance and qualities and the criticism of the changing thing. Briefly, what we call the Self, is, for Hume, simply the collection of mental facts, experiences, ideas, and so forth which would normally be said to belong to the Self; but there is no Self over and above the experiences and ideas, for the experiences and ideas to belong to. A certain group or series of these experiences may, indeed, at some given moment, be called a Self. But this group has no permanence or unity of its own. It is a mere assemblage of experiences. Thus, if we think of the ordinary conception of the Self as the thread of a necklace along which are strung the beads of its psychological states, the effect of Hume's criticism is to affirm the beads but to deny the thread.

Hume's Arguments.

As in the case of cause, Hume presents two kinds of arguments for his conclusion, the one kind derived from experience, the other from reason.

(1) The argument derived from experience consists in an appeal to introspection. Carefully introspect your experiences at any given moment, says Hume in effect, and what do you find ? Not a Self, but a succession of experiences—a thinking, a desiring, a hoping, a fearing, or, in the case in question, a wondering whether there is or is not a Self; but never the Self that thinks, desires, hopes, fears or wonders. The conciseness and elegance of Hume's style render his exposition a model of philosophical writing. I make no apology, therefore, for giving one or two extracts from his argument.

" If," he says, " any impression gives rise to the idea of self, that impression must continue invariably the same, through the whole course of our lives ; since self is supposed to exist after that manner. But there is no impression constant and invariable. Pain and pleasure, grief and joy, passions and sensations succeed each other and never all exist at the same time. It cannot, therefore, be from any of these impressions, or from any other, that the idea of self is deriv'd ; and consequently there is no such idea " . . . There follows a statement of his opponents' position and a direct appeal to introspection to refute it. . . . " There are some philosophers who imagine we are every moment intimately conscious of what we call our *Self* ; that we feel its existence and its continuance in existence. . . . The strongest sensation, the most violent passion, say they, instead of distracting us from this view, only fix it the more intensely, and make us consider their influence on *self*. . . . To attempt a further proof of this were to weaken its evidence ; since no proof can be deriv'd from any fact, of which we are so intimately conscious ; nor is there anything of which we can be certain, if we doubt this " . . . " Unluckily," Hume comments, " all these positive assertions are contrary to that very experience which is pleaded for them ; nor have we any idea of *self*, after the manner it is here explain'd." . . . " For my part " he adds, " when I enter most intimately into what I call *myself*, I always stumble on some particular perception or other, of heat or cold, light or shade, love or hatred, pain or pleasure. I never can catch *myself* at any time without a perception. . . . When my perceptions are remov'd for any time, as by sound sleep, so long am I insensible of *myself* and may be truly said not to exist. And were all my perceptions remov'd by death, and cou'd I neither think nor feel, nor see, nor love, nor hate after the dissolution of my body, I should be entirely annihilated " . . . Hume's conclusion is that " setting aside some metaphysicians of this kind . . . the rest of mankind . . . are nothing but a bundle or collection of different perceptions, which succeed each other with an inconceivable rapidity, and are in a perpetual flux and movement."

(2) The argument from reason is less convincing. First, Hume argues, it is the nature of our experiences to be independent and self-subsistent. Hume, it will be remembered,[1] divides experiences into impressions, which we should call sensations, and ideas, and each of these impressions and ideas exists in and for and by itself. In this respect

[1] See Chapter II, pp. 51, 52.

it complies with the conditions which Hume lays down for the existence of any substance. Existing in and for and by itself, it does not require anything else in which to inhere. Hume, as we have seen, held officially an advanced form of Subjective Idealism. Whatever he may have believed, he maintained that his reason was unable to discover any objects of a knowing mind which were not the impressions and ideas of that mind. To be the object of a consciousness is, then, for Hume, to be an impression or an idea. This extreme Subjectivism enabled him to put forward a further argument. Our impressions, admittedly, are fleeting and evanescent ; but the Self is supposed to be self-identical and enduring. How, then (assuming that impressions and their objects are one) can a fleeting impression introduce me to a permanent Self ? " If," says Hume, " any impression gives rise to the idea of self, that impression must continue invariably the same, thro' the whole course of our lives ; since self is suppos'd to exist after that manner. But there is no impression constant and invariable. Pain and pleasure, grief and joy, passions and sensations, succeed each other, and never all exist at the same time. It cannot, therefore, be from any of these impressions, or from any other, that the idea of self is deriv'd ; and consequently there is no such idea."

Effect of Hume's Criticism.   The view of the Self that results from these criticisms is that suggested by the cinematographic analogy which we have already used.[1] On the screen we see an apparently continuous figure which, though changing, appears to remain the same through change. In fact, we know that what we are looking at is a very large number of separate static figures, the illusion of continuity being produced by the rapid succession of these figures and by their close similarity. Similarly the Self is only a succession of experiences which happen to be contiguous in time and to resemble each other very closely. Or, again, to revert to the metaphor already used, if we think

[1] See Chapter VII, pp. 205, 206.

of the Self as a necklace along which are strung the beads of our various psychological states, the effect of Hume's criticism is to eliminate the thread and to leave only the beads.

To combine this analysis of the Self and the Humian theory of perception, according to which what we know in experience is the series of our own impressions and ideas, is to realise the cumulatively sceptical effect of Hume's philosophy. To revert to the development described in Chapter II, Locke had analysed the process which we call knowledge of the external world into three factors. There were (A), the Self, (B), the experiences of the self which he called ideas, and (C), an external Substance *plus* primary qualities which caused the ideas. Berkeley had eliminated (C) and left only (A), the Self, and (B), the Self's ideas.[1] Hume proceeded to eliminate the Self, (A), and left only (B), the ideas or experiences which would normally be said to belong to it.

The universe, then, for Hume, resolves itself into a series of ideas or experiences which only by courtesy are called yours and mine. Indeed, it is only by courtesy title that you and I can be said to exist. More correctly, then, the universe is a series of experiences which are not experiences of anything and do not belong to anybody. They just occur.

Bearing of Hume's Doctrine on the Free Will and Determinism Controversy.

It would seem, at first sight, rather a curious corollary of the Humian doctrine of the Self that it should be invoked by opponents of Free Will. For opponents of Free Will have almost invariably subscribed to the alternative doctrine of Determinism, and Hume, by casting doubts upon the efficacy of causation, must, one would have supposed, have greatly increased the difficulty of holding determinist doctrines.

Yet on further examination the corollary appears natural enough. The Self as commonly conceived is endowed with Free Will because, as commonly conceived, the Self is a continuing and continuously active spirit possessing a

---

[1] I am ignoring for the moment Berkeley's substitution of God for Locke's Substance (C), to be the cause of the ideas (B).

personality of its own. If we eliminate the continuing personality in favour of a succession of psychological states, it becomes exceedingly difficult not to think of each such state as being dependent upon the preceding one. In fact, to treat the Self as Hume does, is to treat it as if it were like a piece of matter completely analysable into its component parts. It is, in short, to regard it as the aggregate or sum by addition of its components. Now the entity which is typically the mere sum of its component parts is a machine.[1] Exhaustively to analyse the Self into its component states is, therefore, to treat it like a machine with the inevitable corollary of conceiving its mode of working after the model of the working of a machine.

In other words, it is only if we are entitled to conceive of the Self as an enduring entity which is more than the sum of the experiences which occur in and to it, that we shall be entitled also to maintain that it is free.

The Arguments Against Free Will.   Even if we, do so conceive the Self, it will be found exceedingly difficult to maintain the belief in Free Will, so long as our conception of freedom is modelled on commonsense lines. For Free Will, like the commonsense notions of Substance and its qualities, of a changing thing, of cause and effect and of the Self, is something which, if the colloquialism may be pardoned, will not bear thinking about. For directly we begin to think about it, we cannot avoid noticing that all the arguments which occur to us are arguments against it. Just as to think about the Self is to disintegrate it into its component states, so to think about the states is to realise their apparently complete dependence upon a vast number of external factors. It is from the variety of these external factors that the number and variety of arguments which may be adduced against Free Will spring.

The issue between Free Will and Determinism is primarily an ethical one and will not, therefore, receive special treatment in this book, which is concerned with

[1] See Chapter XV, pp. 415–419, for a discussion of the difference between wholes and aggregates.

epistemology and metaphysics. Nevertheless, most of the arguments on both sides of the controversy presuppose and derive from metaphysical positions. They are, that is to say, arguments which are only valid on the assumption that a particular view of the universe is in its broad outlines true. I propose in the course of the survey of metaphysical views which will occupy Part III to mention some of these arguments in connection with the metaphysical positions from which they derive, in order that their relation to and dependence upon these positions may be clearly seen. Thus I have already indicated the psychological arguments for Self-Determinism in the discussion of Mechanism and Teleology in Chapter VII,[1] while further arguments suggested by the conclusions of physiology will figure in the exposition of Materialism.[2] Similarly, arguments for Free Will, which depend upon and presuppose a creative view of mental processes, such as, for example, the view put forward by the philosopher, Bergson, will be presented in connection with Bergson's metaphysical system.[3] For the present, I propose to confine myself to those arguments which base themselves upon conceptions of the Self, and these are almost wholly adverse to Free Will.

One of the most important of these has already been mentioned in connection with our discussion of Teleology and Mechanism. This is the argument known as Self-Determinism,[4] which asserts that every state of the Self is determined by its preceding states.

The Argument from Universal Causation.　This in its turn is only a particular form of the general argument that everything must have a cause. Nothing can come out of nothing, it is said, and nothing, therefore, can happen without something to cause it to happen. One of the best statements of this view is that of the mathematician Laplace :

" We ought, then," he says, " to regard the present state of the universe as the effect of its antecedent state and the cause of the state that is to follow. An intelligence, who for

---

[1] See Chapter VII, pp. 188, 189.　[2] See Chapter XVIII, pp. 513, 514.
[3] See Chapter XIX, pp. 555, 556.　[4] See Chapter VII, pp. 188, 189.

a given instant should be acquainted with all the forces by which Nature is animated and with the several positions of the entities composing it, if further his intellect were vast enough to submit those data to analysis, would include in one and the same formula the movements of the largest bodies in the universe and those of the lightest atom. Nothing would be uncertain for him ; the future as well as the past would be present to his eyes. The human mind in the perfection it has been able to give to astronomy affords a feeble outline of such an intelligence. . . . All its efforts in the search for truth tend to approximate without limit to the intelligence we have just imagined."

It is the same view which is admirably summarised in the following verse from Omar Khayyám :

> *With Earth's first Clay They did the Last Man's knead,*
> *And then of the Last Harvest sow'd the Seed :*
> *Yea, the first Morning of Creation wrote*
> *What the Last Dawn of Reckoning shall read.*

According to this view, whatever happens is the direct result of some preceding happening, the preceding happening is in its turn the result of something else and so on indefinitely, the immediately relevant conclusion being that my present thoughts are the determined result of what some Neanderthaloid ancestor of mine thought a million years ago, just as much and as just as directly as the weather now is the result of the climatic conditions of a million years ago.

The argument appears in theology in the form of the doctrine of the Fall ; the children suffer for the sins of the fathers, and we are born in sin because of what happened in the Garden of Eden. Calvinism with its insistence on pre-destination, affords, perhaps, the most thorough-going example of the application of this deterministic type of argument to theology. Applying it to the problem of the Self, let us restate the doctrine of Self-Determinism.

Self-Determinism Restated. Let us suppose that I am a person continually given to good works ; all my actions, we will suppose, are noble, none ignoble. Now these good actions of mine must, it is said, have some cause. Whence, then, do they spring? Obviously from the nobility of my character. But how was this noble character of mine formed? Clearly not arbitrarily and not out of nothing. Being good is not as easy as all that. How then? By training and discipline and the habit of leading a good life. But a good life is nothing apart from the good actions in which it finds expression. A good life is, in fact, simply one that expresses itself in good acts. Hence a good character is the result of the continuous performance of good acts. But whence do these good acts spring? Obviously from the possession of a noble character, for a good character—as we have seen—is one that naturally results in good acts. Hence at every stage of our career our actions are the determined results of our characters, which in their turn were formed by our preceding actions, which in their turn sprang from the good characters which expressed themselves in them, and so on *ad infinitum*. At every stage, in fact, we act in such and such a way *because* we are that sort of person, and *tout comprendre est tout pardonner*. Travelling backwards on these lines we come to the first actions we ever performed which are the result of the initial character, or potentiality for a character, with which we were born interacting with the environment in which we found ourselves placed.

Now, unless we believe in reincarnation, it seems difficult to hold that we are responsible for the initial character or disposition for a character with which we were born ; more difficult still to hold ourselves responsible for the environment in which at birth we were placed. We may conclude, therefore, that we are responsible neither for our initial character, or disposition to form a character, nor for our initial environment, from which it follows, if the argument which I have outlined is correct, that we are not responsible for our actions or our characters at any stage of our subsequent careers.

The argument for Self-Determinism is strong ; it is also exceedingly difficult to refute, a circumstance which must be my excuse for venturing to traverse from a different point of approach in this chapter, ground already partially covered in the last. The conclusion of our survey is a completely deterministic one ; we are determined, it asserts, by our inherited vital endowment reacting to the environment in which we happen to be placed in accordance with the tendencies initially latent in that endowment. In other words, we are at the mercy of our natural dispositions, which we do not form or even control.

Psychological Determinism.

This mode of thinking is very popular at the present time. It has been developed by modern psychologists and forms the basis, usually unavowed, of the conception of human nature presupposed by psychoanalysis. So developed, it constitutes perhaps the most formidable body of doctrine that those who believe in Free Will have to face, and it is worth while pausing for a moment to consider what precisely in its modern form it asserts, and what are the grounds on which it bases its assertion. Let us take as typical of this school of thought the views of Freud.

Freud, as is well known, holds that the origin and explanation of all conscious events is to be found in the unconscious. Our conscious thoughts and desires are, therefore, the reflections more or less distorted and more or less sublimated of unconscious elements in our nature. We do not know what is going on in the unconscious ; if we did it would not be unconscious, but, in respect of our knowledge of it, conscious ; therefore we cannot control it.

If we do not know it and cannot control it, we are not responsible for it ; therefore, we are not responsible for the particular version of it that appears in consciousness. In other words we are not responsible for our thoughts and desires. Our thoughts determine what we think, our desires what we do. If, in short, consciousness is rightly regarded as a by-product of unconscious processes, it is clearly determined by the processes which produce it. Conscious events are merely the smoke and flame given off by the workings of the subterranean psychological machinery of which we are unconscious.

At this point it may very naturally be objected that no account is being taken of the will. It is true, it may be said, that our desires and thoughts occur to a large extent without our volition ; but whether we encourage them or not is a different matter ; whether we indulge our thoughts and gratify our desires depends upon our wills. It is the function of will to control thought and discipline desire and in exercising this control will is free. Thus in using our wills to control our desires, to choose this and to refrain from that, we are really free agents. Similarly with our tastes ; we cannot, admittedly, guarantee that we shall like doing this or doing that, but we can guarantee that we will do this or that, whether we like it or not. But, if psycho-analysis is right, this traditional account is very far from representing the facts.

Psycho-analysis suggests that the fundamental motive forces of our natures are instinctive and impulsive in character. Now the will is either one among such forces or it is a sublimated version of such a force. It is, that is to say, either an instinctive drive to act in a certain way, or, if it is not, it cannot be brought into operation unless there is an instinctive drive to use it in a certain way. The will, then, is helpless, except in so far as some force which is outside our control enables us to bring it into play.

A Modern Theory of Instinct. This attitude to the will is by no means confined to psycho-analysis. It is prevalent in the writings of many modern psychologists. Professor McDougall, for example, one of the best known of modern writers on psychology, holds[1] that the primary motive forces of human nature are the instincts. We have instincts to behave in certain ways. We act in order to satisfy our instincts, and, without the prompting of an instinct seeking its satisfaction, we can neither act nor think.

" The instincts," says Professor McDougall, " are the

[1] Or used to ; his earlier views about instinct have been to some extent modified in his latest work.

prime movers of all human activity; by the conative or impulsive force of some instinct every train of thought, however cold and passionless it may seem, is borne along towards its end . . . all the complex intellectual apparatus of the most highly developed mind is but the instrument by which these impulses seek their satisfaction. . . . Take away these instinctive dispositions, with their powerful mechanisms, and the organism would become incapable of activity of any kind; it would be inert and motionless, like a wonderful piece of clockwork whose mainspring had been removed."

On this view, then, the instincts play a part analogous to that of the unconscious in Freud's theory. Even if we admit that there is in our mental make-up a separate, independent something called the will, it remains inoperative, unless the urge of instinct is brought into play to set it going. Unless, therefore, we are impelled to use the will to suppress an unruly desire, we cannot in fact suppress it. Now the drive or impulsion to use the will for this purpose is, like our other drives to action, an occurrence which is fundamentally instinctive in character, and neither for this occurrence nor for its strength when it occurs, can we be held responsible.

What happens is that we are aware at the same time of two different urges or promptings to action. The first takes the form of an unruly self-regarding desire; the second is a determination to suppress the unruly desire in the interests of the good of the whole. If the desire is stronger than the determination, there will be failure in what we call will, and we shall be said in common parlance to "give way to our desire." If the determination is stronger than the desire, we shall perform what is called an act of self-denial. This act of self-denial, however, just as truly as the contrary act of self-indulgence, will be an expression of obedience to whatever happens to be our strongest instinctive drive to action at the moment. Hence, whatever the resultant action may be, it must be interpreted as the result of a conflict between two instinctive drives, a conflict in which the stronger will inevitably win.

The truth of this analysis has, it is said, been obscured

by the use of ambiguous phrases such as self-control and self-denial. These phrases suggest that in controlling a desire I am in some unexplained way acting in defiance of my nature. But it is only by drawing upon my own *natural* forces that I can defy my nature. If it were not *natural* for me to restrain my desire, I could not restrain it, so that in self-denial and self-control I am being just as truly self-indulgent as in an indiscriminate yielding to purely self-regarding desires.

Summing up, we may say that, if the view that the basis of all action is instinctive or impulsive is correct, the use of the will to repress desire is only a sublimated version of an instinctive drive to suppress a desire which we instinctively feel to be inimical to the good of the whole. If we desire to pass an examination, we *will* to suppress a desire to go to the cinema when we ought to be studying. But the *will* in this case is nothing more nor less than the expression of the desire to pass the examination, for which we are no more responsible than for the desire to go to the cinema.

Bearing upon Ethics.

A similar conclusion is reached in regard to conscience. If the will has been traditionally regarded as the faculty by means of which we restrain ourselves from the performance of actions which are known to be wrong, conscience is traditionally the faculty by means of which their wrongness is recognised. Conscience is the faculty whereby we prescribe certain things to be right and certain things to be wrong. Its function is to tell us when a desire may be justifiably indulged and when it may not. In virtue of its performance of this function, conscience is looked upon as the keystone of morality.

But morality is a structure built on the twin pillars of praise and blame. If you cannot blame a man for doing wrong, and cannot give him credit for doing right, morality goes by the board. Yet praise and blame are equally illogical, where there is no responsibility for the actions which excite the one and provoke the other. If, therefore, the analysis described above does, as it appears to do, strike successfully at the basis of human responsibility, the feeling of shame at wrongdoing, which is the chief expression of conscience, is a feeling for which we are no more responsible than for the desire to do wrong. If the feeling of shame is stronger than the desire to do wrong, conscience will prove effective in inhibiting wrong action. If, however, it is weaker, we shall act wrongly. Once again there is a conflict between two feelings in which the victory will go to the stronger. For neither feeling nor for the strength of either feeling can we be held responsible, since each is the sublimation of some instinctive drive whose origin is unconscious.

Thus by destroying man's freedom the implications of modern psychology tend only too often to cut away the basis from traditional ethics.

Conviction of Free Will and of the Continuity of the Self.

In spite of the fact that all the more obvious arguments in the controversy between Free Will and Determinism seem to be on one side, we remain for the most part unconvinced, and we are unconvinced very largely because of our consciousness of our own freedom. It is a matter of psychological conviction amounting to psychological certainty first, that if I will to move my right arm, it will in fact move, and secondly, that I might, if I had chosen, have willed to move my left. Similarly, nothing will shake my conviction that I have or am a continuing personality or Self, which owns its psychological states and is the source of its acts of will, but is itself other than they. These convictions of mine must receive due weight, even if our conception of the universe itself must be partly moulded by the necessity of giving them their due. Conceiving the universe within the limitations imposed by this necessity, we may discover that we have incidentally answered the determinists, not by refuting their arguments but by outflanking them.

Let us suppose, for example, that the universe is the embodiment or expression of a principle of life ; that life is essentially creative, and that we must conceive of it, therefore, not as a thing but as an activity, the essence of which is to bring something new into existence by the mere process of its functioning. And by " something new " we shall mean something that was not already contained in, or implied by, or latent in what went before. Life so conceived would be radically different from matter, and the laws which governed its workings would be other than those which operated in the material world. It would not, for example, be subject to the law of mechanical causation. Once we conceive of life in this way, the problem of the free will assumes a different complexion, as we shall see when we come to the philosophy of Bergson.[1]

There are also on the side of Free Will important logical arguments which purport to show that the doctrine of Determinism, in at least one of the forms in which it is commonly put forward, is self-contradictory or, more precisely, that, if it be true, there cannot be any reasons for thinking that it is. These arguments will be found in Chapter XVIII.[2]

As with the freedom of the Self, so with its identity. As Samuel Butler has pointed out, an old man of eighty is from almost every point of view a different being from the young man who at the age of twenty fell in love, from the boy who at the age of nine stole apples from the orchard, and from the baby who at the age of eighteen months was slapped by his nurse. His experiences, his thoughts, his memories, his tastes, his faculties, his reactions to his environment—all are different. Moreover, every item of his physical constitution has changed. The brain is different and so are the heart, the arteries and the veins ; in fact, the stuff of the body is different down to the very last atom. Nevertheless the conviction of identity remains, so that a man will feel entitled to say : " I am the person who at the age of twenty fell in love ; at the age of nine stole apples ; at the age of eighteen months was slapped by my nurse " ; and, further, we know that the conviction is justified. Yet directly we begin to subject the notion of the Self to scrutiny, we can, as we have seen, find no basis for it. Here, then, is

[1] See Chapter XIX, pp. 555, 556.   [2] See Chapter XVIII pp. 534–538.

another antinomy,[1] an antinomy between the conclusions
of the critical reason and the plain fact of an unshakable
conviction.

Hume on Feeling and Reason.   What follows ? We can
take the somewhat heroic line of simply disowning our
reason. This, broadly speaking, was the line followed by
Hume. He did not in fact deny that there was causation
any more than he denied the Self. What he denied was that
reason could find grounds for the belief in them. But,
assuredly, we *feel* that there is a Self, just as we *feel* that there
is a causal relation, and Hume was prepared, when it came
to the point, to accept the testimony of his feelings. " I
have never," he writes in a letter, " defended the absurd
proposition that a thing could come into being without a
cause : all I maintained was only that our certainty of the
falsehood of this proposition arises neither from intuition
nor demonstration, but from another source." That other
source was feeling, which Hume exalts in proportion as he
criticises understanding. In a famous passage in the fourth
part of his *Treatise of Human Nature* entitled " Of the Sceptical and other Systems of Philosophy," he says : " Should it
be asked me, whether I sincerely assent to this argument "
(i.e. that we can have no rational certainty about anything)
" which I seem to take such pains to inculcate, and whether
I be really one of those sceptics who hold that all is uncertain, and that our judgement is not in *any* thing possessed of
any measures of truth and falsehood ; I should reply, that
this question is entirely superfluous, and that neither I,
nor any other person, was ever sincerely and constantly of
that opinion. Nature, by an absolute and uncontrollable
necessity, has determined us to judge as well as to breathe
and feel ; nor can we any more forbear viewing certain
objects in a stronger and fuller light, upon account of their
customary connection with a present impression, than we
can hinder ourselves from thinking, as long as we are awake,

[1] An antinomy, it will be remembered, is a term used by philosophers
to denote a direct contradiction. See Chapter VIII, p. 221.

or seeing the surrounding bodies, when we turn our eyes towards them in broad sunshine. Whoever has taken the pains to refute the cavils of this *total* scepticism, has really disputed without an antagonist, and endeavoured by arguments to establish a faculty, which nature has antecedently implanted in the mind, and rendered unavoidable.

" My intention then in displaying so carefully the arguments of that fantastic sect, is only to make the reader sensible of the truth of my hypothesis, *that all our reasonings concerning causes and effects, are derived from nothing but custom ; and that belief is more properly an act of the sensitive, than of the cognitive part of our natures.*"

Thus when Hume has shown that the most fundamental beliefs of mankind cannot be supported by reason, the moral which he draws is : " So much the worse for reason." A paradoxical conclusion this, coming from one who possessed one of the most powerful intellects among philosophers, as paradoxical as the determination of Plato, their greatest artist, to exclude artists from his ideal State !

The Real and the Apparent Self. But there is another way. Maintaining that our instinctive conviction of the continuity and the freedom of the Self is justified, we may nevertheless assert that the Self which is continuous and free is not the Self as ordinarily understood. By the Self " as ordinarily understood " we shall mean the empirical Self, which is open to introspection, subjected to enquiry by psychologists, and incidentally exposed to the criticisms of Hume. Suppose for a moment we concede that this empirical Self, the Self affirmed by common sense, will not stand examination any better than the physical objects or the Substance affirmed by common sense. What conclusions are we entitled to draw ? One conclusion is that we have discovered another reason for distrusting the whole commonsense conception of the world, and for regarding it as an appearance, a frequently misleading appearance, of a reality that underlies it.

This reality, we shall conclude, whatever else may be

true of it, must be such as to accommodate within its bounds the real Self of whose existence we are so intimately aware and so certainly convinced, the Self which is both continuous and free.

Berkeley and the Self.   But if this real Self is not the one which common sense affirms and of which in ordinary experience we are, presumably, conscious, how are we to conceive it ? Berkeley maintained that the mind has a " notion "[1] of the Self. This "notion" was not derived from experience and was, therefore, explicitly distinguished from the ordinary Berkeleyan " ideas." " What I am myself," says Berkeley, " —that which I denote by the term I—is the same with what is meant by *soul* or *spiritual substance*. But if I should say that I was nothing, or that I was an idea, nothing could be more evidently absurd than either of these propositions." " In a large sense indeed," he continues, " we may be said to have an idea or rather a notion of *spirit* : that is, we understand the meaning of the word, otherwise we could not affirm or deny anything of it." The doctrine of " notions " is thus inconsistent with the main Berkeleyan position,[2] that our knowledge comes from experience and consists of ideas. A " notion " is in fact an example of the *a priori* knowledge which in other connections Berkeley was concerned to deny. Berkeley does not develop his doctrine of the " notional " Self or indicate what he considered to be its features. But the very fact that the " notion " was reached otherwise than through experience—our " notions " are said to be of things " whereof in a strict sense we have not ideas "— that it was in fact known *a priori*, suggests that the Self, of which, Berkeley is affirming, we have a " notion," is other than the empirical Self criticised by Hume, the Self of common sense and psychology.

The Self and Modern Psychology.   Most philosophers would agree that Hume succeeded in showing that, if the

---

[1] He also considered that the mind has a " notion " of God.
[2] See Chapter IV, pp. 111, 112.

existence of a continuing Self is to be effectively maintained, it must be by methods other than that of commonsense examination and enquiry ; and, since from this point
of view, science is only organised and correlated common
sense, we may add, by methods other than those of science.
It is not, in other words, psychology which can reveal to us
the secret of the nature of such a continuing Self, but
metaphysics. And it was in fact by metaphysical methods
that subsequent philosophers, such as Kant and Hegel,
attempted to establish the nature of the real as opposed to
the apparent Self. Kant, indeed, went to the length of
so defining reality, that the real, which he called the
" transcendental " as opposed to the empirical Self, should
be specifically accommodated within its bounds. Kant's treatment of the subject will be described in a later Chapter.[1]

Many have, however, taken and will continue to take the
view that the endeavour to determine the nature of the Self
by *a priori* reasoning is mistaken. It may well be that they are
right. Nevertheless, it cannot be said that the empirical
methods of science have up to the present succeeded in
reaching any very satisfactory results in this particular
sphere. And in favour of the view that the attempts on the
part of philosophers to determine the nature of the Self by
a priori reasoning have not, whatever we may think of their
outcome, so far at least as concerns their *method*, been
mistaken, that, in other words, the question of the nature of
personality is a question which, unanswerable by the methods
of science, is properly to be pursued by those of philosophy,
the following considerations are worth bearing in mind.

(1) It is a fact that psychology is and is likely to remain
the most inexact of the sciences ; it starts from no set of
agreed axioms or postulates ; it is embroiled in a perpetual
controversy over its methods ; it acknowledges no agreed
results ; it assembles no corpus of definite knowledge. The sum
of ascertained psychological knowledge, in so far as knowledge implies a set of conclusions to which all psychologists
would agree, is scarcely less negligible than the sum of

[1] See Chapter XIV, pp. 389-391.

ascertained philosophical knowledge. Whenever psychology does succeed in establishing results which are definite, agreed, and calculable, whenever in fact the psychologist feels himself justified in saying : " Given such and such causes, such and such effects will follow," the results in question turn out to convey information not about the mind or Self, but about the body ; that is to say, they form part not of psychology but of physiology. Examples of such results are Pavlov's celebrated formulations of the workings of conditioned reflexes in dogs, and some of the laws postulated by the behaviourists. Two conclusions suggest themselves. Either, as the behaviourists assert, there is no mind and no Self ; there is only a consciousness of bodily movements which is a by-product of those movements ; or the nature of the mind and the Self, if discoverable, is discoverable by philosophical rather than by psychological methods.

Personality Not Amenable to the Methods of the Sciences.

(2) Nor is it only the present position of psychology which suggests this latter conclusion. It may well be doubted whether questions relating to the nature of the Self and of personality as the essence of the Self, can ever be successfully tackled by the methods of the sciences.

Let us suppose that the various accounts which the sciences could give of the human organism were to be collated. We should begin, let us say, with the physiological account in terms of tubes and pipes, nerves and bones and blood vessels. These, presumably, can be analysed into their chemical compounds, and there is, therefore, a chemical account in terms of molecules and elements. These, again, can be analysed in terms of their atomic constituents, and there is, therefore, the physicist's account in terms of protons and electrons. Beginning at the other end of the scale, we should have to include the psychologist's account in terms of mental events, images, sensations and so forth, with special departmental accounts such as the behaviourist's in terms of language habits and conditioned reflexes, and the psycho-analyst's in terms of unconscious desire and promptings of the libido. From other points of view there is the economic man and there is the median man of the statistician ; there is man from the standpoint of the biologist and man as he appears to the anthropologist. There is also the account of particular individual men to be found in the works of the great novelists. Each of these accounts could in theory be made accurate and complete—complete, that is to say, so far as it goes ; yet each would be couched in different terms. To say that no one of these accounts conveys the whole truth about a man, but describes only some particular aspect of him which has been selected for special attention, would be to state a commonplace.

But more than this is implied by the statement that questions relating to the nature of the Self can never be successfully tackled by scientific methods. It is implied that if all the different accounts, the physiological, the chemical, the physical, the psychological, the behaviour-istic, the psycho-analytic, the economic, the statistical, the biological, the anthropological and the novelist's, were collated, supplemented with other accurate and complete but partial accounts and worked up into a comprehensive survey, they would still fail to constitute *the* truth about the Self. And they would fail to do this, not because some particular piece of information had been left out, or some particular point of view forgotten—for, it would be urged, no matter how complete the collection of scientific accounts might be, *the* truth would still elude them—but because they would remain only a set of separate accounts of differ-ent parts or aspects, and a man's Self is more than the different parts or aspects which are ingredients of it. True knowledge of a Self is not, in other words, the sum-total of the complete and accurate accounts of all its different aspects, even if those accounts could be made exhaustive. True knowledge is, or at least includes, knowledge of the Self as a whole. To know a man's Self as a whole is to know him as a personality, for a personality is the whole which, while it integrates all the parts and so includes them within itself, is nevertheless something over and above their sum.

Now to know a man as a personality is to know him in a manner of which science takes no cognisance.

Transition to Constructive Metaphysics.

The conclusion of these observations is that the philosophers may have been right in endeavouring to establish the nature of the Self by *a priori* reasoning rather than by empirical methods, right, that is to say, in their assumption that the nature of personality belongs to the realm of metaphysics, and right precisely because the Self belongs to an underlying real world and not to the world which appears to common sense. We are then, by our examination of the Self, no less than by the examination of cause, of change and of Substance, led away from the world which we know in sense experience to a consideration of a different world which is revealed, in so far as it is revealed at all, to reason. I shall endeavour in Part III to give an account of some of the efforts which philosophers have made to prescribe the nature of this world, and shall briefly enumerate the main features of the resulting philosophical systems.

At this point, then, we pass from critical to constructive Metaphysics.

LAIRD, JOHN. The Problems of the Self.
ARISTOTLE. Nicomachæan Ethics, Book II. (*Edition in Everyman.* Introduction by J. A. Smith.)
    Contains the doctrine cited in the text as Self-Determinism.
HUME. A Treatise of Human Nature. Book I, Part IV, Section VI. (*Edition in Everyman.*)
RUSSELL, BERTRAND. The Analysis of Mind (especially Chapter I).

A valuable treatment of the problem of freedom from the libertarian point of view will be found in A. E. Taylor's contribution to *Contemporary British Philosophy*, Vol. II, entitled " The Freedom of Man." A sketch of the philosophy of personality is contained in J. M. Macmurray's *Freedom in the Modern World*. My *Philosophical Aspects of Modern Science*, Chapter VIII, may also be consulted.

PART III

CONSTRUCTIVE
METAPHYSICS

INTRODUCTORY : A PRELIMINARY DOUBT

Is Constructive Metaphysics Legitimate ?   If the foregoing criticisms have substance, the world as it appears to our senses is not the world as it really is. There is, that is to say, a difference between appearance and reality. How, then, are we to conceive of reality ? For an answer to this question we must turn to the systems of the great philosophers. We have, that is to say, almost reached the point at which we can proceed to consider the nature of the universe as a whole. Almost, but not quite ; for, before we can begin our exploration, there is a preliminary doubt of which we must seek to dispose, or rather, since it will not be disposed of, to which we must at least accord a frank recognition. The doubt may be expressed in the form of a series of questions. Is the constructive speculation in which the great philosophers have indulged a legitimate pursuit ? Can the human mind, by processes of reasoning and reflection, reveal to us the nature of the universe ? Will it not only succeed in revealing itself, projecting upon the empty canvas of an unknown world its own hopes and wishes, using its reason to invest them with a show of plausibility, and then hailing as reality what it has itself projected ? May it not in short be the case that, when the philosopher sits back in his chair and speculates about the universe at large, his results, while telling us much about the philosopher, tell us little about the universe ; that, valuable as psychology, they are valueless as metaphysics ?

The Philosophical Analysts.   I emphasise the doubts which these questions are intended to raise, because they occupy a prominent place in the minds of modern philosophers. In recent years there has grown up a school, known sometimes as the school of " Logical Positivism," sometimes as that of " Philosophical Analysis," which returns a strictly negative answer to the questions just formulated. Metaphysics as traditionally conceived, it is apt to dismiss as a sophisticated form of myth. The object of constructive metaphysics as traditionally conceived is to throw light upon the nature of the universe as a whole. To quote a celebrated description of Professor Broad's, the procedure of the speculative metaphysician is to take over " the results of the various sciences," to add to them " the results of the religious and ethical experiences of mankind, and then " to reflect " upon the whole." " The hope is," he continues, " that, by this means, we may be able to reach some general conclusions as to the nature of the Universe, and as to our position and prospects in it." If the philosophical analysts are right, this hope is doomed to disappointment, for, in their view, the traditional aim of speculative philosophy, the comprehension of the nature of the universe as a whole, is mistaken, or, at any rate, is unrealisable. The primary object of philosophy, it is said, is to analyse and clarify the meaning of commonsense statements, not in the way in which grammar analyses and clarifies them, but with a view to making it clear what precisely it is that our words *mean*, when they are used significantly. It is possible, although by no means certain, that as a result of this clarification of meaning, we may obtain some information as to the structure of facts.

The Clarification of Meaning.

There are two senses in which words can be said to have meaning. There is the meaning which they have and which we know, when we use them correctly. In this sense most people who can use words with grammatical correctness would be said to know the meaning of the words they use. But there is another sense of the word meaning according to which most people would be said not to know the meaning of the words they are using. What most people habitually do, is to use words in a number of different meanings without realising the fact. To take an example given by Professor Stebbing, we may ask, and philosophers have asked, such questions as " Where are dream images ? ", " Where is the Number Two ? ", and " Where is my pen ? " Of these three questions, the last can be intelligibly answered by the statement " My pen is in this room," that is, in some part of physical space. But dream images are not in physical space, nor is the Number Two. When we reflect upon this fact, we are led to realise that, if the word " where " in the two first questions is being used in the same sense as the word " where " in the third question, then the two first questions are strictly nonsensical. There are, in other words, no answers to them. Presumably, then, there are other senses of the word " where " which might make these two first questions meaningful. But, if there are, does it not follow that there may not also be different kinds of space in addition to physical space ? Thus, it is claimed, the analysis of the correct meaning of words and sentences may often throw light upon philosophical problems.

What is Meant by Analysis ?

Strictly, philosophical analysis does not lead to the discovery of new facts ; nor does the analytical philosopher seek to increase the amount of our knowledge about the world. His purpose is to show more clearly what precisely it is that we are knowing, when we know what would ordinarily be called commonsense facts. In a famous passage in his contribution to *Contemporary British Philosophy* Professor Moore cites a number of propositions, such as " ' The earth has existed for many years past,' ' Many human bodies have each lived for many years upon it,' " all of which assert the existence of material things. " I am not," he says, " at all sceptical as to the *truth* of " these propositions ; " on the contrary, I hold that we all know, with certainty, many such propositions to be true. But," he continues, " I am very sceptical as to what, in certain respects, the correct *analysis* of such propositions is." In other words, Professor Moore is doubtful what precisely it is that we are asserting about the world

when we make commonsense statements which we know
to be true. Now it is this that the philosophical analyst
wishes to discover. He wants to find out what it is that we are
asserting when we say things that we know to be true, and
then to restate our true statements with the utmost clarity
and precision. This, some would assert, is not only the main
but the sole object of philosophy. For example, Wittgen-
stein, one of the most prominent exponents of Philosophical
Analysis, has announced that " the object of philosophy is
the logical clarification of thoughts."

Philosophy so conceived does not merely include, it
resolves itself into, analysis ; it becomes, in fact, Philosophical Analysis, since the traditional function of philosophy, that, namely, of constructing a speculative system in
the sense defined by Professor Broad, must be abandoned,
and the business of obtaining information about the nature
of things be carried on by the piecemeal methods of science.

There is a story of a Chinese philosopher who, having
visited England early in the 1930's in order to discover
from the famous Cambridge philosopher, G. E. Moore, the
nature of the world, remarked mock-regretfully at the end
of his visit that he had learnt very little about the nature
of the world, but a great deal about the correct use of the
English language. This picture of the preoccupations of
Cambridge philosophers is a caricature, which is, nevertheless, a very good likeness.

The More Moderate Claims of Analysis. Even those
philosophical analysts who do not subscribe to the extreme
views just stated would be inclined to assert that the method
of analysis—that is to say, the making clear what it is that
we mean when we make true statements, is an indispensable condition of fruitful philosophising in the speculative
sense. As to whether we can by means of speculative
philosophy throw light upon the nature of the universe as
a whole, analysts of the more moderate school are inclined
to profess agnosticism. But, they would hold, it is certain that
this cannot be achieved, until much more philosophical

analysis has been carried out than has been done up to the present. Much philosophy, they say, is worthless because it persistently makes use of ambiguous words, and many philosophical controversies are unreal because the protagonists are using expressions such as space, time, matter and reality in different senses. These ambiguities, they hold, must be cleared up by analysis before philosophy can go forward.

Author's Comment.   The problems discussed by the school of philosophical analysts are difficult, and their methods of discussion are apt to be highly technical. A detailed treatment of the subject would, therefore, be unsuitable in an outline of this kind. Moreover, the whole subject is in a state of flux. Its origin is too recent for it to have reached any very definite conclusions, and it has yet to outgrow the early stages of controversy in which fundamental questions of the method, purpose, scope and possibilities of Philosophical Analysis are still being discussed.

Most philosophers would, however, find difficulty in accepting the view that the traditional aims of speculative philosophy are chimerical. Philosophical progress, they would say, is admittedly slow, and philosophers seem at times to do little but contradict one another. But what else can be reasonably expected, considering the vastness of the territory, whose boundaries are those of the universe, which the philosopher sets out to explore, and the inevitable intrusion of his personality to colour his map?[1] But whether or no speculative philosophy is a will-o'-the-wisp, we cannot help but pursue it. To cite again the remark of the English philosopher, F. H. Bradley, "metaphysics may be the finding of bad reasons for what we believe upon instinct ; but to find these reasons is no less an instinct," and it is an instinct which appears to grow stronger and not weaker as our species evolves.

Nor is it the case that no progress is made. It is by now, for example, reasonably certain that the Representationalism of Locke offers an incorrect theory of perception, and

[1] See Introduction, p. 17.

IP

that Subjective Idealism cannot be maintained in the form in which Bishop Berkeley maintained it. The present author is not a philosophical analyst, and on this issue his own views are on the side of tradition. I believe, that is to say, that it is at least possible, by following the methods traditionally pursued by philosophers, to reach conclusions about the nature of things which are true. If I did not believe this, I should have little interest in philosophy.

Unless I thought that philosophy had some contribution to make to the answering of such questions as " What sort of universe is this in which we are living ? " and " How ought we to live in it?", I, for one, should have no interest in philosophy. I believe that most philosophers are in similar case. In spite of the scantiness of the light which philosophy has managed to throw upon the constitution of the universe and the status of human existence, in spite of the meagreness of the rules which it has succeeded in drawing up for the right conduct of life, we are, most of us feel convinced, not knocking at a door irrevocably closed, when we look to it to provide understanding and guidance.

The issues raised by the claims of the philosophical analysts lie outside the scope of this book, and I cannot further discuss them here. It seemed right to preface a Part which seeks to give an outline of some of the systems which the great metaphysicians have put forward, with a mention of the doubt which modern philosophers have suggested as to the validity of the whole procedure of the system makers. But the doubt is in its modern statement of too recent origin and the issues which it raises are too much matters of contemporary controversy and discussion, to find an appropriate place in a book of this kind. Whether the philosophical analysts are right or wrong in their view that constructive metaphysics is a form of sophisticated myth-making, it is clearly the duty of one who is seeking to provide a general guide to philosophical thought to include an account of some of the great metaphysical systems that philosophers have constructed. To this task I now turn.

CHAPTER X: UNIVERSALS AND PARTICULARS: PLATO'S THEORY OF IDEAS

Introductory : Definitions. The object of this and the ensuing chapter is to describe the view of reality which was held by Plato (427–347 B.C.). Before, however, we can proceed to develop Plato's view, there is a preliminary question to be discussed. This, the question of the relation between universals and particulars, has bulked very largely in the history of philosophy, although nothing has previously been said about it in these pages. The discussion is introduced here because it was a consideration of this question that was responsible, at least in part, for Plato's distinctive conception of reality.

As is often the case with philosophical terms, no agreed definition of universals or particulars can be given, since our definition of these terms will depend on the view we take of the nature of what is defined, and this in its turn is bound up with our general theory of knowledge and metaphysical conception of reality. We may, however, safely include among particulars the kind of things that are given to us in sensation. What we hold these things to be will, of course, depend on the particular view of sense experience that we adopt. Most philosophers would, however, agree that the patch of red that I am now seeing is a particular. A universal is something which is able to characterise a number of different particulars. The redness which I see in this patch is the same as the redness which I see in that one, although the two patches are different. When we use a word to describe something which, like redness, can belong to a number of different objects or facts, the something may be defined as a universal. Thus whiteness.

humanity, justice, triangularity, are all universals, since many different things and facts can be respectively white, human, just and triangular. But this particular piece of snow, this particular man, this particular legal decision, this particular triangle, are all, as the language we use to speak of them denotes, particulars although their total description may involve the presence of universals. Questions which are discussed by philosophers are " What is the status of particulars and what the status of universals ? ", " What is the nature of the relation between the universal and the particular, when we say of a universal that it characterises a particular, or of a particular that it manifests, exhibits, or possesses a certain universal ? " " What universals are there and what particulars ? " These questions raise very difficult problems which, especially in modern discussions of the subject, tend to become technical. The answers to them are also highly controversial. We are, however, in this chapter, concerned with the metaphysical views of Plato, and I propose only to deal with the questions raised above in so far as an acquaintance with them is essential to an understanding of Plato's philosophy. Let us begin by endeavouring to establish the existence of universals as real entities.

Berkeley and Hume on Abstract Ideas.   That there are such entities as universals has been denied by many philosophers. There are, they have affirmed, no such things. When we are making statements about whiteness, for example, what, in their view, we are thinking about is some one white thing. One might have supposed that a simple appeal to introspective experience would have been sufficient to rule out this view.   Having made it, I, for my part, have not the smallest doubt that thinking about whiteness is an entirely different experience from thinking about snow, for example, or cream. How comes it, then, that such an obvious difference should have been overlooked ?

The denial of universals has usually been maintained by empirical philosophers, who were concerned to throw doubt upon the existence of *a priori* knowledge,[1] and realised that to admit that there could be knowledge of universals was fatal to their position ; for a universal, not being a sensible object (that is to say, an object experienced by means of our sense organs) cannot be known entirely by sense experience. To concede knowledge of universals is, therefore, to concede that there can be knowledge other than that obtained by the senses. Consequently we find philosophers such as Berkeley and Hume vehemently denying that there can be what they call " abstract ideas "—that is, general ideas of things which are not ideas of any one particular thing. Berkeley writes as follows : " When I demonstrate any propositions concerning triangles, it is to be supposed " (supposed, that is to say, by the upholders of abstract ideas which Berkeley is attacking) " that I have in view the universal idea of a triangle ; which ought not to be understood as if I could frame an idea of a triangle which was neither equilateral, nor scalenon, nor equicrural. But only that the particular triangle I consider, whether of this or that sort it matters not, doth equally stand for and represent all rectilinear triangles whatsoever, and is, in that sense, *universal*. All of which," Berkeley ingenuously adds, " seems very plain, and not to include any difficulty in it." " There is," Berkeley replies, " no such thing as one precise and definite signification annexed to any general name, they all signifying indifferently a great number of particular ideas."[2] On this view, when we want to think of whiteness, we first form an image of some particular white object, and then abstract from it any quality which is not shared by all other white objects, at the same time taking care not to draw any conclusions in regard to it which would not equally be true of other white objects.

That this is in fact the way in which we are first led to think of universals, few would be concerned to deny. When we begin to learn geometry, we draw a triangle on the

[1] See Chapter IV, p. 108, for an account of *a priori* knowledge.
[2] It is Berkeley's repudiation of abstract ideas which causes him to deny that we have idea of physical objects. See Conclusion (B), Chapter II, pp. 48, 49.

board and take care not to deduce from the particular example anything which would not be true of all triangles. It is only later, as the result of reflection on the common attributes of a number of triangles, that we are led to form a conception of triangularity, that is to say, of the triangle as such. But to admit that this is *how* we come to think of universals is very far from disposing of the view that we do in fact think of them.

First Arguments for Universals.

For the appeal to introspective experience which, as I have suggested, reports strongly in their favour, may be reinforced by argument. If we wish to avoid postulating the universals whiteness or triangularity, we must ask ourselves how we come to know that things are white or are triangles. Presumably by choosing some one particular white thing or particular triangle and declaring that everything is white or is a triangle which resembles the particular example chosen. But this, as Bertrand Russell has pointed out, is to admit the universal " resemblance." " Since," he says, " there are many white things, the resemblance must hold between many pairs of particular white things ; and this is the characteristic of a universal. It will be useless to say that there is a different resemblance for each pair, for then we shall have to say that these resemblances resemble each other, and thus at last we shall be forced to admit resemblance as a universal. The relation of resemblance, therefore, must be a true universal. And having been forced to admit this universal, we find that it is no longer worth while to invent difficult and unplausible theories to avoid the admission of such universals as whiteness and triangularity."

Additional Arguments for Universals.

Let us now consider some of the questions involved on merits. What is the nature of the object which is in front of our minds when we are thinking about whiteness ? There are, I think, broadly three alternative answers.

(1) That the object about which we are thinking is a particular white thing, or, alternatively, the sum-total of all the white things that we happen to have experienced.

(2) That the object of which we are thinking is an idea or conception in our own minds.

(3) That it is a universal.

Alternative (1) has already been dealt with, in so far as it takes the form of the assertion that I am thinking of *one particular* white thing. If it is asserted that I am thinking of all the white things that I happen to have experienced or of all the white things that there happen to be, the assertion cannot, I would suggest, be seriously entertained. It seems to me introspectively certain that I can think about whiteness without remembering all the white things I have experienced; that, indeed, I can think about it without any effort of memory at all, and I do not know all the white things in the world.

Alternative (2) leads to the conclusion that things would cease to be white when we cease to regard them; that in short, if all minds were abolished, there would be no such thing as whiteness in the world. Yet by ceasing to contemplate a white object one does not appear *prima facie* to have effected any alteration in the qualities of the object.

Idealists, of course, would deny this, and would maintain that the whiteness of an object, in common with its other qualities, is dependent upon its being perceived or known; that whiteness can, in fact, only be or exist for a mind. The term normally used by idealists to denote the sort of entity which we have called " a universal " is " concept," a concept being regarded as a piece of mental apparatus through and by means of which our thinking is performed. This apparatus imposes itself upon whatever the mind thinks about as a seal leaves its impression upon the wax it stamps, with the result that we think about the world as possessing those qualities which are in fact contributed by our minds. This view will be further considered in the chapter dealing with Kant, where some criticism of it will be offered.[1] For the present it is sufficient to point out that, if the mind of the perceiver or thinker is meant, the position reduces itself to the Subjective Idealism discussed in an earlier chapter, which, as we saw, is apt to develop into an unbelievable Solipsism.[2] If some other mind is meant, for example, a world mind or an absolute mind, the solipsist difficulty is, indeed, avoided, but others scarcely less formidable arise. Nor can this view be taken except by those who are willing to commit themselves to the full implications of the doctrine of Objective Idealism.[3]

Alternative (3), that we are thinking of a universal is not open to any of these objections, although, as we shall see later, it raises difficulties of its own.[4] According to this alternative, whiteness is a non-material, non-mental fact, to which all the particular things that are white are related in a peculiar way, and it is in virtue of this relation that the quality of whiteness belongs to them.

That the universe contains an innumerable quantity of non-material, non-mental entities—whiteness, justice, humanity, civilisation, one-ness, two-ness, and the like—is a view which, at first sight, seems startling to common sense. Nevertheless, it may with some plausibility be maintained that it is the only view which affords countenance to modes of thought and speech which common sense habitually employs. A couple of examples may help to elucidate this point.

Universals in Historical Thinking.   It is on the assumption that there are universals that the process known as historical thinking may be most plausibly interpreted. Let us consider a statement of the kind that will be found in any history book—for example, the statement that Cæsar crossed the Rubicon. Of what, it may be asked, are we thinking when we use the word " Cæsar " ? To what does it refer ? Clearly we are thinking of something, since the

[1] See Chapter XIV, pp. 376–381 and (for criticism) 394–401.
[2] See Chapter II, p. 56.
[3] See Chapter XV, pp. 412–428, for an account of these implications.
[4] See Chapter XI, pp. 299–306.

statement " Cæsar crossed the Rubicon " conveys an entirely different meaning to us from that conveyed by the statement " Alexander crossed the Rubicon." We know, for example, that the first is probably true, while the second is almost certainly false. Are we, then, thinking of some physical object ? Almost certainly we are not. Cæsar considered as a physical object has ceased to be, or rather the substance of his body has long ago been diffused through worms, plants, cattle, and human beings, so that to-day it is inextricably mingled with the physical substances of men, creatures and things. Now it is certainly not of this widely diffused substance that we are thinking when we say that Cæsar crossed the Rubicon. Moreover, it may well be doubted whether the physical body of Cæsar can ever have been *all* that a person would have wished to refer to, who made the statement about Cæsar.

Another suggestion might be that we are thinking of Cæsar's mind or spirit, and that the mind or spirit of Cæsar still continues to exist. But apart from the difficulty of understanding how Cæsar's *spirit* could have crossed the Rubicon, historical statements are normally made and understood without entailing any suggestion to the effect that human immortality is a condition of their being true. In fact, they are made and understood by many who would deny human immortality. It would not, then, seem that it is of Cæsar as an actually existing personage, whether considered as a mind or a body or both, that we were thinking when we made our historical statement.

Is, then, the object of our thinking some conception or idea which exists in our own minds ? Let us suppose that this is the case. Then two conclusions would seem to follow. First, since historian A would be thinking about one thing (a conception in his mind) and historian B about another (a conception in his), no two historians could ever think about the same thing. On this basis it is difficult to imagine how they could intelligibly communicate with or understand one another. Now it does seem to be the case that historians sometimes intelligibly communicate. Secondly, if history were only a succession of ideas or conceptions in the minds of historians, the abolition of historians would entail the abolition of history. If no mind were thinking of the fact that the Battle of Waterloo was fought in 1815, it would on this view cease to be a fact that the Battle of Waterloo was fought in that year. The views of some idealists do in fact entail this conclusion. But it is highly repugnant to our commonsense beliefs, and those who adopt it are committed to and must be prepared to accept all the consequences which follow from an extreme Idealism.[1] Moreover, if the view were correct, a generation brought up to believe that the Battle of Waterloo was fought in 1816 would by the very fact of their belief automatically produce an alteration in the date of the battle.

If they are not physical things and are not mental conceptions, we seem to be driven to the conclusion that historical events such as the Battle of Waterloo and historical personages such as Cæsar are, like universals, entities which do really exist in their own right in independence both of the minds that think about them and the physical occurrences that once took place in the spatio-temporal world.

Subsistent Objects.   Some philosophers are inclined to accept this conclusion, and assign to entities such as historical facts and personages a status similar to that which we have just postulated for universals. These philosophers, who are sometimes called conceptual realists, since they assert the independent reality of the facts referred to by the general notions which are usually called concepts, have made use of the term " subsistent objects " to denote all non-material, non-mental entities, such as, for example, Cæsar and the Battle of Waterloo. The significance of the word " subsistent " is that, although those who make use of it regard entities such as universals and historical objects as real and independent factors in the universe, the kind of being they believe them to possess is different

[1] e.g. from the Idealism of Hegel. See Chapter XV.

from that of the physical things which exist in the spatio-temporal world. To indicate this difference, physical things are said to exist while universals and subsistent objects are said to subsist. It must not, however, be supposed that most philosophers, or even most realist philosophers, would endorse this conclusion, or subscribe to the belief in subsistent objects. Many of those who, for the reasons given above, would admit the independent existence of universals such as whiteness or triangularity, would demur to the extension of the arguments to include the wider class of subsistent objects ; they would demur, that is to say, to postulating subsistence for historical personages and events. Even the belief in independently existing universals is very far from being a common belief among philosophers. Thus Bertrand Russell, some of whose arguments in favour of universals were introduced above, has in his later work abandoned the view that universals possess separate and independent being, and there is a tendency among other modern philosophers who were at one time conceptual realists to follow Russell in abandoning a position which they now regard as untenable. Some of the reasons which have led philosophers to reject Conceptual Realism, at least in its more extreme form, will be considered in the next chapter.[1]

Universals in Literary Criticism.   Nevertheless, the arguments for the independent being not only of universals but of subsistent objects seem to me to be strong, and at the risk of being thought to give too prominent a place to my own views in what purports to be an impartial survey of philosophical thought, I propose to supplement the above account with a further illustration indicative of the way in which the view that there are subsistent objects is postulated by the every-day expressions of our language. Let us take, as an example of such an expression : " *Hamlet* is a great play." Of what are we thinking when we use the word " Hamlet ? " Or, to put the question in

[1] See Chapter XI, pp. 302–305.

another form, what precisely is the nature of the entity to which we are applying the epithet " great ? "

Again, various alternatives suggest themselves. It may be said that the entity of which we are predicating the attribute of greatness is the manuscript upon which Shakespeare wrote the script of *Hamlet*, or the first folio edition, or a modern printed text, or the sum-total of all of these. But if all the printed copies of *Hamlet* were destroyed and a company of actors proceeded to play *Hamlet* from memory, there seems no reason to doubt that we should still be entitled to call *Hamlet* a great play and that we should mean something by doing so. The printed texts, even Shakespeare's original manuscript, are nothing more nor less than collections of black marks on a white or yellow background, and it is certainly not of these that we wish to assert greatness.

Similarly with regard to the productions of *Hamlet*. A production may be a bad one ; but no one would be tempted to argue from the fact that the production was bad that the greatness of *Hamlet* was thereby impaired. There is, in fact, a familiar and perfectly well understood distinction between the play and its production, and as the script is in the last resort a series of black marks on a white background, so the production turns out on analysis to be a series of movements on the part of the feet, arms and heads of the players, and of waves of sound travelling through the atmosphere originating in movements in their larynxes.

Is it, then, of some mental entity or set of entities that we are predicating greatness, when we speak of *Hamlet* ? Here again there are two alternatives. We may, it is said, be intending to refer to a set of ideas in Shakespeare's mind. But Shakespeare's mind is no longer in existence. Even if we are prepared to assert that the human mind survives death, and further to assume that the surviving mind of Shakespeare still contains the ideas that expressed themselves in *Hamlet*, it seems reasonably certain that this assertion and this assumption are not involved in the statement " *Hamlet* is a great play." Are we then, to invoke the hypothesis of floating ideas which are not the ideas of any mind but exist as it were *in vacuo*, and affirm that it is to these that we were referring ? The hypothesis seems, to say the least of it, unlikely.

Alternatively, it may be said that we are referring to ideas in our own minds, and in the minds of all those who are performing, or seeing, or reading the play, or at any time have performed, or seen, or read it and remember what they learned, saw, or read. This seems to be at first sight a more plausible suggestion, especially if it be supplemented with the further suggestion that the word " ideas " should in this connection be interpreted in a very wide sense, so as to include all the experiences, spiritual, emotional, and intellectual, which a cultivated person may enjoy on seeing a performance of *Hamlet* or in reading the play.

But (1) it seems to be most improbable that we are in fact referring to all these minds and experiences, most of which are unknown to us, when we make the statement " *Hamlet* is a great play." (2) If we were referring to them, we should, in so far as our own experience is concerned, be paying a totally undeserved compliment to ourselves. For it would be of certain events happening in our own minds that we should be asserting that *they* deserved the epithet " great." Now we certainly do not intend, when we praise a play, to pay ourselves any compliment of this kind. (3) If all those who are seeing and reading, and have seen and read *Hamlet*, were abolished, it would, if this view were true, cease to be a great play. I doubt if anybody who has really admired *Hamlet* believes this. (4) When we make this assertion about *Hamlet*, it certainly seems as if we are purporting to speak and we certainly believe ourselves to be speaking not about our own or about anybody else's experiences, but about something which *is the cause of* these experiences. Now this something is not, at least *prima facie*, itself an experience.

But if it is not of a text or a script or a performance or a collection of floating ideas or a set of experiences in any mind or minds that we are speaking, when we say " *Hamlet* is a great play," to *what* is it that we are attributing the characteristic of greatness ? The obvious answer is that it is to the play itself. And what account are we to give of the play itself, unless we are prepared to regard it as a member of the class of subsistent objects which are neither mental nor material but are, nevertheless, constituent factors of the universe possessing being in their own right.

Caution to Reader.   That the postulation of *Hamlet* as a subsistent object has far-reaching consequences, some of which constitute serious difficulties for this whole line of thought, the present writer would be the first to admit. Some of these consequences, and the difficulties which they entail will be considered in the next chapter. Meanwhile the reader is advised to adopt a cautious attitude towards the arguments which have just been advanced, and to regard them not as proofs of the independent reality of sub-sistent objects, but as examples of the considerations which have led some philosophers to include non-material and non-mental entities as factors in the universe. Now universals constitute one class and, as many would affirm, the most obvious class, of entities possessing this sort of being, and the establishment of the independent existence or subsistence of universals is one of the most distinctive achievements of Plato's philosophy. With this preliminary survey of the ground, I turn to Plato's theory proper.

PLATO'S THEORY OF IDEAS (OR FORMS)

Critical Analysis of the Sensible World.   I have already referred[1] to the two opposed views with regard to the nature of change which were current in Greek philosophy—the view of Heracleitus that everything is in a state of flux ; that change, in fact, is the only reality, and the view of Parmenides that change is an illusion. Plato's Theory of Ideas amounts in fact to an acceptance of both these

See Chapter VII, pp. 171-175, 178.

assertions qualified by a limitation of their scope. Plato, in other words, bifurcates the universe into two departments. The first is a flux of change, Heracleitus's world ; the second a changeless reality, Parmenides's.

Plato's theory starts from a critical analysis of the sensible world which is not in essence different from that which the subjective idealists, Locke and Berkeley, were later to undertake.[1] What sort of knowledge, he asks, do we have of the world which we experience by means of our senses ? Continuously, he points out how fallible and relative this knowledge is. If I put my hand which has been chilled in a blizzard into lukewarm water, I shall pronounce the water hot ; but a man coming out of a hot bath will find it cold. In other words, so far as the verdict of the senses goes, it is both hot and cold at the same time. An elephant will regard a rabbit as a small animal, but to a cheese-mite the rabbit will appear gigantic ; hence the rabbit seems to be both small and large at the same time according to the nature of the creature viewing it. Similarly, with regard to aesthetic and moral qualities. One man will find a picture beautiful which another considers ugly, and an action which seems admirable to one will seem base to another. It is clear, then, that, as Plato put it, objects of sense have no more right to be credited with certain qualities than they have to be credited with the contrary qualities. Whatever grounds there may be for saying that X has the quality A, are equally good grounds for saying that X has the quality B, where B is the opposite of A ; in other words, X has the qualities of both A and B at the same time, or, rather, it has neither of them, but fluctuates about, as Plato says, between both. X, therefore, is of such a character that no quality can be truly ascribed to it ; hence, since X has no definite quality, it cannot be quite real. If X is not quite real, we cannot have definite knowledge of it ; we can only have what Plato calls opinion. It is for this reason that we are enabled to pass contradictory judgements about the same thing as when,

[1] See Chapter II, pp. 39–50.

for example, different people assert in regard to the same picture that it is beautiful and ugly.

Opinion and Knowledge.
The argument leading to this conclusion is a celebrated one in the history of philosophy, and I give at length the following passage[1] from Book V of the *Republic*, which is typical of Plato's mode of philosophising :

" ' Does he that knows, know something or nothing ? Do you answer me for him.'

" ' I shall answer,' he said, ' that he knows something.'

" ' Something which is, or something which is not ? '

" ' Something which is. For how could that which is not be known ? '

" ' Then are we sure of this, in however many ways we look at it, that what is completely, is completely knowable, what in no way is, is in every way unknowable ? '

" ' Perfectly sure.'

" ' Good. Then if there be something so constituted as both to be and not to be, will it not lie between what absolutely is and what in all ways is not ? '

" ' It will.'

" ' Then knowledge is set over that which is, and ignorance of necessity over that which is not ; and over this that is between, must we not now seek for something between ignorance and knowledge, if there is such a thing ? '

" ' Certainly.'

" ' But do we say that belief is anything ? '

" ' Surely.'

" ' A power distinct from knowledge, or identical with it ? '

" ' Distinct.'

" ' Then belief is set over one thing and knowledge over another, each according to its own power ? '

" ' Yes.'

" ' Then is it not the nature of knowledge, being set over

[1] Translation by A. D. Lindsay.

that which is, to know how it is ? But first, I think we had better make this distinction.'

" ' What ? '

" ' We shall say that powers[1] are a certain general class of existences, by means of which, indeed, we and every other thing can do what we can. Sight and hearing, for example, I call powers. Perhaps you understand what I have in mind.'

" ' Yes, I understand.'

" ' Then listen to my opinion about them. In a power I see no colour or figure, or any such attributes as many other things have and in reference to which I distinguish them to myself as differing from one another. In a power I look only to that over which it is, and to what it effects, and on this principle I used the term power in each case ; and any powers which are set over the same thing, and have the same effect, I call the same ; if they are over different things and have different effects, I call them different. What is your practice ? Do you do the same ? '

" ' Yes,' he said.

" ' Then come back to this point, my excellent friend,' I said. ' Do you call knowledge a power, or, if not, in what class do you place it ? '

" ' It is a power, and the strongest of all powers,' he said.

" ' Further, shall we call belief a power or place it in some other class ? '

" ' Certainly not the latter,' he said, ' for that by which we are able to believe, is nothing else than belief.'

" ' But a little time ago you admitted that knowledge and belief are not the same.'

" ' How could any sensible man identify the infallible with the fallible ? ' he said.

" ' Good,' I said. ' Then clearly we have agreed that belief is distinct from knowledge ? '

" ' We have.'

" ' Then each of them has by nature a distinct power over distinct things ? '

[1] We should say " capacities " or " faculties " rather than " powers."

" ' Inevitably.'

" ' But knowledge surely is set over that which is, to know how it is ? '

" ' Yes.'

" ' While the part of belief, we assert, is to believe.'

" ' Yes.'

" ' Does it believe the same thing as knowledge knows ; and can what is known and what is believed be the same ; or is that impossible ? '

" ' Its impossibility follows from our admissions,' he said. ' If different powers are by nature set over different objects, and if belief and knowledge are both powers, each, as we assert, distinct from the other, it is incompatible with this that what is known and what is believed should be the same.'

" ' Then if that which is, is known, what is believed will be something different from that which is ? '

" ' It will.'

" ' Then will belief believe that which is not ? Or is it impossible even to believe that which is not ? Consider. Does not he who believes fix his belief on something ? or is it possible to believe and yet to believe nothing ? '

" ' That is impossible.'

" ' Then will he who believes, believe some one thing ? '

" ' Yes.'

" ' But that which is not, would be most accurately described not as one thing, but as nothing, would it not ? '

" ' Certainly.'

" ' Then do we not necessarily assign ignorance to not being and knowledge to being ? '

" ' That is right,' he said.

" ' Then belief will believe neither being nor not being ? '

" ' No.'

" ' And neither ignorance nor knowledge can be belief ? '

" ' Naturally not.'

" ' Then is belief something beyond these, surpassing knowledge in certainty or ignorance in uncertainty ? '

" ' No.'

" ' Rather,' I said, ' do you think belief darker than knowledge and brighter than ignorance ? '

" ' Yes, very much so.'

" ' Then does it lie within the limits of the two ? '

" ' Yes.'

" ' Then belief is between these two ? '

" ' Just so.'

" ' Then did we not say a little while ago that if we found anything which was and was not at the same time, that it would lie between what absolutely is and what thoroughly is not, and that set over it would be neither knowledge nor ignorance, but that which was found to be between ignorance and knowledge ? '

" ' Yes, and we were right.'

" ' But have we not now found something between these two which we call belief ? '

" ' We have.'

" ' Then apparently we have still left to find that which partakes of both being and not being and which could not rightly be described as either absolutely, and if we find it, we shall with justice be able to say that this is what is believed, so assigning extremes to extremes and mean to mean. Is not that the case ? '

" ' It is.'

" ' Then this having been established, I shall say, That worthy who thinks that there is no real beauty and no Form of real beauty eternal and invariable, but recognises many beautifuls, let him speak and answer—this lover of sights who will let no one say that the beautiful, and the just, and so on are one. " Of all these many beautifuls, O most excellent sir," we shall say, " is there any which will not appear ugly ? or of the just any that will not appear unjust ? or of the holies any which will not appear unholy ? " '

" ' No,' he said, ' they must appear somehow both beautiful and ugly, just and unjust, and so on with them all.'

" ' What of the many doubles ? May they not appear halves just as much as doubles ? '

" ' They may.'

" ' And so with the things we call great and small, and light and heavy, can one of those opposites be attributed to them any more than the other ? '

" ' No, at any moment every one of them may have both attributed to it.' . . .

. . . .

" ' Then do you know what to do with them,' I said, ' or have you any better place to put them than between being and not being ? For they will not appear in greater darkness than that which is not, by exceeding it in not being, nor in greater light than that which is, by exceeding it in being.'

" ' Perfectly true,' he said.

" ' Then we have apparently discovered that the multitude's multitudinous formulæ concerning the beautiful and so on tumble about somewhere between what is not and what absolutely is ? '

" ' We have.'

" ' But we agreed, if any such thing should be discovered, that we should have to call it the object of belief, not the object of knowledge, this shifting intermediate world being apprehended by the intermediate faculty.'

" ' We did.'

" ' Then we shall say that those who look at many beautifuls, but do not see real beauty, and are unable to follow another's guidance to it, and who see many justs but not real justice, and so on, these throughout believe but know nothing of what they believe ? '

" ' The conclusion is inevitable,' he said.

" ' But what are we to say of those who look at all the invariable unchanging realities ? Do they not know rather than believe ? '

" ' That conclusion too is inevitable.'

" ' Then may we not also say that they will admire and love the objects of knowledge, while the others love the objects of belief ? For do you not remember that we said that these loved and admired beautiful sounds and colours and the like, but real beauty they will not tolerate as being anything ? ' "

Summary. To summarise the above argument :—knowledge is set over against that which truly is, opinion against that which both is and is not, ignorance against that which completely is not. The thing which completely is either has or has not certain definite characteristics, and the only relation which knowledge can have to it is that of being aware of them. Knowledge, in other words, must be true, since it truly represents what is. In so far as a thing has no fixed and definite characteristics, we cannot have knowledge of it ; we can only have opinion. This, as we have seen, is the case with the sensible world. The appropriate attitude of the mind to the sensible world is, therefore, the attitude of opinion. Opinions may contradict each other and be at the same time true and false, since that about which they are opinions both has and at the same time has not the characteristics they assert of it. It is established, then, that we do not have knowledge of the sensible world. Nevertheless, as mathematics shows, and, Plato would add, science, we do have definite knowledge. Of what, then, is this knowledge ? Plato answers, of the world of Forms.

The Forms as Constitutive of the Real World. The existence of Forms, sometimes known as Ideas, is established by methods similar to those which we have already employed in demonstrating the presence in the universe of the entities which we have called universals. The Forms themselves are conceived after the model of universals, with three qualifications.

First, they are endowed with a higher degree of reality than that of particular things. They constitute, in short, a real world, whereas the world of sensible things or particulars is, as we have seen, only semi-real. The real world, for Plato, is the assemblage or collection of Forms. And, since they alone constitute reality, Plato endows them with attributes of nobility, almost of holiness. He always speaks of them with reverence, and conceives of them as in some sense constituting the goal of human endeavour as well as the objects of human knowledge.

Secondly, there is a difference between our knowledge of the Forms and our knowledge of particulars. In fact our knowledge of particulars is not, for Plato, entitled to be called knowledge at all. It is of the Forms that we have knowledge as opposed to mere opinion, and the object of philosophy is to elevate the soul from the realm of opinion in which her objects are the fleeting, changing things of sense, into the realm of knowledge, where she may come face to face with the Forms.

Thirdly, the Forms are regarded as the source of the being of particulars. It is the Forms which bestow upon the sensible objects whatever qualities they are found to exhibit, and so endow them with such reality as they possess, that is to say, with semi-reality.

Relation between the Forms and the Sensible World.
In virtue of what relation do the Forms perform this office? The Forms, says Plato, " manifest themselves " in the things of sense, and things of sense, he also says, " participate in " the Forms. The relation, then, which he seems to be suggesting, although his language is not as precise as could be wished,[1] is the relation between a number of moulds or dies and a flux of featureless stuff upon which the dies stamp form and shape. In general, he writes as if he wished us to think of the Forms as constituting a permanent and unchanging structure vaguely discernible beneath the changing flux of appearances, which surge to and fro obscuring without hiding its outlines. These, of course, are only metaphors, and must not be pressed. They are more particularly defective, in so far as they fail to make provision for what was undoubtedly Plato's intention,

[1] See Chapter XI, pp. 295–297, for a criticism of Plato's theory on this point.

namely, to ascribe to the Forms the causation of the world of sensible things : for, he says, the sensible world owes its being to the presence in it of the Forms.

There is, however, a famous passage in the *Timæus*, Plato's great cosmological dialogue, in which he is trying to conceive of the manner in which God created the world, which suggests a somewhat different conception. In the Timæus Plato represents God and the Forms as distinct but co-ordinate realities neither of which is dependent upon the other. God did not, in other words, create the Forms, nor is He dependent upon them, but exists, as it were, side by side with them. Nevertheless, the activities of God in creating the world are dependent on and conditioned by the Forms, in the sense that His knowledge of the Forms gives him the ideal or aim for His activity of creation. What God does, then, is to mediate between the Forms and the flux of becoming, modelling out of the flux things which are made after the likeness of the Forms, or (for Plato's mode of speaking admits of different interpretations) bringing the Forms as it were to birth in the flux. Thus the world of sensible things is the result of the modelling by God of the featureless flux after the likeness of the Forms, or the causing by God of the Forms to manifest themselves in the flux. The whole of this conception belongs, however, to the more speculative side of Plato's philosophy. The relationship between God, the Forms, and the flux of events cannot be precisely stated because it is never precisely envisaged. Plato's ideas of God are vague in the extreme, and when he wishes to speak of Him he drops into the language of myth and metaphor, whereas his expressions when speaking of the Forms are normally as clear and precise as the multiplication table.

The Theory Restated.   It is, indeed, on grounds that are strictly logical that Plato in the last resort bases his theory. That it lends itself very easily to mystical development is true. It is also true that Plato's writings afford some countenance for this development. But the theory itself is independent of the mystical views with which it has often, especially by subsequent philosophers, been linked. It is presented to us as an explanation partly of the problem of Substance, partly of the problem of knowledge. The problem of Substance turns, as we have seen, upon the relation between the matter of things and their qualities. The commonsense notion of Substance can be shown on analysis to resolve itself into the conception of a physical world, which consists of a qualityless core of brute stuff to which qualities somehow become attached. The problem of knowledge arises for Plato from the fact that, if the sensible world contains nothing which possesses stable qualities, it contains nothing which can certainly and definitely be known.

The theory—the point must be stressed, since Plato's view is in this respect frequently misrepresented—is in no sense an idealist one. There is no suggestion that the sensible objects of which we have opinion, still less that the Forms of which we have knowledge, are the products of our own knowing or are dependent upon it. Plato is quite definite on the point that knowledge must always be *of* something. It must, in fact, have an object. In the Dialogue known as the *Parmenides* the suggestion is put forward that the Forms may be mental in the sense of being ideas in somebody's mind, only to be rebutted by the statement that we cannot have an idea of nothing. All knowledge in fact must be directed upon something which is other than and independent of the knower. Plato's Forms, then, are not states of the knowing mind, but objects distinct from it about which it has knowledge. Moreover, in the passage quoted above,[1] we see that Plato correlates different kinds of knowledge with different grades of being. Certain knowledge is of that which truly and completely is ; opinion is about that which partly is and partly is not ; ignorance is of that which completely is not.

What, then, are we to say of that which completely is not ? Here we enter the realm of controversy. For how

[1] See above pp. 272–277.

can we make any affirmation about that which is not?
Plato himself has told us that all knowledge is of, and is
directed upon, something; that we cannot in fact know
nothing ; that which is not must, therefore, presumably
have some sort of being, in order that we may be able to
speak of it significantly at all. It must, to put the point
paradoxically, be " something," even if only in order that
we can say of it meaningfully that it is nothing. For in order
that the statement that it is nothing may have meaning, there
must be something for the statement to refer to. Moreover,
Plato's argument suggests, if it does not explicitly affirm,
that the world of sensible things, the world of semi-reality
derives its being from two sources, the world of reality
and the world of non-reality into which the Forms enter,
sensible objects being the result of the manifestation
of the Forms in a featureless flux. Hence, some conclude
that, when Plato talked of the world of non-being, of that
which completely is not, what he in fact meant was that
which has no discernible qualities or properties, and
cannot therefore be an object for the mind's knowledge.
Assuming this interpretation to be correct, the Platonic
universe consists of Forms, of a featureless stuff in which
the Forms are manifested, and of a sensible world of
physical things owning a reality mid-way between the
Forms and the featureless stuff in which the Forms are
manifested.

The foregoing sketch of one of the most famous theories
in philosophy requires to be supplemented and amended
in three respects before it is complete.

I. THE FORM OF THE GOOD

We have hitherto conceived of the real world as consisting
of an assemblage of Forms. There is apparently a Form
for each of the qualities which may be possessed by a
number of things in common, and with a possible exception
in favour of the Forms of Truth, Goodness and Beauty
which Plato speaks of with an especial reverence, there

is no suggestion of any order of priority among the Forms. There is, however, a celebrated passage in the *Republic* in which Plato accords a quite special position to one of the Forms, the Form of the Good. He is here describing the progress which the soul makes in knowledge of reality. By following certain studies which give proficiency in weighing, measuring and counting, recommended on the ground that they train the soul in accuracy and precision, the soul is gradually elevated from a view of the sensible world to a knowledge of the Forms. The advance here described is broadly speaking that from the level of common-sense to the level of science, at which the world ceases to be a flux of meaningless phenomena and the principles are discerned which govern the workings of phenomena. But in the passage in question a further advance is indicated. Taking the first principles of the science as hypotheses, the soul delves as it were, behind[1] them in search of the grounds for these hypotheses. At the end of its quest it comes upon the Form of the Good. The soul's apprehension of the Form is sharply distinguished from the strictly logical, the purely intellectual process which has led up to it. It is, in fact, described in the language of a mystical vision. Once apprehended, the Form is recognised both as reality and as the explanation of reality. The Form of the Good is, Plato tells us, to the world of Forms what " its offspring," the sun, is to the visible world. Now the sun has a double function. It is both the cause of the being of things and the cause of their being known, the source of the light by means of which the eye sees and the source of that which the eye sees. Similarly in the intellectual world, the Form of its Good is at once the source of knowledge on the part of the knowing mind and the source of the reality of the objects which the mind knows. And just as the sun is not itself light or growth, but is their cause,

[1] This suggestion is worked out by Aristotle, and recalls his conception of Logic as the study which, taking the postulates of the special sciences as hypotheses, seeks to establish the common principles which underlie them all. See Chapter V, pp. 137–139.

so the Form of the Good is not itself that which *is*, nor is it the knowledge of it, but it is the source of both.

What are we entitled to deduce from this passage? First, that the Form of the Good stands to other Forms in the same relation as that in which they stand to sensible things. It is, that is to say, the source of their being. Secondly, that it is a single completely sufficient principle of explanation, from which all the knowledge obtained by the various special sciences is in the last resort derivable. In the light of the knowledge of this principle, were such knowledge attained, the reason why all things are as they are would be understood, and from it, the first principles of the sciences, hitherto treated as hypotheses, would appear in the light of necessary deductions. The Form of the Good from this point of view is a Principle of Sufficient Reason. Apprehending it, we should realise precisely why what is so must be so ; contingency in other words would disappear from the world and necessity would take its place.

The account of the Form of the Good given in the *Republic* is not developed. Nowhere else except in the Platonic myths are we taken beyond and behind the world of assembled Forms, a world which, since the Forms are many, is essentially a pluralistic one, that is to say, a world consisting of many different factors, each of which is independently and completely real. In this passage alone Plato goes beyond the pluralistic conception by suggesting a fundamental unifying principle which is at once the source of the Forms and their logical explanation.

II. ANAMNESIS AND REINCARNATION

As Plato propounds it, the Form of the Good is a mystical rather than a logical doctrine. Mystical also is his theory of anamnesis or recollection, although it too derives initially from a logical basis. The basis is Plato's attempt to answer the question, " How can we ever come to know a new thing, in that sense of the word 'know' in which to know a new thing, is to understand what a new thing is ? " At first sight, the problem is a little difficult to grasp. It is not, indeed, obvious why there should be a problem at all. An illustration may perhaps help to elucidate it. Let us suppose that I am trying to remember a tune that I recently heard at a concert. Various tunes come into my mind and are rejected as not being *the* tune of which I am in search. The experience is a familiar one. But how, it may be asked, can I reject the tunes that suggest themselves, unless I already in some sense know the tune of which I am in search? It is only in so far as I do have this knowledge of the tune that I want, that I shall be in a position to say " This one which has just come into my mind is *not* the tune that I want." In other words, I must be credited with *in some sense* knowing the tune of which I am in search all the time I am trying to think of it.

Plato's theory of anamnesis purports to tell us what this sense is. He points out that, whenever we come to know something on what appears to us to be the first occasion, the fact that we do come to know it presupposes some original acquaintance with what is known. To put this point in another way, we cannot learn something fresh without already in some sense knowing what it is that we want to learn, so that the thing learned is not accurately described as something completely fresh ; the learning of it is only a rediscovery of what is already in some sense known already.

WHAT LEARNING INVOLVES. This is brought out by an illustration in the Dialogue called the *Meno*, where Socrates cross-examines a slave in order to throw light upon the nature of his knowledge of mathematical propositions. The slave is placed before the figure of a square, and Socrates proceeds to question him as to the nature of the square whose area is double that of the original square. Can he, for example, give any information about the side of this double square ? The slave is at first at a loss, and makes a number of false suggestions. He suggests, for example, that the side of the double square is double the side of the original square, but in due course sees his error from " the nature of the thing itself," that is to say, from a simple inspection of the geometrical figure. Finally, he perceives in the diagonal of the given square the side of the double square which he is seeking. He sees this suddenly, and he sees it for himself ; Socrates does not, that is to say, tell him the answer. Socrates's rôle is that of a cross-examiner whose object is to turn the attention of the examinee in the direction of an answer which he must see for himself or not at all. Evidently, therefore, Socrates concludes, the slave had in himself as an original possession the knowledge of which he is suddenly made conscious. Thus " teaching " is a process of directing the attention of the pupil to what he already knows. The teacher does not impart informatoin to the pupil. He merely enables the pupil to convince himself of something which he sees for himself. Similarly learning is a process by which the soul becomes re-acquainted with what it already knows, or knows, but has forgotten that it knows. Learning, then, is the apprehension of inborn knowledge. It is " to recover of oneself knowledge from within oneself."

THE PRE-HISTORY OF THE SOUL. Only on the assumption that learning is " a recovery of inborn knowledge," can the process of coming to know what appears to be " new " be explained. As Plato sums the matter up : we cannot come by new knowledge. For, either we already know the knowledge which we wish to acquire, in which case the knowledge is not new, or we do not know the knowledge which we wish to acquire, in which case we cannot know when we acquire it. But if all the knowledge which we *appear* to acquire is already in some sense possessed by us, how are we to explain the fact of our possession of it ? Plato's answer is to be found in his doctrine of anamnesis or recollection. In contradistinction to the grounds for it, which, as we have seen, are of a logical order, the doctrine is itself a mystical one, which is couched in the language of metaphor and myth. Plato, in effect, conceives of the soul as having pre-existed its bodily incarnation. In a famous myth in the *Phædrus* he pictures it, as yet un-embodied, under the likeness of a charioteer borne on a car drawn by two winged steeds, spirit and appetite. It moves forward with the great procession of the gods towards its goal, where the eternal Forms may be viewed in all their purity unmixed with matter. This goal is described as a " place above the heavens." Failing to control its steeds, the soul " loses its wings " and falls to earth where it becomes incarnated in a body and forgets " this imperial palace whence it came." Thus embodied in the flesh, the soul loses its status as a member of the world of being and enters the world of becoming. Seeing with the eye of the body, it can no longer view the Forms in themselves, but only their manifestation or representation in a material setting. So manifested they serve, albeit blurred and distorted by their material investiture, to remind the soul of the direct knowledge which it had of them in its previous condition, and it is in virtue of this previous knowledge that it recognises the presence of the Forms in material things.

The doctrine applies perhaps with the greatest appro-priateness to the case of aesthetic experience, and receives its fullest working out in relation to the form of Beauty. Why, asks Plato in effect, is the soul thrilled by beautiful things ? Because, he answers, it is reminded by them of the Form of Beauty which it once knew with fullness and directness, but has since forgotten. When it sees beautiful things it again becomes conscious of the Form which they image, albeit obscurely represented in a material medium, and is transported by the unconscious memory of that which the visible image calls up. Plato's theory of æsthetics will be considered at length in Chapter XIII.

The theory entails as a corollary the doctrine of re-incarnation. The soul makes a number of appearances in the world of becoming, with apparent intervals in the world of being. On each occasion of its entry into the world of becoming, it assumes a new shape, appearing sometimes in an animal body, sometimes in a human. Plato's teaching on this subject is, however, always enshrined in the form of myth—the Myth of Er at the end of the *Republic* is a typical illustration—and, although he appears to have believed strongly in the immortality of the soul, and gave reasons for his belief, he brings forward no serious grounds of a philosophical order for his belief in reincarnation. Indeed, it is not perhaps a belief which in the last resort he would have sought to defend by means of logical argument. Nor is there any suggestion in Plato of the view, common in Hindu philosophy, that the soul after a succession of bodily incarnations will be released from its Karma, the law which requires of it moral compensation for its own past misdeeds, and condemns it, until such time as it has fully requited them, to successive bodily incarnations, at the end of which it will pass into a condition of static blessedness which is scarcely distinguishable from a condition of nothingness.

III: ETHICAL AND POLITICAL IMPLICATIONS

IMPORTANCE OF PHILOSOPHY. Plato, however, strongly suggests—and this is the third point upon which I wish to touch—that the progress of the soul is to be measured by its increasing knowledge of the Forms, an increasing knowledge which is represented as a development away from the world of becoming in the direction of the world of being. It is not so much that the soul leaves the first world to enter the second, as that it advances from a knowledge of the first to the second. Herein lies the essence of Plato's defence and commendation of philosophy as the highest pursuit of the human mind. It is by means of philosophy and the special kind of training that philosophy gives, that the soul is elevated from the world of changing perishable things to the world of true and changeless being. Thus Plato describes the function of education, and more particularly of the education of the philosopher, as that of wheeling the soul " round from the perishing world " to the " contemplation of the real world and the brightest part thereof." Thus whereas the attention of the ordinary man is fixed upon the world of becoming, about which he has opinions and only opinions, the attention of the philosopher is fixed upon the world of being, of which he has knowledge. It is in the light of this knowledge that the philosopher is able to judge truly what is good for man and for the community. Hence the claim, which at first sight appears paradoxical, that the philosopher should be entrusted with the government of the Platonic ideal State. It is not, indeed, until " philosophers are kings," that the ideal State can be founded.

THE TWO LEVELS OF MORALITY. Problems of moral and political philosophy do not fall directly within the scope of this book, and no account can therefore be given of the detailed working out of Plato's ethical and political theories.[1] The connection between politics, ethics and metaphysics is, however, for Plato so close, and the principles which inform the government of his ideal State are so directly derivable from his conception of reality and his definition of the philosopher as a man who knows reality, that I have thought it appropriate to insert here a short passage rounding off this sketch of Plato's metaphysics with an indication of its political and ethical corollaries.

Plato's philosopher is very far from being an abstract thinker devoted solely to the pursuit of the speculative life. He is, on the contrary, entrusted with the management of practical affairs in the administration of which, Plato suggests, he will find his duty, if not his pleasure. Plato's most famous Dialogue, the *Republic*, is not a mere collection of theoretical discussions about government, an academic exercise in Utopia-making, but a serious project

[1] The reader who desires to acquaint himself with Plato's moral and political philosophy is recommended to read A. E. Taylor's standard work, *Plato*.

of practical reform, for the inauguration and successful completion of which he looked to the philosopher.

Accepting Plato's definition of a philosopher as a person who knows reality, and knows, therefore, among other things, what Good is in itself, assuming also that philosophers are kings, it will follow that the laws which they prescribe for the governance of the State will embody their knowledge of what is good. Their laws, that is to say, will be drawn up upon the model of the ideal laws which the philosophers have discerned in the world of reality, and they will be, therefore, the best possible laws. Being the best possible, they will constitute a framework such that, by ordering their lives in accordance with it, the citizens will be automatically constrained to do what is good. Not being philosophers, the ordinary citizens will be ignorant of what virtue is and of why they should pursue it ; they will lack, that is to say, a spontaneous and self-conscious morality. But by the mere process of living in accordance with the State's laws they will attain to such virtue as lies within their capacity. Thus, in Plato's State the morality of the ordinary citizen will spring, not from an insight into what is good, nor from a conviction that good ought to be pursued and evil eschewed, but simply from his obedience to public opinion and the laws, an obedience which, as a result of his social training and education, has become second nature.

Plato in effect concedes that the morality of the ordinary man is and must always be conventional, and the concession constitutes his fundamental argument against democracy. The ordinary man is too busy or too stupid to discover his duty or to solve his moral problems for himself ; yet it is essential for him to believe something, and to have some code to live by. He is constrained, therefore, to obtain his morals from the social shop. His sense of right and wrong is formed for him, that is to say, by his social environment as it expresses itself in law and public opinion. At Plato's social shop he will obtain the best suit of morals which he is capable of wearing, by living in obedience to laws which, being framed on the model of those that exist in the real world, enjoin upon him as his duty the highest conduct of which he is capable.

The distinctive feature of this conception of private morality and civic duty is directly derivable from the metaphysical theory. The highest virtue—the virtue, that is to say, which consists not only in having right opinions about what is good, but in knowing why what is good is good—is that of the philosopher. Its achievement depends upon a direct knowledge of the Forms. A lower stage of virtue, the virtue of the " citizen," is the moral condition of a loyal member of a properly trained community. His emotions, his appetites and his sentiments reflect and are in accordance with the laws of right living laid down by his rulers, but he has himself no insight into the grounds or nature of their rightness. The most that can be done, therefore, for the ordinary citizen is by means of education and environment to induce him to perform blindly, as it were, and unselfconsciously those actions which he would perform, if he were really virtuous in the higher sense.

Pull of the Forms.   To return to the metaphysical theory, the notion of the soul of man striving to emancipate itself from the world of becoming, in order to attain to a more complete knowledge of the world of being, is not confined to the human soul. Everything, Plato seems to suggest, is imbued with a similar striving. But while the striving of the soul is for completer knowledge or vision, that of things is for completer reality. Sensible things are, as we have seen, constituted by the manifestation of a Form in a featureless subject matter. The manifestation of the Form, is, however, obscured and distorted by the subject matter, with the result that it is only imperfectly that the sensible world copies the real world. Things in fact do not adequately represent the Forms in which they participate ; they only approximate to them with a greater or less degree of imperfection. Hence, Plato's suggestion that things in the world of becoming are continually trying to manifest more completely the Forms which are present in them. To put the point in another way, since such being as they possess is due to the presence of the Forms in them, they are continually trying more completely to realise *themselves*.

The conception of things as trying to realise and make actual their own real nature which in the world of becoming remains only potential, never more than a suggestion in Plato, is, as we have seen, worked out with greater completeness by Aristotle.[1] It applies, it is obvious, most satisfactorily to the cases of growing and developing things and of manufactured works of art. The idea of a stone trying ever more completely to manifest the Form of " stoniness " may seem strained and absurd, but there is little difficulty about the conception of an acorn trying to become more completely an oak—that is to say, to realise the Form of " oakiness " ; while the conception of the artist as trying to realise in intractable material the vision that inspires or the idea that delights him, is familiar enough. As Plato would say, the sculptor making a statue is trying ever more completely to manifest in stone the Form which he is taking as his subject.

Nor does Plato confine this application of his theory to the construction of works of art. He is quite prepared to think of the bed maker as one who is trying to realise in a material setting his conception of the Form of a bed.

The Reality of Things.

The general suggestion that things are continually striving, subject to the limitations imposed by the material of which they are made, to realise or manifest a Form, and that their growth is, accordingly, prompted by the endeavour to approximate to an ideal standard which is also that of their own real nature, is closely analogous to the conception of teleological causation described in an earlier chapter in connec-

[1] See Chapter VII, pp. 183, 184 and 201-20

tion with Aristotle's philosophy.[1] Both Plato and Aristotle tend to think of the most perfect development of a thing as constituting its " real nature." Both tend to think of this " real nature " as exercising a pull over the thing's less mature phases and determining a development in the direction of an ever greater approximation towards it. The dynamic in the world, in virtue of which things grow and change, derives it is implied—although the implication is never more than hinted at in Plato—from an innate tendency on the part of each thing to realise its particular good. For Plato this particular good is the complete manifestation or realisation of the Form (or Forms) whose presence constitutes the being of the thing.

———————

For a discussion of universals and particulars see Bertrand Russell's *The Problems of Philosophy*, Chapters IX and X, and *Mysticism and Logic*, Chapter X.

The standard edition of Plato is Benjamin Jowett's *The Dialogues of Plato*. The *Republic*, the *Parmenides* and the *Timaeus* are important representative dialogues. Standard works on Plato's philosophy are :

RITTER, C.   The Essence of Plato's Philosophy.

TAYLOR, A. E.   Plato.

NETTLESHIP, R. L.   Lectures on the Republic of Plato.

STEWART, J. A.   Plato's Doctrine of Ideas.

[1] See Chapter VII, pp. 185–187.

*Chapter XI : ARISTOTLE'S CRITICISM: THE WORLD OF SUBSISTENCE : SCHOLASTIC PHILOSOPHY

In this chapter it is proposed to consider some of the criticisms to which Plato's theory and its developments are exposed. These criticisms fall into two categories. There are, first, criticisms which other philosophers have brought against Plato's theory in the form in which he stated it, and there are, secondly, criticisms which may be directed against the whole mode of thinking which leads to the establishment of the independent being of universals. The theory of subsistent objects is in a quite special degree exposed to this latter kind of criticism.

I. HISTORICAL CRITICISMS OF PLATO'S THEORY OF IDEAS

Aristotle's Criticisms.   The best known criticisms of Plato's theory are those advanced by Aristotle. Aristotle adopted, at any rate at the outset of his philosophy, a thoroughly commonsense attitude to the Theory of Ideas. Misled by the admitted fact that things possess common characteristics, Plato had, he complained, attributed to the fact a wholly unjustifiable significance, abstracting the characteristics from the things which owned them, and then elevating the characteristics so abstracted into a separate realm of their own, where they were endowed with mystical qualities of pure being. Common characteristics, Aristotle agreed, are certainly met with in things ; but they are not met with outside them. We never come across " whiteness " by itself, existing, as it were, *in vacuo* ; " whiteness " is always a quality of some white thing. We should not, therefore, he contended, needlessly postulate the existence of entities which are never experienced, but should limit the realm of what exists to those entities which are actually met with in experience, namely, white things. Forms, then, are not mystical entities somehow existing before things, and bringing things into being by manifesting themselves in them ; they are to be found always and only within things, and they are nothing more nor less than those qualities which things have in common.

Aristotle and Theory of Knowledge.   This criticism of Aristotle's is based upon strictly empirical grounds. We do not, he says, *experience* universals or Forms. Therefore we may legitimately deny them. But " experience " in this connection must be interpreted as sense experience, since we can certainly *think* about universals. Aristotle's criticism, therefore, springs from and entails an empirical view of the experience which we have of the external world. That he was by no means oblivious of the *a priori* element which, as we have seen[1], all experience contains, is amply shown by his contribution to the theory of logic.[2] But he is certainly apt when criticising Plato to write as if our knowledge of the sensible world was a matter of sense experience only. Aristotle, indeed, tries hard to be a thoroughgoing empiricist. Invariably he begins his philosophical reflections by adopting the attitude of the man in the street, who is distrustful of metaphysical abstractions and profoundly sceptical of mystical moonshine. This attitude may or may not be the right one. It is a good rule in philosophy to keep as close to common sense as we can ; but it is significant that in almost every case Aristotle turns out in the last resort to be unable to maintain his attitude. Starting from a standpoint which is the antithesis of Plato's, his line of thought leads him on almost every metaphysical issue to adopt positions which are closely similar. A

[1]See Chapter IV pp. 113–115. [2] See Chapter V, pp. 127, 137–140,

philosopher who asserts the existence of a universal Prime Mover,[1] and insists upon the intuitive character of our perception of the first premises of all reasoning[2] is in no position to look askance at *a priori* knowledge, or to discard arguments and disown entities merely because the arguments are not derived from, the entities not found in, the experience of the senses.

The "Third Man" Argument.

But Aristotle has another criticism of a logical order which has considerable historical celebrity. This is known as the "Third Man" criticism. Wherever there are discovered to be two entities possessing a common quality, Plato postulates a Form. Thus the existence of two men with common attributes leads him to invoke a Form of Man or Humanity. Consider, then, says Aristotle, a man and the Form of Man. Have they not attributes in common? Obviously they have, namely, human or mannish attributes. Therefore, on Plato's own showing, we shall have to postulate another Form in which both participate to account for these common attributes. We are, then, now required to postulate two Forms, the Form of Man, in which both men participate, and another Form of Man in which a particular man and the Form of Man participate. The process, it is obvious, can be continued indefinitely. We are, therefore, committed to postulating an infinite number of Forms, wherever Plato would have us postulate one.

Relation of Forms to Particulars.

A more substantial criticism turns upon the relation of the Forms to particulars. This, as I have already noted,[3] is a matter upon which Plato's language is far from clear. Two expressions are commonly used to describe this relation. The particulars are said to "participate in" the Forms, which are also "manifested in" them; and the particulars "copy" or "approximate to" the Forms. When using expressions

[1] See Chapter VII, pp. 201–203.   [2] See Chapter V, pp. 137–139.
[3] See Chapter X, p. 278

of the first type, Plato emphasises the causative function of the Forms in relation to the particulars, the presence of the Forms being regarded as the source of the being of the particulars. When using the second type of expression, he is content to say that the particulars are like the Forms, as like, that is to say, as their status as inhabitants of the world of becoming permits. But the two modes of expression conceal an important difference. The first suggests that the two worlds are continuous one with the other, the Forms entering into and determining the characteristics of sensible things as a pair of glove-stretchers enters into and determines the shape and contours of a pair of gloves. But if this is, in fact, the relation, it is impossible to maintain the clear-cut distinction between being and becoming upon which Plato insists. Plato is most emphatic on this point, which, more than any other feature of his theory, has proved a stumbling-block to critics. The world of Forms, he insists, is aloof and apart, and has no continuity with the world of becoming. The whole world of becoming could, indeed, be swept away without producing any modification in the world of Forms. How, then, it may be asked, can this world of aloof and changeless being enter into the sensible world of changeful becoming ? How, indeed, in any event, can that which is real, namely, the Forms, be credited with the capacity to enter into relations with that which is semi-real, relations of so intimate a type that that which truly is, namely, the Forms, is actually postulated as the inmost core and essence of that which partially is and partially is not. If, on the other hand, we think of the world of becoming as owning no causal relation with the world of being, but merely as imitating or copying it, while the aloofness of the Forms is preserved and the difficulty of envisaging a mode of connection between two different orders of reality disappears, we find that we are running counter to the most explicit statements on the subjects by Plato himself. The Form of the Good, he says, is like the sun ; it is the source of the being of the sensible, as the sun is of the visible world. Again, imperfect approximations to the Forms which appear in the world of becoming, for example, imperfectly just acts or imperfectly straight lines, derive whatever justice or straightness they possess from the presence of the Forms in them.

Moreover, to postulate two separate worlds, one of which tries to be as like the other as the nature of its subject matter allows, is, the critics complain, to say the least of it, an untidy way of conceiving the universe. The universe may, of course, be such as this interpretation of Plato's view suggests ; it may, that is to say, consist of two separate although related worlds. But it would certainly be an odd chance if it were. Some have gone so far as to discern in Plato's writings two different theories of Forms, an earlier and a later, the difference between them being illustrated by the two modes of conceiving the relation between the Forms and the particulars. According to the earlier theory, the two worlds are continuous, the particulars participating in the Forms. The later theory drops continuity of being and envisages the relation as one of imitation only. The evidence for this view is not, however, very convincing.

Sources of Plato's Theory.

The truth of the matter seems to be that Plato was led to elaborate his theory by reflection on two rather different types of experience, moral experience and mathematical experience. The question with which he was concerned was, " What conclusions do the fact that morality and mathematics are as they are entitle us to draw as to the nature of reality ? " Both goodness and mathematics were, he considered, to be interpreted teleologically[1] with reference to some ideal goal or standard which gave meaning and reality to such imperfect approximations to it as were to be found in the characters of men and the figures of geometry. A good man, in other words, was always trying to realise a degree of goodness beyond what he had attained. A triangle was

[1] See Chapter VII, pp. 185, 186.

always trying to achieve as much triangularity as the inadequacies of the materials of which it was constructed —lines, for example, which had breadth as well as length, intersecting at points which had magnitude as well as position—permitted. But, while the goodness of the good man could reasonably be represented as due to the presence of some principle of goodness within him, inspiring his actions and encouraging him to compass an ever greater degree of virtue, it was a little difficult to think of a triangle drawn on the blackboard as literally harbouring in its structure the Form of triangularity. It might copy the Form, approximating to it as nearly as its physical limitations allowed, but it seemed a little far-fetched to endow it with an informing dynamic principle, a principle which was nothing less than the Form itself striving to express itself in and through its visible representative. Hence, while the facts of moral experience indicated and even demanded the relation of participation, the principle of goodness informing the character and make-up of the moral man, the facts of mathematics pointed rather to the relation of copying or imitation. Proceeding on the basis of this suggestion, we may conceive of Plato as stressing at one time the one type of relation, at another the other, according to whether his attention was chiefly directed upon ethical or mathematical facts.

The Motionlessness of the Forms.   The most serious criticism of all is directed against the apparently static and changeless character of Plato's world. Even if the *existence* of sensible things can be explained in terms of Plato's formula, their *motion*—that is to say, their coming into existence and their going out of existence—it is said, cannot. Suppose that we agree that the Form of Whiteness is the cause of there being white things, the Form of Triangularity the cause of there being triangles, and so on. Now since the Forms themselves are immutable and motionless, the world which copies them ought also to be immutable and motionless. The world of becoming ought, in fact, if it imitates the Forms, to be as static as the Forms themselves. Yet one of the outstanding characteristics of the sensible world is that it is a changing world. Things in it change and decay, come into existence and perish. Whence, it may be asked, on Plato's view, is the principle of change to be derived ? If things come to be and again cease to be because of the manifestation of Forms in and their withdrawal from them, why should a changeless Form manifest itself and withdraw ? What, in other words, is the principle which determines the appearances and disappearances of the Forms in the sensible world ?

The criticism is, then, that Plato makes no attempt to explain why, if the Forms are the cause of the being of sensible objects, these objects should arise, develop and decay. The obvious explanation would seem to be that there is some principle of motion in the Forms themselves. But this Plato emphatically rejects. It was this absence of any source of movement in Plato's world which partly led Aristotle to postulate God as a principle of movement, the Prime Mover of the Universe.[1] Change and development in things can then be attributed to the pull which God exerts over the world as, in its yearning and love for Him, it seeks ever to know Him more fully and to approach Him more closely. It is in virtue of this movement that, in Aristotle's view, the Forms which are first potential in things are made actual.[2] Thus the world's yearning for God supplies in Aristotle's philosophy the principle of motion which Plato's is said to lack.

II. CRITICISMS OF CONCEPTUAL REALISM

Difficulty of Setting Bounds to its Application.   The above criticisms are directed against the particular form of Conceptual Realism embodied in Plato's Theory of Ideas. There is, however, a further criticism which may be urged against the more general doctrine of Conceptual Realism,

[1] See Chapter VII, pp. 202, 203.   [2] See Chapter VII, pp. 181–183.

which asserts the real and independent existence or subsistence of concepts or universals. This criticism arises from the difficulty, once the separate existence of Plato's Forms has been established, of setting bounds to the application of the arguments which establish it. As I have already pointed out, it was by reflection on the implications of moral experience and mathematical facts that Plato was originally led to formulate his theory. So far, then, as these two spheres are concerned, we are on comparatively safe ground. But Plato himself extended the application of the theory of Forms to account for the coming into existence and development of physical things. In the *Republic* we are bidden to postulate a Form wherever several things are called by the same name ; thus Plato speaks specifically of the Form of a bed in which all beds participate. Are we then to postulate Forms for every class of particular things ? Apparently not : for in a famous passage in the *Parmenides*, where the question is put to Socrates, whether there are Forms of " hair, mud and dirt, or anything else that is foul and base," Socrates answers that there are not. Unfortunately, however, once Plato's line of argument is adopted, it is very difficult to see why there should not be such Forms. We can, for example, think of hair which is not any particular hair, of mud which does not exist in any particular place, and so on. Moreover, we can go further and think of mythical creatures such as griffins and unicorns. Are we then to postulate Forms for these, Forms of which we should, presumably, have to say, that they do not at the moment happen to be manifested in any particular instances ?

The Independent Being or Subsistence of Relations. The question has been exhaustively discussed by modern philosophers, more particularly in connection with the views of the Austrian philosopher, Meinong, who maintained the theory of subsistent objects outlined in the previous chapter,[1]

[1] See Chapter X, pp. 266, 267.

a theory which Meinong did not hesitate to apply to so-called unreal existences.

Let us suppose that we adopt a realist view of perception and maintain that the objects of sense experience are independent of the knowing mind. It seems logical to extend this view to all forms of consciousness and to assert that, if the objects of those acts of consciousness which constitute sense experience are other than the mind,[1] the objects of those acts of consciousness which are judging, thinking and imagining, must also be " other." Hence, " concepts " including universals, laws, numbers and relations are non-mental, but are nevertheless real ; they are objects of thought, which exist in their own right, just as, according to realist theory, the objects of sense exist in their own right.

Let us consider, in this connection, the case of relations. Bertrand Russell, whose views on this issue have already been referred to, has argued for the independent subsistence of relations such as those expressed by the words " on," " under," " to the left of," " to the north of." The following quotation from his early work, *The Problems of Philosophy*, illustrates this line of argument. " Consider such a proposition as ' Edinburgh is north of London.' Here we have a relation between two places, and it seems plain that the relation subsists independently of our knowledge of it. When we come to know that Edinburgh is north of London, we come to know something which has to do only with Edinburgh and London : we do not cause the truth of the proposition by coming to know it, on the contrary we merely apprehend a fact which was there before we knew it. The part of the earth's surface where Edinburgh stands would be north of the part where London stands, even if there were no human being to know about north and south, and even if there were no minds at all in the universe." Bertrand Russell's argument presupposes the assumption, which we have just agreed provisionally to make, that the idealist

[1] It is precisely this that, as we have seen in Chapter III, all realists maintain.

interpretation of the expression " Edinburgh is north of London " is to be rejected. The fact which we wish to assert when we make use of this expression is not, then, given this assumption, a mental one. " But," Russell continues, " this fact involves the relation ' north of,' which is a universal ; and it would be impossible for the whole fact to involve nothing mental if the relation ' north of,' which is a constituent part of the fact, did involve anything mental. Hence we must admit that the relation, like the terms it relates, is not dependent upon thought, but belongs to the independent world which thought apprehends but does not create."

In *The Problems of Philosophy*, Bertrand Russell[1] postulates independent universals, not only for substantives, adjectives and relations, but for verbs and prepositions. " Nearly all the words in the dictionary," he says, " stand for universals." This seems inclusive enough, but we cannot stop even here.

The Independent Being or Subsistence of " Unreal"
Objects.   That this is so will be seen, if we consider the case of so-called " unreal " creatures such as griffins and unicorns. We cannot in such cases adopt Berkeley's theory of abstract ideas, and say that, when we are thinking of griffins, we are thinking of some particular existent griffin which we happen to have seen, since we will assume that nobody has ever had sensory experience of such a creature as a living griffin. Yet, as Professor Moore has pointed out, when I am thinking of a unicorn, what I am thinking of is certainly not nothing : " If it were nothing, then when I think of a griffin I should also be thinking of nothing, and there would be no difference between thinking of a griffin and thinking of a unicorn. But certainly there is a difference ; and what can the difference be except that in the one case what I am thinking of is a unicorn, and in the other

[1] His views on this subject, as already noted (see Chapter X, p. 267), have altered, nor would he now argue for universals which are separate from particulars. Indeed he rejects the whole notion of a world of subsistence.

a griffin ? " The inference seems to be that a unicorn must have being in order that it may be thought of, and it must further be thought of as being something different from a griffin. Therefore, the universal " unicorn " exists or subsists, even if its only ascertainable attribute is its property of being an object of people's thought.

The view can be pushed to even greater extremes. For example, the experience of thinking of a " golden mountain " is different from that of thinking of a " red-headed square." We are, it will be remembered, provisionally adopting the realist hypothesis, which insists that the objects of our acts of thought are different from the acts by means of which we think of them. Neither a " golden mountain " nor a " red-headed square " is a psychical act. Therefore they must have pseudo-existence, or what Meinong calls subsistence, in order that they may serve as the objects of the acts of apprehending them, since on no other assumption can we account for the differences of the two experiences which are involved in apprehending them.

Now let us suppose that we string together a number of letters, e.g. ABYS, to constitute a meaningless word. What ABYS, or an ABYS, is, I shall assume we do not know. But a thought of ABYS is certainly different from a thought of OBES. Therefore ABYS must stand for something, if only in order that it may be significantly thought about by me.

The conclusion here verges on the absurd, and it may be taken as reasonably certain that it is false. Of the many objections to which it is exposed it will be sufficient to mention two. It makes no suitable provision for error,[1] since whenever we assert anything or think about anything, that which we assert or think about must, if the conclusion is true, in some sense *be* ; and it peoples the universe with hosts of existential or " subsistential " entities every time a human being chooses to think. Its effect is to endow with a kind of shadowy existence to which it gives the name of " subsistence " the whole world of imaginative possibility. Not only does the world of subsistence contain this desk with

[1] See Chapter XVI, pp. 432–438, for a discussion of Truth and Error.

three drawers at which I am writing, but it contains an exactly similar desk with four drawers, a similar desk with five drawers, and desks with every possible variation of drawers, tops, sides, colours, shapes and so forth, and with all possible permutations and combinations of the variations. Now there is, so far as I know, no logical objection to this multiplication of entities in the universe. But most people will, I imagine, find it strictly unbelievable. The whole theory of subsistent objects is, indeed, in danger of falling within the category of what Dr. Broad has defined as " silly theories "—that is to say, theories which nobody would dream of propounding outside a philosophical lecture-room.

Theory of Descriptions.   Moreover, there is an alternative theory which purports to tell us what it is that I am referring to, when I use such words as "humanity," "justice" and so forth, without doing such violence to our commonsense beliefs as the postulation of innumerable subsistent objects. This is Bertrand Russell's theory of descriptions. I have already referred to the view of universals which appears in Bertrand Russell's early book, *The Problems of Philosophy*, and shown how it may be logically developed into the theory of subsistent objects. It was partly because of this logical development that Bertrand Russell was led in subsequent books to abandon the theory of the independent reality of subsistent objects both real and unreal in favour of what is known as the " Theory of Descriptions." Let us consider a case in which the appearance in a sentence which we can understand of a word or words standing for a non-existent entity would be regarded, on the subsistent object theory, as requiring us to postulate an unreal subsistent object denoted by the word or words. For example, such sentences as " the King of France exists " and " the King of France is bald " have meaning, and convey meaningful information about a non-existent entity. Russell's Theory of Descriptions requires us to translate the first sentence as follows : " There is someone who is King of France, and there is no other person who is King of France." This sentence may be true or false ; in fact it is false. But it does not, as did the former theory, ascribe existence to an unreal entity ; nor does it require us to hold that there is a subsistent object, the King of France, on the ground that existence can be meaningfully ascribed to the King of France, and that this would not be possible unless the King of France was something. The second sentence may in terms of the Theory of Descriptions be translated as follows : " There is someone who is King of France and is bald, and there is no other person who is King of France." Given that the sentence can be so translated, the necessity for postulating a subsistent object disappears. Negative sentences introduce complications of their own without invalidating the theory. " The King of France is not bald " may, according to the theory, have one or other of two meanings ; either the meaning " There is someone who is King of France and is not bald, and there is no other person who is King of France," in which case it is false, but does not involve a subsistent object ; or the meaning " There is no one who both is the only person who is King of France and is not bald," in which case it is true, but again does not postulate a subsistent object. These sentences illustrate what Russell calls "definite descriptions," a name which he gives to almost any English phrase beginning with the word " the," such as " the King of France." I do not propose to enter here into a general account of the Theory of Descriptions which is difficult and technical, but sufficient will have been said to indicate the methods by which the necessity for postulating subsistent objects can be avoided. It is worth mentioning that Russell's Theory of Descriptions was one of the starting points of the school of Logical Positivism to which reference was made in the Introduction to Part III.[1]

Realism in the Middle Ages. It is, however, by no means certain that the need for a Conceptual Realism which bases

[1] See pp. 253, 254.

itself upon the existence of universals is entirely eliminated by Russell's theory, however successful this may be in disposing of unreal subsistent objects. In one form or another, indeed, Conceptual Realism appears as an ever recurring strand in the web of philosophical thought, and it seems unlikely that its critics will ever succeed in finally disposing of it. During the early Middle Ages it constituted whãt was in effect the official philosophy, when the realists were criticised by the rival school of Nominalism on much the same lines as those on which Aristotle criticised Plato's Theory of Ideas.

SCHOLASTICISM

The Essences of Mediaeval Realism. The distinguishing philosophy of the Middle Ages, known as Scholasticism, is a blend of the philosophies of Plato and Aristotle, a blend which, in the three centuries during which it flourished (from the eleventh to the fourteenth centuries A.D.) exhibits progressively more of the influence of Aristotle and progressively less of that of Plato. Initially Scholastic philosophy was predominantly realist in outlook and abounded in entities such as essences and potentialities, principles and causes conceived more or less after the likeness of the Platonic Forms. These entities were conceived not as ways of representing facts or as the properties of things, but as independent agencies which are responsible for the occurrence of the phenomena they were invoked to explain. Because a stone fell to the earth when dropped, realist mediaeval philosophers were inclined to say that it possessed a " principle of gravity " which caused it to seek the earth's centre ; the fact that quinine prevents a cold would be explained as due to its possession of a " cold-forbidding essence," conceived in the likeness of a Form, with which the material of quinine had combined.

One school of mediaeval philosophers, the realists, continued to maintain this Platonic doctrine in all its completeness, affirming that the Forms were principles of substance existing apart from physical objects and from minds. In addition to the Forms, there were also, they held, the general ideas we have of them ; there is, for example, a Form of whiteness, and there is also our general idea of whiteness, and since it is not necessary, on the realist view, for a Form to manifest itself in or to combine with matter in order that it may exist, there are Forms which have no material manifestation. Thus, for the realist, chimerical entities, like unicorns, existed in the world of Forms, and Conceptual Realism was logically committed to the absurdities into which we have followed the theory of subsistent objects.

The nominalists, the opponents of the realists, did not deny that we can form general notions of things, nor that there are factors in the external world from which these notions are derived. But, like Aristotle, they refused to assign to these factors independent existence, asserting that they are merely the common qualities observed in groups of physical objects, whiteness being the common quality possessed by both snow and cream, but not being something over and above the snow and the cream which are white. Hence, the nominalists contended, our general notions are derived from an inspection of physical objects and do not precede such inspection. William of Champeaux (1070–1121) was a leading realist ; Roscellinus (1050–1122), the teacher of Abelard, the protagonist of the nominalists. Abelard (1079–1142) attacked both Realism and Nominalism, but his own views inclined more to Nominalism than to Realism.

Views of St. Thomas Aquinas.

Both Realism and Nominalism were ultimately superseded by the philosophy of St. Thomas Aquinas (1227–1274), which may be regarded as the most mature expression of the thought of the Middle Ages. St. Thomas Aquinas's account of substance and of the relation of substance to the qualities which substance exhibits, is a typical scholastic doctrine, and deserves to be described in some little detail. St. Thomas's thought is largely influenced by that of Aristotle, with the result that in his philosophy the Forms, though still retained in name, are mere semblances of their Platonic originals, a Form being regarded not as an entity distinct from the material world, but as that which subsists in and only in the matter to which it gives its shape and qualities. For St. Thomas Aquinas, the universe is composed of a union between matter and forms.[1] The matter (*materia prima*) is itself without form, but it is united with forms of various kinds which have been fixed by the Creator. The result of the combination is a particular kind of substance endowed with qualities,[2] and it is this particular kind of substance which we call a material object. Matter may combine with a number of forms either successively or together, but the forms cannot themselves be transmuted into one another, except by divine agency. Thus, change in a piece of matter is due to the withdrawal of one form which previously combined with it, and its replacement by another. The green leaf in spring is the same as the yellow leaf in autumn, so far as its matter is concerned, but the form of greenness with which it was combined has given way to the form of yellowness.

Among the forms which a material object may exhibit, there is one that St. Thomas Aquinas called " the substantial form." The substantial form is that which makes the object what it is; in the case of a leaf it would be "leafiness," in the case of a jug, " jugginess " and so forth. A thing's substance is the union of its *materia prima* with its substantial form. Any other qualities which it may possess, those, for example, in virtue of which we call the jug white or black, tall or squat, are termed accidents, since they are not essential to the jug's being a jug, and are due to the accidental union of the jug with the forms of whiteness or blackness, tallness or squatness.

The ability of matter to change, that is to say, to take on a new form, arises from what is called its " potentiality."

[1] I shall henceforward drop the capital F, the smaller letter being more appropriate to the diminished dignity of the forms in St. Thomas's philosophy.

[2] The resemblance of this view to Aristotle's theory of Form and Matter (see Chapter VI, pp. 162, 163) is obvious.

This potentiality is latent until it is brought into play by an external act.[1] Thus, if St. Thomas were asked to give an account of what happens when water is boiled and turns into steam, he would say that the potentiality of the matter of which the water is composed to take on the substantial form of " steaminess," has been transformed into actuality by the exposure of the water to the heat of the fire.

As one reads St. Thomas's views, one cannot help noticing how the full-blooded Forms of Plato, the inhabitants of a perfect and changeless world, which alone possess the full title to be called real, have been watered down until they have become nothing more than the shaping agencies of the *materia prima*. That they cannot exist without the matter to which they give shape is clear from St. Thomas's doctrine of the soul. Man is a combination of soul and body, the body being the substance, which owes its qualities to the imposition of various forms upon the *materia prima*, and the soul being the substantial form. Conformably with his doctrine of matter and form, St. Thomas insists upon the necessity of the body to the soul, in order that there may be a soul at all. Hence, the soul could not survive the death of the mortal body, unless it were provided with a new and glorified body. But it is with precisely such a body that, he teaches, it *is* provided at death.

SUMMARY OF PRESENT OPINION

Two questions remain for consideration. First, what is the present state of philosophical opinion in regard to the subjects discussed in this and the immediately preceding chapter ? It is not easy to say. Like most philosophical problems, those raised by universals, their nature, status and relations to the sensible world, have never been settled and are, perhaps, incapable of settlement. The same may with truth be said of the particular form of Conceptual Realism entailed by Plato's Theory of Ideas and of the extremer

[1] The relation to Aristotle is again close (see Chapter VII, pp. 181–183).

developments which have extended the theory to include unreal, subsistent objects. While, however, many philosophers who belong to the realist school would be inclined to concede existence to universals, such as whiteness and justice, they would demur to postulating subsistent objects for natural objects and manufactured things. They would deny, for example, a subsistent oak, or a subsistent bed, and they would certainly deny that there were subsistent objects of unreal entities such as griffins and golden mountains. Some, however, including the present writer,[1] starting from a realist view of perception which maintains that the objects of our immediate sense experience are sense data,[2] have suggested that physical objects may appropriately be regarded as subsistent. We do not, they point out, experience the table with our senses. We only experience hard surfaces, brown colours, oblong shapes. Nevertheless, we certainly *think of* the table. We think of it, for example, as being Chippendale or oak or as worth a certain price, and we think of it as something of which we falsely believe ourselves to have sense experience. Hence arises the suggestion that the table must rank as an object of thought, rather than as an object of sense. But to say that it is " an object of thought " is not to say that it is in any sense "ideal." On the contrary, the arguments used above[3] are invoked to show that it is an independent factor in the universe, known by mind, but not dependent on mind for its existence.

Secondly, it may be asked in what sense the foregoing can be construed as a criticism of Plato's theory. The answer is that the theory of subsistent objects is a logical development from Plato's premises and a logical extension of the scope of his arguments. Given that the arguments for the Forms of justice and of whiteness are valid, it is difficult to see why they are not also valid, first, for the Forms of hair and mud, and, secondly, for golden mountains and red-headed squares. Granted that we reject these latter as absurd, we must either find some satisfactory halting-place

[1] See my *Philosophical Aspects of Modern Science*, Chapter VI.
[2] See Chapter III, pp. 92–95.   [3] See above, Chapter X, pp. 262–269.

in the argument, or we must abandon the Platonic theory of Forms from which they take their rise. Yet no satisfactory halting-place readily suggests itself, and it may well be that none can be found.

———————

Aristotle's Metaphysics *(Clarendon Press)*, with an introduction by W. D. Ross.

Meinong's theory of subsistent objects may be studied in R. Findlay's *Meinong's Theory of Objects.*

Bertrand Russell's *Introduction to Mathematical Philosophy* contains arguments and conclusions which have led many to dispense with the notion of universals as independent real subsistents. His *Mysticism and Logic,* Chapter X, may also be consulted. W. P. Montague's *The Ways of Knowing,* Chapter IV, summarises recent thought on the subject.

Scholastic Philosophy.

DE WULF, M.   History of Medieval Philosophy.
D'ARCY, M. C.   Thomas Aquinas.

*CHAPTER XII : DEVELOPMENTS AND APPLICATIONS OF PLATO'S THEORY OF IDEAS

1. The Philosophy of Modern Physics

Introductory. The last chapter was devoted to criticisms of Plato's Theory of Ideas and of later developments of the theory. In spite of these criticisms, many philosophers would maintain that the theory embodies important philosophical truth. This is the view of the present writer. I propose, therefore, in this chapter and the next, to endeavour to illustrate and to support the Platonic view of the world by showing how it may be fruitfully applied in certain spheres of contemporary discussion and controversy. I will select for this purpose the spheres of modern physics and of aesthetics.

It is frequently said that twentieth century philosophy has witnessed a revival of Platonism. One of the most comprehensive philosophical systems that our age has produced, that of Professor Whitehead,[1] is quite explicitly a development and application of Platonism in the light of modern knowledge, and especially of modern scientific knowledge. Whitehead's most substantial book *Process and Reality*, is introduced with a statement of the author's belief " that the train of thought in these lectures is Platonic." He goes further and describes the whole " European philosophical tradition " as consisting of " a series of footnotes to Plato." Without subscribing to this somewhat extreme view, we may well find significance in the fact that recent developments in the view of the external world sponsored by physics have tended to endorse the philosophical theories

[1] See Chapter XX, for an account of Whitehead's philosophy.

of two of the greatest philosophers—Plato and Kant. The bearing of the developments of modern physics upon Kant's philosophy will be considered in a later chapter.[1] What is their relation to that of Plato ?

Physicists' Accounts of the External World.

In order to answer this question it will be necessary to glance very briefly at the accounts of the external world given by modern science. Philosophers have devoted a considerable amount of attention to the philosophical implications of modern physics, and modern physicists are noted for their continuous, if not always fortunate, incursions into the field of philosophy. It is only fitting, then, that I should include in these pages some reference to matters of such considerable contemporary interest. The fact that, following White-head's hint, the reference is introduced in the form of " a footnote to Plato " must, I fear, be ascribed to bias in favour of that philosopher on the part of the author. Bias, though from the austere standpoint of complete impartiality it cannot but be deplored, is less deplorable, if avowed.

There is to-day no single and agreed description of the external world which physics studies. One thing, however, is agreed ; the external world consists partly of matter. What, then, is matter ? Matter is a kink in space-time, an electron " mush," a wave of probability undulating into nothingness, a collection of charges of electricity which are not charges in anything, a system of spatio-temporal events whose qualities are exclusively mathematical. A world of matter so conceived is so shadowy and insubstantial that some physicists are inclined to follow Berkeley or Kant, and to regard it as an emanation from or a construction of their own minds—it is variously described as an inference from events in the brain and the body, a projection from consciousness, a phenomenal[2] selection made by consciousness from a noumenal[2] world—and assert that reality is in its fundamental nature mental, as

[1] See Chapter XIV, pp. 362, 363.
[2] These words have a technical significance in Kant's philosophy which will be explained in Chapter XIV (see p. 381).

unhesitatingly as their predecessors announced fifty years ago that reality was material and mind a creation of matter.

The External World Practically Qualityless.

Without at this point following the physicists into the realm of metaphysical speculation, we may pause to note one common feature of all these varying accounts of the physicist's world. They are all couched in terms of extreme simplicity. The external world asserted by science is for the most part nearly—it is not quite—homogeneous. Sir Arthur Eddington has described how the physicist is required to divest himself one by one of his sense-organs, when he wishes to establish contact with his world. Divested of ears, nose, palate and skin, he is, it is true, permitted an eye, but since everything that he observes is through a microscope or a telescope, only one. Nor is it difficult to see why the physicist's sense-organs may be dispensed with ; for the qualities which in our ordinary daily life the sense-organs seem to reveal to us—colour, solidity, sound, smell, temperature—are, in the physicist's world, simply not " there."

Take, for example, heat. A gas, we are told, consists of molecules of about a hundred-millionth of an inch across, with comparatively large spaces between them, moving about in all directions with an average speed measured in hundreds of yards a second. The molecules meet and collide, and in consequence of their collision the gas has a certain temperature. If the gas is placed in a flame or hot body, the molecules of which it is composed will gain in energy, moving rapidly and colliding more violently. Imperceptibly the temperature of the gas goes up ; heat, as we say, is generated. But the cause of this heat is the greater energy of motion of the molecules ; or, as a textbook on physics would put it, heat *is* nothing but the energy of motion of molecules.

Similarly, sound is said to be caused by, or alternatively to *be*, waves in the atmosphere. These waves vary in length, in frequency of vibration, and in mode of vibration. Variations in length determine the loudness, in frequency of vibration the pitch, and in mode of vibration the quality of the sound. Sound, then, is produced by atmospheric waves. Atmospheric waves are described as regions of pressure and rarification in the atmosphere moving forward with a certain velocity ; and the movement of such a region of atmosphere is the cause of, or simply *is*, sound. Thus the properties of the atmospheric waves which the sounding body gives out determine the character of the sounds which are heard.

Most significant of all is the case of colour. Modern physics deals with immense numbers of electro-magnetic waves, which, so far as their intrinsic characteristics are concerned, differ from each other only in point of speed, wave-length and frequency. In terms of their wave-lengths and frequencies they are graded in the electro-magnetic spectrum. The rays which are called " light rays " occupy only a small part of this spectrum, at one end of which are located the so-called cosmic rays, and, at the other, wireless waves whose wave-length is measured in hundreds of yards. We may express this by saying that in the scale of wave-lengths and frequencies, according to which waves are arranged in the electro-magnetic spectrum, there is a certain section of waves which are—or which have effects which are—visible ; these are called light waves.

Light, therefore, is, or is caused by, a certain set of wave-lengths of varying frequencies in the electro-magnetic spectrum. Within this section of wave-lengths which are, or which cause, light, certain subsections are earmarked for the different colours. Thus, just as light-waves constitute a section of the waves graded by the electro-magnetic spectrum, most of which are not visible, so each colour is constituted by a sub-section of waves of particular frequency and wave-length falling within the light section.

But these sub-sections of waves are not themselves coloured.

What is Left ?   If scent, sound, colour, and, we may add, texture, taste and smell, are not really " out there " in the physicist's world, what is ? It is extremely difficult to say. Mathematical physics postulates a world of point events ; it takes four numbers to specify a point event uniquely, and a minimum amount of structure may, therefore, be postulated for the world, that is to say, of mathematical structure. From this minimum structure of point events and the relations between them, the mind—according to the most popular contemporary form of physico-philosophical speculation—builds up the world of varied qualities we know, concentrating upon those point events which fall into patterns which interest it, or which it finds significant. That such a conception lends itself to idealist interpretation is sufficiently clear. For, as I pointed out at the end of Chapter VIII,[1] the sort of world we know, will, on this view, depend upon the sort of minds we possess. Minds differently constituted would make different selections, resulting, it is obvious, in different worlds.

Without necessarily subscribing to these idealist implications, we have, it seems, no alternative but to accept the account which physicists give of their world as being fundamentally mathematical in character. Qualities it has, in so far as number, velocity, and spatio-temporal position— although the last is no longer so precise as could be wished— can be considered qualities ; but for the rest it is featureless. Endow Locke's Substance[2] with mathematical characteristics, and one might say that the external world of the physicists has been reduced to Locke's Substance. Itself divested of qualities, it has become a mere substratum to support the qualities which mind projects into it. To quote again the celebrated phrase in which Whitehead sums up Locke's philosophy of nature : " Nature," on this view, " is a dull affair, soundless, scentless, colourless ; merely the hurrying of material, endlessly, unceasingly."

The Modern Atom.   The above conclusions are chiefly suggested by reflection on the implications of relativity theory. The picture of the outside world derived from a

[1] See Chapter VIII, p. 227.   [2] See Chapter II, pp. 40, 41.

study of the atom is not fundamentally different. Atoms, we are given to understand, are the fundamental constituents of matter. Yet the atom is not known ; its existence is inferred from the effects upon the surrounding environment of the energy which it generates when it changes.

" The idea that there is a little hard lump there, which *is* the electron or proton, is," according to Bertrand Russell, " an illegitimate intrusion of commonsense notions derived from touch. For aught we know, the atom may consist entirely of the radiations which come out of it." The atom, in fact, has become an underlying Lockeian Substance,[1] in which the physical events which are observed may inhere or from which they emanate, but which is never itself observed. Now matter is composed of atoms, and what is true of atoms is true of matter. " Matter," therefore, to quote an epigram of Bertrand Russell's, has become " a convenient formula for describing what happens where it isn't."

If the atom resolves itself into the effects which the atom, if it existed, would produce, when it changes on the surrounding spatio-temporal field, what are we to say of the surrounding spatio-temporal field ? Precisely what we have said about the atom. In so far as there are effects in that field, they take the form of occurrences or events. These occurrences or events are physical ; therefore they will ultimately be susceptible of the same analysis as that which is applicable to the atom.

To quote Russell again ; " There is a certain air of taking in each other's washing about the whole business. Events in empty space are only known as regards their abstract mathematical characteristics ; matter is only an abstract mathematical characteristic of events in empty space." In other words we describe what is happening at place A in terms of the events at place B ; we describe what is happening at place B in terms of the events at place C, and so on indefinitely.

In so far, then, as the conception of matter has historically connoted the notion of substance, we must conclude that

[1] See Chapter II, pp. 40, 41.

modern matter is not material. The concept of material substance, in fact, has faded out of modern physics, and has been replaced by that of emanations from a locality. For substance X being defined in terms of its effects on substance Y, substance Y in terms of its effects on substance Z, and so on indefinitely, matter itself (if the mixture of metaphors may be forgiven) is perpetually dangled like a carrot before the nose of the inquiring mind. It is a something to which the mind is ever being led, but which it never reaches.

The External World as Inferred.

But the doubts suggested by modern physics as to the possibility of our knowing an independently existing outside world are not confined to atomic theory. We do not, physicists seem to be agreed, directly know atoms ; the atom, they tell us, is known only as the result of an inference. But do we directly know physical objects ? Is the physical object known by some method other than inference ? As we saw in the first chapter, if physics is to be believed, it is not.

Let us revert to the scientist's description of the machinery of perception at which we briefly glanced in the first chapter.[1] We there took, as an example, the combined accounts which a physicist and a physiologist would give of the events which occur when a man looks at a star on a dark night. We pointed out that, if the physicist and the physiologist were right, the man's belief that he was actually seeing the star involved a double inference. Of the first inference the contemporary educated man is ordinarily aware. He is aware, that is to say, that the interval of time required for the passage of the light rays to the earth is sufficiently large to make it probable that it is *not* the star which is the immediate object of vision. The first inference is, then, from the fact that we have the sensation of seeing a yellow patch to the conclusion that there must be a physical object, a star, which is in some way responsible for the patch ; the second, from the fact that the brain and visual apparatus are being stimulated in a certain way to

[1] See Chapter I, pp. 31–36.

the existence of an external "something" to cause the stimulation. Both inferences may be mistaken ; in fact, directly we venture to make any statement as to the nature of an external world supposed to be revealed to us in perception, we are liable to fall into error. To quote Bertrand Russell : " We are less likely to be mistaken if we say that the surface of the eye is being stimulated in a certain way, and still less likely to be mistaken if we say that the optic nerve is being stimulated in a certain way. We do not eliminate the risk of error completely unless we confine ourselves to saying that an event of a certain sort is happening in the brain ; this statement may still be true, if we see Jupiter in a dream."

Conclusion : the Underhat Philosophy.

The conclusion, whose truth is normally recognised when we are looking at stars, is involved no less when we are looking at objects on the earth. It is only because the interval of time during which the physical and physiological machinery is functioning is, in the case of ordinary perception, very short, that the fact that there *is* an interval tends to escape notice. But the example which we cited from Bertrand Russell in the first chapter, in which a physiologist is conceived to be looking at a patient's brain,[1] makes it sufficiently clear that, so far as physics and physiology are concerned, the only possible conclusion is that the event which is the immediate cause of our sensations, is one which occurs in our own brains. For this reason, the title of "Underhat Philosophy" has been applied to the conclusion which some thinkers[2] have sought to derive from their examination of modern science, the conclusion, namely, that the only things that we can know are events taking place " under our own hats." Whether this somewhat repellent solipsistic conclusion is justified or not, there can be little doubt that, if the scientists' account of perception is to be taken at its face value, we have no *direct* knowledge of the physical world. *Some* cause there must be to start the chain of physical and

[1] See Chapter I, p. 32. [2] Noticeably, at one time, Bertrand Russell.

physiological processes which results in perception ; but of the nature of that cause we have and, on this view, can have no knowledge. Certainly we do not know its qualities, since, if the physicist is right, these are engendered by the mind as the result of the cause's impact upon the brain and nervous system. It is not only the familiar, secondary qualities of touch, colour, temperature and sound which in Sir Arthur Eddington's language are " fancies " projected by the mind into the external world. " Permanence," the " structure " of familiar things, and their " substantiality," are all regarded by him as products of the mind's faculty of " world building." The " some cause," therefore, subsides like the atom into the rôle of a Lockeian Substance ; it is a mere featureless something, owning in its own right none of the qualities we believe ourselves to perceive. To sum up in Eddington's words, " Its substance has melted into shadow. . . . It remains . . . an unknown quantity which the mathematical symbol X stands for."

Idealist Implications. What conclusion does this scientific reduction of the physical world to a comparatively featureless medium, a flux of events, suggest for philosophy ? Or, to put the question in another way : Whence, if the qualities of things do not really belong to them, in the sense of being " out there " in the world, are they to be derived ? The usual conclusion, the familiar answer, is the idealist one. It is the mind which, it is said, projects into the world the qualities which it finds. This, it will be remembered, is Locke's answer. " Thus," to complete the quotation which I cited above from Professor Whitehead, " Nature gets credit which should in truth be reserved for ourselves : the rose for its scent, the nightingale for his song, and the sun for his radiance." This, as we shall see in Chapter XIV, is also broadly Kant's. It is also, as we have already seen,[1] Sir Arthur Eddington's. In a famous passage he likens the mind to an editor sitting in his office and weaving a picture of the outside world from the " code messages

[1] See Chapter I, pp. 34, 35

transmitted along the nerves into its (the mind's) sanctum."

This answer may, of course, be the true one. There are, however, two reflections which it inevitably suggests. First, it is impossible to stop at the point at which Eddington and other physicists sometimes seem to wish to stop. If the qualities of things in terms of and by means of which we know them are mental, then the underlying substratum, the " unknown quantity which the mathematical symbol X stands for," must be mental too. To assert a material substratum is to assert more than we know ; to assert an unknown one is, as Berkeley showed in his criticism of Locke,[1] to assert nothing at all, since, if the substratum cannot be known, it cannot be known to exist. Thus the idealist interpretation cannot call a halt in mid-course ; it must be pushed all the way, until the world that science studies is pronounced to be mental through and through. And not only the world that science studies. For—and this is my second observation—whatever grounds there are for pronouncing the scientific world to be ideal, apply equally to the world of sense. As we saw above, not only the atom, but the star, must, according to the physicist's account of the processes involved in its perception, be regarded as an inference from events happening elsewhere. Moreover, the world of science has evolved by gradual and historically traceable stages from the world of sense ; it cannot, therefore, in the long run, belong to an order of existence different from that of the sense-world. If, then, there are good grounds for regarding atoms as ideal constructions, these apply no less to tables and chairs. In other words, the qualities of things are imposed upon them by the mind.

Whether the reader will feel able to accept this interpretation will depend upon his attitude to idealist philosophy as a whole. He will, therefore, do well to suspend his judgement, until he has made acquaintance with the views of the great idealist philosophers, Kant and Hegel, of whom Hegel in particular made a sustained attempt—the most comprehensive in the history of human thought—to interpret

[1] See Chapter II, pp. 43, 44.

LP

the whole of the known universe in terms of pure mind. Most philosophers have embraced Idealism in one form or another, and, although the present writer is not an idealist, he fully recognises the strength of the idealist case, especially in its application to the problems raised by modern physics which are at present under consideration. Our immediate concern, is, however, not with Idealism but with Plato. The programme with which I started this chapter was to endeavour to show how Plato's theory of Forms could be fruitfully applied to the elucidation of the problems raised by modern science. This programme I must now try to carry out.

Re-introduction of Plato.

Plato's scheme, as we have seen, postulates two ingredients in the composition of the sensible world, immaterial Forms and a featureless medium in which they are manifested. Translating the development described above into Plato's language, we may say that the progress of modern physics is one in which the physicist penetrates ever farther through the sensible qualities of things to reveal the featureless medium which underlies them. Already, as we have seen, he has stripped the material world of all qualities except the severely mathematical ; and of the severely mathematical, velocity and spatio-temporal position can, it appears, be assigned to particles only in a very doubtful sense. If they have the one, they must, it seems, dispense with the other.

Many have taken the line that the future advance of science will result, if it has not done so already, in the complete elimination of the need for a medium. Everything, as these scientists would say, everything, as Sir James Jeans does say, will be completely describable in terms of mathematical law. Now to say that everything will prove ultimately susceptible of exhaustive analysis in terms of mathematical law implies, presumably, that nothing would in the analysis be left over which would be unamenable to law. Can this suggestion, the suggestion that the world of brute fact will one day be analysed away altogether and be replaced by law, be accepted ? It seems highly doubtful. For there must, it seems, in the very nature of things, be a resistant intactable something in the universe, which, *from the very fact that it is that to which laws apply, is itself other than law*. This element of brute-given is, I should say, irreducible, and its presence sets a definite limit to the advance of science.

There Must be Something for Science to Apply to.

The procedure of science is to take the given phenomena of the sensible world, and to analyse and correlate them with a view to exhibiting an apparently chaotic diversity of happenings as exemplifying the workings of law. Success in this undertaking enables us to understand and to predict. The understanding is of the immediate causes of the phenomena ; the prediction is of their recurrence, given the same causes, in the future. As it advances, science succeeds in bringing an ever greater area of that which is initially given to the senses under the aegis of an ever-diminishing number of laws. As its researches are pushed farther and farther back, what was formerly accepted as " brute-given " is shown to be amenable to law and brought within the scientific fold. But science will never succeed in dispensing with the necessity for postulating a something which is regarded as that to which at any given moment its laws are applicable, and this something, from the very fact that it is *its workings and consequences* which scientific law determines, must itself be other than the operations of law. It must, that is to say, be unamenable to and unreachable by the operations of law at the particular stage which science happens then to have reached. Granted that it may subsequently become amenable, yet it can only do so by giving way to a new something which assumes the rôle of " brute-given " in its place. The following quotation from Professor A. E. Taylor puts the point clearly.

" We have to appeal in all our explanations of the actual not only to ' laws ' but to ' collocations.' Science, which hates to accept anything whatever as mere bare ' given fact,'

is always trying with much success to reduce the ' collocations ' with which it starts as given to mere consequences of
' laws.' " It reduces the collocation which appears as
brute-matter to elements ; the collocation of elements to
atoms ; the collocation of atoms to charges of positive or
negative electricity. " But every success in such reduction
is achieved at the price of acquiescence in some assumption
of an earlier and more ultimate ' collocation.' Without
' collocations ' which have to be taken as ' brute fact,' as
there, we do not know how or why, the functional depend-
ences we call 'laws' would reduce to functions without any
arguments, and would thus become as insignificant as the
symbol f or φ before a blank. Here we clearly come upon an
inevitable limit to the whole work of scientific explanation."

The Forms and the Featureless Medium. Science, then,
analyses the world into a comparatively featureless and,
therefore, unknown X, into collocations, stuff, matter—the
name we give to it is immaterial—and the laws which
govern its behaviour. Increasingly, all positive statements
that can be made about the world belong to the category
of the law ; diminishingly are they statements about the
qualities of X. X, in fact, as we have seen, comes to bear
an increasing resemblance to Locke's Substance.

Now let us compare the position reached by science with
the outline which I have given of that of Plato. Plato's view,
as we have seen, envisages the need of a substance or stuff, as
a medium in which the Forms can manifest themselves. This
medium is featureless, all the qualities we perceive in the
sensible world being due to the presence in it of the Forms.

The present tendencies of science seem to confirm Plato's
conclusion. What science has done is to divest " matter "
of the characteristics which we perceive, and to leave " out
there " in the external world only a featureless substance.
Two alternative ways of dealing with the characteristics
then present themselves. We may say either that they are
mental, being constructed or projected by the mind ; or we
may take Plato's hint and ascribe them to the presence in a

medium of immaterial Forms. Thus the difference between thinking and sensory experience is that in the activity of thinking we explore the world of Forms and map out the relations which we discover to hold between them ; in sensory experience we are aware of the Forms as imperfectly manifested in a medium. If this suggestion has any validity—and it emanates from no higher authority than that of the author—it has the additional advantage of outflanking one of the most difficult problems in modern philosophy, namely the problem which we discussed in Chapter III of the relation between physical objects and sense data.[1] On the view here suggested the problem does not arise, since *all* our sensory experience is an experience of Forms manifested in a quality-less medium.

Support from Evolutionary Theory.

Nor, though the argument has hitherto been devoted exclusively to physics, is this the only science which lends itself to fruitful applications of Plato's theory. The conclusions of modern biology may also be fitted into his metaphysical framework. The dominating conception of the modern biologist is still the evolution of species. Something there is which we call a species, which from generation to generation passes through a series of small modifications which biologists trace and whose causes they discuss. But what precisely is this something ? What, that is to say, is the species itself, whose successive members are said to exhibit the modifications ? Not, it is obvious, any one of the individual members of the species who successively appear and whose gradual divergence from some initial type is usually regarded as evidence for the theory of evolution. Nor is it the aggregate of these individuals. For it is not of a chaotic collection of creatures, some dead, some living, that we are speaking when we say of a species that it evolves or is modified. Are we not, then, driven to postulate a common nature or form of the species which, as evolution proceeds, is gradually and, it may be, increasingly revealed. If this is so, the process of evolution

[1] See Chapter III, pp. 95-99.

may be described as the gradual revelation of a form in a subject matter, and we shall be entitled to say that later individuals approximate to the form of the species or manifest it more completely than the earlier.

This suggestion must, it is obvious, be treated with caution, since it entails the flattering conclusion that a modern civilised man realises or reveals the nature of the human species more completely than his Neanderthalian ancestor. If, however, we are prepared to countenance this suggestion, we shall be committed to a conception very like Plato's—a conception, namely, of an underlying form or type which manifests itself in the many members which make up a common class or species, but which is never exhausted by its individual manifestations. The suggestion cannot be developed here, but it will serve to indicate a possible application of Plato's ideas in the realm of evolutionary theory. Briefly, it would be suggested that the ideal of the perfect dog, like that of the perfect man, is laid up in heaven, the process of development which we call evolution being nothing but the gradual approximation to the ideal type on the part of decreasingly imperfect representatives ; or, to change the metaphor, the gradually increasing revelation of the ideal type in the imperfect approximations.

Books dealing with the philosophical questions raised by modern physics are :

Books by scientists :
EDDINGTON, A. S.   The Nature of the Physical World.
                            New Pathways in Science.
JEANS, SIR J.   The New Background of Science.
LEVY, H.   The Universe of Science.

Books by philosophers :
WHITEHEAD, A. N.   The Concept of Nature.
BROAD, C. D.   Perception, Physics and Reality.
                        Scientific Thought.
JOAD, C. E. M.   Philosophical Aspects of Modern Science.

CHAPTER XIII: DEVELOPMENTS AND APPLICATIONS OF PLATO'S THEORY OF IDEAS

2. The Philosophy of Aesthetics

Introductory.   In this chapter it is proposed to consider the application of the conclusions of Plato's Theory of Ideas in the realm of aesthetic theory. The philosophy of aesthetics is primarily concerned to find the answers to such questions as " What do we mean by the word ' beauty ' ? ? ", " Is there a criterion or standard by reference to which we can assess and compare the aesthetic merit of different works of art ? " " What part is played by the mind in the appreciation of beauty, and how far can beauty be considered an expression, or a creation or a characteristic of the mind ? " It is not possible within the limits of a single chapter to deal adequately with any of these questions. Moreover, my treatment will be determined throughout by the considerations which have led me to undertake it. My primary purpose in undertaking it is, that is to say, to exemplify and apply the metaphysical view described in the tenth chapter : this purpose should be borne in mind throughout.

1. THE PLATONIC THEORY OF AESTHETICS

Plato's Account of Beauty.   A celebrated passage in Plato's Dialogue, the *Symposium*, describes the journey of the soul in search of beauty. Diotima, the prophetess, is instructing Socrates in the pursuits which must be followed by those who wish to know the Form of Beauty.

A man begins by appreciating the beauty of one beautiful

object or shape. His capacity then advances to the stage in which he can appreciate several beautiful objects, and realises that the beauty in one is the same as the beauty in another. The next stage is the appreciation of abstract beauty, that is, the beauty of laws and institutions.

But the knowledge of the Form of Beauty is not yet. He must persevere until he has achieved aptitude in the study of the abstract beauty of stage three. We learn, moreover, in the seventh book of the *Republic* that the method by which a man approaches nearer to the true vision of the Form, is by an arduous study in that branch of knowledge which is furthest removed from illusion, that is, in the exact sciences of measuring, weighing and counting, called the Theories of Numbers, Geometry, Stereometry,[1] and Astronomy ; and it is for the reason that he has had no training in these exact sciences, that it is said of the artist in the tenth book that he will never attain to a perception of the Form itself. After long study of the exact sciences the seeker will be rewarded with a sudden apprehension of the Form. This is described in the *Symposium* in the language of a mystical vision : " And at last the vision is revealed to him of a single science which is the science of beauty everywhere." In the seventh epistle Plato says that the knowledge of the Forms cannot be put into words like other kinds of learning, but that suddenly, after much study and prolonged pursuit of them, light, whereby they may be beheld, springs up in the soul like flame from a fire. This final apprehension, then, is an intuition, a mystical flash entirely divorced from the purely logical and mathematical processes of thought and study which necessarily precede it. The vision follows logically from and is conditioned by the leading-up process. But in itself it is distinct and unique, involving both immediacy and separation from self.

Then, says Plato, will it be seen that all other beautiful things are beautiful, only in so far as they participate in the true being of Beauty. In the *Phaedrus*, moreover, we are told that the Form of Beauty alone of all the Forms appears in

[1] Theory of Solids.

this world as it really is. A man cannot attain in this life to absolute Wisdom or absolute Justice ; but he can apprehend absolute Beauty. The doctrine of Recollection[1] is then invoked to explain how, when the soul knows beauty on earth, it is only recognising that with which it has already been familiar in its discarnate state.

Psychology of the Creative Process.

Modern psychological theory supports the Platonic account of the aesthetic process, more particularly in respect of its recognition of two distinct stages, the first a stage of sustained intellectual effort, the second an ensuing flash of intuitive apprehension, which are very similar to those affirmed in the *Symposium* and the *Republic*. A brief account of modern psychological work on the subject may serve a useful purpose in developing the Platonic view.

In a well-known work, *The Art of Thought*, Professor Graham Wallas summarised the information which modern psychology has obtained with regard to the processes involved in the birth of new ideas in the world of thought and original inspiration in that of art. His summary goes beyond Plato's account in that it distinguishes *four* stages in the process which leads to the making of a new generalisation, the discovery of a new formula, the devising of a new invention or the conception of a new work of art. The first is that of Preparation, during which a particular problem is investigated in all directions ; the second, that of Incubation, during which no conscious thinking is done in connection with the problem or work of art with which the creative thinker or artist is concerned ; the third, consisting of the appearance of the " happy idea," together with psychological events accompanying that appearance, is called Illumination ; and the fourth, embodying the working out and application of the idea in thought or the execution of the work of art, Verification.

Particular stress is laid upon the importance of Incubation as a preliminary to Illumination. Professor Wallas

[1] See Chapter X, pp. 283-287.

speaks of the many men of genius who have done their best work after a period of idleness. But the period of idleness must itself be preceded by a spell of hard thinking, during which the intellect is working at full pressure. To adopt the language of modern psychology, we may say that consciousness during the Preparation stage propounds a problem, collects the relevant data and explores different avenues for a possible solution. A period of rest ensues during which the problem and relevant data are transferred to the unconscious. That the unconscious may work effectively, consciousness must, so far as possible, be unoccupied. The solution is worked out by the unconscious, and appears in due course in consciousness as the " happy idea " of the scientist and the inspiration of the artist.

The conclusion bears out Plato's hint in the *Symposium*. Wallas like Plato stresses the fact that the " happy idea " which succeeds the period of hard thinking is of an entirely different order from the thinking itself. It outruns the thinking, and, although it is led up to, is far from being necessitated by it. The mind, in other words, makes a definite jump, and it is for this reason that in the sphere of science a subsequent process of " Verification " is necessary.

Objective Theory of Beauty Stated.   But while Plato makes an important contribution to our knowledge of the nature of aesthetic experience, the distinguishing feature of his theory of aesthetics is his insistence upon the fact that such experience, whether it be creative or appreciative merely, is always in its essential nature a process of discovery. There is, he affirms, a Form of Beauty ; by following an appropriate training we can achieve a knowledge of the Form. We can also reproduce in sound, paint or stone images of that which we have known. Differences in aesthetic judgement are, therefore, not purely subjective differences, *mere* differences of taste ; they are differences of knowledge. The aesthetic knowledge of some will be truer than that of others, and of some knowledge it can be affirmed that it is false. It is this suggestion, which entails what in modern phraseology is termed the " objectivity of beauty," which I shall proceed to develop.

II. SUBJECTIVITY AND OBJECTIVITY

Philosophical discussions of aesthetics turn largely upon the question whether aesthetic judgements are always subjective, or whether it is at least possible for them to be objective, even if they are rarely so in fact. Most moderns appear to have an instinctive predilection for the subjective view.

The terms " subjective " and " objective " are frequently used in philosophical discussion ; nor is their use confined to philosophers. It is not surprising, therefore, to find that they have a number of different meanings, and, since those who engage in controversies on aesthetics do not always employ these words with the same meanings, such discussions normally lose themselves in a tangle of words. A real difference of view may of course separate the disputants ; but if it does, it is rarely that it is laid bare. Let us, then, begin by trying to define a sense in which the words " subjective " and " objective " can be used with some degree of precision. A subjective judgement we will define as a judgement to the effect that the experience of the person making the judgement is being modified in a certain way—in other words, that something is happening in or to " the subject." An objective judgement we will define as a judgement to the effect that the world external to the person judging is characterised by a certain quality. Whether there can be objective judgements in the sense defined may be a matter of controversy. But, if there are such judgements, it is this, namely, that the world is being characterised by such and such a quality, that we shall understand them to mean.

Examples of Subjective Judgements.   Now most people would be inclined to say that *prima facie* some judgements are subjective, some objective. If X judges " These gooseberries are sour," while Y judges " These gooseberries are sweet," most people would say that what X and Y are in fact judging about is not some quality which is characterising or is possessed by the gooseberries, but the effects produced by the gooseberries on their respective palates. The palates being different, the effects produced are different, and, as a consequence, the qualities of the experiences of X and Y respectively are different. Hence the judgement " These gooseberries are sour " does not contradict the judgement " These gooseberries are sweet," since each of the two judgements is *about* something different. The two judgements are, therefore, according to the definition given above, subjective judgements. Again, most people would say, although not perhaps with the same degree of conviction, that the two judgements " The colour of the sea is now blue " and " The colour of the sea is now green " were subjective, since that to which they referred would not be some quality, namely blueness or greenness, which was characterising the sea, but the effects produced by the sea (or, to be scientifically precise, by the light waves proceeding from the place where the sea is) upon the respective retinas of the two persons making the judgements. These effects would be complex effects, to which the conditions of light, the respective positions of observation, and the different characteristics of the retinas and general visual apparatus of the persons in question would contribute. For example, one of the two persons might be colour-blind, so that the colour of the sea would appear differently to him and to a person of normal vision. Because these complex physical and physiological conditions were different, so too, it might be said, would be the experiences of the persons judging.

I say that the degree of conviction in this case would probably be less than in the case of experiences originating in the palate, for the reason that there is a general presupposition to the effect that the colour of things really belongs to them in some sense in which their tastes, for example, whether they are sweet or whether they are sour, do not. Most of those who had any acquaintance with the idealist arguments mentioned in the first and second Chapters of this book would, however, be inclined to deny that things *really* possess colour, and would, therefore, class the judgements "The sea is now blue" and "The sea is now green" as subjective in fact, if not in form. They would, that is to say, maintain that the only statements about colour that we are *really* entitled to make are such statements as : " The sea *looks blue to me*," or " the sea *gives me an experience of blueness*," and " The sea *looks green to me* " or " the sea *gives me an experience of greenness*," statements which are subjective in form as well as in fact.

Examples of Objective Judgements. At the other end of the scale we may, as examples of *prima facie* objective judgements, instance mathematical judgements. When somebody judges that $3 + 2 = 5$, or that $7 \times 7 = 49$, he is purporting to assert something about the relations that hold between numbers. He would not ordinarily be taken to mean " I am so constituted that I happen to think that $3 + 2 = 5$, but somebody differently constituted is perfectly entitled to assert that $3 + 2 = 6$."[1] He means, and would normally be understood as meaning, that anybody who thinks that $3 + 2 = 6$ is simply wrong, and that this *is* what he means any schoolboy who took advantage of the undeniable subjectivity of many judgements to assert his inalienable right to maintain that $3 + 2$ does equal 6, would very quickly discover to his cost.

Another example of a *prima facie* objective judgement would be a judgement about the temperature of a room. If I say " The temperature of this room is 75° Fahrenheit," most people would hold, that my judgement admits of being either right or wrong in a sense in which the judgement " This room seems to me to be unduly hot," or alternatively

[1] This statement would not, of course, be accepted by those who hold that the laws of mathematics are primarily descriptions of the way in which the mind works. See the discussions on Laws of Thought and Laws of Things, Chapter V, pp. 144–150.

" unduly cold," does not admit of being either right or wrong. The first judgement, in other words, purports to say something about the conditions prevailing in the room, the second about my personal reactions to these conditions. It may, of course, be the case—it almost always is the case— that psychological or physiological conditions prevailing in me determine the kind of judgement I shall pass about the temperature of the room. If, for example, I have recently emerged from a hothouse, I shall probably judge it to be lower than I would, if I entered it from a refrigerator. But, although subjective conditions may determine the precise judgement that I actually pass, they do not prevent the judgement from being at least in intention an objective one, of being, that is to say, a judgement which purports to assert something about certain conditions which are existing in the world independently both of me and of the judgement, and most people would say that, since the actual temperature of the room can be measured by a thermometer, there is a perfectly precise sense in which a judgement to the effect that it is so and so can be objective and right, while another judgement to the effect that it is something else would be objective and wrong. Moreover, one judgement would also be said to be more nearly right than another, if it was nearer to the thermometer reading.

In some cases a *prima facie* objective judgement would appear to shade into a *prima facie* subjective judgement and *vice versa*. If I am standing on a railway bridge and looking down at the railway line immediately below me, I shall judge " These rails are parallel." If I look as far as I can along the track, I shall notice that the lines *appear to* converge. Now this apparent convergence I believe to be what I call an optical illusion. Hence, while I should describe the judgement " These railway lines are parallel " as an objective judgement, I should regard the judgement " These railway lines converge at a certain distance along the track " as subjective. Yet the lines to which the two judgements purport to refer are the same lines, and there must, presumably, be a point somewhere along the track at which the objective judgement ceases to be made and is superseded by the subjective judgement.

Subjective and Objective Theories of Aesthetics.   Now the question upon which philosophical discussions of aesthetics mainly turn is whether aesthetic judgements such as " This picture is beautiful," " That symphony is great," " Keats is a better poet than Miss Wilcox," " Shakespeare is a greater playwright than Noel Coward," are objective or subjective. Do they in fact refer to and make a statement about some intrinsic quality possessed by the work of art or writer under judgement, or do they merely report the subjective preferences and prejudices of the judger? On the first assumption, works of art possess a quality which we will call provisionally their " beauty," just as truly as they possess the quality of squareness, if they are pictures, of loudness, if they are symphonies. On the second assumption, there is no difference in point of meaning between the judgements "This is a good picture" and "This is a picture which I happen to like." The two judgements, in fact, are saying the same thing in different ways, and the view of the commonsense man who " knows nothing about art " but " knows what he likes," is entitled to as much respect as that of the lifelong critic. In fact, neither the commonsense man nor the critic really succeed in telling us about the picture at all. Each is only reporting his own experiences.

III. SUBJECTIVIST THEORIES OF AESTHETICS

1. EXTREME SUBJECTIVISM

One of the best known statements of the extreme subjectivist attitude to the problems of aesthetics will be found in Tolstoy's (1828–1910) *What is Art*, published in 1897. The conclusion of Tolstoy's discussion is that the value of any artistic whole, whether poem, picture, symphony or statue, depends entirely on its effect upon the persons who perceive it. Art, for Tolstoy, is the communication of emotion. When a man tells a story, composes a song, or paints a picture, with the object of communicating to others an emotion he has felt himself, then there is art ; when the emotion is fresh and springs from a fresh and vivid attitude to the world, then there is great art. The art which professes to aim at being beautiful, but which really seeks only to arouse pleasure, is not art at all. Such, in Tolstoy's view, has been throughout the period of recorded history the nature of the so-called art of the bourgeois and upper classes. Tolstoy concludes that, since Russian peasant songs have communicated emotion to numerically more persons than has Shakespeare's *King Lear*, which, incidentally, Tolstoy thought a wicked and vicious play, they are greater art than *King Lear*. The extreme subjectivist theory which results from this view may be stated as follows. The beauty of a work of art—be it a poem, a piece of music, or a painting—is to be assessed entirely by reference to what people think about the work of art in question. In order to decide which of two works is the greater, we have simply to count heads and find out which is appreciated by the greater number of people. For beauty is not objective, or inherent in works of art ; it is a quality of the effect produced by them on those who are brought into contact with them. Beauty, in fact, is a subjective experience, the function of the artistic product being simply to produce a sense of the beautiful in the people who regard it. Just as warmth according to Idealism is not an attribute of fire, but is the effect produced by the fire on the senses, so beauty is an effect produced on the aesthetic sense.

IMPLICATIONS OF THE SUBJECTIVIST VIEW. Tolstoy, it is clear, is perfectly right on his premises in declaring that, inasmuch as Russian peasant songs have a wider appeal than *King Lear*, inasmuch, that is to say, as they produce a feeling of pleasure in numerically more people than *King Lear*, they are to that extent greater works of art. The young mechanic who contemplates Botticelli's Round Madonna in the National Gallery and, finding it to be productive of less pleasure than a magazine cover which features bathing belles, dismisses it as unimportant, has passed as correct an aesthetic judgement as that of the art connoisseur who prefers the Madonna ; in fact, he has passed a more correct judgement, since more people undoubtedly derive satisfaction from the contemplation of the bathing belles than of the Round Madonna.

The bearing of this view upon music is no less startling. Most contemporary persons undoubtedly prefer jazz to Bach. Therefore, the composers of jazz have succeeded in communicating emotion to more people than has the music of Bach. Therefore, according to the argument, jazz is greater music than Bach's.

Now it should be noted that this somewhat repellent conclusion cannot be refuted by logic, just as no conclusion based on consistent reasoning from extreme subjectivist premises,[1] can be refuted by logic. But, although it may be logically irrefutable, there is not the least reason to suppose it to be true.

THE APPEAL TO THE EXPERTS. The usual method of refutation has lain in an appeal to the alleged consensus of opinion amongst experts. It is said that people who have technical knowledge of music, who have studied it all their lives and who as a result have formed mature tastes, who have, moreover, in the course of their study listened both to Bach's music and to Jazz a great many times, unhesitatingly prefer the former.

There is, it might be urged, a real consensus of opinion as to the value of all great works of art—Shakespeare and Beethoven are often instanced in this connection—and this consensus is a sufficient guarantee of the correctness of the judgement it embodies. An appeal is made also to the effects of time. Jazz is ephemeral ; Bach, it is said, will live.

The difficulty attaching to this kind of answer lies not only in the controversy that exists amongst experts as to

[1] See remarks on Solipsism, Chapter II, p. 56.

the merits of any work that may be instanced, but also in determining the choice of the selected experts whose views shall be privileged to form the consensus. What exactly constitutes an expert? An expert is not simply a man who knows about music. Many people who are not experts in the sense required by the present argument, inasmuch as they *do* prefer Jazz to Bach are, nevertheless, skilled musicians who have spent their lives in the study of music and whose profession it is to compose it. Again an expert is not a man who agrees unfailingly with other experts as to the merits of an acknowledged great piece of music. It is a commonplace that experts differ amongst themselves, and the controversy amongst rival musicians over any and every piece of music is far more obvious than any alleged consensus. In fact, it turns out in the long run that the experts, according to whose judgement we feel justified in elevating Bach above Jazz, are simply the people who happen to prefer the former to the latter. Thus this refutation of aesthetic subjectivism fails, owing to the difficulty of defining the expert. The attempted refutation has in fact involved itself in a vicious circle. Its argument may be expressed in question and answer form as follows : " By what criterion are we to judge Bach superior to Jazz?" Answer: " By the consensus of opinion among experts who unanimously prefer it." " By what criterion are we to select these experts whose judgement is to be trusted ? " Answer : " They may be known by virtue of the fact that they prefer Bach to Jazz."

2. MODIFIED SUBJECTIVIST POSITION

A view which is sometimes advocated is that beauty consists in a certain relation between the mind and the aesthetic object. Objects, it is said, cannot be beautiful if there is nobody to appreciate them, since the existence, no less than the experience, of beauty necessarily involves the co-operation of a mental element. Beauty, in fact, only comes into being when the mind makes contact with objects of a certain class, beauty being a quality that supervenes on the union of mind and object, in virtue of a certain harmony between the two. This view is commonly found in association with a monistic metaphysic,[1] which asserts that wholes are both more than and more real than the sum of their parts. This assertion is, as we shall see, made more particularly in regard to the whole which is an act of knowledge, of which the knowing mind and the known object are constituent parts.[2] It is of such a whole, it would be said, that beauty is a characteristic. This view is highly congenial to idealist modes of thought and is the sort of view that would be advocated by the large number of philosophers who would regard it as inconceivable that any quality, whether beauty or its opposite, squareness or roundness, green or blue, could belong to a world of objects which is not being perceived by any human mind. There is no short way of answering this contention, provided that those who advance it are prepared to accept *all* the consequences which it entails. What these consequences are, I shall try to show in Chapter XV.

3. Dr. I. A. Richards's View

Subjectivist views in some form or other are extremely prevalent in modern thought. One of the best known statements of them will be found in the work of Dr. I. A. Richards. In his *Principles of Literary Criticism* and *Foundations of Aesthetics*,[3] Dr. Richards has put forward the view that what we call beauty is emotional satisfaction. When we say of a thing that it is beautiful, what, in his view, we mean is that certain impulses in ourselves are brought by the contemplation of it to a state of emotional equilibrium or harmony. Because of this condition of equilibrium we experience satisfaction and postulate the presence of beauty in that which has caused it. But such postulation is only a projection into the outside world of our own feelings.

[1] See Chapter XV, pp. 412–428, for an account of Monism.
[2] See pp. 424–426.
[3] *Foundations of Aesthetics* was written in conjunction with Mr. C. K. Ogden.

This theory has a psychological background from which it cannot be divorced. Man's psychological life, it is pointed out, consists very largely (if not wholly) of a constant play of impulses, which are partly excited by the stimuli coming from his environment. Now these impulses are often inharmonious ; they conflict. It is desirable, therefore, to systematise them : " A complete. systematisation," says Dr. Richards, " must take the form of such an adjustment as will preserve free play to every impulse with entire avoidance of frustration." " In any equilibrium of this kind," his account concludes, " however momentary, we are experiencing beauty." The fact that all our impulses are harmonised and integrated, that " as we realise beauty," we for the moment " *are* the whole complex of our impulses," is said to be the explanation of the detachment so often noted as a characteristic of aesthetic experience. The state of equilibrium is further described as being active, and in this respect it is distinguished from irresolution. Irresolution is a mere balancing of equally strong impulses, which " sustain severally their independent phases," whereas in " equilibrium " the active impulses " do yet sustain one state of mind." But, although the phrase, " we need not have experienced Beauty " is used, as though Beauty were, in truth, an object of experience, no mention is made anywhere in the account of *the object* of aesthetic enjoyment, the work of art. It is thought sufficient that an account of aesthetics should be given in terms of states of mind.

IV. CRITICISM OF SUBJECTIVIST THEORIES

It is obvious that the theories briefly outlined above are incompatible with Plato's view that beauty is objective, since they do in fact deny the existence of any objective element or factor which is present in and common to all types of beautiful objects, and which remains present and common whether a mind happens to be appreciating those objects or not. Since the primary purpose of this chapter and the last is to expound and develop Plato's Theory of Ideas in its application to different departments of contemporary philosophical enquiry, I propose to offer certain criticisms of the theories in question before proceeding to a positive application of Plato's view, since, if these theories are right in their main contention, no such application can hope to be successful.

Criticism of Dr. Richards's Views.

I will begin with the third form of the subjectivist view which I took from Dr. I. A. Richards's work. The question with which we are concerned is " What do we mean by the word ' beauty,' when we affirm of a particular work of art that it possesses beauty ? " Regarded as an answer to this question, Dr. Richards's position seems to be open to four different objections.

(1) Nobody supposes that, when I apprehend a square piece of wood, squareness is a characteristic of my apprehension ; nor, when we say " this piece of wood is square," does there seem any reason to suppose that we mean to assert something about a state of mind and not about the piece of wood. If this is the case in regard to the proposition " this piece of wood is square," there seems to be no reason why it should not be the case in regard to the proposition " this picture is beautiful." That there may be doubt as to the proper analysis of the proposition and doubt as to the proper meaning of the word " beautiful," is true. But that the proposition does not purport to assert something about a state of mind and does purport to something about the picture, there can be, I think, no doubt. Moreover, in practice it is clear that, when one praises the beauty of a picture, one does not mean to say something complimentary about a process going on in one's own mind. Nobody would be prepared to accept as an adequate description of the merits of a house an account of the feelings of those who were looking over it with a view to living in it ; yet *mutatis mutandis* it is precisely to such a description that

Dr. Richards's account commits us in respect of the beauty of pictures.

(2) If Dr. Richards is correct, what we mean by calling a picture beautiful is that there is a certain equilibrium among our impulses, when we enjoy it. Now that this equilibrium may be achieved in aesthetic appreciation, and that it is an important characteristic of the mental state of a person enjoying aesthetically, nobody would wish to deny. It may be the case either (a) that equilibrium between impulses is a *necessary condition* of my enjoying aesthetically, or (b) that it is *the result* of my enjoying aesthetically, or (c) that it is an *invariable*, or at least a *frequent accompaniment* of my enjoying aesthetically. But to assert that either (a) or (b) or (c) is the case, is certainly not equivalent to asserting that equilibrium of the impulses *is* aesthetic enjoyment, still less that it is what we *mean* by beauty or aesthetic value.

(3) The view that all that we *mean* by beauty is that there is an equilibrium of impulses in the person experiencing it, has difficulty in explaining the circumstance that works of art which are valued in one age are neglected in another. If to say that a work of art is valuable means only " there is an equilibrium of impulses in all or most persons who are brought into contact with it," and if sometimes (e.g. in an age when the work is appreciated) there is equilibrium and sometimes there is not, we must suppose that the value of a work of art (and not merely the estimation in which it is held) varies from age to age, and that, if the world relapsed into savagery, it would have no value at all.

(4) We "realise beauty," says Dr. Richards, when all our impulses are harmonised. That harmonisation of impulses is not what we *mean* by beauty, has been pointed out in (2) above. But let us suppose that such harmonisation is a psychological condition which either invariably accompanies aesthetic appreciation, or is its cause, or its effect. Now Dr. Richards nowhere maintains that *any and every* object is capable of producing this effect. (I take the second of the three alternatives (a), (b) and (c) for the sake

of shortness, but the argument is unaffected, if the harmony of impulses is *the cause* or the *invariable accompaniment* of beauty.) It is, therefore, we must presume, only objects belonging to a certain class which he would regard as the appropriate objects of aesthetic estimation. Every such object is, therefore, on Dr. Richards's view, distinguished by a certain property, the property, namely, of being able— able, presumably, under certain conditions—to effect a harmony of impulses in the person appreciating it. Now this property is truly a property of the object. It is not, that is to say, an event in the psychology of the appreciator, since it is the cause of such an event, nor is it a relation between the appreciator and the object. What, then, can the property be ? Before I try to answer this question, it is necessary to deal with a possible objection. Hitherto we have assumed, what Dr. Richards has implied, that it is only objects of a certain class which are capable of evoking aesthetic emotion. But many would deny this. All objects, they would say, are capable of being regarded aesthetically. This assertion would, I think, be made by many modern art critics, who lay stress upon the fact that the practical restriction of fine art to music, painting, sculpture, pottery, and textiles is in the nature of an historical accident. Given the right situation and circumstances, given also an appreciating mind in the requisite state of sensibility, then, they would say, it is always possible that there should be aesthetic emotion. Suppose that we grant this contention, which is certainly not open to logical refutation. What follows ? That all objects and all arrangements of objects possess a property such that, when a mind in the right condition of sensibility is brought into contact with them, there is aesthetic emotion, that is to say, if Dr. Richards is right, harmony of impulses ; or, more shortly, all objects and arrangements of objects possess the property of evoking in certain circumstances aesthetic emotion in minds which are in the right condition of sensibility. What, then, we may now repeat the question, can this property be?

Plato's answer would be " the property or characteristic

of being beautiful, which the object possesses in virtue of its participation in the Form of Beauty." Before I proceed to develop this answer, I propose to supplement the treatment of Mr. Richards's views by a more general criticism of subjectivist views, as formulated in the two versions of subjectivist theory, the more and the less extreme, which were outlined in (1) and (2) above.

General Criticism of Subjectivism.

1. First, it is only on the basis of a thoroughgoing idealism that even a modified subjectivism such as that described in (2) on pages 338, 339 above is tenable. The realist to whom it was suggested that beauty is a characteristic of compound wholes, of which the mind and object each constitute integral parts, would be immediately prompted to ask " Is not the table something different from my knowledge of the table ? " He would answer that it certainly is different ; indeed, he would go further and assert that it is only possible for me to know the table because my knowledge of the table is not the table.[1] " If therefore I abolish my mind," comes his next question, " do I also abolish the table or my knowledge of the table only ? " ; and his answer must be, " My knowledge of the table only." He would then apply exactly the same argument to a beautiful object, and draw the conclusion that, if we abolish a knowing mind, we abolish not the beauty of the object known, but only the appreciation of that beauty. Unless, then, we are prepared to identify beauty with the appreciation of it, and assert that they are synonymous terms, the conclusion that beauty is a relation between the mind and object, and not something inherent in the object is inadmissible. That such an identification cannot be correct seems to the present author self-evident. If, for " beauty," we can read at will, " appreciation of beauty," we are, as I suggested above, driven to conclude that when we admire a beautiful sunset, we are only admiring our own admiration of the sunset, with the corollary that we never make contact with the real

[1] See Chapter III, pp. 74, 80, 81, for an elaboration of these contentions.

sunset at all. Aesthetic appreciation becomes in this view an emotion of approval for something which is happening in our own minds.

The Mysterious Character "X".

(2) The fourth of the criticisms urged against Dr. Richards's view[1] may also be used against any form of Subjectivism. It is not asserted that it is upon the union of mind with *any* known object that beauty is said to supervene, but only upon its union with objects of a certain class, those, namely, which, when rightly appreciated by a mind in a certain condition or state of development, are capable of evoking aesthetic appreciation in the mind in question. Now the property of belonging to a certain class is a property which the object possesses in its own right, independently, that is to say, of its entry into relation with a mind. If we call the property (X), we may say that it is only objects which are independently qualified by (X) which are capable of entering into a relation with a mind such that aesthetic emotion is aroused. But in thus postulating the independent possession by an object of a property which is essential to the occurrence of what is called aesthetic experience, we are in fact affirming the objective basis of aesthetic value. If, however, it is maintained that all objects are capable of entering into the requisite state of union with a mind, then the property (X) must be universally postulated.

(3) It is important to notice that any view which, while refusing to subscribe to the extreme Tolstoyan conclusion, seeks, nevertheless, to compromise with subjectivism, can be reduced to the more extreme position which it seeks to avoid. Let us, for example, subject to critical examination the modified view[2] that beauty is a property neither of A (the picture) nor of B (the mind), but of R, when R is the relation between A and B. Now the relation of the mind to a picture which it appreciates is obviously different from its relation to a picture which it dislikes. R therefore varies as A varies ; it also varies as B varies, since the same mind

[1] See pp. 342, 343 above.   [2] See pp. 338, 339 above.

may entertain different feelings towards the same picture at different times. Since R varies with B, it is partly dependent for its characteristics upon the characteristics of B ; hence beauty, which on this view is a characteristic of R, turns out on analysis to be dependent upon *a prior* characteristic of B. Beauty, therefore, is not an objective entity existing independently of mind in its own right ; it is a characteristic of a relation, which varies with and is, therefore, dependent upon the existence of a certain attitude of mind, or, more accurately, of certain states of feeling. Aesthetic value, in other words, on this view, no less surely than on the more extreme view, is subjective. The extent to which it will characterise the relation between a mind and a particular work of art depends, that is to say, at least in part upon the sentiments which the perceiver experiencing the work in question entertains in regard to it ; if these sentiments are hostile, or if they are negative, the relation will not be the required character, and we are not entitled, therefore, to say that the work of art is beautiful.

Value of Uncontemplated Beauty.   (4) Let us suppose that all people in the world are abolished but one. Let the sole survivor of humanity—and for the moment we will assume that there is no such thing as a divine mind—be confronted with the Sistine Madonna of Raphael. This picture, it will be said by subjectivists, is still beautiful because it is being appreciated. Suppose, further, that in the midst of the last man's contemplation of the picture he too is abolished. Has any alteration occurred in the picture ? Has it experienced any change ? Has in fact anything *been done to* it ? The only change that has occurred is that it has ceased to be appreciated. Does it, therefore, automatically cease to be beautiful ? Those who hold the subjectivist position must maintain that it does, and, as I pointed out above, there is no logical disproof of their contention. Yet, although it cannot be disproved, I maintain that it fails to make provision for the undoubted fact that we all of us do feel that it is better that an uncontemplated Madonna should exist than an

uncontemplated cesspool. The existence and prevalence of this sentiment is well brought out in the following passage from G. E. Moore's *Principia Ethica*.

" Let us imagine one world " (he says) " exceedingly beautiful. Imagine it as beautiful as you can : put in whatever in the world you most admire—mountains, rivers, the sea, trees, sunsets, stars, and moon. Imagine all this combined in the most exquisite proportions, so that no one thing jars against another, but each contributes to increase the beauty of the whole. And then imagine the ugliest world you can possibly conceive. Imagine it simply as a heap of filth, containing everything that is most disgusting to us for whatever reason and the whole, so far as may be, without one redeeming feature. . . . The only thing we are not entitled to imagine is that any human being ever has or ever by any possibility can see and enjoy the beauty of the one or hate the foulness of the other. . . . Is it irrational to hold that it is better that the beautiful world should exist than the one which is ugly ? "

The answer that it is irrational requires a certain amount of intellectual hardihood, nor, outside the philosophical lecture-room, would the answer be likely to command assent. We do, that is to say, believe in our hearts that beauty is better than ugliness, even if there is nobody to enjoy it, and although the amount of weight which should be given to an instinctive belief of this kind is a matter for discussion, and although no philosopher would assert that, even if such an instinctive belief were universal, it constituted anything in the nature of proof, yet we are, I should say, entitled to take it into account as a factor lending support to the view that beauty is objective. Plato would probably explain this universal prepossession in favour of uncontemplated beauty in terms of the doctrine of Recollection.[1] In any event the presupposition exists, and the view that it is the reflection of some factor in the nature of things to which the human mind responds is by no means lightly to be dismissed.

[1] See Chapter XI, pp. 285-287.

Let us now proceed to develop a positive theory of aesthetics on the basis of Plato's Theory of Ideas.

V. DEVELOPMENT OF AN OBJECTIVE THEORY OF AESTHETICS

Clive Bell's Theory of Significant Form. The fundamental aesthetic problem may be most appropriately stated in the form of the following question : " Why is it that certain forms, colours and sounds, when arranged and combined in certain ways, profoundly move us, and move us in a particular manner, while a different arrangement of the same forms, colours and sounds moves us not at all ? Why," to take a concrete example, " does the statement of the theme of a Bach fugue thrill us to ecstasy, while the notes which constitute the theme, when played haphazard or in reverse order succeed only in producing dissonance or dullness ? " Perhaps the best modern treatment of the subject from the Platonic point of view, is that contained in Mr. Clive Bell's celebrated book *Art*. I do not mean that Mr. Bell is explicitly an advocate of Plato's Theory of Ideas, but all that he has to say on the subject of aesthetics not only falls within the framework of the Platonic hypothesis, but constitutes a forceful and vivid application of Plato's theory of objective beauty to the interpretation of the significance of works of art and the practical problems of art criticism. What, in fact, Mr. Bell does is to derive from an aesthetic position which is in all essentials that of Plato a criterion or standard of artistic value of which art criticism stands badly in need. Mr. Bell's view is developed more particularly in regard to the visual arts, but with the requisite changes in point of detail it could be made equally applicable to music. " The starting point for all systems of aesthetic experience," Mr. Clive Bell tells us, " must be the personal experience of a peculiar emotion. The objects that provoke this emotion we call works of art." The emotions produced by works of art may differ in quality and differ in intensity. But they are all of the same type, and to emotions of this type we give the name of "aesthetic." Unless we agree that works of art all possess this common quality of provoking aesthetic emotion, and unless we also agree that works of art and only works of art do provoke it, it is clear that when we speak generically of works of art, as if they were objects belonging to a certain class, we are talking nonsense. However they may differ in form, subject, or manner of appeal, unless they have this common quality they are not works of art at all.

A work of art produces aesthetic emotion in virtue of the fact that it possesses significant form. To the question "What does Mr. Bell mean by significant form?", I shall return in a moment. For the present it is sufficient to say that the immediate cause of the possession of significant form by a work of art is the experiencing of a certain emotion felt by its creator, an emotion to which it gives expression. It is the fact that the artist has felt this emotion while the copyist has not, which explains the otherwise inexplicable circumstance that, while a picture may move us profoundly, a reasonably exact copy or a photograph of the same picture will move us not at all.

This emotion felt by the artist, which is the indispensable condition of the presence of significant form in the picture, is an emotion for something which the artist has seen. The something seen will be, in its first description, an ordinary physical object—a face, a landscape, or a building—but I use the words "in its first description" in order to indicate the fact that it is not as a face, a landscape, or a building that the artist sees it. The ordinary man sees an object in relation to its possible utility to himself, and in so doing sees only as much of it as it is necessary to see for the purpose. Emotion may, of course, be felt for the object when seen in this way, but it is not the object itself which causes the emotion. An object seen as the ordinary man sees it may be a medium for conveying emotion, but it is not for it that the emotion is felt. Thus the face of a loved woman may provoke the emotion of jealousy, the sight of a pointed revolver the emotion of fear, but these emotions are felt not for the object considered as an object, but for the train of ideas which the object arouses.

Differentiation Between the Artist and the Ordinary Man.

We do not in fact in ordinary life see things in themselves ; we see them in relation to the purposes which we wish to fulfil in regard to them, and as means to the fulfilment of those purposes. The artist, and the artist alone, sees an object not as a means to something outside itself but as an end in itself ; and, in saying that he sees it as an end in itself, I mean that he sees it as a combination of significant forms. It is precisely thus that those of us who are not artists see works of art, when we see them rightly. Thus a possible definition of an artist from the point of view of Mr. Bell's theory is a man who feels for natural objects the sort of emotion which the non-artist feels only for works of art.

Consider, for example, the case of the typical Dutch picture. Apparently a coloured photograph of a simple scene, in which every detail is accurately reproduced—it is a difficult exercise to try to state in what respect a Vermeer differs from a coloured photograph—it is invested with a significance which the scene itself lacks. Or lacks for most people ! For Vermeer, presumably, differs from most people in being able to see in the scene the significance which we cannot observe save in the picture. What he has done is to drag it forth from the irrelevant setting in which it lurked, and throw it into high relief. He does not create beauty ; he is the midwife who brings to birth the beauty that is latent in things.

We may now advance a step further and hazard the view that it is because the artist has transferred to canvas the significant form which he has discerned in the material object, that we obtain from his picture the same emotion as that which he obtained from the object ? In other words, just as we see works of art as ends in themselves, divorced from purpose, unrelated to utility, so does the artist see material objects. They are to him, as pictures are to us, not means for conveying an emotion but objects of emotion.

Now the power to see objects continuously in this way, not as related to the purposes of life, but as combinations of significant forms and hence as objects which arouse aesthetic emotion, is a very rare one besides being from the strictly evolutionary point of view a mistake. " Biologically speaking," as Roger Fry puts it, " art is a blasphemy. We were given our eyes to see things, not to look at them."

The view that objects can be seen as ends in themselves—that is to say, as combinations of significant forms —is not one which is easy to expound in a few sentences. It may be that no amount of exposition can render it intelligible to those who have never felt an emotion for objects seen in this way. But most people do, in fact, from time to time get a vision of objects as pure form. There are occasions for most of us when we see a landscape not as so many fields, cottages and trees, but as a combination of colours and forms, and have experienced the thrill that we normally obtain only from works of art. You look, for example, at a tree on many occasions and notice it only as possible timber, or as an elm, or as dangerous ; or you do not notice it at all. Then comes a day when you *suddenly* notice that it is beautiful : and it is the same with a picture ; its beauty *suddenly* strikes us.

In such moments it may be conceived that we see with the eyes of the artist, obtaining from material objects the peculiar emotion in virtue of which those gifted with the artist's power of expression are enabled to create pictures which possess significant form. The word " create " is used here loosely, because it signifies what the artist is commonly supposed to do. But if beauty be an objective quality of things, is creation the name properly to be ascribed to his activity ?

What is Significant Form ?   This question can only be answered by examining a little more in detail what is meant by the words " significant form." The formal significance of a thing has been defined as the significance of that thing considered as an end in itself. When we consider an object as "an end in itself," our minds become aware of that in it which is of greater importance than any qualities which it may have derived from its human associations or power of satisfying human needs. They become aware, in short, of the reality which is behind it, and which is latent in it. It is this reality, and not the object in which the reality is manifested, that thrills the artist to ecstasy, and it is the emotion felt for reality which he conveys to us when he succeeds in transferring to canvas his vision of reality as a combination of pure forms. And now the argument has reached a point at which it can return to Plato.

Behind the world of sensible objects, imperfectly manifested in them and overlaid and distorted by the sensuous material in which they appear, lies, so Plato asserted, the world of Forms. To this world he gives the name of reality, because it alone possesses perfect and immutable being, while the world of which our senses make us aware is, as we have seen, designated semi-real by reason of the fact that it is imperfect and continuously changing. The question of the relation between these two worlds is no doubt a source of difficulty.[1] Whether or no the Forms are the *cause* of the existence of sensible objects, they stand, nevertheless, in a necessary relationship to them, the relationship being one which may be metaphorically expressed by the statements that they lie behind the appearances of visible things, endow them with their characteristics, and give them the peculiar significance of which Mr. Bell speaks. When, therefore, it is said that the artist views an object as a combination of pure forms, what is meant is that he possesses the capacity to discern the element of reality which is latent in the object, to disentangle it from the sensuous material in which it is embodied, and, by expressing his vision of it in his picture, to enable us to glimpse the pure form which he has visualised.

It is for this reason that, though the form of artistic expression changes from age to age, the feelings which

[1] See Chapter XI, pp. 295–297.

great art awakens have been the same in every age. The forms of art are inexhaustible, but they all lead along the same road of aesthetic emotion to the contemplation of the same ultimate reality. It is for this reason, too, that questions of aesthetic criteria, of the sources of the work of particular artists, of the schools to which they belong, or of their influence upon their successors are irrelevant to aesthetic appreciation, and it is not necessary to know how, when, or by whom a work of art was created in order that the vision of the reality which it imperfectly reveals may be enjoyed. Art, on this view, is a window through which we gaze upon reality ; the panes vary from age to age and sometimes they are bright and sometimes dim, but the view which they offer is eternally the same.

Art as the Window of Reality.   And since art enables us to glimpse a reality which lies outside the realm of that of which we are normally aware, the emotions which it arouses are not of this world. Aesthetic emotion is emotion felt not for this world but for reality ; it is, therefore, unlike all other emotions, being both unanalysable and unique. It is for this reason that we speak of the quality of remoteness in art. For so long as the vision which art vouchsafes endures, we are shut off from the interests which this world begets. Our anticipations and regrets, our hopes and fears, are alike arrested. It is as if we were enabled for the moment to escape from the stream of life and, forgetful of the turmoil of want and desire, of striving and seeking which life involves, to be at peace upon the banks.

Some have held that the emotion which we obtain from works of art is an emotion of the same kind as that felt by the mystic, and for the reason that it is felt for the same object. But while the mystic's vision of reality would seem to be direct, in that it is achieved by the contemplation of the mind without the aid of the senses, the artist's is indirect, since he uses and uses of necessity sensuous objects as the medium in which reality is seen and through which it is approached. The mystic's vision, moreover, is at times

MP

continuous and prolonged ; the artist's is tantalisingly brief. Hardly are we aware that the veil has been lifted, before it is withdrawn ; hardly is the vision glimpsed, before it passes, and passing, leaves a feeling of indefinable long-- ing and regret. Thus aesthetic emotion is at once the most satisfying and the most unsatisfying of all the emotions known to us ; satisfying because of what it gives, unsatisfy- ing because it gives so briefly, and, in the act of giving hints at greater gifts withheld. It is on some such lines as these that the view that beauty is objective may be worked out in relation to the facts of aesthetic experience. As we have seen, the view in question originates with Plato, and the foregoing is in effect little more than a development of hints and suggestions thrown out by him in various pas- sages in the Dialogues.

Summary. It is time to draw together the threads of the above discussion by appending a series of conclusions. First, as to the meaning of the word " beauty " : when we say " this picture is beautiful," we are asserting, even if we cannot satisfactorily define its nature, a necessary con- nection between the picture and the Form of Beauty. The existence of this connection is a condition of our judgement being true. The existence of the physical picture is also, of course, a condition of the judgement's being true, but it is not sufficient for its truth. It is not enough that the picture should exist ; it is necessary that the Form of Beauty should be manifested in it.

Secondly, as to the criterion of value in a work of art : this is different from the purpose of the artist, and has no connection either with what the artist may have in his mind, or with the effect he may be aiming to produce, (with what is sometimes called his ideal) or with his success in communicating emotion to or arousing emotion in an audience, or with any judgement of appreciation or the reverse that any person or body of persons, expert or other- wise, may pass upon the work of art produced.

The criterion of the value of a work of art lies outside the work of art and is to be found in the Form of Beauty. If the Form manifests itself in the work, the work is beautiful ; if not, not. Whether it will do so or not, depends not upon the artist's intention or upon his power of expressing that intention, but upon his capacity for vision. If he possesses the capacity for vision, in virtue of which he is able to disentangle the manifestation of the Form of Beauty from the physical setting in which it appears, then the work which he produces will possess that quality of significant form in virtue of which we say that it has aesthetic value. If he does not, no amount of training, no mastery over technique, will enable him to produce beautiful works. There is— the fact is obvious—no known formula for securing the manifestation of the Form in a work of art. If there were, art would not be art but science. We may, however, following Plato's hint, suggest that the best method of approach to beauty, which is also the best recipe for the construction of valuable works of art, is strict discipline by the artist in the exact sciences of measuring, weighing, and counting.

The Incalculable Element in Art. Translated into modern terms, this means that an artist who has perfected himself in the technique of drawing and painting, who has mastered the theory of harmony and the rules of orchestration, or who pays strict attention to requirements of rhythm and metre, will be more likely to produce a work of beauty than one who sets about his task uninstructed and without study. But such training and study will not enable the artist to command the Form, or to ensure that beauty will clothe his work. The coming of the Form knows no law. It is the incalculable element in all art ; it can neither be compelled nor cajoled.

And this would seem to be the reason for the fact, so often noted, that works of the greatest elaboration and technical skill are yet not great works of art. This explains also why beauty attaches to the work of some men who disregard all the rules, and throw all canons of taste overboard, whilst it eschews the laboured productions of those who follow rigorously and with perfect taste the best traditions of the elders. But it is equally true that the Form of Beauty is more likely to be attracted where a knowledge of technique is present than where such knowledge is absent, and that, other things being equal, knowledge and skill are more likely to produce works of beauty than the so-called inspiration which is too often devoid of them.

This is as far as Plato takes us. In the last resort the apprehension of the Form, in virtue of which the artist is enabled to produce work of aesthetic value, is left unexplained. Effort and training help, but they are not sufficient ; whether the artist's efforts will be rewarded by a vision of reality, it does not lie with him to determine. But this at least is certain, that if his vision does not penetrate through to the Form of Beauty, however fleeting the glimpse, then he will not, except perhaps by lucky chance, produce work of aesthetic value.

Apology for Personal Bias.

I am conscious that some part of what has been written above involves a greater intrusion of personal views than may be considered justifiable in a book of this kind. The theory of the aesthetic process that has been outlined is, indeed, very far from being held by all or even by most philosophers, and it is at least open to question whether Plato's Theory of Ideas would be developed along precisely the above lines by any other philosopher.

Two considerations may be urged in mitigation, if not in complete justification, of this intrusion of the personal. In the first place, I have thought it desirable to exhibit the implications of Plato's metaphysical view in their relation to topics of current philosophical discussion and controversy. One of these is the correct interpretation of the findings of modern physics ; another the nature of the process known as artistic creation and the meaning of aesthetic judgements. The very fact that these are issues of current controversy precludes the possibility that there should be any accepted view in regard to them. Upon such issues the expression of a personal view is, perhaps, less open to censure than in those departments of the subject where some degree of agreement exists, or in which, even if there is disagreement, the opinions of opposing schools of thought and the differences between them have been clearly defined by centuries of philosophical discussion. The force of this apology is strengthened, if the field is one in which the application and development of Plato's metaphysics can be shown to be particularly fruitful. This I believe to be pre-eminently the case in regard to the field of aesthetics.

In the second place, philosophers have of recent years become increasingly conscious of the debt which philosophy owes to Plato—Professor Whitehead, indeed, as we have seen, characterises " the European philosophical tradition " as " a series of footnotes of Plato "—and Plato's theories, or theories which derive from Plato, bulk largely in contemporary discussion. This is particularly true of the two fields in which I have sought to apply and to develop the Theory of Ideas. In the field of the philosophy of science, the most discussed view at the present time is that of Professor Whitehead.[1] The most distinctive feature of Professor Whitehead's philosophy is the postulation of eternal objects which, entering into the flux of events, confer upon the physical world the characteristics which it is seen to possess. Thus Professor Whitehead's eternal objects bear a strong resemblance to Plato's Forms, both in respect of their intrinsic nature and of their relation to what Plato called the world of becoming. At the beginning of his most substantial metaphysical work, *Process and Reality*, Professor Whitehead owns and welcomes the analogy, and refers to Plato as his chief teacher. " If," he says, " we had to render Plato's general point of view, with the least changes made necessary by the intervening two thousand years of human experience, in social organisation, in aesthetic attainment,

[1] See Chapter XIX for a brief summary of some of the leading ideas in Professor Whitehead's philosophy.

in science and in religion, we should have to set about the construction of a philosophy of organism." This task he has himself attempted. As regards the content of the present chapter, current discussions of aesthetics and ethics turn largely upon what is known to-day as the problem of Value. There is a widespread modern tendency to affirm that Goodness and Beauty are ultimate Values, and to interpret the special significance of morals and art in terms of their presence in the world. Many thinkers follow Plato in affirming these values to be independent factors in the universe, apprehended by mind, but not owing to mind the fact of their being. Hartmann's three-volume work on Value, *Ethics*, the most substantial contribution made to the subject in recent years, is definitely Platonic in outlook. Thus interpretations and applications of Plato are in the philosophical climate of our times, and there seemed to be no good reason why the fashion should not be followed to the extent of including two such interpretations in this book.

PLATO. Symposium.

BELL, CLIVE. Art.

TOLSTOY, L. What is Art?

OGDEN, C. K., AND RICHARDS, I. A. The Foundations of Aesthetics.

RICHARDS, I. A. Principles of Literary Criticism.

BOSANQUET, B. The History of Aesthetics.

ALEXANDER, S. Beauty and other Forms of Value.

CARRITT, E. F. Philosophies of Beauty.

WALLAS, G. The Art of Thought.

*Chapter XIV : OUTLINE OF KANT'S PHILOSOPHY

I. THE MATTER AND MANNER OF KANT 1724-1804

Introductory : Difficulty of Exposition.   I come now to a chapter which I have found more difficult to write than any of the others. For this there are two reasons. First, Kant's thought is intrinsically difficult, and makes use of conceptions which are not readily grasped. Secondly, his exposition is exceedingly obscure. His method of writing is abstract and diffuse ; he rarely condescends to use examples to illustrate his meaning, and his meaning itself changes in a bewildering way. Kant's thought, like that of most of the great philosophers, developed and, as the development took place, his views on matters of fundamental importance changed. Kant does not, however, usually take the trouble to inform us of the fact, which the reader is left to divine for himself on discovering to his surprise that a particular position which Kant happens to be maintaining is quite different from a position he formerly maintained. Nevertheless, such is the obscurity of Kant's writing that the reader can never feel quite sure that it *is* different. It always remains a possibility for the reader to reckon with that he has simply failed to understand what Kant is saying.

The understanding of Kant is not made easier by the fact that his philosophy seems at times to contain arguments for every philosophical position which the imagination of man can conceive, and for every possible permutation and combination of conceivable positions, so that the exasperated reader continually finds himself driven to ask "Now which of these positions do you really hold, since, if you hold this one, you cannot possibly hold that one ? "

All this makes it a matter of some difficulty to find out what Kant really did believe, and subsequent philosophers, while agreeing that his thought was exceedingly important, have rarely been able to reach agreement as to what precisely it was. The amount of expository and critical writing that Kant has evoked is prodigious, but it cannot be said that this vast corpus of explanation and criticism has succeeded in reducing Kant's views to a clear, simple and agreed statement.

A further difficulty of a more personal character has beset the writing of this chapter. When the author of a book which aims at giving an impartial and disinterested survey of a controversial subject is conscious of bias, he will do well to avow it. I have already avowed a bias in favour of Platonic philosophy, and given a somewhat personal interpretation of its application to aesthetic theory. I have now to make a further confession, this time of unfavourable bias. Without actually subscribing to the dictum of a famous modern philosopher, who announced that "Kant is the greatest disaster in the history of philosophy," I find his general position no less unsatisfactory than his method of expounding it is exasperating. I do not think that the universe is as Kant conceived it, and I do not think that philosophy ought to be written as he writes it.

Explanation of Kant's Mode of Writing.

So much having been said by way of avowal of bias, which it is hoped the reader will remember to discount, I must endeavour to redress what will seem to many the unfairness of the foregoing comments by drawing attention to certain considerations which explain, if they do not justify, the peculiarities of Kant's manner and go far to justify the importance currently attributed to his matter. These observations, in so far as they relate to Kant's manner, I take from the Master of Balliol's recent book on Kant,[1] which, indeed, I have largely followed in the exposition of Kant's ideas.

Kant's most important work is the *Critique of Pure Reason*.

[1] *Kant*, by A. D. Lindsay (published by Benn).

He pondered over this work for eleven years. At the end of this period he still remained dissatisfied with his conclusions, but, alarmed at the delay in bringing out his book, which had been frequently announced and long expected, he proceeded to write it out in some four or five months. He was at the time lecturing for about fifteen hours every week, and under these conditions he must, Professor Lindsay calculates, have written about five pages a day. Working at this rate he must, it is obvious, have utilised material collected during the preceding eleven years, so that the *Critique*, as we know it, embodies his thought at various stages of development during the whole of that period. Secondly, as regards the numerous and sometimes incompatible alternative arguments which Kant gives for the same position, it is important to bear in mind the fact that he was a university teacher who was engaged in lecturing for from fifteen to thirty hours a week for a period of about twenty-five years. Kant was regarded as a lucid and attractive lecturer by those who found the *Critique* intolerably difficult, and the reason for the difference may well have been that in his lectures he employed the work of a somewhat arid philosopher, Baumgarten, as his text-book, and relied upon his own intellectual resources for comment and illustration. In the *Critique* he had to "introduce into his writing the element" which in his lecturing "had been supplied by the text book." Thus his readers had to swallow the powder without the jam.

More important is Kant's conception of philosophy as essentially a process of criticism. Philosophical thinking was for him the process whereby the mind reflects upon its own operations. His object in writing was, therefore, to make his readers think philosophically, that is, to undertake the process of reflection necessary to enable them to understand what Kant was saying and they were thinking. Kant's object, in fact, was, in his own words, to teach his pupils "not philosophy but to philosophise." Hence the number of different arguments addressed to his readers, whom, lecturer-like, he treats almost as if they were hearers. " It is," says Professor Lindsay, " as though Kant were saying, 'If that will not make you see it, perhaps this will.'" Hence, though Kant's main position remains in the view of his more friendly critics fairly constant, the arguments he uses in developing it change.

Contemporary Popularity of Kant.

As regards the matter of Kant's philosophy, it is only fair to say that this has been held in the highest estimation by the very great majority of his successors. It is usually said that Kant's thought effected a revolution in philosophy, and most philosophers to-day would assign to him a place among the great thinkers of the world, which only Plato, Aristotle, and perhaps Hegel, would be judged worthy to share.

Kant's thought, moreover, has a peculiar appositeness at the present time, since, of all metaphysical positions, that which he adopts is most favourable to the view of the physical world suggested by modern science.

As I pointed out in Chapter VIII,[1] the difficulties in the commonsense conception of causation exposed by Hume are now widely recognised by physicists themselves. The notion that one piece of matter can exert an influence over another from which it is separated by intervening space-time is regarded with suspicion by contemporary physicists ; the whole conception of force operating from a distance is, indeed, suspect. As the commonsense notion of a world of things separated by space and time whose motions are governed by laws which are independent of any observer grows increasingly difficult to maintain, it is inevitable that some other conception should be substituted. A number of suggestions are in the field, of which the one which is at once the most prominent and most plausible is that the objects with which science deals are in some sense mental constructions or, rather, mental abstractions, the physicist having, as it were, made them up, or carved them out for himself by abstracting from the real world only those qualities with which, in his capacity of physicist, he is

[1] See Chapter VIII, pp. 225-228.

competent to deal. All the rest, it is said, he ignores. Nor on this view is the procedure of the common man radically different from that of the physicist. He, too, abstracts from reality those aspects of it with which he is, as it were, capable of coping. But he does more than abstract. He imposes upon reality the characteristics in virtue of which he does cope with it ; only, in fact, in so far as he imposes these characteristics upon it, can he know it at all. Thus the mind is regarded as a lawgiver to nature. Such concepts as that of causation and action at a distance do not, it is said, really belong to the world as it is ; they only appear to hold in the world that we know because the mind has, as it were, put them there as a condition of knowing it.

Suggestions of this type continually recur in the thought of modern physicists. Purely scientific in origin, and put forward in the course of the attempt to resolve some of the difficulties with which contemporary physics finds itself beset, they owe nothing to philosophy. Yet it is precisely these same suggestions which, in a highly developed and elaborate form, constitute the basic contentions of Kant's philosophy. It is not without reason that modern scientists should affirm that Kant's metaphysical views afford a more hospitable structure than those of any other philosopher for the accommodation of the conclusions to which increasingly they find themselves driven, or that J. B. S. Haldane, devoting a chapter to Kant in his book of popular scientific essays, *Possible Worlds*, should insist that modern scientific developments make Kant's views "more important now than when Kant arrived at them a hundred years ago."

How Far is Kant Constructive ?

One further matter must be mentioned before I proceed to attempt an outline of Kant's system. I have included this chapter on Kant in the part devoted to "Constructive Metaphysics." Yet, strictly speaking, metaphysics does not, in the sense in which I am using the term, exist, for Kant. Metaphysics, as I pointed out in an earlier chapter,[1] is usually described as

[1] See Chapter VI, pp. 155, 156.

the study of the world of reality, of reality, that is to say, in contradistinction to the commonsense world of appearance. So conceived, metaphysics is sometimes called, and was called by Kant, " transcendent metaphysics." Now, for Kant, there can be no such study, since—it is the salient feature of his philosophy—the world of reality, is for him unknown and must remain unknown. Therefore, although he admits " immanent metaphysics," the study of reality, in so far as it is included in the world which we know, he denies the possibility of " transcendent metaphysics." The point is, however, an academic one. For Kant, although denying that we have knowledge of reality, if the word " knowledge " is interpreted in a strict sense, considers that we possess intimations of its nature in other forms of experience, notably in moral experience. Moreover, the view of the world with which he presents us is noticeably different from that which is taken for granted by common sense. He is thus, in all but the most strictly technical sense of the word, a metaphysician, and his methods are such as have been used by all the great metaphysical philosophers.

II. KANT'S PROBLEM

Retrospect.   In order to place ourselves at the starting point of Kant's philosophy, we must take a brief historical retrospect. In an earlier chapter[1] we raised and discussed the question, " Why should the laws of our thinking apply to the behaviour of things ? " The laws of logic and the formulæ of mathematics are mental products in the sense that the knowledge of them belongs to and is reached by minds ; some philosophers, as we saw in a previous Chapter,[2] have held that they are also mental descriptions, that is statements about the way in which the mind works. When we believe that three and two make five, that every effect must have a cause, and that a tree cannot both be and not be a beech, we do so, they have asserted, only

[1] Chapter V.   [2] See Chapter V, pp. 146-148.

because our minds are made like that. It is, they say, conceivable that creatures with minds differently constituted—Martians, for example, or white ants—might take different views. At any rate, they would conclude, there is no *necessary* reason why the universe should be of such a kind as to conform to the way in which our minds happen to work, why, in other words, the truth that three and two make five, a truth reached by human mental processes, should apply to the behaviour of non-human things.

Success of Science. The question at issue is raised in an acute form by the possibility and the success of physical science. The procedure of the scientist occupies a position midway between reasoning and sense-experience. Like mathematics or logic science makes use of reason, but unlike them, it checks the results of its reasoning by an appeal to sense-experience ; scientific conclusions, in short, must be verified. The existence and validity of mathematics provide no relevant problem, for here reason operates entirely within her own sphere and the results at which she arrives have not to be checked by experience. Again, there is no relevant problem in the fact that sense-experience should be possible, since we have five senses through which this experience comes. The puzzle is why the conclusions of the former should apply to the raw material provided by the latter ?

That they do, in fact, apply, the success of science demonstrates, the method of science being to apply the formulæ arrived at by reasoning process to the prediction of events and the behaviour of things. Science arrives, for example, at a general law like the law of gravitation, and predicts that the behaviour of things which have never been experienced will conform to it. And, when the experiment is made, they do, in fact, conform. A scientific law is, in other words, the result of the application of mathematical and logical reasoning to actual experience, and the problem is, why should things behave according to the expectations which reasoning leads us to form of them ?

Now Kant's answer to this problem brings us back to the controversy between rationalists and the empiricists, at which we have already glanced in Chapter IV. That there is a distinction between the things we know in sense-experience and those we know by means of our understanding, between the pairs of objects which the child adds together to make four and the general proposition that two and two make four, is obvious. Since, then, our general ideas are other than the individual particular experiences we get through our senses, our question may be rephrased : Why should our general ideas, which are *a priori*, be true of or apply to the things we immediately experience ; why, to take a concrete example, should such general laws as that two things which are each equal to a third thing are equal also to one another, or that, if A follows from B and B from C, then A also follows from C, apply to the things we know by means of our senses ?

Rationalism and Empiricism both Defective.

It was this problem which, more than any other, had led to the controversy between the rationalists and the empiricists. The rationalists had tended to reason away the actual stuff of our sense-experience ; they were concerned with the world as it ought to be, not in the moral sense of the word " ought," but in the sense in which ought implies necessity. In mathematics, for example, everything follows necessarily from everything else, and there is no place for anything which just is, and which could not, therefore, have been deduced from something else. Hence, the rationalists, when faced with brute-facts, such as the fact that a substance with the chemical composition of sugar happens to be sweet, a combination which just is, but which is not rational, tended to ignore it. They left out, that is to say, the observation of actual facts. The empiricists, realising that no amount of reasoning will give us information as to the nature of what exists, and that if, therefore, we want to know what the world is actually like, we must go and see, relied entirely upon sense-experience for knowledge, affirming that there was nothing in knowledge which had not previously been in sense-experience. Just as the rationalists made no provision for our observation of actual facts, so the empiricists made no provision for our knowledge of the general principles governing our observation, in virtue of which we arrange, compare, group together, or select from what we observe in order to form general conceptions. When pressed, they would, no doubt, have admitted the existence of these general conceptions, but on their premises they were totally unable to account for them. Thus, if the empiricists were right, reasoned knowledge was impossible ; if the rationalists were right, it would be impossible to explain how there were things to know. Nevertheless, it is perfectly clear that we do reason about and arrange our sense impressions, and that conclusions reached by mental processes do, in fact, apply to the world around us. The problem was, therefore, to find a *modus vivendi* between the rationalists and the empiricists, a *modus vivendi* which would reconcile the empiricists' insistence upon the observation of actual fact as the raw material of our experience, with the general principles of reasoning which, as the rationalists had shown, were used in working up this raw material into knowledge.

Kant's Reconciliation. It is to the solution of this difficulty that Kant applied himself. Given the problem that our senses provide us only with the raw stuff of experience, but that we, nevertheless, form general principles to which nature is found to conform, Kant's solution consists in effect in denying that the stuff of experience really is raw. In point of fact, he says, we never do have experience of nature, as nature is in herself. The stuff of our experience is not raw material coming to us direct from the outer world and revealing the outer world as it is, but a composite stuff, which has already been worked up and modelled by our minds in the process of becoming our experience. This being so, it is only to be expected that it should conform to the general laws which our minds prescribe. The rationalists' principles of reason apply, therefore, to the empiricists' raw material of experience because the material is not raw after all, but, if I may be forgiven the metaphor, has already been " cooked " in the process of reaching the understanding. Thus what we know is not nature as she is, but nature to which our minds have already given meaning. In this world of " meaning," which is the world that we know, the laws of thought apply simply because this is a world in the formation of which thought itself has assisted. Whether they apply to things in themselves, we do not know ; but this is of no importance since we never know things in themselves.

Kant's great contribution to philosophy is, therefore, to stress the activity of the experiencing subject. The mind in perception is not passive, but active. It acts as a lawgiver to nature, prescribing to the world we know the forms and conditions under which it shall appear to us. Thus, when we come to ask how it is that we already have knowledge *a priori* about the world which appears to us, Kant answers that it is because the same knowledge has been at work in the formation of what appears. The law of universal causation is admittedly a product of the understanding, but it is universally valid in the world we know, since the world we know is also a product of the understanding. Thus we know *a priori* of things only what we have ourselves put into them.

I have thought it well to make this preliminary survey of the ground to be covered, since an advance knowledge both of the problem and of the Kantian solution of it may perhaps facilitate the understanding of its more detailed statement, orienting the reader, as it were, by the points of the Kantian compass. We must now proceed to a more detailed exploration of the same ground.

Analytic *a Priori* Knowledge.

Those philosophers who, prior to Kant, had proceeded by *a priori* methods (Descartes, Spinoza and Leibnitz) had considered knowledge to be in essence analytical. Mathematical knowledge is, as we have seen, the typical form of *a priori* knowledge, and the achievements of mathematical knowledge were conceived to have been won by a process in which the mind developed the implications of certain initial postulates, axioms and definitions. The implications were, it was thought, somehow contained in the postulates, axioms and definitions to begin with, so that, if one knew these, there was a sense in which one also knew, although one's knowledge might not be explicit, all that they implied. Thus learning mathematics was a process of " digging out " the full implications of something that one knew already. It was, in other words, a process of analysing what was already given. Now it is perfectly true that the fact that the angles at the base of an isosceles triangle are equal is already given in or implied by the fact that the triangle is isosceles, so that we may say with equal justice, " An isosceles triangle is one that has equal angles at its base," and " A triangle which has equal angles at its base is isosceles." Each fact implies the other, so that, whichever of them one starts with, it will reveal the other to anybody who takes the trouble to " dig out " all its implications.

Whether *all* mathematics is of this kind may be open to question. But *some* mathematics certainly is, and the rationalists, who had been inclined to regard all knowledge as mathematical in character, tended therefore to think of *a priori* knowledge as analytical. It was a making clear or explicit of the implications of what one already somehow knew. And if the question were put " How did one come by this prior knowledge ? ", the general answer was Descartes's, that the mind possesses initially, as it were, certain " innate ideas " in which or by means of which this knowledge was, as it were, stored up. A man had only to develop these ideas and the knowledge would reveal itself. *A priori* knowledge, then, was analytical. It was also necessary, since, if A is implied or contained in B, then, so long as B is as it is, A cannot be other than it is.

Locke's Theory of Knowledge.   The empirical philosophers (Locke, Berkeley and Hume) had regarded knowledge

not as an analysis but as a synthesis. It was, that is to say, a putting together of experiences that were initially given as separate. To know a thing was to observe the fact of a number of separate " ideas "[1] habitually going together. These separate, simple ideas, which we find habitually going together, we associate[2] to form " complex " ones. Thus we find habitually going together in our experience a number of ideas of simple qualities—of whiteness, of coolness and of fluidity, for example. These we associate together, give them a general name, proceed to suppose some support or substratum for the qualities which produce the ideas in us (Locke's Substance[3]), and as a result say that we know milk. Thus the knowledge of milk is the result of a synthesis, the putting together of several simple and separate ideas. Hume, the most logical of the empiricists, did not attribute this " putting together " to the activity of the mind ; it was, for him, rather a kind of automatic associating on the part of the ideas themselves. The ideas associated themselves together by the mere fact of happening to occur together, and a " complex " idea was the result. Locke, less logical, thought of the mind as active in the process. It manipulated the simple ideas, the raw materials, of experience, and synthesised them to make complex ideas. Thus our knowledge of general ideas and of the principles which they embody is, for Locke, the result of the manipulative activity of the mind, which puts together the simple ideas, the raw materials of our experience, and produces ideas such as those of humanity and civilisation which are its own voluntary creations. In the interests of accuracy it should be pointed out that Locke also believed that the mind is initially provided with certain " abstract ideas," the examination and analysis of which is the origin of mathematics. But his successors, for example,

[1] See Chapter II, p. 39, for the special sense in which the word " ideas " was used by the empiricists.
[2] The language used in the text is appropriate to Locke. Hume regarded the ideas as associating themselves together. See p. 54.
[3] See Chapter II, pp. 40, 41.

Berkeley,[1] had little difficulty in showing this view to be inconsistent with Locke's empirical premises.

Let us proceed to a comparison of the two views of knowledge, the rationalist and the empiricist, the view that our knowledge of the fact that an isosceles triangle has equal angles at its base is a digging out of the necessary implications of the given fact that the triangle is isosceles, and the view that our knowledge of the fact that gold is yellow is an observation of the fact that certain qualities happen to go together, or is the result of such observation. We shall notice that not only is the first judgement analytical and *a priori*, while the second is synthetic and empirical, but that the first is necessary, while the second is contingent. There is, so far as we can see, no *necessary* reason why a substance which has the specific gravity of gold should be yellow ; we just notice that it is so.

Hume's Sceptical View of Knowledge.

Hume, taking the view that *all* knowledge was empirical, did not hesitate to draw the conclusion that no knowledge could be certain. If we assume with Hume that all knowledge is derived from sensation, and that it is nothing but a putting together or rather a " going together " of the ideas which are given in sensation, Hume's conclusion seems inescapable.

Herein lies the significance of his sceptical analysis of causation.[2] He denied that a knowledge of causation could be either demonstrated by reason or elicited from experience, precisely because he held a view of the nature of knowledge according to which what we know is limited to impressions derived from the senses,[3] and ideas which are copies of the impressions. Thus, in denying knowledge of causation, Hume was only developing the implications of the empiricist theory of knowledge, namely, that knowledge was a putting together of ideas which happened to go together in sensation, with more logic than the other

[1] See Chapter X. pp. 260, 261 for Berkeley's criticism of Locke's theory of " abstract ideas."

[2] See Chapter VIII, pp. 207–211.   [3] See Chapter II, p. 51.

empiricists. If the empiricist theory of knowledge was correct, then it was indeed the case, as Hume maintained, that our belief in causation could have no better basis than custom and feeling.

The Significance of Hume's Conclusion.

Kant, coming to the problem with different and fundamentally rationalist prepossessions, was unable to accept Hume's conclusion. Nevertheless, he was impressed with Hume's proof that the principle of causation could not be proved by pure reason, that it was not, in other words, discoverable by a process of analysing the knowledge which we already possess. Moreover, although not derived entirely from experience, since, like all general laws, it outruns experience, causation does undoubtedly apply to experience. The connection which we call " cause and effect " appears, therefore, to be both certain and necessary, like the *a priori* knowledge of the rationalists, and also to be synthetic like the " put together " knowledge of the empiricists, in the sense that it is a putting together of ideas of cause and ideas of effect which are given separately. Moreover, the law of causation, although owing to the accident of Hume's criticism it served to rivet Kant's attention upon the problem, waking him, as he put it, " from his dogmatic slumbers," was only a special case of a wider difficulty, the difficulty referred to above of understanding how science is possible.

The Validity of Science.

For science, too, outruns experience. When we make scientific judgements and formulate scientific laws, we are not merely experiencing and observing. In a sense, no doubt, we are describing what we see. But we are doing more than this. We are also describing what, under certain given circumstances that we are prepared to specify, we shall see. What science enables us to affirm is not merely that H_2O produces water now, but that H_2O will produce water to-morrow, that, in other words, hydrogen and oxygen, if associated together in the right proportions and in the right environment, will always and in all circumstances produce water. A scientific law is a statement to the effect that under certain conditions which are stated certain events will be experienced. It enables us, therefore, to calculate and to predict. It is for this reason that scientific laws can be verified. Thus in making scientific judgements the mind outruns experience. It lays down, that is to say, what, given certain circumstances, future experience will be, and it does this because it feels in a position to assert that, given the circumstances, reality will behave in a certain way and will do so *of necessity*. Admittedly the law may turn out to be wrong, but there is always an element of generality in it which cannot be wrong, and this general element is also the element of necessity. It is not necessary that acid should cause litmus paper to change colour, but it is necessary that every event should have a cause, and the general statement about cause must be true, and we must know that it is, before the particular statement about the litmus paper can be truly made, for the reason that it is *implied* in the particular statement. In virtue of its inclusion of this *general element*, a scientific judgement or law thus possesses both the characteristic of *a priori* knowledge, the characteristic, namely, of being necessary, and the characteristic of empirical knowledge, the characteristic, namely, of being synthetic—that is to say, of applying to a number of different experiences all of which, it affirms, will conform to the judgement or law in question.

Kant's Statement of the Problem. Now Kant's problem was, " How do such judgements come to be made, and how do we come to know that they are true ? " " How," to put the question in the celebrated form in which he asked it, " are synthetic *a priori* judgements possible ? " Let us consider a little more closely the precise terms in which he formulates the problem. At first sight they are rather surprising ; yet in the light of the preceding discussion their general significance should be clear enough. Let us suppose that we agree that scientific judgements are synthetic in the sense that they are reached, not by a process of analysing the implications of experience which is initially given, but by a process of going out beyond what is given, of putting together, that is to say, the results of a number of different experiences. Why, then, is not Kant's problem simply " How are synthetic judgments possible ? " ; why qualify with the words " *a priori* " ? The answer is because of the element of necessity in science. Scientific laws, as I have remarked above, share the characteristic of mathematical laws of purporting to be universally true. Unlike mathematical laws, however, they are not in fact always true in respect of all that they assert. Nevertheless, as I have emphasised, they always contain a necessarily true element. But how, it may be asked, can a law purport to be always true, be, nevertheless, in fact sometimes false, yet always contain a necessarily true element ? The point is admittedly confusing and requires further elucidation.

The Element of Necessity in Science.

Strictly speaking, scientific judgements are not, like mathematical judgements, theoretically certain. They are certain enough for all practical purposes, but theoretically they are liable to be upset. Later evidence may be discovered which will lead to their revision. Newton's law of gravitation, for example, was regarded as certain for nearly three centuries ; recently we have been taught by the Theory of Relativity that the universe does not behave quite as Newton supposed. Nevertheless, though a particular scientific formula may be upset, there *is* an element of necessity about scientific judgements. The precise content of any particular judgement may turn out to have been mistaken ; but, as I pointed out in the illustration of the litmus paper and the acid, there are certain general principles involved in the making of the judgement which are never mistaken. Now it is these general principles which constitute the *a priori* element in synthetic judgements and with which Kant is especially concerned.

The realisation of this element of necessity and of universality in science is one of the greatest achievements of the Greeks. Thales, travelling in the East, found that the Egyptians possessed certain rough rules of land measurement. Every year the inundation of the Nile obliterated the landmarks, and the peasants' fields had to be marked out afresh. The Egyptians had invented a method of dividing up the land into rectangular areas, in order that they might cope with the floods. Thales was not interested in the marking out of fields, but he saw that the method could be detached from the particular purpose for which it had been used, and generalised into a method for calculating areas of any shape. Thus the rules of land measurement were converted into the science of geometry, the conversion depending upon the recognition of precisely that element for which Kant was seeking to provide. A few further examples may help to elucidate the point. Let us suppose that we are applying the principles of trigonometry to the laying out of a tennis court. We know, of course, that any measurements that we may make will be only approximate, and that the result will also be only approximate. But the fact that it is possible to arrive at even approximate results implies that the trigonometrical principles upon which we have been working are themselves absolutely true, and, what is more, that they can be applied in practice. Again, there are different systems of coinage by means of which a given amount of money may be variously estimated. But whatever system of coinage we may happen to adopt, the rules of arithmetic by means of which we estimate the amount in terms of the coinage remain invariable. They also remain applicable. Again, all scientific judgements to the effect that A causes B are approximate and liable to be upset. But the principle of causation, which affirms that there is some sense in the assertion that one thing does cause another, is recognised as being both universal and applicable. These examples may help us to see how all scientific judgements, even though they may themselves be inaccurate, presuppose the operation of certain universal and necessary principles which are recognised as being both true and applicable to the particular facts about which the judgements are made.

Restatement of the Problem.

We are now in a position to state Kant's problem in an intelligible form. The world which we know by means of our senses is fragmentary and chaotic, and the facts which it contains are accidental and contingent. They might just as well be otherwise. The rules which the mind obeys when it reasons, the rules of mathematics and logic, are fixed and necessary. Clearly, then, the latter have not been derived from observation of the former. Yet the former obey the latter. If they did not, science would be impossible, science being, as we have seen, simply applied logic and mathematics. Kant's problem, then, is simply, how and why do the facts obey the laws. How is it that scientific prediction is possible and that mathematics applies to the world? How, in other words, can empirical, synthetic judgements, that is to say, judgements about the behaviour of what is observable, come to have the status of *a priori* judgements, that is to say judgements about what is intuitively perceived to be necessary? The problem, in fact, is the one at which we have already glanced in another connection in a previous chapter[1] when we asked, " How do the laws of thought come to apply to the behaviour of things? "

Kant's Answer.

Kant's answer is broadly as follows :

(1) An element of thought as well as a sensory element is involved in all our knowledge of the external world. We never merely observe and experience ; we always go out beyond what we observe and contribute to it, organising it, interpreting it, comparing and correlating it with knowledge already existing, and fitting it into a framework of relations and connections.

(2) The instruments of this organising, interpreting, comparing, correlating and fitting are certain principles of

[1] See Chapter V, pp. 144, 145.

thought which are necessary and universal—in fact, the *a priori* principles which we have been discussing.

(3) These principles, which constitute the *a priori* element in all sensory experience, are not so much principles governing actual experience as principles which prescribe the conditions of possible experience. They refer to our sense-experience, it is true ; but only in the sense that they set the conditions which our sense-experience must satisfy, if it is to be intelligible. We find that all experience conforms to certain conditions. Why ? Because these conditions are such as the mind which experiences has laid down. They constitute a framework within which all our experiencing must fit, and not only our experiencing but also our thinking, since, for Kant, thinking and experiencing cannot be disassociated. Our business is, then, to find out what are the conditions with which all experiences must comply.

Hence the main purpose of Kant's philosophy is to determine the principles or conditions in terms of which we can understand things. His concern is not to observe objects as a scientist might do, nor is he interested, as were the empirical philosophers, in discovering the precise nature of the psychological elements which constitute our knowledge. What, he wants to know, are the *universal* principles governing all experience, such that all objects which are observed or known must conform to them, inasmuch as these principles are the conditions to which, by virtue of the fact that they *are known*, all known objects will conform. What, in fact, are the principles of the possibility of experience ?

Significance of Kant's Question. Before we proceed to enlarge on Kant's answer to the questions he has set himself, let us pause to consider the significance of the form in which he has chosen to state them. The question in which our investigation of Kant's problem has culminated is, " What are the general principles to which all things that are known by human minds will conform ? " The formal question with which we started was, " How are synthetic *a priori* judgements possible?" What is the relevance of the one question to the other? The answer—the terms of it are mine, not Kant's—is broadly as follows.

If you can show that all experience conforms to certain conditions which have been prescribed to it by the mind, then you may expect to find that all experience will exhibit certain assignable characteristics, those, namely, which it derives from the fact of its conforming to the conditions, just as if you pour a number of different metals in a molten state into a set of square moulds to cool and set, they will all, whatever the substances of which they are composed, possess the common characteristic of being square. These characteristics which all experience will exhibit, will, therefore, be necessary and universal characteristics, and in virtue of their necessity and universality, they constitute the *a priori* element in our experience. Nevertheless they really are characteristics of *experience*; it is, that is to say, our experience of the outside world that they are characterising and informing. Kant expresses this by the word "synthetic." Our experience is not just the mind's experience of itself; it applies to something outside the mind; our knowledge is not always, like analytic knowledge, reached by analysing what we know already. It is sometimes a knowledge of something we did not know already. The notion of cause, for example, is not contained in that of event—yet we know that every event has a cause. Thus our experience is both *a priori* and synthetic. It both obeys the laws of thought and applies to and enables us to predict the behaviour of things. And it does this precisely because the things which it reveals to us, since, in order that they may be experienced at all, they must conform to the framework of the general principles which the mind prescribes, will all bear upon them the hallmark of the human mind.

III. KANT'S SOLUTION

The Forms of Intuition.   Let us suppose that I am born with a pair of blue spectacles permanently affixed to my nose;

everything that I see will be blue, and I shall affirm, therefore, that blueness is a universal property of things. In this
I shall be mistaken ; blueness, in the case in question, will
not be a property which belong to things in their own right,
but a quality imposed upon them by the peculiar conditions
of my seeing ; that things should appear to me to be blue,
will be, in other words, a condition of my seeing them at all.
To apply the metaphor, the mind, according to Kant, is
fitted with a number of different sets of mental spectacles
which insensibly transform everything that the mind knows,
just as, in the instance given, the blue spectacles altered
what my eyes saw. In point of fact, Kant held that there
are two different kinds of mental spectacles. The first
which he called " Forms of Intuition," are time and space.
All our sense impressions are subject to time, and all those
which come to us from outside to space. As a consequence,
time and space pervade everything that we know of the
external world.

When we experience the external world, what is actually
given to us is a crude, formless stuff, which Kant calls
" matter." This stuff is apprehended under the Forms of
Intuition, as a result of which the things we perceive appear
to us to be related together in time and in space, so that
everything we know is here or there, and then or now.
Thus " in the phenomenon," says Kant, " I call what
corresponds to the sensation the matter of the phenomenon,
and that which causes that the manifold of the phenomenon
is perceived as arranged in specific relations, I call the
form of the phenomenon." " Space " he says, elsewhere,
" is nothing except the form of all phenomena of outer
sense." As the result, therefore, of the operations of the
first set of mental spectacles, the world appears to us to be
in time and in space.

The Categories.   The second set of mental spectacles,
which Kant called " Categories " or " Principles of Understanding," now comes into play. Examples of these are
quality, quantity, substance, and causality. It is in virtue

of the Categories that everything we know possesses certain universal attributes. When we come to reflect on the nature of the things we know, we realise that each has substance, is of a certain quantity, exhibits certain qualities, and is at once the cause and the effect of something else. For example, iron turns into rust, burnt wood into ash ; but something remains the same in spite of the differences through which the iron and the wood pass. This " same " element we identify with the substance of the thing. Hence arises the Category of substance. Again the burnt wood which turns into ash cannot turn into anything else ; it is determined to turn into ash. Hence arises the category of causality. When, therefore, Kant says we apprehend the raw material of experience under the forms of the Categories, he means that the mind combines what comes to it from without with a series of contributions provided by itself. Thus it invests things with quantity and quality ; it also interposes connections and relations between them. " Experience " says Kant, " is possible only through the representation of a necessary connection of perceptions " ; and the necessary connection is the work of the mind. Hence, the object we know is a composite object ; it consists of a non-mental ingredient, a sort of raw stuff or material which has been worked up by the Forms of Intuition and the Categories into something which we can not only know but recognise.

It is by means of the Categories, that is to say, that we can recognise the black shape surmounted by a pink blob that we see in the street as a man. Or, to put the same point in a general form, the recognition of sense data as constituting or belonging to physical objects[1] is an example of the mind's activity in " Categorising " the raw material of sense-experience.

The above by no means exhausts Kant's account of the mental operations which we perform upon the raw material which is given to us in sensation, but it will serve to indicate the unceasing mental activity which he believes to be a continuous accompaniment, or rather an integral part of

[1] See Chapter III, p. 95.

experience. The world as we know it, the world, that is to say, that our minds have insensibly transformed in the process of knowing, is called by Kant the world of *phenomena*. Of this world Berkeley's conclusions are, at least in part, true ; its existence, that is to say, depends upon its being known, and, if it were to cease to be known, it would cease to exist. Of this world, the world of everyday experience, Kant says, it " does not exist in itself independently of the series of my ideas."[1] But to the world as it is, the world that is independent of our knowledge, called by Kant the world of *noumena*,[2] Berkeley's conclusions do not apply.

Reconciliation of Idealism and Realism.

I have already tried to show how Kant's system mediates between Empiricism and Rationalism, recognising the claims of both in a system which transcends both. Our *a priori* knowledge applies, he explained, to the world we know, simply because it is in part the architect of the world we know. But his system mediates no less between the claims of Idealism and Realism. It is in the first place a repudiation of Berkleyan Idealism. I said above that, so far as the phenomenal world was concerned, Kant was, with occasional lapses into inconsistency an example of which I indicate in a footnote,[1] prepared to subscribe to Berkeley's conclusions. The statement, useful for expository purposes in the context in which it appeared, now stands in need of amplification. Kant never believed that all that we know consists of our own ideas, that our knowledge, in other words, is limited to the contents of our own minds. On the contrary, he is careful to point out that we only become conscious of ourselves by knowing something which is other than ourselves. We do not, for example, *invent* the notion of a world outside ourselves, projecting it, as it were, from

[1] This, at least, is his main position. But, as I pointed out at the beginning, Kant is apt to change his positions. He does so on this point. Thus in the second edition of the *Critique of Pure Reason* we find him saying that the world of *experience* (my italics) must exist independently of our *individual* minds.

[2] " Noumena " is an untranslatable word ; it is usually understood as meaning " things in themselves."

our own inner consciousness which has engendered it. On the contrary, it is, he insists, given in our every-day experience. We begin with the consciousness of outside things; it is only subsequently that we become conscious of our own mental states. Kant was careful to make this clear at the very outset of his philosophy. " Whatever," he writes in the first paragraph of the first part of the *Critique of Pure Reason*, " the process and the means may be by which knowledge reaches its objects, there is one that reaches them directly and forms the ultimate material of all thought, viz. perception. This is possible only when the object is given, and the object can be given only (to human beings at least) through a certain affection of the mind." But what interpretation are we to place upon the ambiguous phrase " given only . . . through a certain affection of the mind " ? In so far as he asserts that some element other than ourselves is implied in our experience of the outside world, Kant is a realist who repudiates Berkeley's subjective Idealism. In so far, however, as he affirms that this " something other " is never experienced as it is independently of us, but is moulded by the Forms of Intuition and the Principles of Understanding, he is an idealist, since he is implying that the world as experienced is not *completely* independent of ourselves and would, therefore, disappear, if we ceased to experience it. Admittedly it is *partially* independent ; it contains, as it were, a core of " otherness " which is given from outside. But we cannot separate this core from its context of " mental conditioning," and discern it as it really is in itself. For any particular part of our experience which might be represented to be the element of alleged " otherness " would have to be experienced in order to be recognised as " other," and in the process of being experienced would be insensibly transformed by the activity of the experiencing mind. Hence, what we experience is infected through and through by the contributions made to it by our own minds. Nor is there any way either of knowledge or of perception by means of which this " *cordon sanitaire* " of " mental infection " can be broken.

The Relation of Knowledge and Perception.   Before
we conclude our survey, it is worth while to emphasise the
significance of the phrase " either of knowledge or of perception." Let us recall some of the considerations which were
set forth in the first and second Chapters[1] in illustration
of the apparently misleading and partial character of our
perception of the outside world. It is not merely that what
we see changes with our position, with the light, with the
state of our visual apparatus, and so forth ; no less important is the fact that we do not, from any position or in any
light, see the whole of any object. We do not, for example,
see the whole of a table, but only a part of its top and a
couple of its legs. It is probable that we have never actually
seen the whole of any single thing ; we rarely see its *other*
side or its *under* side, and, even if we see its inside, we cannot
at the same time see the whole of its outside. If, then, the
world of which we have direct sensory experience were all
that we knew, we should know very little. In fact, however,
we are very far from being content with it, and bring in our
minds to supplement the evidence of our senses. In all sorts
of ways we go out beyond what we see, supplying the other
side of the table, the inside of the box, and so on. This
activity of the mind in supplementing the fragmentary data
of perception has been regarded by many philosophers as
an activity which enlarges our view of reality. It is by the
mind rather than by the senses, they have affirmed, that
we know the world as it really is, and understanding can
correct the faults of perception. We have seen how Plato,
for example, regarded perception as introducing us to a
half real world of becoming, in contradistinction to knowledge by means of which we achieve an entry into the world
of real being. But this is not Kant's view. For him neither
understanding nor perception gives us knowledge of the
real nature of things. All that understanding can do is to
give us information about our *possible* perceptions. If I
examine any scientific judgement—for example, that water

[1] See Chapter I, pp. 25-30, and Chapter II, pp. 41-47.

freezes at such and such a temperature—and reflect upon what the judgement means, I shall find that one of the things that it means is, "under such and such conditions, for example, if the temperature drops to below 32° Fahrenheit, I shall have such and such perceptual experiences." In other words, the organised knowledge of science does not enable me to pass from a world of experience to a world of thought. It enables me to pass from what I am experiencing now to what under such and such conditions I shall experience. Science, in other words, enables me to predict. But its predictions are limited to the world of our possible experiences. This is the meaning of one of Kant's characteristically obscure phrases, to the effect that the "concept," that is to say the sort of notion of which the scientist makes use, "is a function of unity in our representations."

Summary and Recapitulation.

We are now in a position to attempt a brief summary of Kant's theory of knowledge.

1. Each of us is in direct contact with reality ; but we do not perceive reality exactly as it is. For example, what we immediately perceive is already given to us arranged in space and ordered in time. Moreover, what we experience changes as we ourselves move in space and as our consciousness moves on in time. Now this space and this time are provided by us.

2. I have just used the phrase "immediately perceive." But there is in fact no such thing as "immediate perception." From the outset the mind goes out beyond what it perceives, embroiders it and makes judgements about it. In so doing, it utilises its notions of space and time to prescribe the character of its future perceptions. "If," I say to myself, "I walk round the table, I shall perceive the other two legs, surmounted by the edge of the other end of the top." Thus I am enabled to connect not only what I see at one time with what I see at another, but what I see at one time with what I believe I should see, if I were to change my position in an appropriate way. Thus time and space, the Forms of Intuition, are an indispensable

apparatus for enabling the mind to form its notion of physical objects.

3. Although the process which culminates in the experience of physical objects is begun by the Forms of Intuition, it is not yet completed. It is not enough that I should perceive that *this* is the edge of a piece of wood surmounting two legs, and that I should know that, if I were to walk in a certain direction, I should see another edge of wood surmounting another pair of legs; it is not enough, that is to say, if I am to recognise that I am in the presence of a table. I must be able to compare what I am now seeing and what I am now representing to myself that I should see, if I were to walk to the other end of the room, with similar experiences on past occasions, and to contrast my present experiences with different experiences on past occasions. Thus when I affirm of anything " This is a so-and-so," my mind is advancing still further beyond what is actually given to me from outside, making a comparison between what I perceive now and other things perceived by me in the past which are like it, and contrasting it with yet others which are different. Thus in saying " This is a table," I am implying that it is not a chair; I am implying that it is like other objects that I have called " table " in the past, and I am implying that I know what sort of experiences I shall have of it, if, for example, I rap it, burn it, chop it up, or bark my shins against its legs. In a word, I am implying that *all* that is involved in being a table, its origins, its causal properties, its points of likeness to and difference from other things, will hold good of the object I am now experiencing. All these experiences, though I may have them at different times and in different places, are comprised in my assertion, " This is a table." Now these implications are the work of the Principles of Understanding, which are what we should now call, and Kant himself often called, " Concepts." It is by means of Concepts that we arrange and order the fragmentary data that we perceive, and are enabled to anticipate what, under given circumstances, we shall perceive. And this we can do

because our Concepts connect up one set of our experiences with others, or, if the metaphor be preferred, because our Concepts constitute a clearing-house to which all our experiences are automatically referred for sorting, filing and co-ordinating with the information already stored there. " Concepts," says Kant, " depend on functions. By function I mean the unity of the act of arranging different representations under one common representation. Perceptions," he continues, " without Concepts are blind "— that is to say, they would not take us beyond the material which is immediately given to our senses—" Thoughts without contents are empty "—that is to say, Concepts have no meaning apart from the perceptual elements which they unify.

4. The processes involved in our knowledge of physical objects—for example, in our recognition that " This patch of oblong black colour which I now perceive is or is part of the object, table"—are involved in all acts of knowledge. By the use of language and writing we can enlarge our knowledge, so that we are in a position to anticipate what sort of experiences we shall have under various sorts of conditions which are not yet realised. But our knowledge still conforms to the same formula. We are still, that is to say, going out beyond what we immediately perceive and piecing it together with what, under various conditions, we and other people have perceived. This is the method of science. Science is a process by means of which, starting with what is perceived by us here and now, we end by predicting what would be our perceptions in certain circumstances which we are in a position to specify. Science, then, like ordinary sensory knowledge, of which, indeed, it is only a methodical organisation, is not about things in themselves, but about the possibilities of our sensory experience.

5. Thought, then, does not directly apprehend the nature of things. All that it can do is to fill out the discontinuous and fragmentary nature of our perceptions by fitting our perceptions into a correlated scheme. The principles of thought described in Chapter V, which logicians have

formulated, are principles whereby we synthesise our perceptual experiences. Being universal, they apply to all experiences and hold, therefore, of necessity of the world we perceive. In this sense the laws of thought are the same as the laws of things, if the word " things " is interpreted to mean the things we experience. But they do not apply outside and beyond experience. They do not give us knowledge of reality.

6. We are now in a position to grasp the significance of the famous Kantian distinction between phenomena and noumena. The laws which govern the workings of nature— for example, the law of cause and effect—are really valid if we interpret them as being, in Kant's terminology, " grounds of the possibility of experience." We cannot deny them without denying the elementary distinctions in our life ; for example, the distinction we make between things which merely succeed each other and those which, as we say, *cause* each other, without which our experience would be a chaos. But they do not apply beyond the bounds of experience. What may be beyond these bounds we do not and cannot know, since, if we were to make the attempt, that which as a result of the attempt we succeeded in knowing, would by the very process of being known be brought within the framework of our Concepts and thus insensibly transformed, in that it would bear upon it the hallmark of the Principles of Understanding. What it was before it received that hallmark, we cannot tell. Hence we know only the world of phenomena, which is the world as it appears, after it has passed through the sieve of our Concepts. The world of noumena, of things as they are independently of us, must remain unknown. In so far, then, as metaphysics is defined as the study of reality, metaphysics is impossible.

IV. KANT'S MORAL THEORY

Qualification of the Epistemological Position. It has been objected to Kant's philosophy that it contains no assertion which he does not subsequently qualify. This, it is said, is true not only of his individual statements on particular topics, but even of his general position. This general position, as we have just seen, involves a denial of the possibility of knowledge of reality, but we must now hasten to add the qualification that the denial only holds good, if the word " knowledge " is interpreted in a strict sense to mean " intellectual apprehension." For Kant did in fact believe that we make contact with reality in moral experience, and that intercourse with the real world, denied to the knowing mind, was achieved by the moral sense.

Kant's moral theory is a peculiar one, and, although it is no part of my purpose to include a survey of ethical philosophy in this book, some account of it must be given because of the key position which it occupies in relation to Kant's metaphysical conception of reality.

The Unique Rôle of the Will in Kant's Philosophy. Kant divided man's psychological faculties into three main groups, the senses, the intellect, and the will. The senses and the intellect are, as we have seen, precluded from a direct knowledge of reality by their introduction of an *a prior* element into the raw material of sensory experience, an element contributed by the mind and present from the first. Thus, sensuous experience and intellectual knowledge both give information about a world whose connections and relations have been inserted by ourselves. But, when we *will* something, we obtain, Kant held, a kind of knowledge which is neither sensuous nor intellectual. We are not in willing making contact with a phenomenal world upon which we have imposed the Categories of our own minds, nor do our moral experiences reach us through the forms of space and time. The exercise of the will is a free activity in virtue of which we can use our sensuous and intellectual knowledge as we please. It brings also a sense of emancipation from the law of cause and effect which dominates the world of phenomena, no less than from the laws of logical necessity which constrain the operations of the reason.

The Self from the Standpoint of the Sciences.

In so far as we act in accordance with desire, Kant held that we are not free. If we consider our actions from the points of view of biology, of anthropology, or of psychology, it is very difficult to resist the conclusion that they are determined. The biologist sees a man as a member of a particular species which happens to have evolved, endowed with a general inheritance of impulse, faculty, and desire, which is characteristic of his species. The anthropologist sees him as a member of a particular race which has reached a certain stage of development, possessing the intellectual and emotional equipment appropriate to that race at that stage of development. The psychologist applies to the individual a mode of treatment similar to that which the biologist applies to the species and the anthropologist to the race. He treats him as a being endowed initially with a certain psychological and physiological make-up. He is scheduled as having such and such congenital tendencies which develop in such and such an environment, and he is pictured, as a result, as growing up into an adult person possessing such and such a nature with such and such tastes, prepossessions, prejudices, desires, and thoughts. These, taken in sum, determine both the states of his consciousness and the actions in which they express themselves. Analyses of the individual along these lines have already been given in preceding chapters[1]; and, inevitably, their outcome is the philosophical doctrine of self-determinism sketched in Chapter VII. To analyses of the Self in terms of the concepts of the special sciences Kant was prepared to subscribe. In so far as human beings are considered from the point of view of biology, anthropology and psychology, in so far, that is to say, as they are considered from the empirical standpoint of the special sciences, there can, he held, be no doubt of their complete subjection to the law of cause and effect. They are, therefore, completely determined. " Man," Kant wrote, " is

[1] See Chapter VII, pp. 188, 189, and Chapter IX, pp. 237-241.

one of the phenomena of the sense world, and he, too, is in so far one of the nature causes whose causality must stand under empirical laws. As such, he must have an empirical nature. . . ." But, as we have already seen, the law of cause and effect holds only in the phenomenal world. If, therefore, there were some other standpoint which yielded a profounder view of man, if, for example, we could conceive of him as possessing a noumenal as well as a phenomenal nature, then determination by causal laws would not apply to his noumenal nature. Unfortunately we cannot so conceive him without in the very process transferring him, as it were, to the phenomenal world by imposing upon him the limitations of our conceiving. But, though we may not be able intellectually to conceive, we can, Kant held, experience within ourselves something which is not phenomenal. This leads to one of the most important features of Kant's theory, the distinction between " the empirical or phenomenal Self," which is the Self studied by the sciences, and " the transcendental Self," which is the source of moral experience.

Man's Noumenal Nature Expressed in Moral Experience.
Kant employed a number of subtle arguments to show that the transcendental Self is unique. It is only to the empirical Self that the disintegrating arguments we considered in Chapters VII and IX apply. The transcendental Self, which, as we shall see in a moment, is also the moral Self, is a unity.

Now the empirical Self is a chaos of wishes and desires. As creatures of desire we belong, Kant agreed, to the phenomenal world, and our feelings and actions are as completely determined as the movements of matter in the physical world. But when we act in accordance with the law which our moral will prescribes, we escape from the phenomenal world and establish contact with reality. In so far, in fact, as man wills freely in accordance with the laws of his own nature, he is noumenal ; that is to say, he wills as a member of reality. For the feeling of moral obligation is something which cannot be accounted for on phenomenal lines. Psychology can tell us what we are and what we want to do ; it cannot tell what we ought to be and what it is our duty to do. The conception of " ought " is on an entirely different plane from the conception of " is." It presupposes that when we have finished with our analysis of a man's antecedents and character, the analysis which tells us what he " is," and how, in virtue of the fact that he is what he is, he is naturally disposed to act, we can still assume that it is in his power to act differently. We can still say, " Yes, I agree that, given his heredity and constitution, he had a strong instinctive tendency to act in this way and every justification for obeying his natural instincts ; nevertheless, I still maintain that he ought to have acted in *that* way," and in saying that " he ought to have acted in *that* way," we are also implying that he was free to act " in *that* way," since it is nonsense to say that a man ought to do what he cannot do. Thus the consciousness of moral obligation is " inextricably bound up with the consciousness of the freedom " of the Self that wills, which is the transcendental Self. One knows, Kant insisted, " that one can act because one is conscious that one ought, and thus one knows in oneself the freedom which—without the moral law—had remained unknown." It is for this reason that Kant, in speaking of our obligation to do our duty, employs the phrase " the categorical imperative." Whereas most of our actions are conditioned by an " if "—*if* we want so and so, we must act in such and such a way—and so are " hypothetically determined," the obligation to do our duty is governed by no such condition. We ought, we feel, to do it, whether we like it or not, and we shall continue to feel this, even if we habitually fail to do it.

Uniqueness of the Concept of " Ought."

Now this consciousness of *ought* is a unique fact of a kind which is not anywhere to be found in the phenomenal world. " Obligation," Kant says, " expresses a sort of necessity . . . which occurs nowhere else in nature. It is impossible that anything in nature *ought to be* other than in fact it is. In truth, obligation—if one has before one's eyes only the succession in nature—has simply and solely no meaning. We can as little ask what ought to happen in nature as what attributes a circle ought to have." Hence the unique position which Kant gave to what he called the good will which is the source of moral action. "There is," he maintained, "nothing in the world—nay, even beyond the world, nothing conceivable, which can be regarded as good without qualification, saving alone a good will." The moral will is thus by its very nature outside the causal sequence which operates universally in the phenomenal world. Nor can its content, that is to say, the course it prescribes, be derived from the phenomenal world. The very fact that it takes no account of likes and dislikes, that it is indifferent to circumstances, suggests that it is not the reflection of likes and dislikes, nor the product of circumstances. Whence, then, is it derived? Kant answers, from the nature of man regarded as a moral being. Hence man as a moral being is not a part of the phenomenal world, but is a member of the noumenal world. For this reason, when he obeys the moral law, he is spoken of as obeying a law that comes from himself, from himself, that is to say, considered as a real and rational being and not as a member of the world of causes and effects. This obedience to the moral law, which is also moral freedom, is something which cannot be explained. For explanation is the work of understanding, and whatever the understanding understands is *ipso facto* exhibited as phenomenal.

Nevertheless, the sense of moral obligation is a fact, a fact which, Kant has tried to show, derives from the noumenal world, the corollary being that in virtue of our ability to recognise its promptings and obey its commands, we, in respect of our transcendental Selves, own membership of that world.

Working out of the Theory.   So much for the metaphysical bearing of Kant's moral theory. With the details of its working out we are not here concerned ; nor are they particularly helpful. A very brief statement will serve to round off the account already given.

What the moral will prescribes is that we should act in every case upon general principles which are intuitively recognised to be morally binding. These general principles are of the kind which everybody acknowledges irrespective of their needs and circumstances, for example, that we should not tell lies, that kindness is better than cruelty, honesty better than deceit; and so forth. Nor are they in any way opposed to reason. On the contrary, if we investigate the deliverances of our wills by means of the reason, we realise that the general principles which the will prescribes are the only ones which are not self-contradictory. There is, for example, no contradiction inherent in the precept that everybody should tell the truth ; but if everybody were to lie, nobody would believe anybody else, and there would be no point, therefore, in lying. This is what Kant means by saying that wrong conduct is self-contradictory ; it cannot be universalised without stultifying itself. Hence Kant's famous precept : " Act only according to that maxim which you can at the same time will to be a universal law."

Unfortunately this doctrine gives us little guidance in the actual circumstances of daily life. Kant affirms, for example, that the will prescribes truth-telling as a categorically binding general principle ; as such it admits of no exceptions. But there are occasions in which the telling of a lie may be justified in actual life, on the ground that the consequences of truth-telling would be harmful. Ought we, for example, to tell the truth to a potential murderer who asks where an innocent person whom he proposes to kill is hiding ? Most people would say that we ought not, but, whatever view we take of the matter, Kant's universally binding principles afford us little practical assistance. It is often no less difficult to know what our duty is, than it is to do it, and Kant does not help us here. Moreover, it seems difficult in practice to decide between alternative courses of action except by reference to their consequences, and this alternative criterion of right conduct, which the Utilitarians stressed, is implicitly excluded by Kant's moral system.

V. COMMENT AND CRITICISM

Kant's philosophy is so important in itself and has had so great an influence on subsequent thought, that it would be unfair to the reader to leave it without giving some indication of the criticisms to which subsequent philosophers have subjected it. From the extensive body of commentary which Kant's doctrines have provoked, I propose to select three criticisms, of which the first two are directed against internal inconsistencies in the Kantian doctrine and must, therefore, be met by those who accept Kant's main premises and endorse his main conclusions, while the third springs from entirely different premises and presupposes a wholly different approach to the problem of knowledge.

1. Criticism of Kant's Theory of Reality

The Kantian doctrine may be summarised in the following propositions.

A. All our knowledge includes a sensory element.

B. Sense-knowledge is incapable of apprehending reality; it can know only the world of our experience, and in the world of our experience the mind has already inserted universal connections and relations.

C. Non-sensory knowledge is admittedly conceivable, and if we possessed it, it might give us knowledge of a noumenal reality—" the concept of a noumenon, that is, of a thing which shall be thought wholly through a pure understanding, not as an object of the senses but as a thing in itself, is not at all contradictory : for one surely cannot assume that sensibility is the only possible form of intuition."

But, D, we do not possess it, the concepts which constitute our thought being only a framework into which our sense perceptions must fit.

Two criticisms arise. The first, which is purely formal, is as follows : Kant is not really denying, as he appears to be, that reality cannot be known. We know at least two things about it, namely, that it is not self-contradictory (see quotation in C above), and that it is such as would be revealed to pure understanding unmixed with sensory elements, if there were such a faculty. But there is no such faculty ; therefore nothing can be known directly about noumenal reality ; therefore, it cannot be known about it that it is not self-contradictory, and that it would be knowable by pure understanding.

Secondly, and more importantly, it cannot be known that reality exists and that it underlies and is the partial cause of the world of phenomena. Kant's position in this respect is open to a criticism similar to that which we brought against the Representationalism of Locke.[1] Again we are presented with three entities—(a) the knowing mind, (b) the world of phenomena, and (c) the noumenal world which underlies the world of phenomena (b) and is its partial cause, the other cause of (b) being the contributions made by our own minds *via* the Forms of Intuition and the Principles of Understanding. (a), we are told, knows and always knows (b), but never knows (c). (a), then, cannot know anything about (c). How, then, can (a) know that (c) exists, or that it has the property of underlying and being the cause of (b). Admittedly, Kant might reply that we know reality in moral experience. But it seems reasonably clear that moral experience does not in itself inform me that reality is a collection of "noumena." This information is only reached by *interpretation* of moral experience, and such interpretation is the work of the understanding.

Appearance and Reality. To many philosophers the distinction between appearance and reality has always seemed to be inadmissible. If a thing exists, they would affirm, it is real, and no one thing can be more real than another. There cannot, in fact, be degrees of reality.

[1] See Chapter II, p. 43.

However, most of those who have thought fit to make the distinction have insisted that there is no absolute gulf between the two realms ; that reality not only underlies but manifests itself in appearance, as the spirit of a personality may inform a face, or a general policy the measures of a Government.[1] You have only to study the phenomenal world sufficiently closely, they maintain, and you will discern the nature of that which, while it transcends, is nevertheless immanent in it.

Kant, however, refuses to adopt this method of resolving the difficulties raised by the distinction between appearance and reality. Closely to study the world of phenomena is not for him to discern the outlines of reality in a flux of shifting appearances, for the reason that reality is in no sense given in the world of phenomena, and cannot, therefore, be disclosed by a study of it. On the contrary, since to think is to interpose connections between our sense experiences, the mind thus contributing elements which are not derived from the outside world, the more we think about phenomena, the further we drift from reality.

Hence the distinction between appearance and reality is presented by Kant in a particularly obnoxious form. To put the point in another way, Kant's philosophy more than that of any other thinker is exposed to the criticism that, if we do not know reality, we have no grounds for postulating it as a part cause underlying the world of appearance.

2. CRITICISM OF KANT'S THEORY OF THE SELF

Similar difficulties arise in regard to the notion of the Self. Kant bifurcates the Self as he bifurcates reality. There is, on the one hand, the ordinary daily Self of which we become aware by introspection, the " phenomenal " or " empirical " Self ; and there is, on the other, the transcendental Self, the source of moral experience, which prescribes to us our duty and is a member of the real world. Both Selves are known. The empirical or phenomenal Self is the one revealed to introspection ; the transcendental

[1] This in effect is Hegel's view. See Chapter XV, pp. 419-421.

Self is known in moral experience. In virtue of his ownership of the first Self, man is a member of the phenomenal world. He is, as we have seen, "one of the phenomena of the sense world, and he, too, is in so far one of the nature causes whose causality must stand under empirical laws." But he is also transcendental : " On the other hand—in consideration of a certain capacity—he is a purely intelligible object." Now the expression " purely intelligible object " is always used by Kant to describe ultimate reality, the noumenal world which is independent of our consciousness. Moreover, Kant goes out of his way to speak of the " intelligible character " of the moral Self as " the character of the thing in itself."

This doctrine, taken in conjunction with Kant's general position, suggests the following reflections.

Reality as a Kingdom of Moral Selves. It is inconsistent, since, having been informed that we cannot know " things in themselves," we are now told that we know the moral Self and that this is a " thing in itself." This much, then, at least we know about the noumenal world—it contains one moral Self, namely, the Self of the knower. In fact, however, Kant goes considerably further than this. The fact of morality, he points out, implies the existence of other people in intercourse with whom the moral Self finds occasion for its exercise. Robinson Crusoe on his desert island, with nobody to steal from, to lie to, to do violence to, to overreach, or to betray, and, as a consequence, with no occasion for the exercise of the virtues of honesty, truthfulness, kindness and fair dealing, is not a completely human being, since one side of his nature, namely, the moral, is atrophied. It is only necessary, then, to examine what Kant called " the content of the moral law " to realise that it implies intercourse with other people. Now the moral law cannot, Kant contends, consist of a merely academic injunction. Its " ought " is meaningless, unless it implies " can." To say that it is our duty to carry out its implications means, then, that we are free to carry out its implications. Therefore, there must be other moral

Selves in relation to whom we can exercise and fulfil our own moral self: " Act," says Kant, in a famous passage, " so as to use humanity both in thine own person and in the person of another, always as an end, never merely as a means." The conclusion seems to be that the ends and aspirations of the individual regarded from the standpoint of the moral law have no meaning, except in so far as he belongs to a society of related moral Selves, which Kant designates by the word "humanity." These moral Selves he describes as " a kingdom—the systematic union of different reasoning beings through common laws." Since these other Selves are moral, they are, also, according to the preceding argument, noumenal. Therefore, we are now in a position to assert that reality consists of a number of moral Selves upon whom Kant subsequently proceeds to confer the attributes of holiness, happiness and immortality. He also includes God in this world. The conception of an unknowable reality has, it is obvious, receded very far into the distance.

The Distinction Between Selves Inadmissible. The above conclusion is derived very largely from Kant's moral theory which presupposes a distinction between the transcendental (real) and the empirical (phenomenal) Selves. Can this distinction be maintained ? What, it is important to know, is the relation between the two Selves ? The answer is obscure. Kant says that the " empirical character is the mere manifestation of the intelligible." One is tempted to wonder whether this description is compatible with the account of the empirical Self as the product of a long chain of biological and psychological sequences of cause and effect, a mere cork bobbing upon the waves of impulse and desire ? How, one might ask, could such a Self be described as a " manifestation of the intelligible," that is, of the real Self ? But is this description of the empirical Self in any event adequate ? Surely not, since it leaves moral experience out of account. Admittedly Kant makes provision for this by turning it over to the noumenal Self. The result is to leave us with two Selves, separated from and confronting each other, the one real and moral, the other phenomenal and amoral. But (*a*) the distinction is surely inadmissible. I am conscious of myself in moral experience in exactly the same way as I am conscious of myself in any other kind of experience. Moreover, moral experience shades into other kinds of experience by imperceptible degrees. To drive a wedge of absolute difference between moral experience and other kinds of experience, assigning them to different worlds and endowing them with different kinds of reality, is plainly incompatible with these obvious facts. (*b*) Moreover, the distinction cannot be maintained. The transcendental Self, we are told, determines and prescribes to the empirical. In so far as it does this, it produces causal effects upon the empirical. The causal relation belongs to the phenomenal world. Therefore, by virtue of the effects it produces in the phenomenal world, the transcendental Self loses its character of being purely real and purely transcendental.

3. REALIST CRITICISM OF KANT

The above difficulties arise from internal inconsistencies in the Kantian philosophy. If some of the things that Kant says are true, others, it is suggested, cannot be true. But how far can we accept the philosophy as a whole?

The peculiarity of Kant's theory of knowledge lies not so much in the fact that he regards the object known as a composite, part of which is derived from what is, presumably, the noumenal world, part contributed by ourselves, as in his assignment of the respective parts. The crude material given in sensation—colour, texture, and so forth—comes, he holds, from outside. The arrangement of the material in space and time and its connections and relations are supplied by ourselves. The element that we supply is *a priori* and necessary, the result being that we may rest assured that everything that we experience will conform to the mind's laws, because the mind has imposed upon it those characteristics in virtue of which it conforms. Hence the element of necessity in, for example, mathematics. All known things will conform to the proposition that seven and five make twelve, because the fact of their conformity is an element contributed by our minds.

But what if our minds change ? They have, it is obvious, changed in the past, and it is probable they will do so in the future. Nor, if the laws of mathematics are, as Kant thinks, primarily laws governing the workings of our mind and not laws governing the relations of numbers, does there seem to be any necessary reason why our minds should not change in respect of their arithmetical conceptions. Thus, if our natures were so to evolve that our remote posterity adopted the view that seven and five made thirteen, the behaviour of the world of phenomena would presumably, if Kant is right, bear out the view of posterity. Whether it would in fact do so or not, I am unable to say, but the mere possibility seems to destroy that element of necessity which Kant claimed for mathematical and scientific judgements.

Are Relations Mental ? Apart from this difficulty, can we accept the view that the relations between phenomena are contributed by the mind ? Let us consider such a relation as " to the north of." Edinburgh, we say, is to the north of London. If Kant is right, this relation is contributed by the mind, and what it in fact relates are all possible experiences by minds of Edinburgh and of London. If there were no experiences, then there would be no relation. To eliminate experiencing minds is, then, to eliminate the relation between Edinburgh and London. But is it, in fact, the case that Edinburgh would cease to be to the north of London, if there were nobody to know that it was ? I do not believe that it is, although I cannot see any way of convincing anybody who wishes to maintain the contrary. To take another example given by Bertrand Russell : " It seems plain that it is not thought which produces the truth of the proposition ' I am in my room.' It may be true that an earwig is in my room, even if neither I nor the earwig nor anyone else is aware of this truth ; for this truth concerns only the earwig and the room, and does not depend upon anything else." These considerations would have no weight with Kant, because he would be unwilling to recognise the possibility of the existence of things which were known by a mind, but which, nevertheless, were not dependent on the fact of being known for their existence. The point at issue illustrates the fundamental difference between Realism and Idealism. A realist finds no difficulty in admitting this possibility ; indeed, he would probably accept it as a self-evident fact, although he might perhaps hesitate to affirm that what did exist in independence was a physical object.[1] To the idealist, on the other hand, it is self-evident that anything which exists must also be an object of knowledge. Kant did not go so far as to assert this, since he admitted the existence of the noumenal world. Nevertheless, it is to this conclusion and to nothing less than this that the whole trend of his philosophy points, and this was in fact the conclusion that Kant's successors, and in particular Hegel, were concerned to maintain.

Kant's *Critique of Pure Reason* is translated by F. Max Muller. There is also an edition in Everyman with an introduction by A. D. Lindsay. Norman Kemp-Smith's *Commentary on Kant's Critique of Pure Reason* is the standard work on Kant, but is difficult. Easier are :

LINDSAY, A. D. Kant.
CLARKE, NORMAN Introduction to Kant's Philosophy.

[1] See Chapter III, pp. 89-95, for the view that what exists in independence of mind is sense data.

*Chapter XV : OUTLINE OF HEGEL'S PHILOSOPHY: MONISTIC IDEALISM

Introductory. Like Kant's, Hegel's (1770–1831) philosophy is very difficult. It is also exceedingly philosophic; it exhibits, that is to say, in the most eminent degree the method of abstract, speculative ratiocination directed to the establishment of conclusions remote from commonsense reality which is usually, whether in approbation or in disapprobation, associated with philosophy. Hegel's method, in short, is that of sustained abstract reasoning divorced from observation, and it is the most outstanding example of this method in the history of philosophy. The conclusion that he reaches is that reality is a unity which is Spirit or Person.

His philosophy falls into two parts, negative and positive. The negative part consists of a criticism of rival philosophies which maintain that ultimate reality is unknown, or which hold that it consists of a number of separate limited realities. The positive part seeks to establish the fact that reality is Spirit or Person. It will be convenient to divide our exposition of Hegel into three parts, dealing respectively with his method, his negative teaching and his positive philosophy. We shall, then, embark upon a general discussion of Monism, the metaphysical doctrine which asserts that the universe is a single whole or unity, of which Hegel's philosophy is the most celebrated example.

I. THE HEGELIAN METHOD

The Hegelian Triad. The Hegelian method is offered to us as an instrument, the only possible instrument, by the use of which the human mind can reach truth. Let us suppose that somebody entertains a particular idea or doctrine which is wrong. It can, Hegel holds, be shown by careful examination to be self-contradictory, since in the course of our examination of the doctrine we shall be led to envisage the opposed doctrine which denies and refutes it. May we, then, substitute for the original doctrine this opposed doctrine? Hegel answers that we may not, since the opposed doctrine can be shown to be no less faulty, and therefore no less prone to self contradiction, than the original doctrine. Where, then, does truth lie? In a third doctrine which unites, but unites on a higher plane, the essential features of the original doctrine and its opposite. This third doctrine will, however, on analysis, itself be shown to be inadequate, and liable, therefore, to self-contradiction : and as in the preceding cases, the complete analysis of it will be found to have revealed its contrary. The contrary will be no truer than the third doctrine, although both— that is to say, both the third doctrine and its contrary—in so far as they are more comprehensive, will embody more truth than the original doctrine with which we started and *its* contrary. The next stage is to consider whether the third doctrine and its contrary cannot be united on a higher plane. If we are successful in so uniting them, we shall have built up a fifth doctrine to which, although it is more comprehensive than any of its predecessors, there will still be opposed a contrary doctrine. This process continues indefinitely. Thus the mind is driven forward by the movement of its own analytical thought to ever wider and more comprehensive formulations of truth. Since at each stage of the process it is found that a complete criticism of a doctrine involves an analysis of it which reveals its contrary, it follows that the most effective manner of disposing of any false doctrine is to analyse it in such a way as to make it refute itself. The process just described is called " the Hegelian Dialectic," the combination of two partial doctrines and a third in which they are united being known as " the Triad."

Examples of the Dialectic. The Hegelian Dialectic cannot be considered in isolation from Hegel's metaphysical position. Hegel, as we shall see, holds that the universe is a whole or unity, in which complete truth and complete reality are merged. Just as anything which is less than the whole is regarded as possessing only partial reality, so any doctrine which is less than the whole truth about the whole is regarded as being only partially true. Since no doctrine which the human mind is capable of entertaining can embody the *whole* of truth, no doctrine is entirely true. This is not merely to assert that no doctrine is the whole of truth ; it is to insist that no doctrine is completely true even in respect of that part of truth which it asserts.

Since all doctrines are faulty, they direct the attention of the mind which adequately analyses them to their contrary or refuting doctrines. Let us metaphorically conceive of the world of thought as a circle. Then at whatever point of its circumference the mind enters it, by the mere process of adequately analysing its own conceptions it will find itself driven in the direction of the Hegelian Absolute, the embodiment of all truth, which lies at the centre.

The actual examples which Hegel gives of the Dialectic at work are not as clear as could be wished. They are also, unfortunately, highly technical. The following, which are adaptations[1] rather than transcriptions of Hegel's own examples, will, however, serve to indicate the kind of process which he has in mind.

(1) Pure Being, unqualified by any characteristic, since it cannot be thought about, turns out to be Nothing.

(2) But Nothing is not really Nothing, since it can in fact be thought about. Therefore (3) neither Pure Being nor Nothing is a satisfactory concept, since each points forward to something beyond itself. This something, which is reached by associating both the concepts and transcending them, is " Determined Being," that is, Being which is qualified by certain determinable characteristics.

[1] The examples here given are not in fact to be found in precisely this form anywhere in Hegel.

Another example which has an important bearing upon Hegel's theory of knowledge, to which, indeed, it is the key, is derived from the conception of the Self and the Not Self.

The Self and the Not Self.

Let us start with the commonsense conception according to which the Self is a self-contained entity sharply distinguished from the rest of the universe, the Not Self, which it knows, but which is other than it.

Now this doctrine, Hegel insists, clearly will not do. To begin with, how does the Self know itself at all ? Only by reason of the fact that it distinguishes itself from the Not Self. Knowledge of the Not Self is, therefore, essential to knowledge of the Self, nor can there be one without the other. Thus knowledge of the Self is empty of content, unless the Self be taken to include the Not Self. Starting from the other side, Hegel shows that the Not Self is nothing without the Self, since, if there were no Self to know it, the Not Self, which is by definition that which is distinguished from the Self that knows, could not be. Here, then, are two concepts, the concept of the Self as a separately existing entity, and the concept of the Not Self as a separately existing entity, each of which reveals itself on analysis as meaningless without the other ; and, not only as meaningless, but as self-contradictory, in the sense that each, when carefully scrutinised, is found to demand for its completion the incorporation of the other, which is its opposite. That which results, the synthesis of both, is neither Self nor Not Self, but an act of knowledge[1] of which the Self which knows and the Not Self which is known are distinguishable but not separate aspects. Although the synthesis " act of knowledge " is reached as the conclusion of the preceding argument which began with an investigation of the two apparently more elementary concepts of Self and Not Self, the concept " act of knowledge," once it has been reached, is seen to be

---

[1] See below, pp. 425, 426, for the importance of acts of knowledge in Hegel's philosophy.

logically prior to both the limited concepts with which we actually started, but which are now revealed as aspects of it. Not only is it logically prior to, it is more concrete than, that is to say, it is fuller and richer because more inclusive than, our original concepts. It is, then, more real than either of them. The doctrines with which we have just made acquaintance—that the more concrete is more real than the less, that knowledge is of the concrete, and that knowledge itself is logically prior to both knower and known—are distinctively Hegelian. They belong, however, rather to the metaphysical than to the logical side of Hegel's philosophy, and will be developed in a later section.[1]

Comment and Criticism.

It will be convenient to introduce at this point one or two comments on the Hegelian method just outlined. Hegel attached very great importance to his method, which he regarded as an integral part of his philosophy. Moreover, since, on his view, the distinction between knowledge and its objects, and, therefore, between logic and metaphysics, is unreal, his theory of method, though primarily a theory of logic, is also a theory of reality. Again, the method does not merely describe reality ; it actually helps to constitute that which it describes. Reality itself, that is to say, may in one of its aspects legitimately be regarded as behaving like the Hegelian triad.

Nevertheless, many philosophers have held that the Hegelian method is in no sense an essential pre-requisite of Hegel's metaphysical views, and that it is quite possible to hold that the universe is in its general structure such as Hegel conceived without at the same time concurring in Hegel's belief that the Dialectic is the sole, or even the most suitable, method of finding out what the universe is like. Furthermore, in spite of the large claims made on its behalf, the method is in practice surprisingly unfruitful. Hegel used it with apparent effect, but it has been suggested that its effectiveness in his hands arose very largely

[1] See below, pp. 419-426.

from the nature of the problems to which he applied it. These problems were technical in character and possessed great interest for Hegel. But many would refuse to regard them as real problems at all. On the antinomies of thought which actually puzzle and disturb men's minds, it throws singularly little light.[1]

For example, many people have wanted intensely to know whether our minds are free. Now directly they begin to think about freedom, they are impressed by the strength of the arguments which are hostile to freedom. As I pointed out in an earlier chapter,[2] all the obvious arguments are arguments for Determinism, and it is exceedingly difficult to discover any purely rational grounds for believing in freedom. Nevertheless, in spite of these arguments, most of us are convinced that we are free. Here, then, is an antinomy between our innate conviction of freedom and the apparently unshakable arguments for Determinism. Applying the Hegelian method, we ought to be able to resolve this antinomy by synthesising the two opposing doctrines and producing—what? The answer, I suppose, should be, "By producing limited freedom." But limited freedom is in the view of many a meaningless concept—we are, they would say, either free or not free, or partially free, and, if partially free, completely free in respect of some of our thoughts and actions, and not free at all in respect of others—nor is it clear in what way limited freedom could be evolved as the synthesised version of no freedom and complete freedom. Other time-honoured controversies on matters in regard to which men have been passionately convinced of the truth of each of two contrary conclusions, and been able to find apparently good arguments in favour of their convictions, are no more satisfactorily resolved by the Hegelian method than the controversy between Free Will and Determinism.

---

[1] An antinomy is a contradiction. Thus where there are two doctrines each of which seems to be true, since we can find no flaw in the arguments for it, but which are such that if one of them is true then the other cannot be, there is said to be an antinomy.

[2] See Chapter IX, p. 234.

II. OUTLINE OF HEGEL'S POSITION

A. His Negative Doctrine

This consists of a disproof of two widely held views about reality, each of which had been maintained by some one or other of Hegel's predecessors.

1. REALITY IS NOT NECESSARILY FEATURELESS. The first of these views is that Reality must be featureless—must be, that is to say, destitute of properties of any kind. This contention recalls Spinoza's proof that Substance must be unlimited,[1] with its corollary, although Spinoza did not, as we have seen, draw the corollary, that Substance is without feature or determination. Broadly, the argument is as follows. To attribute any feature to Reality is to limit it, since it is to deny to it the non-possession of that feature. For example, to say of Reality that it is round or white or noble, is to exclude from it the features of squareness, blackness and ignobility. But if Reality is unlimited, it cannot, it is said, lack any feature ; or rather (to make the same assertion in another form), it must lack all features, since to ascribe to it any feature, is to deprive it of the opposite of the feature ascribed. Reality must further be unknowable, since to be known is to be endowed with qualifications or features.

Hegel has little difficulty in disposing of this view. A featureless Reality is nothing at all. " Pure Being," as Hegel calls this hypothetical, featureless Reality, is neither in space nor in time, neither organic nor inorganic, neither conscious nor unconscious, neither matter nor spirit. It is, in fact, nothing. But actual Reality is not nothing, because, first, it contains my consciousness which is now thinking about it, and, secondly, it is being thought about, even if not very successfully thought about, by me. It possesses, therefore, the attribute of consciousness and the attribute of being thought about by consciousness.

[1] See Chapter IV, pp. 123, 124.

2. REALITY IS NOT NECESSARILY UNKNOWABLE.

Since it cannot be proved that ultimate Reality is without features, it is not inconceivable that ultimate Reality should be known. But what of Kant's contention that Reality is in fact unknowable, a contention resting on the argument that, since the objects of our knowledge are fettered by the forms of our consciousness to which they must conform, we can never know things as they are independently of our consciousness ? This position is, as has already been pointed out, naturally congenial to modern science. The Reality we know, says the physicist in effect, can be shown to be very largely the product of the abstracting and projecting activities of our own minds. As scientists, we abstract from what is given those qualities with which alone scientific method is competent to deal ; we project into what is given other qualities which own no counterpart in external reality. Thus the world that science studies is a phenomenal world. Behind the phenomenal world there may be an underlying world of Reality, but to this the mind can never penetrate. Hegel answers that those who postulate such a Reality do, in fact, succeed in preserving inviolate its unknowability. Kant, for example, holds that " things in themselves " are the causes of our sensations, and that they are many. In other words, they are thought of in terms of the concepts of plurality and causation and are not, therefore, strictly unknowable. Furthermore, they are, as we have seen, conceived of by him as moral Selves. Any attempt to postulate an unknown Reality behind the phenomenal world which is known will be found, says Hegel, similarly to contradict itself.

But why, in any event, should such an unknown Reality be postulated ? The only function which it performs is that of being the cause of the known phenomenal world. But to postulate an unknown cause does not help matters. Consider, for example, the scientific concept of electricity. Electricity is nothing more nor less than a something which is postulated to explain the occurrence of electrical phenomena. But, since we do not know what electricity is, its introduction does not help matters. In the interests of economy of mystery, we should be better advised to accept as unexplained the electrical phenomena that we observe, than to invoke an unknown principle of explanation, namely electricity, to explain them. The argument here, then, is that an unknown Reality, which is introduced to explain phenomena, does not in fact perform the function required of it. It simply substitutes an unknown cause of phenomena for unexplained phenomena.

The conclusion is that ultimate Reality is not unknowable, nor is it featureless. How, then, are we to conceive it?

B. His Positive Doctrine

DESCRIPTION OF THE ABSOLUTE. The ultimate Reality which Hegel postulated is usually termed "the Absolute." The Absolute is an underlying principle of logical arrangement which may be conceived under two aspects. In the world it expresses itself as a principle of order and priority which governs all existing things; in human thought and experience it expresses itself as the idea of the order in the world. The principle not only expresses itself universally throughout the world and our experience; it *is* the world which it permeates. There is, that is to say, nothing which is not the principle. The principle is, therefore, a whole or unity, the totality of all existence and of all thought. This whole includes time and all that occurs in time. It includes, therefore, the passage of events that we call history and the human experience which is knowledge of the events. Since the principle which is the whole exhausts the universe, and since the process which is called history is a part of the whole, history must be something which the whole has projected from itself, so that it comes to be distinguishable in thought, though it is not distinct in fact, from the whole in which it occurs and to which it belongs. The knowledge of the process of history which is human experience is similarly a projected part of the whole. The process of history, or, if the phrase be preferred, the passage of events, is thus a progressive revelation to the whole of its own nature, a revelation which takes the form of experience in finite minds.

SIGNIFICANCE OF SELF-CONSCIOUSNESS IN THE ABSOLUTE. But mind is self-conscious ; therefore, the whole is conscious of itself. The activity of the whole may, therefore, be conceived under two aspects. It projects from itself what may, from the partial standpoint of human experience, be viewed as other than itself, that is to say, the process of events that we call history, and it is aware of itself. But both forms of activity and the products of them— that is to say, both the events which are known and the knowledge of them—remain within the ambit of the whole. As in self-consciousness the Self is both the subject that knows and the object which is known, so the absolute whole both constitutes the objects of its knowledge by externalising itself and knows the objects which it has externalised. These objects are not, however, as with Kant, the members of a phenomenal world cut off by an impassable gulf from Reality ; they remain eternally within the self-conscious unity of the Absolute which both produces and knows them.

PHILOSOPHY AND RELIGION. A final and rather surprising characteristic of the Absolute principle is the characteristic of deity ; the Absolute, which is pure spirit, owns, in fact, as at least one of its aspects, the aspect of Godhead. Hegel often writes—although the assertion of personality seems difficult to reconcile with the notion of unlimitedness—as if the Absolute were personal God. That Reality is a whole and a unity, we have already emphasised. That it is a unity of thought, is an implication of the statement that it is a knower of the objects which are also itself ; that it is self-conscious, is a presupposition of the unique relations postulated between knower and known and between them and the unity within which both knower and known fall.

The assertion that the Absolute is all these things is not equivalent to the further assertion that it is God, but it is at least not incompatible with that further assertion. The characteristics in question are, indeed, perfectly feasible attributes of deity. The further step which consists in the assertion that they are, in fact, attributes of deity is taken not by philosophy but by religion. Since the Absolute is all and philosophy is the exploration of the Absolute, it follows that the objects of philosophy and of religion are the same,—" the Notion of God," says Hegel, " is identical with Being "—but their methods are different. While the method of philosophy is thought, that of religion is intuition. We may have an " immediate assurance " of God and of ourselves as related to God, an assurance which, though it may be supported and even reached by philosophical argument, is independent of argument. Philosophy, in fact, is the sustained endeavour to demonstrate the truth of which religion makes us immediately aware. Thus religion is our personal relation to that which philosophical thought affirms. The lower forms of religion conceive of this relation as external ; the soul never loses its sense of otherness in relation to the God of whose existence it is assured. Philosophy, however, which teaches that everything is an experience of the Absolute within which it falls, denies this externality and insists that the God of religion must include the Self which knows Him. The higher forms of religion—for example, the religion of the mystics—corroborate this conclusion of philosophy, and the mystic enjoys a direct personal experience of the unity which philosophy demonstrates.

III. MONISTIC PHILOSOPHIES
The Arguments for Monism

The arguments by which the position outlined above is supported are very various and are apt to be technical. Monism, which asserts that the universe is in some sense a whole which is also a unity, and that the apparent plurality of things is in the last resort illusory, was a view very widely held during the nineteenth century, and a number of monistic philosophers advanced a variety of arguments in support of what are in essentials very similar metaphysical positions. Fichte and Schelling in Germany, F. H. Bradley and Bernard Bosanquet in England, and J. Royce in America, were all monistic philosophers, whose conceptions of the universe belonged to the same school.[1] There were important differences on points of detail—Hegel, for example, was attacked by both Fichte and Schelling—but from the standpoint of modern Realism, all three philosophers would be classed as holding broadly the same cosmic view. These philosophers produced a very substantial body of philosophical writing, all of which is dominated by the same metaphysical tendency. I propose briefly to run over some of the main lines of thought leading to the monistic position, without confining myself to those actually followed by Hegel. Of the ensuing arguments it can be said that all of them appear in the works of some one or other of the philosophers mentioned, although the actual form in which they are here presented may occasionally differ from that adopted by any of these philosophers. I propose, in other words, to try to present what may be described as the highest common factor of the thought of these various philosophers in the most easily comprehensible form.

A. The Axiom of Internal Relations

This may be stated as follows. The relations which relate terms are an integral part of the terms they relate. If we consider such a statement as : " This emu's egg is bigger than that hen's egg," it would normally be said that the fact which the sentence expresses consists of two separate entities—the emu's egg and the hen's—and of a relation, namely, the relation of being greater than, which is asserted to hold between them. The two eggs, we should say, are distinct from each other, and distinct also from the relation which relates them. Moreover, they can come into and pass out of the relation in question without suffering any alteration in their own being or nature. If, for example, emus ceased to lay eggs, and if all existing emus' eggs were destroyed, there would, it would commonly be said, be no alteration in the hen's egg. This, the view of common sense,

[1] Fichte, 1762-1814 ; Schelling, 1775-1854 ; Bradley, 1846-1924; Bosanquet, 1848–1923; Royce, 1855–1916.

is denoted by the statement that relations are external to their terms, and it is precisely this that the Axiom of Internal Relations denies.

Taking the instance given, the advocates of internal relations would point out that, unless a hen's egg were smaller than an emu's, unless it were browner than a pigeon's and larger than a sparrow's, unless it were more brittle than rubber and more oval than a billiard ball, it would not be the egg it is. Hence, its attributes of " being smaller than," " being browner than," " being larger than," " being more brittle and more oval than " literally constitute its nature. If it did not possess these attributes, it would be a different egg. But each of the attributes in question presupposes the existence of something else to which, in virtue of its possession of the attribute, the egg is related. If there were no emus' eggs, pigeons' eggs and sparrows' eggs, no rubber and no billiard balls, these attributes of a hen's egg could not be its attributes. Therefore the relation of the hen's egg to other things and, by consequence, the existence of these other things, constitutes part of the being or nature of the hen's egg. Again, it is a truth about the egg that, if kept too long, it will smell ; another truth that together with eleven other similar eggs it will fetch 1s. 6d. in the market. Now these truths about the egg entail the existence of yet other sorts of things—time, for example, smell, markets and money. And, once again it is insisted, unless these truths were true about the egg, it would not be the egg it is. Thus every entity is related to other entities by relations each of which helps to constitute the being both of it and of the other entities to which it is related. These in their turn are related to yet other entities, so that everything in the universe is bound up with everything else in a network of relations which are not distinct from the things they relate, but penetrate into their being and make them what they are. Change a thing and you change its relations ; you change, therefore, everything in the universe. Change the relations of a thing and you change the thing. The universe on this view may be likened to an enormous reverberating chamber, in which any whisper, however faint, in any part, however remote, echoes and re-echoes throughout the whole. It follows that a book upon the table is not the same book as it is upon the floor, and that the clock upon the mantelpiece will be altered, however slightly, every time a tiger is shot in the jungle. This may seem at first sight a somewhat extreme statement, yet it is a necessary corollary of any doctrine which asserts that the reality of the universe is that of an interrelated unity which is also a whole.

B. Wholes and Parts

Upon the implications of the phrase "interrelated unity," I have already commented, but the word " whole," as used in this connection, also has a technical significance which must be elucidated.

WHOLES AND AGGREGATES. A heap of stones by the roadside is an aggregate. Withdraw one stone from the heap and the heap remains unchanged, except in respect of the fact that it contains one stone fewer. The items, that is to say, the separate stones in the heap, are not, as Hegel would say, organically related to each other. Now let us consider a human being. He, too, is an aggregate of material units —of flesh and blood, nervous tissues, and organs. But in addition to being the sum of these constituents, the human being has, as we have seen,[1] a personality of his own which is more than the arithmetical sum-total of the constituent parts of his body. Take a heart, a pair of lungs, a pancreas, a backbone, take, if you will, all the principal parts from a living body, and then endeavour to put together again the body from which they have been taken. You will find the task impossible ; for the whole to which they belong has been destroyed by their withdrawal and cannot be re-constructed. Moreover, a heart laid out on a dissecting-table —that is to say, considered by itself in isolation from the rest of the body—is literally different from what it was, when it functioned in the body to which it belonged, since

[1] See Chapter XI, pp. 248-250.

it is shorn of the relations in which it formerly stood to the other members and to the body as a whole. Two conclusions follow. First, wholes, as opposed to aggregates, are more than the arithmetical sum of their parts ; secondly, the nature of the parts is actually determined by the wholes to which they belong.

THE NATURE OF PARTS DETERMINED BY WHOLES. If a whole determines the nature of the parts by virtue of the relations in which they stand to it and it to them, then to analyse the whole in the sense of breaking it up into its component parts is to do violence to the parts. Moreover, having isolated the parts from their relations, to examine them in this isolated state, as a scientist does, is to give an incorrect because insufficient account of their real nature. The conception of the whole or unity figures very prominently in monistic philosophy. It is important, therefore, that it should be understood, and I venture to append a few more examples which help to illustrate it. It is commonly said that a movement of a symphony is a whole or unity. What, precisely, is entailed by this description ? That, if one of its phrases were taken away, there would be left not merely the movement minus the particular phrase, but a mere succession of musical sounds whose aesthetic value had evaporated, simply because their pattern had been destroyed. An aesthetic whole, in other words, like the human body, is not only the sum of its parts, but is something more than their sum, and this " more," though dependent on the assemblage of the parts for its physical[1] existence, is not itself contained in them. The whole, in fact, is a something added, like the bloom on a rose or the flush on the cheek of perfect health. Yet just because it *is* dependent on the parts for its existence in the physical[1] world, the subtraction of any one of the parts destroys the whole.

Now consider the parts ; consider, in particular, the phrase which we have conceived to be taken away from the symphony. If it is played in isolation, its effect upon the hearer

[1] I stress physical existence because, as we shall see below, the Hegelian doctrine stresses the *logical* priority of the whole to the parts.

is totally different from that which it made, when it occurred as an integral part of the developing movement of the symphony[1] ; different and less important, less significant. And, as in the parallel case of the abstracted heart or lungs on the dissecting-table, the difference arises from the fact that the phrase has been divested of its relations to the aesthetic whole of which it once formed a part. Torn from its context, it is no longer the same, because its context—its relations to the whole and to the other parts—entered into and literally made it what it was. Thus to remove any part from an aesthetic whole is not only to destroy the whole, but radically to alter the part.

THE PERVASION OF THE PARTS BY THE PATTERN OF THE WHOLE. One way of putting this is to emphasise the fact that an aesthetic whole is distinguished by a certain pattern or form, and that this pattern or form pervades the parts. That there is an obvious sense in which an aesthetic whole is the embodiment of a form or pattern, we have seen in a preceding chapter.[2] The statement of the theme of a Bach fugue, for example, consists normally of no more than a dozen notes. To strike them at random upon the piano is to start a chain of physical processes of which the physicist and the physiologist between them might give a reasonably satisfactory account. It would be satisfactory in the sense that it would include everything of importance that could be said about them. Arrange the same notes in such a way that they form the statement of the fugue's theme, and, hearing them, you may be thrilled to ecstasy. The actual physical and physiological events that occur, the sound waves that travel through the atmosphere, the vibrations of the ear-drums, are the same in

[1] If anyone doubts this, let him play the *stretto* of a Bach fugue or the concluding chords in the fugue without playing the fugue which precedes them. Played thus by themselves, the mounting complexities of the culminating *stretto* sound thin, the profound appeasement of the final chords unconvincing. They have lost what, for want of a better word, I can only term their " significance." They no longer matter where once they mattered enormously.

[2] See Chapter XIII, pp. 348, 349.

both cases. It is only their sequence which is different. The order and sequence of the physical events, the pattern and form of the work of art which they represent, is, in other words, an essential ingredient in their value.

PICTURES AS WHOLES. Similarly, with a picture. From one point of view, from the point of view of physics and chemistry, a picture is merely a collection of coloured paints arranged on a canvas background. Of these paints the chemist gives an adequate, the physicist a more ultimate though, perhaps, less adequate, analysis. The physicist and the physiologist could also tell us exactly what happens when, as a result of light waves of specified lengths and frequencies travelling from the place where the picture is towards the retinas of our eyes, we see the picture, and recognise that it is, let us say, a picture of a woman with a white ruff and a red and purple dress posed against a blue and green background of hills and trees and holding a pink-coloured baby. From this point of view, the subtraction of one mass of coloured paint from the sum-total of the paints collected together in the area which is the canvas makes a purely arithmetical difference. There is just so much less paint of that particular colour. But this, it is obvious, is not the point of view that matters. From the point of view that matters—that is to say, from the point of view of the picture considered as an object of aesthetic interest and value—the subtraction destroys most of the interest and most of the value ; and it does this because it destroys a whole. For a picture, like the human body and the symphony, while from one point of view it is the sum-total of its constituent parts, is from another more than its parts. While it is dependent upon them, it is not exhaustively ana-lysable into them. Hence to remove a part, is to destroy the whole ; for perspective, proportion, balance, harmony, in a word, form, are of the essence of the whole, and all these are shattered by the removal of the part. Finally, the part con-sidered by itself, the draperies of the Madonna, for example, cut out of the canvas and painted or pasted on to a featureless background, while they may retain technical interest for the painter or the art critic, have lost their aesthetic value.

The human personality, whose scientific analysis was given in an earlier connection[1] illustrates the same point. A person is the sum of his parts, is dependent upon them and is yet more than them, so that, just as to take away a heart is not merely to leave a living body *minus* a heart, so to take away a faculty is not only to leave a mind *minus* an idea, an emotion, or a memory ; it is to destroy a person. It is hoped that enough has been said to illustrate the peculiar significance of the words " whole " and " unity," —the two terms are often used interchangeably by monistic philosophers—and the important consequences which follow from the statement that the universe is itself a whole or unity. One of these consequences is that no single thing in the universe can be adequately known or properly understood when it is treated, as it is treated, for example, by science, in abstraction ; that is to say, divorced from the context of the whole in which it appears. So to treat it, Hegelians urge, is to falsify it, for the reason that, so treated, it is not really itself.

WHOLES PRIOR TO PARTS. Two points in particular must be emphasised before complete justice is done to this important conception. The first is in the nature of a correction. In the illustrations given above I have spoken of the parts as coming together to make a whole. The movement of a symphony is, I said, " dependent on the assemblage of the parts for its physical existence." As an illustration of the Hegelian conception this is incorrect, in so far as it implies that the parts precede the whole which comes into existence only as a result of their association. In everyday life, it is true, we construct wholes by putting together parts, and this is true even of the painting of pictures and the scoring of symphonies. But of mental wholes this is not true. We entertain our ideas, we form our plans as wholes before we begin to express them in the series of actions which give them effect, and the wholes of monistic philosophy are in

[1] See Chapter IX, pp. 248, 249,

this respect like mental wholes—in fact they *are* mental wholes. The wholes emphasised by monistic philosophers are, therefore, logically prior to their parts. They are there, as it were, to begin with, and being there, proceed to express themselves in parts whose natures they pervade and determine. They are not in the process of historical time brought into being by their parts.

A Socialist Government committed to a scheme of Socialist reconstruction is, we will suppose, elected to power. It proceeds to take over the banks, to nationalise coal, transport, and cotton, to establish a National Investment Board. All these measures may, from one point of view, be considered as separate, although related, governmental acts. From another and more fruitful point of view, they are the expressions of an underlying policy. Here, we may say, is the fundamental ground plan of the Socialist conception of society pervading and determining the character of all that the Government does. It is, therefore, immanent in all that the Government does. If we were ignorant of the ground plan, we should, perhaps, be unable to understand the interrelation between the various measures undertaken by the Government. It is only when they are regarded as items in the execution of a policy which is prior to, is immanent in and yet transcends them, that their mutual relevance can be grasped. Nevertheless, though ignorant of the ground plan, we might, if we were sufficiently expert politically or endowed with a sufficiently acute political insight, be able to divine the ground plan from the acts.

It is precisely this work of divination that the Hegelian philosopher must seek to perform in relation to the ground plan of the universe. Faced with a manifold of fragmentary and apparently uncorrelated events, objects, persons and thoughts, he must seek to incorporate them, or rather, to see them as incorporated in the wholes of which they are parts and in the contexts in which they can alone be understood. For, taken as isolated, as science, for example, would take them, or common sense, they are not completely intelligible, for the reason that they are not completely real.

Thus it is the task of the philosopher to penetrate below the surface of things in order to divine the meaning and the significance that underlie them. Proceeding by the method of the Hegelian Dialectic, he combines opposed doctrines into the meaningful truths of which they are the partial expressions, and sees apparently fragmentary facts as mutually related parts of wholes in which alone they possess meaning and significance. His activities may, then, be likened to those of a detective engaged in reconstructing a crime from fragmentary clues. The Absolute develops by expressing itself in an infinite multiplicity of partial representations. These, which to the practical man are the apparently isolated objects and events of daily life, are treated by the philosopher as clues to the plan of the whole which underlies them and is expressed in them. But just as the crime precedes the clues which the detective discerns and follows, so the whole precedes the parts which the philosopher traces back to their context in the whole. To follow the analogy a little further, the crime is first conceived as a whole by the criminal, and the conception then receives expression in the various actions which are required for its realisation. This, if the disrespect implied by the analogy may be pardoned, is the activity of the Absolute. The detective, taking actions as his clues, endeavours to infer the nature of the plan which alone will give them meaning. His activity, then, may be likened to the activity of the philosopher. But the absolute whole is prior to its expressions of itself in the manifold of the world of appearance. The fact that we have to begin with the world of appearances, and that our thought has then to traverse in reverse direction the developments by which the Absolute came to be manifested in it, is a limitation arising from the partial character of our minds, which are themselves partial expressions of the Absolute.

CONCRETE AND ABSTRACT. Secondly, the whole is more real than its parts, and more real because more concrete. The use of the word " concrete " in this connection is technical. A thing's concreteness is proportional to the mass and richness of the ingredients it contains, to the number of the elements that go to make it what it is. The type of universal exemplified by the Platonic Forms, Hegel would have criticised on the ground of abstractness. The Forms, as Plato conceived them, are, for Hegel, as they were for Aristotle, mere abstractions from the particular things which they characterise. And, in the degree that they are abstract, in that degree also they are not real. As with Platonic universals, so with scientific and mathematical laws. Divorced from the instances which exemplify them, the things to which they apply, these are nothing at all ; apart from their instances, they have no being. But if scientific laws and mathematical truths, moral maxims and social generalisations, if the whole class of entities to which in Chapter X we gave the names of universals, are empty shells without their instances, the instances are nothing without the universals. A physical thing, as we have seen in an earlier chapter,[1] is analysable in terms of the qualities it exhibits and the attributes it possesses, and these qualities and attributes are due to the presence of the universals which characterise it. Shorn of its universal qualities, its blueness, its hardness and so on, a thing would be nothing at all ; even if it retained some sort of shadowy existence as a Lockean[2] substance, it would not be possible to have knowledge of it. Thus, we reach again the Kantian conclusion that, while concepts or universals without particulars are empty, particulars without universals are blind.

DEGREES OF REALITY. What, then, is real ? The combination of the two—that is to say, the whole thing in which universal and particular are distinguishable but not separable aspects. The " concrete universal," concrete in the sense that it contains and gathers up into itself both the abstract universal of Platonic philosophy and the raw stuff of sense experience, is the model for Hegel's conception of reality. It is the concrete universal, he insists, which is given

[1] See Chapter VI, pp. 160, 161.   [2] See Chapter II, pp. 40, 41.

in experience, which actually exists, which is real. It is only reflective thought which subsequently proceeds to distinguish in it the two aspects of abstract universal and particular.

Thus, the Hegelian solution of the problem set by Plato's philosophy[1] of the relation between particular and universal is in effect a denial of the existence of the problem. If, he says, we start by conceiving of the particular and the universal as two separate entities, we shall never be able to bring them together. But it is a mistake so to conceive them, for they are not initially separate. They are initially given as members of a whole which transcends them both. The problem of the relation between them does not, therefore, arise, any more than the problem of the relation between two facets of a crystal arises.

While the concrete universal, being a whole which transcends its abstracted aspects, is more real than they, it is, nevertheless, not completely real. To a profounder view it too is revealed as an aspect of a whole which, since it comprehends and transcends it, is more concrete and, therefore, more real than the concrete universal which we have been considering. Hegel thus introduces the conception of degrees of reality, according to which one whole is represented as being more real than another in proportion as it gathers into itself and comprehends more elements. Ultimate and complete reality is to be found only in the whole which contains *all* other wholes as its parts, thereby achieving a degree of concreteness by comparison with which all other wholes are seen to be abstract ; and they are abstract, because it is only in so far as they are *abstracted from* the whole of wholes to which they belong, and in which alone their real nature is revealed, that they can be said to possess separate being in their own right. Now such abstraction is, as we have seen, a falsification of their real nature. Therefore, the *separate* being which they appear to possess in their own right is not real but illusory. The only thing which is entirely real is the whole of wholes, which is the Absolute.

The two doctrines outlined above, the doctrine of internal

[1] See Chapter XI, pp. 295–297.

relations and the doctrine of wholes and parts, have far-reaching applications which ramify through the whole structure of monistic philosophy. I have space here to mention only one or two of the most important.

Corollaries

1. JUDGEMENT. At Bradley's theory of judgement we have already glanced in another connection.[1] Bradley, it will be remembered, defines judgement as " the act which refers an ideal content to a reality beyond the act." Whenever we assert something, we are, he holds, ascribing a predicate to a subject,[2] and this subject is continuously the same, namely, Reality. The combination of subject and predicate is further regarded as a whole or unity which is more real, because more concrete, than the two aspects of it, the subject and the predicate which it transcends. It is also logically prior to them, in the sense in which, as we have seen, the whole is prior to its parts. Thus the analysis of judgement is invoked to support the general Hegelian position that everything is ultimately one, that this " one " is a single whole or unity, and that the apparent " manyness " of the world we know, the many thoughts and things, the many subjects and predicates, which we normally assume to possess a separate existence, are to be interpreted as aspects of the underlying whole.

2. OUR KNOWLEDGE OF THE EXTERNAL WORLD. Perhaps the most important corollary of the conception of wholes as logically preceding and transcending their parts is its application to the problem of knowledge, and, in particular, to our knowledge of the external world. In the early chapters of this book various theories of the nature of this knowledge were discussed. The problems involved are, it is obvious, exceedingly difficult, nor are philosophers in agreement as to their solution. What, for example, is the function of the mind in knowledge? Does it create the objects it knows, or does it contribute to them, or is it

[1] See Chapter VI, pp. 167, 168.
[2] See Chapter VI, pp. 166–167, for an elucidation of the terms "predicate" and "subject."

merely aware of them ? What again is the nature of the object known ? Is it a physical thing, a collection of atoms and electrons, a sense datum or a set of sense data, a colony of souls, or a set of ideas in the mind of the knower ? As I have already pointed out, whatever answer we give to these questions must in the long run depend upon and be determined by our general philosophical position. Kant, who, as we have seen, maintained a metaphysical distinction between the world of noumena and the world of phenomena, insisted that we know only phenomena, whose general characteristics, temporal and spatial, qualitative, quantitative and causal, have been contributed by our minds. Hegel's answer similarly presupposes his general metaphysical position. The problem, he maintains, arises from a false presumption. This is that knowing mind and known object are two initially separate things which are somehow brought together by the relationship of knowing. Once this mistake is made, we are faced with the problem of determining what sort of relation this relation of knowing may be. This problem, he holds, is strictly insoluble. Hegel's own approach to the problem is *via* the Axiom of Internal Relations and the concept of wholes. Knowing mind and object known constitute, he holds, an example of a whole or unity, and this wholeness is initial ; that is to say, it precedes the distinction between mind and object. In accordance with the Axiom of Internal Relations, we shall regard knowing not as an external relation which has been tacked on to the mind and the object and somehow cements them together, but as a constituent part of the terms which it relates. Given that the knowing mind, the knowing relation and object known constitute a whole or unity, what sort of whole is it ? Hegel answers that it is a whole of knowledge. Knowledge is thus logically prior to the aspects, mind and object, which are distinguished in it, as a triangle is logically prior to its angles and sides.

Nor is the priority merely logical ; it is confirmed by the evidence of experience. The raw material of our experience, that which is, as it were, actually given to us, is neither a mind nor an object, but the knowledge of an object by a mind. A mind which knows, but knows nothing, is itself nothing ; an object which is not known is also nothing. We start, then, with a mind knowing something, this something being the object known ; we start, in other words, with an act of knowledge. This knowledge admittedly implies a distinction between the subject which knows and the object which is known. It has, in other words, two sides to it. But the distinction is not something which is outside the act of knowledge ; it falls within it. It is not a distinction between two initially separate things which have somehow been brought together. It is a distinction made within a whole between the parts or aspects of the whole which are recognised as contained in it, even while they are distinguished. The whole, the whole of knowledge, is real and exists ; minds and objects are abstractions from knowledge, and, if regarded as existing separately in their own right, false abstractions.

THE NATURE OF THE ABSOLUTE. While all acts of knowledge are thus treated as wholes, a special and, in Hegel's philosophy, a specially significant example, of knowledge is that which we ordinarily term self-consciousness. In the initial sketch of Hegel's completed doctrine, I emphasised the twofold character of the Absolute idea which, externalising through innumerable partial representations of itself the process of history, proceeds, by means of those expressions of itself which are partial human minds, to know its own externalisations. The passage of events which we know as history is, therefore, a progressive revelation to itself of its own nature. What the Absolute knows is itself ; and, since the Absolute is all that there is, it is not possible that it can know anything but itself. Moreover, since, as we have seen, knowledge is a whole which is logically prior both to knowing mind and to known object, the Absolute of knowledge is logically prior both to that aspect of the Absolute, which is the known passage of events, and to that aspect of itself which is knowing. Thus the Absolute may be most correctly described as an Absolute of knowledge.

THE SIGNIFICANCE OF SELF-CONSCIOUSNESS. Now the model of this conception is to be found in the fact of individual self-consciousness. The individual who is self-conscious is at the same time both subject and object. He projects from within himself both that which is known, the self or object of consciousness, and that which knows, the self which is conscious. Yet the individual is logically prior both to the conscious knowing self and the self which is object of consciousness. These exist not as distinct and separate entities, but as distinguishable aspects of a whole, which contains and transcends them. Thus the self-conscious self illustrates both the Axiom of Internal Relations and the doctrine of wholes and parts. Self-consciousness, moreover, is fundamental in all knowledge. All consciousness is self-consciousness, since we cannot know a thing without being aware of the fact that we know it. Thus self-consciousness is a whole within which all other forms of consciousness fall. For this reason, it achieves a greater concreteness, because a greater inclusiveness, than any other whole of knowledge. It embodies, therefore, in accordance with the doctrine of the concrete and the abstract, a higher degree of reality than other types of knowledge, all of which, when considered apart from the self-consciousness in which they occur, are infected by various degrees of abstraction. For the above reasons, self-consciousness affords an appropriate model for our conception of the Absolute. I do not mean to suggest that Hegel first made an independent examination of the facts of self-consciousness and then decided, " The Absolute must be like that." I am suggesting rather that, having established by a process of logical reasoning the monistic nature of the universe as a unified whole developing through the expression of itself in partial manifestations, he finds in human self-consciousness the one thing of whose existence we are most certainly assured and of which we have, so to speak, an inside view, a highly satisfactory illustration of his cosmic conception. It is natural, then, for an expositor who is endeavouring to explain the general character of the Hegelian universe, to invoke our experience of self-consciousness as at once an aid to the imagination and as evidence of the conception. Self-consciousness, in fact, is a microcosm of the Hegelian macrocosmos which happens to be available for the inspection of all. One important Hegelian philosopher, the late Professor McTaggart, maintained that Hegel meant by the Absolute nothing more nor less than a society of self-conscious beings, and although this is not the normal interpretation, it indicates the importance which the concept of self-consciousness assumed for Hegel.

IV. SUMMARY AND COMMENT

Hegel's Philosophy as a Culmination.   The above constitutes a brief account of some of the leading ideas of Monistic Idealism. During the last century Monistic Idealism commanded a larger measure of agreement among philosophers than has been accorded to any other philosophy since the Middle Ages. It constituted the logical development of two separate streams of thought. One of these is the thought of the English empiricists, Locke, Berkeley and Hume, the other, the thought of the Continental rationalists, Descartes, Leibnitz and Spinoza. These two streams of thought, first brought together by Kant, were developed to their logical conclusion by Hegel and his followers. About Hegel's conclusions, indeed, there is a sense of finality. It is difficult to see how any further advance could be made along the lines which Hegel followed.

The Idealism of Locke, Berkeley and Hume is usually known as subjective, because its main common contention is (with certain reservations in the case of Locke and Berkeley) that everything that is known is in the mind of the subject that knows. This position, pushed as it was by Hume to its logical conclusion in Solipsism, was justly regarded as intolerable. The Idealism of Hegel is usually called objective, because, while retaining the assertion that everything that exists is mental or at any rate is of the same nature as thought, it abolishes the notion of the individual mind, or rather transcends the individual mind in the act of knowledge, which is itself but an aspect of the whole of knowledge. The act of knowledge has an objective as well as a subjective side, and, since, as we have seen, knowledge is the ultimate reality of the Hegelian universe, knowledge may justifiably be entitled objective : it does not, that is to say, depend upon any particular mind for its existence. On the contrary, mind itself is but a partial aspect of objective knowledge. Similarly the object is not dependent, as it is in Berkeley, upon being known for its existence. It is an integral part of knowledge and so of Reality.

Thus, for the Idealism of Hegel, the solipsist impasse reached by Subjective Idealism does not arise, since the distinction between the knowing individual mind and other individual minds which the earlier idealists had taken as ultimate is transcended.

The differences between the many things of the common-sense world are similarly resolved by means of the Axiom of Internal Relations. The universe is not, as Leibnitz, for example, held, a colony of separate experiencing units, or as Plato held, an assemblage of Forms vaguely ranked under the Form of the Good, or as Kant held, a collection of things in themselves or noumena ; it is a single substantial unity, comprehending within the ambit of its being the world of appearance in which it expresses itself. The objective idealistic Monism affirmed by Hegel's metaphysic is, in fact, the most comprehensive scheme of the universe that any philosopher has hitherto devised. If it is true, it may justly claim to explain everything, both everything that exists and every mind that knows, in terms of its fundamental principle the Absolute.

Critical Comment. But is it true ?

Detailed criticism falls outside the scope and intention of this book. Nevertheless, the reader who has no previous acquaintance with the subject must in fairness be informed that the Hegelian philosophy, which was dominant in the nineteenth century, is no longer dominant to-day. Criticism of the Axiom of Internal Relations has brought its Monism under suspicion, while the close scrutiny which modern philosophers have given to the problem of perception has proved damaging to its Idealism. If, for example, the realist view of perception, which we described in the third chapter, is in essentials correct, then the objects of sensory experience are not dependent upon any mind for their existence, and an interpretation of the universe in terms of mind, which insists that knowledge is a universal cosmic characteristic, can no longer be sustained. Thus for one reason or another most philosophers would to-day find difficulty in accepting Hegelianism. The monistic universe is, indeed, uncongenial to the general temper of our times. There is to a twentieth-century mind something dead and static about the Hegelian Absolute. The charge of deadness is not, it must in fairness be conceded, justifiable. Because the universe is a complete and unified whole, it is not, say the Hegelians, either a static or a finite whole. On the contrary, it is ever new in its continual expression of itself in finite terms, and, since none of its terms can express it adequately, each expression of itself is different. But, seeing that, although immanent in each partial expression, it retains nevertheless its character of infinite totality, it cannot itself be supposed to change, that is, to be historical in character, since history presupposes change in that which it records. This conception has been variously attacked under the name of " the block universe " by William James and the pragmatists,[1]—William James dubbed the Absolute with its all-embracing intimacy a " large sea-side boarding-house with no private bedroom in which I might take refuge from the society of the place,"—by the realists and by the modern neo-idealists. It is attacked because, by locating the Absolute with which Reality is identified behind and beyond our finite experience, it makes Reality transcend our experience and so precludes the possibility of our knowing it ; because by making the Absolute the immanent spring from which all thought rises, as well as the all-embracing sea into which all thought merges, the universal presupposition of experience, as well as the final synthesis of experience, it renders progress non-existent and change

[1] See Chapter XVI for an account of Pragmatism.

unreal ; and because, for this very reason, Reality becomes an embodiment of thought as a passive structure and not an expression of thinking as an active principle.

In general, Hegelianism appears to the twentieth-century mind to belittle individuality, to minimise the differences between things, to make insufficient allowance for the existence and the integrity of brute-facts which happen to be humble facts, as, for example, that this notebook in which I am writing is two inches to the left of that ink-pot, and to fail to make due provision for change.

Thus it is no accident that those philosophers who may perhaps with the greatest justice be regarded as the legitimate descendants of Hegel, the Italian neo-idealist philosophers, Croce and Gentile, while retaining the view that mind is fundamental in the universe, substitute for the " thought " of Hegelianism a dynamic process of active " thinking." Eliminating the completed Absolute at the back of things, they concentrate on the immediacy of our changing individual experience. For them mind, active, self creative and object creating, is literally the only thing in the world ; besides mind there is nothing, neither an all-generative Absolute at the beginning nor an all-absorbing Absolute at the end. Space precludes any account of this, the most recent, development of Idealism. Here, then, we must take our leave of idealist philosophies.

Hegel's Science of Logic translated by Johnston and Struthers is the standard translation of Hegel. *Hegel's Logic of World and Idea* translated with an introduction by H. S. Macran is a smaller work containing two of the more important parts of Hegel's logic. William Wallace's *The Logic of Hegel* and W. T. Stace's *The Philosophy of Hegel* are important expository and critical works. F. H. Bradley's *Appearance and Reality* and J. McTaggart's *Nature of Existence* are the most important works by English philosophers belonging to the objective idealist school. Bernard Bosanquet's *Knowledge and Reality* may also be studied. A. C. Ewing's *Idealism* contains a comprehensive criticism of Objective Idealism ; Chapter IV on the Theory of Internal Relations may in particular be read with advantage.

Chapter XVI: DEVELOPMENTS AND APPLICATIONS OF HEGELIANISM

1. The Problem of Truth and Error: Pragmatism

I. CORRESPONDENCE AND COHERENCE

Introductory. It will be convenient to introduce a chapter on truth and error, one of the most vexed problems in philosophy, at this point, since one of the most widely held theories of truth, the Coherence theory, presupposes and supports the monistic view of the universe described in the last chapter. There are, broadly speaking, three main theories of truth, namely, the Correspondence theory, the Coherence theory, and the Pragmatic theory. I shall say something about each of these theories in turn. The adequate discussion of any theory of truth raises metaphysical questions, just as its acceptance commits the acceptor to a certain metaphysical position. Broadly speaking, the Correspondence theory is held by realists, the Coherence theory by idealists, and the Pragmatic theory by pragmatists. Nevertheless I propose to state, and, so far as possible, to discuss, these theories without traversing their metaphysical background more than may be absolutely necessary. A treatment on these lines, while conceivably open to the charge of superficiality, has very considerable advantages from the point of view of clarity. Moreover, with the exception of Pragmatism, of which some account will be given in the second part of this chapter, the philosophical positions underlying the theories to be discussed have been treated in more or less detail in other chapters.

Statement of the Correspondence Theory. I propose to introduce the statement of this theory by enumerating certain considerations upon which it is based. The truth of these considerations seems to the present writer self-evident, although they are very far from being admitted by all philosophers. In particular the supporters of the Coherence and the Pragmatic theories of truth would, as we shall shortly see, reject some of them. Nevertheless, they are, I think, such as common sense would on reflection be prepared to accept.

First, truth is a property not of facts, but of judgements or propositions. Secondly, the presence or absence of belief in the judgement made or proposition asserted has no bearing upon the question of its truth or its falsehood. For hundreds of years almost everybody believed in the truth of the proposition "The earth is flat." But the prevalence of this belief did not make the proposition true. The truth and falsehood of propositions and judgements are, therefore, independent of belief : they are also independent of any attitude on the part of any mind or body of minds. Thirdly, although truth is a property of judgements or propositions, whether the judgement or proposition will or will not possess the property of being true depends on something other than the judgement or proposition, namely, upon the existence of a certain fact or set of facts. Thus the proposition, " There is a pebble blue in colour and one inch in diameter touching the east side of the fourth column from the landward end of the South Parade Pier at Southsea," is rendered true or false by the existence or non-existence of a pebble possessing these characteristics and occupying this position. Fourthly, and here we come to the statement of the Correspondence theory, a judgement or proposition is true, if and only if there is a fact such as the proposition asserts or the judgement judges. Hence, the meaning of truth is correspondence with fact. Fifthly, the meaning of truth so defined is different from the fact whose existence makes the proposition true. It is also different from the considerations which lead us to regard the proposition as true. For example, we may often be led to believe a proposition to be true because the belief gives us emotional satisfaction, and we may, and often do, produce invalid reasons or manufacture evidence in favour of the proposition because of the emotional satisfaction which belief in it confers. " Emotional satisfaction " is not, however, what we mean by truth, nor does the fact that a belief induces it make the belief true. The meaning of truth is further different from the way in which we come to discover that a proposition is true. For example, the meaning of the truth of the proposition, "The train leaves King's Cross at 10 a.m. for Edinburgh," is that there is a complex physical fact which the sentence used in the enunciation of the proposition expresses, and that this complex physical fact corresponds with the proposition. But I come to *believe* that the proposition is true as the result of looking up the train in a time-table, and I come to *know* that it is true by being at King's Cross and seeing the Edinburgh train leave the platform at 10 a.m. As I said above, these considerations seem to me on reflection to be self-evident, and I expect that most of my readers will on reflection agree with them. Nevertheless, it is exceedingly difficult, when discussing the problem of truth and error, not to make assumptions or to draw inferences which, whether explicitly or implicitly, deny some one or other of them.

Limitations of the Correspondence Theory.   In favour of the view that the meaning of truth is correspondence with fact, it may be said that it is precisely this that most people do in fact mean by the word " truth," when they make ordinary judgements in the course of their daily life. Let us, for example, take the case of an ordinary perceptual judgement. If I judge " This book is red," most people would agree that what I am wishing to assert is that there is before me an object, namely, a book, and that this object is red, and they would further agree that my judgement is true, provided that there is before me an object such as that which the judgement asserts. Now it is obvious that this

view entails a realist theory of perception. It entails, that is to say, that there are such things as books, that they are meaningfully described as red, and that I do directly apprehend them by means of my senses. It is probably also implied that the book is independent of my act of apprehending it, and that it is what it is, apart from its relations to all the other things in the universe and to the universe as a whole. The Correspondence theory, therefore, implicitly denies the Axiom of Internal Relations.

Now idealist philosophers do not believe any of these things. They believe that our apprehension of the book as an isolated object is partial, imperfect, and misleading, and that our fuller knowledge of it is, to quote one of them, " a revolution in which the book is swept away and determinate connections between determinate universal concepts are substituted." Further, they do not believe that the book can be isolated from its relations or considered as a separately existing entity. If the book depends for its being upon its relations with other objects, some of which are not known, and if, as a consequence, we do not know the book in its entirety exactly as it is, we cannot completely know the fact with which our judgement is to correspond. It is clear, then, that the Correspondence theory of truth cannot be held by a monist or by an idealist. To put the point in another way, it is only if we are content with a realist theory of perception which does not depart too radically from the tenets of common sense, that we can consistently hold the Correspondence theory in its simple form.

Arguments in Favour of Correspondence.

Nevertheless, the consideration that Correspondence provides a meaning for truth which is precisely such as we intend our judgements, when we make them, to bear, is exceedingly important, and provides a strong argument in favour of the theory. When I judge " there are twenty people in the room," what I believe myself to be affirming is a fact, namely, the presence of twenty people. If the number present were twenty-two, I should regard my judgement as false because the fact was one with which it failed to correspond.

Correspondence, again, is the obvious criterion, when, confronted with two rival judgements, we want to know which of the two is the truer. If, for instance, A says that B is six feet high and C says that B is five feet eleven inches, and we take a tape measure and measure B's height and find that the tape measure shows it to be six feet, it is quite obvious that there is a sense in which A's judgement is more correct than C's. And the meaning of the word " correct " as applied to A's judgement is that the judgement corresponds with the measurement given by the tape of something which we may describe as " brute-fact," while C's judgement does not.

Now it is quite true that this test is a purely empirical one, that we have adopted the standard of feet and inches as a convenient way of measuring, and that the height of six feet as given by the tape measure may, therefore, be a height that only exists in relation to ourselves. Yet granted all this, and granted as a consequence that the true judgement so arrived at may be devoid of full meaning and significance, there still remains an important sense in which the Correspondence theory of truth, when the test of correspondence is applied to determine the relative truths of two judgements of isolated fact, does express exactly what we mean when we say of one of them that it is " the truer."

Historical Judgements. The Correspondence theory also appears to advantage as affording a meaning for truth when applied to historical judgements.

If I judge that Nelson was shot in the chest, my judgement is true primarily because of its correspondence with the meaning of certain printed words written in the page of a history book. So far admittedly the judgement takes us very little way. How, we want to know, did those particular words come to be there? How, to put the question in another way, did the judgement they embody come to be passed? Because, presumably, of a fact that somebody witnessed. Now the judgement can only be doubted on the ground that this fact was other than what it asserts. The fact might be either (1) that Nelson was not shot, or (2) that he was not shot in the chest. Now it does not seem to be open to question that the only way in which we can possibly ascertain which of the three judgements, Nelson was not shot, Nelson was not shot in the chest, and Nelson was shot in the chest is true, is by an appeal to the testimony of eye-witnesses. If there was once a fact, the perception of which by eye-witnesses corresponded with the judgement "Nelson was shot in the chest," then that judgement is true because of that historical fact and for no other reason.

Objections to the Correspondence Theory.

Let us now consider the objections to the Correspondence theory. There is, first, the objection, already referred to, that the Correspondence theory involves a somewhat naïve theory of perception on the basis of which alone it is tenable. It is not clear how much weight should be attached to this objection. Even if there are no such things as red books, or even if we do not perceive them in the simple way which common sense supposes, it will not, therefore, follow that the meaning of truth is not correspondence with fact. It is, of course, the case that we should in this event have to revise our notions of what constitutes fact, and many judgements which are generally accepted as being true would have to be modified. But it does not follow that the meaning which the Correspondence theory gives to truth is not its correct meaning, merely because many judgements which we have been accustomed to think true turn out to be false. As we have already seen, most philosophical theories entail the conclusion that our commonsense notions are faulty, and it is a little unfair to bring this as a special charge against the Correspondence theory of truth.

A more serious objection to the theory was first suggested by Aristotle. It may be briefly stated as follows : The Correspondence theory asserts that a judgement is true, if it corresponds with a fact. Now the fact is either known or not known. If it is not known, we cannot know that the judgement corresponds with it. If it is known, it is, to say the least of it, unnecessary to make a judgement about it, to refer to the known fact to establish that the judgement about it is true, and then, having established that it *is* true, to conclude that the fact which it asserts must exist. For the conclusion that the fact exists because the judgement which asserts it is true, must already have been assumed in the course of the chain of reasoning which is involved in establishing the conclusion. Nor, unless it is assumed, could the chain of reasoning validly occur. The difficulty here is similar to that which attaches to Representationalism.[1] Either I know directly the fact with which my true judgement is to correspond, or I do not. If I know it directly, what need is there for me to pass a true judgement about it, in order that the judgement may correspond with it? If I do not know it directly, how am I to know that my judgement does correspond with it? The theory, in fact, postulates two entities, (A) and (B), of which we know (A) but do not know (B) ; but, if we do not know (B), we can never know that (B) corresponds with (A). A true judgement, therefore, is either superfluous or unauthenticated. Even if we were to admit the validity of this objection, it is not certain that it would be fatal to the Correspondence theory. The fact that the theory involves a roundabout way of establishing something that we must be assumed to know already, does not entail the conclusion that the meaning of Truth is not correspondence with fact.

Coherence and Monistic Idealism.

The Coherence theory maintains that the meaning of truth is coherence with the general structure of beliefs about the universe as a whole. It is usually advocated by idealist philosophers, and constitutes an essential part of the Monistic Idealism described in the last chapter. For monistic idealists the correspondence of judgement with fact is not and cannot be the meaning of truth, since there are no facts in the strict sense of the word

[1] See Chapter II, pp. 43, 44.

with which judgements can correspond. An isolated fact plucked from its context is not, for a Hegelian, a real fact at all, and no judgement, therefore, which seeks to correspond with it can be true. Let us take such a fact as that constituted by this particular square red patch, at which I am now looking. Supporters of the Coherence theory would not deny that the judgement that the patch is square and red is, so far as it goes, a true judgement : but they would deny that the patch so conceived is a real constituent of the world. For the reasons given in the last chapter, they would denounce it as an abstraction. To give an adequately comprehensive account of the square red patch in the context in which, as actually experienced, it appears, we should have, say the Hegelians, to include within the account all the relations which the patch has to its context, since, if it did not have these relations to the general context in which it appears, it would not be the patch that it is, but a different one. The fact that the patch appears in a context is, therefore, of fundamental significance for the understanding of its reality.

For the Hegelian idealist, as we have seen, everything which exists exists in a system, a system which in the last resort is the Absolute. In a system so conceived everything implies and is implied by everything else. Consequently we can only truly know a thing, if we understand all that it implies, and no judgement made about the thing which ignores all the other things which the thing implies can be a completely true judgement. To put the point shortly, we may say that everything transcends and reaches out beyond itself to embrace all the other things to which it is related. No judgements about the thing which presuppose that it exists in isolation can, then, be true. Now judgements such as those which the Correspondence theory declares to be true do entail this presupposition.

Significant and Non-Significant Judgements.

This conclusion is commonly embodied in the assertion that judgements about isolated physical or historical facts are devoid of significance. The meaning of the expression "lack of significance," when applied to a judgement, can be most readily grasped by taking, as an extreme example of a non-significant judgement, the case of a man who judges that in 1934 the name of the Chancellor of the Exchequer began with a C, but believes that the Chancellor was Mr. Churchill. There is, it may be said, a formal sense in which such a judgement is true. But since it presupposes and expresses a false belief, it is devoid of significance. Now it is easy in this case to see that the term "lack of significance," when applied to a judgement, means among other things that the person making the judgement has ignored all the relations of the thing about which the judgement is made to other things. In the case in point, this "ignoring" leads him into error directly he passes beyond the judgement made and proceeds to make others. But, in the view of the idealist critics of Correspondence, the case cited only affords a glaring example of a defect common to all commonsense judgements : for it is precisely this same charge of lack of significance that is brought by supporters of the Coherence theory against the ordinary judgements of common sense and history.

In order to realise the import of this criticism, let us consider in a little more detail, as an instance of an historical judgement, the judgement that Nelson was shot in the chest. Now such a judgement might be made by a person who was totally ignorant of English history ; it is clear, nevertheless, that there is some sense in which it would be true. But it would certainly fall short of the *full conception* of what we mean by truth. Nobody would deny that the significance of the judgement "Nelson was shot in the chest" would be increased, if we knew what manner of man Nelson was, what he was doing on shipboard, how he came to be shot, and so forth. Now such knowledge clearly involves a knowledge of Nelson's relations to the context of history, and to say that a judgement is not significant means, therefore, that it is a judgement about something which has been arbitrarily abstracted from its context for the purposes of the judgement. It is just in so far as such a something is not entirely real, that, supporters of the Coherence theory would say, the judgement about it cannot be entirely true.

The Whole as More than the Sum of its Parts.

But there is a further criticism to follow. In another connection I tried to show[1] that the complete knowledge of a man can never be reached by collating an infinite number of theoretically complete scientific accounts of his various aspects, on the ground that a man is more than the sum of the various departments or aspects of him that science studies. Similarly, the full knowledge of all the facts which may have occurred during a period of history is, it might be said, very far from constituting a real understanding of the period. For a period of history is more than the isolated facts that it contains ; it is a whole which includes the facts but transcends them. It is of such a whole that a good student obtains what we may call " a general comprehension." In the light of this comprehension, he is able to gauge the relative importance of various events, to estimate the influence of personalities, to allow for and to trace the interplay of causes and motives, and to display that kind of familiarity with events and their causation which we denote by this phrase " an understanding of the period." This " general comprehension" will be different in different historians, so that no two historians will give the same impression of any given period. But though the impressions conveyed by two historians may be different, they may each be true and each equally true. Now, we cannot, it is said, deny the application of the word truth to this general comprehension ; yet, inasmuch as a general comprehension is something over and above the various judgements of isolated historial fact which go to make it up, its truth cannot be established by Correspondence alone.

Similarly, with regard to the truth about a circle. The third book of Euclid contains a number of perfectly true propositions about the " circle as such" considered as an

[1] See Chapter IX, pp. 248, 249.

isolated figure, and it might be possible to increase these so that all the truths about the "circle as such" were known. But these truths do not constitute the whole truth about a circle. The circle is also a conic section and bears relations to hyperbolas, parabolas and to other conic sections. Hence further truths remain to be ascertained about the circle considered as a member of a whole or series, which are over and above the truths about the "circle as such," and these further truths about the circle as a member of a whole or series cannot be established by regarding truth simply as Correspondence between judgements and isolated facts or between judgements and perceptions of isolated facts.

The Truth about a thing, in fact, is not an aggregate of all the true judgements about it. The true judgements may be formally true, but they are incomplete, and it is just in so far as particular judgements of fact do and must fall short of the whole Truth about a thing, that, it is said, the Correspondence theory fails.

Considerations in Favour of the Coherence Theory.

Now, while the Coherence theory does not purport to give us the whole Truth about a thing, it does, say its supporters, make provision for the fact that isolated, partial judgements about its various aspects do not and cannot constitute the whole Truth about it; what is more, that they cannot claim to be completely true. For, if reality can, as Hegelians maintain, be regarded as a systematic organic whole, the parts of which are related teleologically to it, if no one fact can be understood by itself, but only in relation to the whole of which it forms a part, it is quite obvious that no judgements about any part of reality can be known to be true, unless we know what the whole means. As this is humanly impossible, it would seem that isolated judgements about particular things cannot ever be known to be completely true. This contention has the merit of meeting the requirements of a number of different metaphysical views.

Let us suppose, for example, that we are convinced by the arguments used in Chapter X in favour of the existence of

Platonic Forms such as the Forms of Truth, Justice and Beauty. The Forms themselves can never be completely known : hence, judgements about particular things which participate in these Forms, and which by virtue of their participation comprise an ultimately unknowable element, cannot be known to be quite true. This conclusion squares with practical experience. Differences of opinion with regard to the merits of works of art are numerous and apparently irreconcilable, and only a dogmatist would be prepared to claim absolute truth for any particular aesthetic judgement. Now these differences are precisely what we should expect, if works of art, by virtue of their participation in the Form of Beauty, contain an unknowable element.

But, although the Coherence theory denies absolute truth to any artistic judgement, it is claimed on behalf of Coherence that it provides a useful test by reference to which we may grade different judgements in respect of the degrees of truth which characterise them, in such a way as to distinguish those which are more true from those which are less. For the conception of degrees of reality, described in the last chapter, obviously carries with it the notion that there may be degrees of truth. There is a celebrated case, frequently referred to in philosophical textbooks, of a Chinaman who was taken to a Queen's Hall concert and started to leave after the tuning-up of the orchestra, which he thought was the concert. Now, although it may be urged that there is no known certain standard by an appeal to which the aesthetic judgement implied by the Chinaman's departure can be pronounced to be false, it is less likely to be true than the judgement which prefers the concert, since it is inconsistent or incoherent with the general consensus of musical opinion. Thus, in practical matters, the test of the truth of a judgement becomes, on the Coherence theory, consistency with other judgements passed by persons who are qualified to judge.

Objections to the Coherence Theory.

There are, unfortunately, objections to the Coherence theory no less strong than those which we have noted in the case of Correspondence. In the first place, the Coherence theory, as we have seen, asserts that, since no fact taken in isolation is absolutely real, no judgement about a fact can be absolutely true. The only judgement which, presumably, would be entirely all inclusive, which would, that is to say, take into account *all* the relations of the fact about which the judgement was passed to everything else in the universe, would be a judgement which the Absolute passed about itself, and it is only, therefore, to such a judgement that the description " absolutely true " could be applied.

The argument that, until we know reality as a whole, we can never completely know the truth of any particular judgement, applies inevitably to the Coherence theory of truth. On its own premises, then, we can never know that the Coherence theory of truth is true. It may of course be replied that Coherence still remains valuable as a test of the truth of practical judgements in cases where absolute truth is not required. Yet it is as applied to practical judgements that, as we have already noticed, the Coherence theory is most palpably deficient. It despises the truth of isolated judgements of fact, charging it with being formal merely and lacking in " significance." How much substance is there in this charge ?

I endeavoured above to indicate the sense in which the word " significance " is used. I cannot pretend that the attempt was very successful. " Significance " is, it must be admitted, an ambiguous word, whose meaning cannot be defined with precision. But, whatever its precise meaning may be, it may well be doubted whether it is the same as that which we wish to convey by the word " truth." Significance, in fact, is one thing and truth is another. It occasionally happens in science that each of several hypotheses can be regarded as affording an equally probable explanation of certain facts, or that several possible accounts can be given of a certain phenomenon, each of which fits in sufficiently well with the general structure of our beliefs and views about what is antecedently and on other grounds probable. Now all these hypotheses and all these accounts might, I think, be justly termed equally significant. Nevertheless, it is fairly clear that, by calling them significant, we do not in the least mean to imply that they are necessarily true.

Criticism of Self-Consistent Systems.

It might be said that the notion of " consistency " rather than that of " significance " best conveys in practice the meaning of Coherence. Consistency is something that we normally predicate of hypotheses, interpretations, explanations and theories.

In this connection the word " consistent " may refer either to a theory's general consistency with all existing knowledge, or to the internal consistency of the theory with itself. Let us consider each possibility separately. As the preceding pages bear witness, several different philosophical systems have from time to time been advanced purporting to explain and to describe the universe, each of which, in so far as it is consistent with all existing knowledge, may, if truth can be equated with consistency, be regarded as being equally true. Clearly, these systems cannot all be true. One may be true, and, in that event, the others must be false. Now, it is obvious that a certain characteristic must apply to the true one, which is absent from the others, namely, the characteristic of squaring with the facts. It is equally obvious that the Coherence theory, if interpreted in terms of general consistency, provides no means of recognising this characteristic, nor of discriminating the true consistent theory from the various false consistent theories. Provided they are all equally consistent, they are all, for the Coherence theory, equally true. But that they should be so, is clearly a defect in the Coherence theory.

The test of self-consistency is no more helpful than that of general consistency. Some philosophers have held that systems were true, not so much because they were Coherent with our general knowledge of the universe, as because all their parts were consistent with one another. A fatal objection to this view is constituted by the fact that there have been several perfectly self-consistent philosophical systems which, nevertheless, contradicted one another. Each of these, on the "self-consistency" theory, would have to be regarded as equally true. In fact, however, it is highly probable that no one of them is true.

Similarly, there are a number of systems of space, Euclidean space, or Riemann's space, each of which is theoretically self-consistent. Yet there is clearly a sense in which one of these systems of space corresponds with fact and the others do not. Thus correspondence with fact supplies an overriding condition which even the most self-consistent system must satisfy.

Reply to Criticisms : The Argument from Completeness.

It would, of course, be urged in reply by advocates of Coherence, that philosophical and spatial systems which, although they may appear to be self-consistent in the light of our present knowledge, are, nevertheless, untrue in the correspondence sense of the word " untrue," that is to say, failure to correspond with known facts, are not really self-consistent but only seem to be so. It is only because they are incomplete, it is said, that they achieve a false appearance of self-consistency.

The argument proceeds as follows : the further the bounds of our knowledge extend, the more will it be seen that only one system is really coherent, and that only one system is, therefore, ultimately true. Other coherent systems which appeared to be coherent with the knowledge we formerly possessed, will be shown to be unable to assimilate fresh facts about the universe, or will only be able to assimilate them by eliminating features of difference and reducing themselves to the common pattern of the one true coherent system.

The resulting single coherent system will, it is said, also correspond with all the known facts. In the end, as thought approaches the Absolute, in which, as we have seen, truth and reality are merged, the distinction between system and fact will vanish and correspondence will become identification.

Whether we shall find this reply acceptable, will depend upon our attitude to the system of Monistic Idealism described in the last chapter. If Monistic Idealism provides a true picture of the universe, then it may very well be the case that the Coherence theory of truth is ultimately defensible in terms of the Absolutist conception.

Coherence Stultifies Itself.   But a final difficulty, at which we have already glanced, remains. Accepting Monistic Idealism, we shall defend the Coherence theory on the ground that it is in the last resort only for absolute and ultimate truth that it provides a meaning. Its failure to give a meaning to the truth of the judgements of perception and history will then be understandable, since, on the basis of the Absolutist theory of the universe, such judgements, being partial, are not completely true. But must we not in this event judge the Coherence theory by its own high standard, and point out that, just in so far as it seeks to provide a meaning for ultimate truth, it cannot itself be true ? No one pretends that the Coherence theory, even if it is true, constitutes in itself the whole of truth, and yet it is the Coherence theory itself which tells us that nothing short of the whole of truth is true.

So long, in fact, as we recognise that the Coherence theory, being incomplete, is not wholly and absolutely true, there will always remain the possibility that its incompleteness, and, therefore, its untruth may be found in just that part of it which asserts that truth is one and single, and that this one and single truth is to be found only in the Absolute. Thus there will always remain the suspicion that, if we knew the Coherence theory completely, if, that is to say, we could cease to regard it as an isolated theory and could contemplate it in the context of that indivisible monistic system with which, it asserts, it is related by relations which are themselves parts of it and of the system, we might find it asserting that there are several truths all of which are true, and that complete truth *may* be found short of the Absolute.

II. PRAGMATISM

Anti-Intellectualism of Pragmatism. Pragmatism emerged as a distinct philosophy, or, more correctly, as a distinct philosophical attitude in the latter years of the nineteenth and early years of the twentieth centuries, when a number of philosophers adopted pragmatic modes of thought as a protest against the Monistic Idealism which was dominant at the time. Its main exponents were C. S. Peirce (1840–1914), William James (1842–1910) and Professor John Dewey in America, and Dr. F. C. S. Schiller (1864–) in Great Britain. The distinctive feature of Pragmatism is its theory of truth, a theory which identifies truth with utility. But in order that the full bearing of this identification may be understood, some account must be given of the pragmatists' general approach to traditional philosophy and in particular of their theory of perception.

This account is rendered difficult by reason of the fact that Pragmatism is not so much a definite and compact philosophical theory, as a characteristic of a philosophical attitude. This attitude expresses itself in the view that personal considerations affect all knowing, and that logic and even metaphysics are, therefore, dependent upon psychology. The view that allowances must always be made for the personal factor in any account of knowledge, is maintained in opposition to the traditional theory of knowledge, which holds that the knowing faculty can be studied in isolation and that a man's view of the universe, even if it is to some extent coloured by the desires he entertains and the purposes he wishes to fulfil, does not necessarily depend upon such considerations.

A good example of the pragmatists' general approach to traditional philosophy is the criticism of the syllogism described in an earlier chapter,[1] a criticism which, it will be remembered, insists that this traditional formulation of

[1] See Chapter V, pp. 140, 141.

the laws of reasoning does not in the least represent the way in which people do in fact reason. This criticism of the syllogism is only a special case of a general attack upon what is called intellectualist logic, because of its alleged refusal to acknowledge the influence of the personal element in all reasoning processes. Reasoning, the pragmatist insists, is not an abstract process conducted by a hypothetical faculty, the intellect, which functions as it were *in vacuo* independently of the rest of our faculties ; it is dominated throughout by personal and emotional factors.

The Atomistic Theory of Perception.

Our account of Pragmatism may conveniently begin with the consideration of a theory of perception, advanced by William James, to which most pragmatists would, I think, be prepared to give general adhesion. The theory begins with a direct denial of that view of the perceptual process which was common to the English philosophers Locke, Berkeley and Hume, a view criticised by William James on the ground of its undue atomism. According to Locke,[1] Berkeley and Hume the objects of perception consist, broadly speaking, of a number of distinct and separate ideas or impressions. Let us restate what is in effect Locke's view. When we are brought into contact with what is called a physical object, a table for instance, the table produces certain stimulating effects upon our sense organs. These effects are conveyed by the nerves to the brain where we become conscious of them as ideas, and it is these ideas, each of which is a distinct and separate entity, which are known by the mind and which form the subject-matter of our knowledge. Thus, when we think we perceive the table, what we in fact experience is a series of isolated sensations, sensations of hardness, smoothness, coolness, squareness, brownness and so forth ; we never perceive the table itself. The implications of this psychology when logically developed, speedily lead, as we have already seen, to the position of Solipism.[2]

Kant—I am summarising the gist of the pragmatists'

[1] See Chapter II, p. 39.   [2] See Chapter II, p. 56.

Pp

criticism—endeavoured to avoid the solipsist impasse by endowing the mind with an apparatus of faculties, which perform the function of welding together the chaotic material presented to us by our senses into a coherent and intelligible whole. The mind, it will be remembered, on Kant's view, works up our fragmentary sensations into unified wholes, by means of the Principles of Understanding. But what right had Kant, ask the pragmatists, to legitimise the mind's impudence in tampering with its sensations? Why should the sensations conform to the Categories, and why should the constructional process, by means of which connections are interposed between the originally unconnected, result in anything but a complete falsification of reality? Rightly or wrongly, then, the pragmatist refuses to take shelter in the elaborate structure erected by Kant, and insists that, if we accept the premises from which Locke and Berkeley started, there is no way of escape from the scepticism in which Hume finishes.

W. James's Account of Perception. But, William James asked, is it after all necessary to accept these premises? And the distinctive feature of the pragmatist position consists in the assertion that it is not. So far, in fact, from the atomistic psychology being true, it is, according to the pragmatist, the exact reverse of the truth. The atomists had said that experience is composed of distinct sensations between which the mind interposes connections. William James retorted by asserting that experience comes to us as a continuous whole in which the mind interposes distinctions. " Consciousness," in James's words, " does not appear to itself chopped up in bits." On the contrary, it is a "*continuum*," in which the relations between the different elements are experienced just as truly as directly as the elements related.

Whereas Berkeley's analysis of the proposition " the egg is on the table " asserts a group of isolated ideas of sense qualities which are associated together to form an egg, a group of isolated ideas of sense qualities which are associated together to form a table, and a piece of mental jugglery which interposes the relation "on" between them, William James's analysis asserts, first, a continuous stream or flux in which the egg, the "on," and the table are all alike experienced as an indistinguishable whole, and, secondly, a piece of mental activity which subsequently separates the egg from the table, and postulates a distinct relation of *on-ness* between them. Thus, according to the pragmatist view of perception, the essence of mental activity is to break up and separate that which is originally a continuous whole. This separation is effected by means of what are called mental concepts, of which the concept of the relation "*on-ness*" is an example, and it is effected for the purposes of action. A world of experience which was a vast indeterminate flow would prove difficult, if not impossible, to live in, and it is necessary, therefore, in order that we may act, that we should discriminate the flow of experience into eggs and tables and their relations. Thus all our mental processes bear a definite relation to action. This brings us at once to a new and important point.

Activity of Mind in Perception.

In analysing experience the mind is active. Not only does it discriminate but it selects, not only does it select but it adds, and it selects and adds in accordance with the interests of the perceiver and in relation to the purposes which he has in view. The analysis which we make of our experienced *continuum* is thus the expression of a choice and is conditioned by the will. What is real for us consists of a reality which we ourselves have made, and we have made it of such and such a kind because it is precisely that kind of reality which best serves our purpose.

Thus the pragmatist psychology emphasises two important points : (*a*) Experience is a continuum which is broken up and analysed into objects and their relations by the activity of the mind.

(*b*) This analysis is not arbitrary, but is dictated by the interests, the purposes, and, we may add, the temperament of the perceiver. The reality that results is one that it is useful to us to perceive. The establishment of the important principle of the influence of " usefulness " or " purpose " in conditioning perception, lies at the basis of the pragmatist view of logic, which results from an extension of the same principle.

If what we believe to be real depends upon what it is useful for us to believe to be real, may not the same principle determine what we believe to be true ?

Pragmatic Theory of Truth.   Modern psychology has shown how great is the influence of our wishes in determining our beliefs. The smoker believes that tobacco ash is good for the carpet, the angler that fish, being cold-blooded, do not mind having their throats dragged out of them by a hook—or do not mind very much—because these beliefs are such as they would wish to be true. We are, the fact is, alas, only too obvious, prone to regard our own emotional satisfaction as constituting evidence for the truth of the belief which provides it. Reflection may, indeed, insist that our own attitude to our beliefs cannot possibly affect their truth, and invoke the second of the considerations cited at the beginning of this chapter[1] as a warning against erecting what most of us would regard as humiliating evidence of human fallibility—it is because we are not yet sufficiently rational, we might say, that we mistake the promptings of our wishes for judgements of probability—into a theory of the meaning of truth. Yet this, in fact, is precisely what Pragmatism does. For the essence of the pragmatic theory of truth is the identification of truth with emotional satisfaction. Starting from the proposition, " people hold beliefs to be true which are emotionally satisfying," Pragmatism proceeds to the entirely different assertion, " a true belief *is* one which is emotionally satisfying," or, as it is usually put, " a true belief is one which works." How does Pragmatism justify the taking of this further step ?

[1] See p. 433 above.

Truth Gradually Established by Experience. The words true and false are, it is pointed out, only applied to beliefs with regard to which a question has arisen. When the question does arise, " Is it true or false ? " we answer it in some such way as this : " If the belief furthers the purpose which led us to ask the question, it is true ; if not, false." Hence the meaning of the words true or false is the furthering or not furthering of the purpose which led to the asking of the question " Is such and such a belief true ? "

Now it is clear that the extent to which a belief furthers a purpose can only be ascertained by experience. Hence the truth of a belief is not immediately established : if, however, we proceed upon the assumption that a belief is true, and find that this assumption is warranted by the consequences which follow the adoption of the belief, if, in short, the belief works in practice, then it becomes progressively more and more true ; so that the truth of a belief which has stood the test of experience over a long course of years, such as the belief in the law of gravitation, becomes *for all practical purposes* established. Since all experience is finite, no belief can be said to be absolutely true ; but this fact need not disturb us. Absolute truth is a figment of the logicians ; it is of no importance in practice. Every belief, then, is a truth claim. By acting upon the belief we test it, and if the consequences which follow from adopting it are good, if they promote the purpose in hand and so have a valuable effect upon life, the truth claim of the belief is validated. Hence we make our own truth just as we make our own reality, the truth of the beliefs we hold and the reality of the objects we perceive being equally relative to our purposes.

" The ' true,' " says William James, " is the name of whatever proves itself to be good in the way of belief and good too for definite assignable reasons." We are now in view of the fully developed theory. James states it as follows : " The ' true,' to put it very briefly, is only the expedient in the way of thinking, just as the ' right ' is only the expedient in the way of our behaving. Expedient in almost any fashion : and expedient in the long run and on the whole, of course."

At this point the inevitable objection arises ; although we may agree that true beliefs usually work and false beliefs do not, it is not the fact that a belief works that makes it true. What we mean by a true belief is a belief that squares with the evidence. Scientific laws are held to be true because they conform with all the known evidence, and only for so long as they conform ; this is clear, if for no other reason, from the fact that when fresh evidence is discovered with which the law does not conform, the law is modified or another law is substituted in its place.

The implication would seem to be that science requires a Correspondence theory of truth.

The Pragmatist's Treatment of Science.

But Pragmatism has little difficulty in rebutting this argument derived from the assumed needs of science and turning it to its own advantage. For the practice of the scientist affords, in the pragmatist's view, an illuminating example of the very procedure which, he insists, is involved in the formation of all our beliefs. Scientific laws are not, he points out, in reality laws at all. A scientific law claims *prima facie* to embrace not only all the phenomena that have occurred in the past, but all the phenomena of the same type which can possibly occur in the future. But, since the future is unknown, we cannot tell that a scientific law, however well it has worked in the past, will necessarily hold good in the future : hence, the so-called laws of science are properly to be regarded as hypotheses or postulates. A postulate is a man-made hypothesis which purports to explain all the facts known at the time. It is a product of free choice, dependent upon the will and modifiable by the will. Having formed a postulate the scientist looks around for facts to support it. If the process of selection from the stream of experience produces facts which verify the postulate, the postulate may be said to have worked, and its claim to truth is thereby enhanced. If the facts

reject the postulate, it is modified or abandoned. Now all
scientific laws are postulates of this kind. Originally formed
to fit the facts known at the time, they become progressively truer as more and more facts are found to conform
to them. Thus no scientific law is either finally or absolutely true ; in the words of Sir J. J. Thomson, it " is a
policy, not a creed," and its truth, which is continually
subject to review, is tested by the consequences which
attend its application to reality, and progressively validated
or invalidated by the results of the test.

Criticism of Intellectualist Logic.

As with the laws of
science, so with those of logic. The pragmatic concepts of
purpose, usefulness and verifiability are invoked to reinforce the criticism of the traditional concepts of intellectualist logic. An example of this criticism in its bearing
upon the Syllogism was given in Chapter V. Its effect is
to establish the conclusion that all reasoning is relative
and provisional ; relative in the sense that it is undertaken
with a definite object to serve a definite purpose, provisional in the sense that it is always liable to be overturned
by a sudden failure to apply to new circumstances.

Reasoning, the pragmatist insists, cannot in practice be
divorced from purpose ; and the truth of all laws, whether
of science, of mathematics, or of logic, is only established by
the consequences which attend their adoption. As for the
logic of traditional philosophy, it is dismissed as barren and
academic. It is charged with only attaining to certainty
at the cost of novelty, and only conforming to the demands
of reason because it fails to conform to the facts of reality.

Pragmatist Metaphysics.

Although Pragmatism has no
official metaphysical creed, a theory purporting to give
an account of the nature of facts and their formation which
has been advanced by Dr. Schiller is worth including
here, not only because of its intrinsic importance, but
because it is typical of an attitude to reality which is fairly
common in non-philosophical twentieth-century thought.
For Pragmatism has affected the popular consciousness

in a degree only less than that of psycho-analysis. As we have seen, great emphasis is placed by Pragmatism upon the influence of the will in perception. We carve out of the flux of reality the facts that interest us by means of concepts formed by the mind for that purpose ; and, although we cannot altogether deny the existence of a certain brute substance which is the subject-matter of this perpetual vivisection, the substance of reality is unknown and remote, while the facts which are known are, so to speak, dressed up and " faked " for our delectation by the mere circumstance of our perceiving them.

Thus the act of perception, which alters the fact perceived, in a very real sense creates it. All knowing is relative to doing, and that which in point of fact determines whether a fact gets known is the suitability or non-suitability of the fact for the purposes of our action. And, since our knowledge of the fact brings the fact into existence as a separate constituent of reality, everything that is known is affected by the fact that we know it : no fact, therefore, is independent of our knowledge of it. This conclusion accords well enough with the pragmatic theory of knowledge, for, if all knowing is for the purposes of action, our knowledge of a fact necessarily involves our acting upon the fact known. It is only disinterested knowledge, whose existence, as we have seen, the pragmatist denies, that could be conceived of as not altering or affecting that which it knows.

Knowing as Fact Making.

The conclusion is also in complete agreement with the pragmatic theory of truth : it reinforces it and is reinforced by it. How is this agreement effected ? Belief in a fact, as we have seen, alters the fact. If the belief alters the fact in harmony with our wishes, then the belief works and becomes, according to the pragmatic theory of truth, a true belief : the fact is, accordingly, a real fact. If, however, the belief in the fact alters the fact in such a way as to be inharmonious with some of our wishes, the belief in the fact has not completely worked, and is, therefore, replaced by a modified belief which alters the fact in some other way. If the modified belief produces satisfactory consequences, the modified belief is *ipso facto* truer than the original belief, and the fact formed by the modified belief is, therefore, more real than the original fact. Thus reality is continually being made just as truth is continually being made, the essential factor, in the creation of truth and reality alike, being the ability of the belief which is true and of the fact which is real to satisfy the wishes which led to the belief being entertained and the fact being created. Thus complete truth and complete reality are to be found together at the end of the road which leads to the complete satisfaction of our wishes, and the axiom " Man is the measure of all things " has been faithfully maintained as the touchstone of the pragmatist philosophy in psychology, in logic, and in metaphysics.

Criticism of Theory of Perception.   As I have indicated the main criticisms to which the Correspondence and the Coherence theories of truth are exposed, I must, in common fairness, mention some of the objections which are usually brought against the Pragmatic theory of truth. They are, in my view, decisive. Let us begin, first, with the pragmatic theory of perception upon which the theory of truth largely depends. The pragmatist, as we have seen, regards experience as a continuous flux or stream from which the mind selects certain aspects according to the interests of the perceiver, and then proceeds to work them up into the chairs and tables of everyday existence.

But if experience is really an indeterminate flux or blur, as void of distinction, say, as a sheet of white paper, it may be asked why the mind should carve out of it certain objects rather than others. Why, for example, should my mind carve out a chair instead of a rhinoceros as the object upon which I am now sitting, unless there is some distinctive mark or feature in reality itself in virtue of which I do in fact say " chair " and not " rhinoceros " ? Is it not, then, necessary to assume, as most philosophers have assumed, that reality is not wholly featureless, not wholly without differentiation, but contains within itself certain rudimentary distinctions which form the basis upon which mind builds the structure of the world known to science and to common sense? Whichever view of the matter we take, however, Pragmatism finds itself in a dilemma. Let us consider the two alternatives separately.

1. If, on the one hand, it is true that mind can arbitrarily carve out of the flow of experience whatsoever it pleases without let or hindrance from reality, if, in short, mind can, as the pragmatist holds, make its own facts, how is it possible for facts so made to thwart the purposes of the maker?

Pragmatism, as we have seen, regards scientific laws as postulates which are progressively verified or invalidated by their success or failure in conforming with the facts. But, if we select our own facts, in what sense is it possible for them not to verify the postulates we have formed? Pragmatism, which holds that some postulates work and become true while others fail to work and are therefore abandoned, obviously envisages the possibility of facts sometimes conforming to a hypothesis and sometimes failing to do so: yet it is equally obvious that the psychology of fact-making upon which Pragmatism is based rules this possibility out of court.

It is difficult to see, therefore, how on pragmatist premises any postulate or truth claim, as it is called, can fail to make good, seeing that, whatever the consequences its adoption involves, the postulate, being arbitrarily selected from the flow of reality to serve our purposes, must necessarily have the effect of serving those purposes. But, if this is the case, the Pragmatic theory of truth is convicted of the very defect which it imputes to its rivals, the defect, namely, of failing to provide a criterion by which true beliefs are to be distinguished from false beliefs.

Criticism of Theory of Reality.   The assumption that mind makes its facts by selecting from the indeterminate flux of experience is attended by difficulties no less serious for the pragmatist's view of reality, than those in which it involves the Pragmatic theory of truth. It follows, as we have seen, from this assumption that mind constructs its own facts, pronouncing that to be real which it has " conceived after the likeness of the heart's desire, the product of a human purpose." Only those facts are real, then, which further our purposes.

Now it is undoubtedly and unfortunately true that many facts thwart our purposes. How do these facts come into being ? The pragmatist, who defines a real fact as that which is selected because it serves our purposes and is, in fact, made real because it serves them, is driven to assert that disagreeable facts are in some sense illusory. The steps by which he arrives at this result are as follows : the only facts we recognise are those which we have ourselves selected : we select facts which serve our purposes ; therefore, either (a) it is impossible for us to know facts which do not serve our purposes ; or (b) if this conclusion proves contrary to experience, those facts which we know but which do not serve our purposes must be unreal facts : they are appearances only. Hence we are committed to the time-honoured distinction between the world of appearance, which is the world of experience, and the world of reality, a distinction as complete as that established by the philosophy of Hegelian Idealism, the criticism of which first brought pragmatism into the philosophical field. It is only in the world of reality that the pragmatist doctrine of " real facts " holds good, and the world of reality is unfortunately not the world we know. The whole doctrine, therefore, reduces itself, in Bertrand Russell's words, " to the proposition that it would be heavenly to live in a world where one's philosophy was true "—a proposition which no philosopher would desire to controvert.

Distinctions as Actually Given in Reality.

2. Let us now consider the second alternative.

Some pragmatists might, if pressed, admit that the flux

of experience is not entirely featureless. They might concede that rudimentary marks or articulations are actually given in reality, and that it is the function of mind by selection, emphasis, and amplification to work up the embryonic distinctions which exist in reality into the fully developed world of objects with which common sense is acquainted. Perception, then, would, on this view, consist of recognising and working up distinctions which are already " there," not of introducing distinctions which are not " there." But, if this view of reality is taken, it is clear that our selection of fact can never be completely arbitrary. If the stuff of reality is composed of rudimentary objects which are given, and are given in a certain juxtaposition, and of rudimentary events which are given, and are given in a certain order, then it is clearly possible for the view of reality constructed by one mind to be either more or less correct than the view of reality constructed by another. Greater correctness would appear to be constituted by greater approximation on the part of the world of objects as constructed, to the world of rudimentary distinctions, as given : lesser correctness by an arbitrary construction which to all intents and purposes ignored the features of the presented reality.

But the notion that there may be a rudimentary order in reality which is given and not made, involving as it does the assumption that one man's view of reality may be truer than another's, suggests, indeed it necessitates a different conception of the meaning of truth. If, in fact, there is some sense in which A's view of reality, being largely based on the rudimentary features of the given, is truer than B's which largely ignores them, is not this sense precisely that which is asserted to be the meaning of truth by the Correspondence theory of truth, the sense, namely, in which a true view of reality is one which corresponds with reality ?

Criticism of Theory of Truth.   This consideration at once suggests a criticism of the essential doctrine of Pragmatism, the doctrine that the meaning of truth is " that which gives emotional satisfaction." It has been suggested by critics of Pragmatism, notably by Bertrand Russell, that this definition of the meaning of truth springs from an ambiguity in the use of the word " means."

Let us first of all, following Bertrand Russell, consider two propositions in which the word " means " is used in the two different senses which it is capable of bearing. We can either say (1) that " cloud means rain," or (2) that " *pluie* means rain." Now the sense in which " cloud means rain " is different from that in which " *pluie* means rain." We say that a " cloud means rain " because it possesses the causal properties and characteristics of being liable to produce rain ; we say that " *pluie* means rain " because the words " *pluie* " and " rain," both of which are symbols for communicating what is in our thoughts, happen to be symbols for communicating the same thought in the minds of two different people. Now the sense normally given to the word " means " is the latter sense, and the question " What is the meaning of truth ? " can therefore be paraphrased, " What is it that we have in our minds when we say that a belief is true ? "

Now let us consider the pragmatic definition of truth in the light of these two possible meanings of " means."

The pragmatist begins by enquiring why it is that we affirm a certain belief to be true. He answers this question, and, in the light of modern psychological developments, we may agree that he answers it approximately correctly, by stating that we affirm those beliefs to be true which further our purposes. From the proposition that " a belief which furthers our purpose is a belief which we affirm to be true," he deduces the further proposition, with which we may also agree, that " the fact that a belief furthers our purposes causes us to affirm that belief to be true."

Having reached this stage, he proceeds to deduce one more proposition, and, in order to make this further deduction, he utilises the first meaning of " means " as defined above. He notices, that is to say, that there is a sense in which, if A *causes* B we may affirm that A *means* B, and applies this sense of the word " means " to his definition of truth. He then deduces from the proposition " belief furthering our purposes causes us to think belief true," the further proposition " furthering our purposes " is what truth *means*.

Having established this proposition, the pragmatist claims to have satisfactorily defined the meaning of truth. And it must be admitted that he has defined it, but only in terms of the first sense of the word " means " referred to above, the sense, that is to say, in which a cloud *means* rain because a cloud *causes* rain. But we agreed that this is not the sense in which we commonly use the word " means," and, in particular, it is not the sense which we have in mind when we ask, " What is the meaning of truth ? "

If, then, we agree that there is a distinction between (a) what we have in mind when we say a belief is true, and (b) what causes us to say that a belief is true, it is clear that the pragmatic definition of the meaning of truth, which may be correctly given as an account of (b), is not the correct interpretation of (a). It follows, therefore, that the meaning of truth must be something other than " furthering our purposes."

Truth Not Man-Made. If the meaning of truth is something other than what the pragmatist asserts, if the truth of a belief is not to be identified with its usefulness, the theory that truth is man-made, the theory, namely, that truth is created by a progressive verification of the beliefs for which truth is claimed, also falls to the ground.

The pragmatist, it will be remembered, draws a distinction between a belief which has not yet been tested by the criterion of whether it works—such a belief being called a truth claim—and a belief whose consequences have been found to be satisfactory, the truth of which is said to be validated or established. But the psychological argument, which the pragmatist invokes in support of his theory of truth, only shows that the beliefs which further our purposes are those which we persist in calling true after reflection, and that we do so persist for the very reason that they further our purposes. But unless we identify the truth of a belief with the properties which a belief must possess in order that we may call it true, the fact that we persist in holding a belief after reflection does not mean that the belief is true. Many beliefs which have been held by large numbers of reflective men over considerable periods, such as the belief that the earth is flat, have been shown to be not wholly true by the test of Correspondence with reality.

The Pragmatic theory of truth, then, may reasonably claim to be on safe ground in so far as it asserts, (1) that we tend to hold those beliefs to be true which are emotionally satisfying ; (2) that we persist in holding a belief to be true, if the consequences of its adoption are found to be satisfactory. It is incorrect in making the further assertion (3) that those properties, such as the property of having satisfactory consequences, which cause us to regard a belief as true, are the same thing as the truth of a belief.

Popularity of Pragmatism.

I have devoted some little space to a criticism of the doctrines of Pragmatism in general and of the Pragmatic theory of truth in particular, because the relativism and subjectivism which they embody has in recent years enjoyed a widespread vogue. The theory of evolution has led to the view that everything is relative ; species, for example, are not fixed, but are changing continually into other species. Even the laws which govern the physical world are, it appears, in some sense relative to an observer. On the negative side, the decline of the belief in supernatural religion has produced an instinctive hostility to absolutes and ultimates of all types. If this world is all, then it is a natural presumption that there can be no valid standards of thought, conduct or reality, other than those which are the products of the human mind. But these change as the human mind changes. The subjectivist theories of beauty described in Chapter XIII exemplify this attitude in its bearing upon the theory of aesthetics. The modern psychology of instinct and the views of psycho-analysis represent the same attitude in its application to ethics.[1] The relativism which in aesthetics denies the existence of absolute beauty, in ethics denies that of absolute good and right. We do not admire things because they are beautiful, or approve them because they are good ; they are beautiful because they are admired, good because they are approved. Finally, in the sphere of logic, Pragmatism subjects truth also to the domination of the human mind, and insists that in the long run that alone is true which it suits human beings to think true. The bearing of this attitude and of the conclusions in which it finds expression upon our general view of the universe and of the status of human beings within it is obvious. Pragmatism has ministered to human complacency by assuring human beings that right and wrong, beauty and ugliness, reality and unreality, are not external facts, features of the universe to which human beings must in the long run subject themselves, but are the products of human consciousness and, therefore, amenable to human desires. Pragmatism is, indeed, just such a world view as the triumphant nineteenth century, dazzled by its own achievements, might have been expected to evolve. It seems doubtful, however, whether it will survive the twentieth.

RUSSELL, BERTRAND   The Problems of Philosophy
    (Chapter XII for the Correspondence Theory).
JOACHIM, H. H.   The Nature of Truth
    (For the Coherence Theory).
JAMES, WILLIAM   The Meaning of Truth
    (For the Pragmatic Theory).

A. C. Ewings's *Idealism*, Chapter V, may be recommended for a comprehensive treatment of the subject as a whole and in particular for a criticism of Coherence. John Wisdom's *Problems of Mind and Matter*, Part II, Chapter XI, treats the subject from the modern analytical point of view.

[1] See Chapter IX, pp. 238–242, for development and illustration of this generalisation.

CHAPTER XVII: DEVELOPMENTS AND APPLICATIONS OF HEGELIANISM

2. The Philosophy of Dialectical Materialism

Introductory. It may appear at first sight a little surprising to introduce a chapter on Dialectical Materialism as a development of Hegelianism. Dialectical Materialism, announced by Karl Marx (1818–1883) and Friedrich Engels (1820–1895), and developed and expanded by Lenin, Bukharin, and others, has already transformed the social and political institutions of a sixth of the inhabitants of the planet, and in the opinion of many good judges may shortly be expected to produce similar re-arrangements among a large proportion of the other five-sixths. Is it not, then, it may be asked, a little pedantic to represent a doctrine of such prodigious practical importance as a pendant to a philosopher whose work is difficult, comparatively unread, and largely out of date—to treat Dialectical Materialism, in fact, as a footnote to Hegelianism? The answer is that nothing of the sort is here intended. The most important and the most original parts of Marx's teaching are economic and political. But this book is not a book about either economics or politics. Its concern is philosophy. Moreover, from its scope and intention that part of philosophy which deals with the good life for the individual and for the community and with the nature of the State, is deliberately excluded. It is obvious, then, that those aspects of Marx's thought which are relevant to the theme of this book are unimportant relatively to the main body of Marxist doctrine. We are concerned, in fact, with the metaphysical foundation of Dialectical Materialism, and this, the more strictly philosophical part of Marx, derives more or less directly from Hegel. What follows, then, is not an exhaustive account of the thought and work of Karl Marx. It is an attempt very briefly to indicate the philosophical background, usually termed Dialectical Materialism, of Marx's thought, and it will confine itself to the strictly philosophical assertions that Dialectical Materialism embodies.

I. MARX'S INTERPRETATION OF THE HEGELIAN DIALECTIC

What Marx Adopted from Hegel. Marx explicitly accepted Hegel's theory of Dialectic as a mode of reaching truth, but qualified his acceptance by saying that the Dialectic, " must be turned right side up." What, then, did the Dialectic, when " turned right side up " amount to ?

1. First, it involved the general view, which Marx took over from Hegel, that all development, whether of thought or things, is brought about through a conflict of opposing elements or tendencies. This doctrine, as we have already seen, is two-sided. It is a description of the way in which things come into being, develop and behave, and it is a description of the way in which we come to learn the truth about them. For Hegel the two processes, the development of things and the discovery of truth, were aspects of the same reality ; but whereas he gave logical priority to the second, Marx, holding, as we shall see, that thought is in some sense a reflection of things, emphasised the priority of the first.

2. Secondly, the dialectical process involves a continual series of ups and downs. One tendency by its very success generates its opposite, so that at the very moment of its apparent triumph its opposite begins to gain upon it. To take one of Marx's own examples :—the nineteenth century saw the development of an increasingly triumphant and increasingly extreme Individualism. But Individualism throughout the whole period of its advance was generating Collectivism, which first entered the field as a formidable

rival at the very moment of Individualism's apparent triumph. Since in coming to fruition any tendency or movement prepares the way for its opposite, the right understanding of the tendencies operating in society at any given moment depends upon a knowledge of the processes which have brought that society into being.

But the movement from one tendency to the other is not simply that of a see saw. The later tendency is truer than the earlier because it takes it into account and includes it. Thus the conflict of opposing tendencies both in thought and in events is no less fruitful than necessary, since it leads to a development in the direction of truth and reality.

There is, however, no finality about the process, which is endless.

3. Up to this point, no more has been involved than a logical application of the Hegelian Dialectic to the interpretation of history. But when we ask the question, " What is the motive force of the whole process, the initiative from which the development through opposites proceeds ? " Marx makes a radical departure from Hegel.

In Hegel the driving force of the dialectical process was engendered by the developing ideas themselves. But, as Marx points out, ideas which are not ideas in any mind, are figments. Ideas can only exist in the minds of individual persons, and an idea in the mind of an individual is, for him, always the expression or reflection of something else. Individuals, in fact, are only the instruments of this something else, which Marx identifies in the last resort with movements or changes in the physical world. " With me," he says, " on the contrary" (that is, in contradistinction to Hegel), "the ideal is nothing else than the material world reflected by the human mind and translated into terms of thought." This quotation indicates the bridge by means of which Marx passes from Hegelianism to the Materialism in which his distinctive contribution resided. Before, however, we proceed to describe Marx's distinctive form of Materialism, there are two additions to be made to our account of the dialectical process as he conceived it.

The Conflict of Opposing Tendencies. Events, we have been told, occur as the result of the conflict of opposing tendencies. The truth about events, that is to say, the correct interpretation of history, is reached by the understanding of both the opposing tendencies and of the result of their conflict. Just as in the world of thought, to pursue a tendency to its logical conclusion is to reveal its opposite, so in the world of fact the very success of one movement tends to call into existence *its* opposite. Thus Feudalism produced Capitalism by creating the bourgeoisie, who, by reason of the expansion of industry and the growth of commerce, were presently to destroy Feudalism ; and Capitalism, by reason of its creation of a class-conscious proletariat, is forging the instrument of its own destruction. But while from one point of view—looked at from the outside as it were—the tendency is a one-sided development which is seen to call its opposite into existence to correct its one-sidedness, from another—viewed as it were from the inside—the tendency is itself seen as a synthesis of opposites. Thus each system of society contains its opposite within itself, and it is the opposition between it and the opposite it contains which leads to the disruption of the system and to its supersession by another.

Marx's celebrated announcement of the contradictions of Capitalism, by reason of which he was led to prophesy its eventual supersession by Communism, was a logical working out of this conception. Capitalism, for a variety of reasons into which we cannot here enter, tends to increasing trustification and monopolisation. The trustification and monopolisation of industry would, Marx thought, lead to a diminution in the number of capitalists, and those who had been squeezed out by the process would sink into the ranks of the proletariat. In this way Capitalism, by the process of its own development, would tend to make capitalists fewer and proletarians more numerous, thus bringing into being the forces which would ultimately compass its own destruction.

Again, Capitalism is driven, by the discovery of new

industrial techniques, to increase production. Now Marx's theory of surplus value taught that Capitalism by its very nature pockets all, or at any rate most, of the profits of industry, leaving to the workers only a bare subsistence wage, which will never vary very much in the direction either of increase or of diminution. If this theory is correct, the home workers will be unable to provide a market for the products of expanding Capitalism, owing to their lack of purchasing power. Thus capitalists will be unable to find an outlet for the products of their increasingly developed industrial technique within the boundaries of their own States, and, as a result, will be driven to look for markets abroad. The discovery and exploitation of such markets will become the major object of the foreign policies of States of which, in virtue of their economic power, the capitalists are in control. The capitalist State is therefore driven, by reason of its search for foreign markets, to adopt a policy of Imperialism. This brings it into conflict with other capitalist States embarking upon similar policies for similar reasons. Competing imperialist policies lead to war. Thus once again Capitalism is exhibited as being driven by the contradictions inherent in its own nature—in this instance the contradiction between its need to obtain markets for its products and the increasing insufficiency of the home market consequent upon the appropriation by capitalists of surplus value—to embark upon policies which lead to its own supersession. This characteristic Marxist doctrine affords a good example of the dialectical process, according to which any given system leads to its own supersession by the generation within itself of those opposing tendencies which will overthrow it.

Marxism not Completely Determinist.

The question is often raised whether the dialectical process so envisaged entails a complete Determinism. Is the movement of the process inevitable, in the sense that, given sufficient knowledge, an observer could at any given moment predict its outcome ?

Marx's answer appears to be that it is not. If the conflicting tendencies were operating in a vacuum, screened from the influence of all irrelevant factors, and there worked out their conflict undisturbed, each phase of the conflict would, he agrees, be determined. What is more, the rate of its development would be determined and therefore predictable. In fact, however, the two conflicting tendencies, though they may be the dominant forces at work within the matrix of any particular system, are not the only ones. There is always a variety of other forces and tendencies which may cut across the operation of the two dominating tendencies, impede or facilitate their working out, blur the outlines of their opposition and confuse the outcome of their conflict.

Moreover, the two tendencies which are distinguished in thought do not exist in fact in the abstract purity with which thought envisages them. It is not merely that they are related to and affected by other contemporary tendencies. They contain their own distorting and obscuring factors within themselves. As we have seen, nothing in the Hegelian philosophy is ever completely itself. It is pervaded through and through by " otherness," an otherness which, according to the Axiom of Internal Relations, is introduced into the very essence of its being. This is true of the tendencies and movements which constitute the dialectical process as it occurs in history. There is no such thing as Capitalism as such, or Communism as such ; there are no pure classes and no pure individuals. Marx does not make the mistake often attributed to him of conceiving of the individual *merely* as a representative of his class, whether proletarian or bourgeois, exclusively swayed by class ideology and invariably voicing class sentiments. Marx's definition of a real individual would be, a focal point for a set of social relationships, just as a thing, for Hegel, is a focal point for a set of internal relations. But it is not with the individual, as he really is in his concrete actuality, that Marx is concerned. "Individuals," he says, "are dealt with *only in so far as they are the personifications* of particular class relations and class interests " (my italics). Marx, that is to say, is conceding that an individual is more than the personification of a class, and that class relations and interests are themselves unreal entities in so far as they are abstracted, as thought cannot help but abstract them, from the social context in which they appear.

Also Marx would agree—it is, indeed, as we shall see below, a presupposition of his theory of knowledge—that human nature is not static, but changing. The individual, then, as he is in concrete actuality, is a changing, even, Marx might perhaps concede, a capriciously changing individual. Nevertheless, it is with individuals and class relations in the abstract, that is, with the " abstract," static individual standing to his class in an unchanging relation which is " abstracted " from all the other relations into which he enters, that Marx's theory is concerned.

Have his Predictions been Falsified ?

The point has practical importance in connection with the frequently-made assertion that Marx's prophecies have been falsified by history, and that the whole conception of the Marxian Dialectic may, therefore, be dismissed as invalid. Marx's doctrine of " increasing misery " is often cited in this connection. As Capitalism develops, so, Marx taught, the lot of the proletariat will become progressively worse. In fact, however, since Marx's time, wages have risen and the working classes of the nations of Western Europe are slightly but definitely less poverty-stricken. Does the fact constitute a criticism of the Marxian diagnosis ? Marx's answer would be that it does not. ' It is only,' he would say, ' in so far as Capitalism is postulated as an isolated system operating *in vacuo*, that it produces the effects I have described. In fact, the tendency, or rather the group of tendencies which, taken together, constitute capitalist society, has developed *pari passu* with another set of tendencies which make for collective control and modify, therefore, the development of the first set. As Capitalism has developed, so has Trade Unionism. The effect has been to confuse the broad outlines of the structure of developing Capitalism, and to mitigate the full force of its distinctive effects. It is only of Capitalism unmodified by other tendencies—that is to say, of pure Capitalism existing in abstraction—that the doctrine of increasing misery may be truly predicated. But Capitalism so conceived is a figment. The special circumstances which modify " pure Capitalism " vary, of course, from case to case. In England, for example, the abstract workings of pure capitalism have been modified by a contingent circumstance, the existence of the British Empire. Thus, the real proletariat of England has been created in her colonies and dependencies, upon the population of which the English working class is in a sense parasitic.'

Marx's conception of the State offers another example of this rather confusing distinction between a thing as it is in concrete actuality and the thing considered *as such*, that is, the thing postulated as an abstraction by thought for its own purposes. Marx conceives of the State *as such* as the repository of power in the community ; it is the supreme coercive force in the background, nor can it lose this attribute of forcefulness without ceasing to be itself. Even under the dictatorship of the proletariat, the State will continue to wield such force, and the condition of Communism proper, when the necessity for force has been superseded, is described by Lenin as a condition in which the State " withers away." Of the State Marx continually speaks—indeed, he defines it—as an " instrument of class domination." Critics have pointed out that, even if from one point of view the State may justly be described as such an instrument, it is in fact more than this. The criticism would not disturb Marx. ' It is only to the State, in so far as it really *is* a State,' he would say, ' that the description can be justly applied. In so far as the simplicity of my theoretical conception of the State has been obscured in practice, in so far as the underlying structure of the capitalist State is traversed by the incipient organisation of social control and modified by the effects of class conflict, the

State is no longer completely itself. It has become more than itself, and my definition of it is, therefore, no longer completely true of it. The State, in other words, can become more than an instrument of class dominance, but only in so far as it becomes more than itself.' Marx, in other words, would invoke the Aristotelian conception of the nature of a thing,[1] as that which is realised only in its purest form, to justify his refusal to regard the partially collectivised State as a State at all.

II. MARX'S MATERIALISM

I pointed out above that the agencies of the movement of the Marxian Dialectic are not, as in Hegel, ideas, but material forces. This statement must now be expanded. The expansion brings us to what is known as the materialist, or sometimes as the realist conception of history. The treatment here may be conveniently divided into two parts. There is, first, Marx's peculiar and distinctive form of Materialism ; there is, secondly, the application of the doctrine to the interpretation of history.

Materialism in General. Materialism is a doctrine which assumes many forms. Common to all of these is the view that mind is not an independent and spontaneous activity in the universe, but that its workings are ultimately determined by the movements of some non-mental entity which it registers and reflects ; this non-mental entity is usually conceived to be the physical body. Many materialists deny the existence of mind altogether ; but all materialists concur in denying mental initiative. Marx was a materialist only in this second sense. He divided all previous and contemporary philosophers into two main classes, the materialists who believed matter to be both logically and chronologically prior to mind, and the idealists who maintained that mind was logically and chronologically prior to matter. Marx professedly belonged to the first of these classes. He

[1] See Chapter VII, pp. 186, 187.

was avowedly a materialist. Most of the arguments for Materialism are derived from the discoveries which have been made by the special sciences, especially the sciences of physiology, psychology and biology. Of these I shall give some account in the next chapter. Marx's form of Materialism, however, owes very little to science. Moreover, in spite of his broad division of philosophers into classes according to the priority they give to matter or to mind, his own form of Materialism is less concerned to emphasise the dependence of the mind upon matter, although such dependence is entailed, than the impossibility of disinterested thought and knowledge. All knowledge, Marx affirmed, is for the sake of action. Indeed, it is a form of action. As Bertrand Russell, from whose book *Freedom and Organisation* I have adapted much of the ensuing exposition, has pointed out, in this respect Marx's doctrine approximates much more closely to that of the pragmatists than to that of the scientific materialists.[1]

Marx's Theory of Knowledge.

The following quotation from Marx's *Eleven Theses on Feuerbach* will indicate his main philosophical position :—" The chief defect of all previous Materialism—including that of Feuerbach —is that the object, the reality, sensibility, is only apprehended under the form of the object or of contemplation, but not as human sensible activity or practice, not subjectively " (as, Marx intends to say, it ought to be). " Hence it came about that the active side was developed by idealism in opposition to materialism."

What this quotation affirms is that we cannot apprehend an external object merely as object. We apprehend it, presumably, in order that we may act in regard to it. The Materialism which Marx is criticising here is the Materialism of the eighteenth century. This conceived of matter as being at once the cause and the object of sensation. Its significance and, from Marx's point of view, its error reside in its attitude to the mind which it regarded as

[1] See Chapter XVI, especially pp. 451-455.

completely passive in sensation. The mind, for the eighteenth and early nineteenth century materialists, was like a piece of wax receiving in the form of sensations the impressions made upon it by the external world. It was against this kind of materialism that Marx in the quotation given above was protesting. There is no such thing, he insists, as a knowing which is a *mere* contemplation of the outside world. The human being is like a coiled spring waiting to uncoil itself in action at the first touch of a stimulus from without. As the starting point of its action, it knows or is aware of the stimulus ; but this knowledge, like the release of the spring, is only incidental. The true purpose of the human being's activity is not to know the stimulus but to change it. " Philosophers have only *interpreted* the world in various ways," Marx complains, " but the real task is to *alter* it." This is not to deny that we can know the outside world ; in certain unrepresentative moments we may even be content with a mere knowing. But the knowing is not an end in itself ; we know in order to act. Knowledge cannot be understood, nor does it occur independently of its relation to action, the object of which is to change what is known. A cat does not merely know a mouse ; a farmer does not merely know a field of standing corn. Their real concern is not with knowledge, but with action, and the " knowing " is only an incident in a chain of events which ends in action. Action changes the environment acted upon ; it also changes the agent ; thus neither human nature nor the world is static ; a continuously changing agent knows a continually changing environment, and, by reason of his knowledge, gives it the impetus to further change. If knowing is the preliminary to action, matter is, for Marx, its opportunity. He conceives of matter as a kind of raw material which is known in order that it may be transformed by the knowing individual into a completed product. There can, then, be no such thing as disinterested thought, thought which is merely concerned to know, and objective truth is a figment. " The question whether objective truth belongs to human thinking is not," Marx insists, "a question of theory, but a practical question. The truth, that is the reality and power of thought, must be demonstrated in practice. The contest as to the reality or non-reality of a thought which is isolated from practice, is a purely scholastic question." Since the purpose of knowledge is to change matter, that kind of knowledge is true which changes it successfully—that is to say, in accordance with the purposes which led us initially to concern ourselves with it. Finally, since knowing is continuous and changes what is known, the world is itself continually changing. As what is known changes, so does the knowledge that we have of the world. Hence both truth and reality develop, and, since it contains the principle of development within itself, Marx feels justified in appropriating Hegel's word " Dialectical " to describe his own philosophy of Materialism.

Distinctive Character of Marx's Materialism. The views just described, which would now be denominated Instrumentalism rather than Materialism,[1] are not usually associated with Marx, since they receive little expression in *Capital*, his most widely read work. Moreover, there is some reason to think that Marx may have modified them later in his life. Little trace of them is to be found in his collaborator, Engels, who adopted the more old-fashioned Materialism of the eighteenth century, according to which the process of knowing the outside world is one in which external things make imprints upon the knower's mind in the shape of sensations and ideas. Moreover, Lenin, in his *Materialism and Empirio-Criticism* which is ostensibly an application and development of Marx's philosophy, makes no reference to them, his version of Materialism approximating much more closely to that of Engels, than to that of Marx. Nevertheless, it cannot be doubted that the activist theory of knowledge described above, which insists that knowledge is indissolubly bound up with action

[1] The philosophy of Instrumentalism has been recently popularised in America by Professor John Dewey.

and alters the reality known, is the outstanding and distinctive feature of Marx's *philosophy*, as opposed to his theories of history and economics. Moreover, in affording a justification for the ascription of the epithet " Dialectical " to his Materialism, it provides the necessary basis for the application of Dialectical concepts to society. It was because his philosophy contained this promise of change and development as a universal and inalienable feature of things, that Marx was enabled to represent society as necessarily evolving by means of the dialectical process. Society is not static, but evolves by the confrontation of the opposed tendencies which it develops, because matter is not static ; and matter is not static because it is continually being changed in the process of being known. To the social and historical applications of Marx's philosophy we must now turn.

III. ITS APPLICATION TO SOCIETY: ECONOMIC DETERMINISM AND THE MATERIALIST CONCEPTION OF HISTORY

Fundamental Principles.　　Marx proceeds to apply the philosophical ideas outlined above to the interpretation of history and to the analysis of society. The gist of the resulting doctrine is contained in the following quotation from Marx's collaborator, Engels.

" The materialist conception of history starts from the proposition that the production of the means to support human life and, next to production, the exchange of things produced, is the basis of all social structure ; that in every society that has appeared in history, the manner in which wealth is distributed and society divided into classes or orders, is dependent upon what is produced, how it is produced, and how the products are exchanged. From this point of view the final causes of all social changes and political revolutions are to be sought, not in men's brains, not in man's better insight into eternal truth and justice, but in changes in the modes of production and exchange. They are to be sought, not in the *philosophy*, but in the *economics* of each particular epoch. The growing perception that existing social institutions are unreasonable and unjust, that reason has become unreason, and right wrong, is only proof that in the modes of production and exchange changes have silently taken place, with which the social order, adapted to earlier economic conditions, is no longer in keeping. From this it also follows that the means of getting rid of the incongruities that have been brought to light, must also be present, in a more or less developed condition, within the changed modes of production themselves."

The two most salient features of the doctrine just outlined may be illustrated by two further quotations. First, the conflicts which lead to changes in society are not conflicts in anybody's mind. It is not in human desires and thoughts, but in the processes of production, that the ultimate springs of change are to be found.

" This conflict between productive forces and modes of production is not a conflict engendered in the mind of man, like that between original sin and divine justice. It exists, in fact, objectively outside us, independently of the will and actions even of the men that have brought it on. Modern Socialism is nothing but the reflex in thought, of this conflict in fact ; its ideal reflection in the minds, first, of the class directly suffering under it, the working-class."

Secondly, all the various elements which go to make up the cultural life and institutions of a society, ethical, religious, legal, and aesthetic, are the by-products of its fundamental economic structure.

" It was seen that *all* past history, with the exception of its primitive stages, was the history of class struggles : that these warring classes of society are always the products of the modes of production and of exchange—in a word, of the economic conditions of their time ; that the *economic* structure of society always furnishes the real basis, starting from which we can alone work out the ultimate explanation of the whole superstructure of juridical and political institutions as well as of the religious, philosophical, and other ideas of a given historical period."

Relationship of Men to Things and Men to Men. The doctrine just summarised may be most conveniently developed in the form of a series of propositions.

First, in order to satisfy their need for warmth, food, shelter and clothing, men have learnt to perform certain operations upon things, those things, namely, which are the raw materials of production. There is, thus, from the outset a fundamental relationship in a society between men and things.

This relationship involves a corresponding relationship between men and men. There will be division and specialisation of labour, there will be rights which have been taken by or conceded to certain men to exploit certain things, and there will be corresponding prohibitions preventing other men from exploiting them. There will, in a word, be ownership of some things by some men and deprivation in respect of these same things for other men. But these other men, although they do not own things and have no rights in respect of them, may and will perform operations upon them under the control and direction of those who are their owners; the owners may even compel them to perform these operations. Now the different ways in which things are operated upon under different forms of ownership, and the different operations which men perform upon things lead to different forms of relationship between men and men. Thus the relationship between men and men depends in the last resort upon the way in which, at any given period in the development of a society, things are owned and worked.

Class Basis of Society. Marx holds, as a matter of fact, that during the period of recorded history, the relationship between men and men has remained fundamentally the same. This relationship is one of exploitation, and because of it, society is divided into two antagonistic classes. But though it remains the same in fact, this relationship of exploitation assumes a variety of different guises. By reference to the variations in its form Marx distinguishes three main phases in the historical development of societies. These are the phases exemplified respectively by slaveholding societies, feudal societies, and capitalist societies. In the first two, the relation of exploitation is clear. Whether it assumes the form of the relation of owners to slaves, or of feudal lords to serfs, it is unconcealedly a relation between those who own the raw materials of wealth and as a consequence possess economic and political power, and those who, whether as slaves or as serfs, transform these raw materials into usable commodities. This second class pays to the first a tribute which takes the form of what Marx calls "surplus value," in return for the permission to operate the raw materials which the first class owns, and receives as payment for its labour only a bare subsistence wage. Under Capitalism the relation between the two classes remains fundamentally unaltered, but it is cut across and obscured by a miscellany of confusing facts—the fact for, example, that production is for sale rather than for immediate use, the introduction of the middleman as a link between producer and consumer, the growth of political freedom symbolised by the concession of the vote to the exploited classes. All these developments obscure what, Marx insists, remains the fundamental fact in every capitalist society, namely, that most men are still only allowed to work on condition that they pay tribute to the owners of the means of production.

Thirdly, that which determines the development from one phase of society to another is a change in the relationship between men and things, or, more precisely, a change in the way in which men treat raw materials in order to satisfy their needs. From time to time new techniques are introduced, and these determine new forms of society.

Inventions are made, men's skill improves, knowledge of matter increases. As a result, new ways of organising the resources of production are adopted, and these determine new forms of economic organisation. Thus, economic systems, if they are to keep pace with the developing resources of production, need to be continually modified.

Relativity of Ethical and Legal Codes and Logical Concepts.

Fourthly, at any given stage in the development of society, its moral and legal systems reflect its fundamental economic structure, being conditioned by the need of the exploiting class to justify the peculiar form of relationship between the two classes, that is to say, the peculiar form of exploitation of one class by the other, which the prevailing stage of economic technique brings into being. Political institutions and legal systems and the political and legal ideas by means of which men justify and support them, are thus relative to and determined by the economic structure of society. They are at once its product, its prop, and its mirror, and in respect of each of these three activities their nature is determined by the particular phase of economic development which they support and reflect. As with the political and legal systems of society, so with its moral consciousness. Slavery and serfdom were approved by the societies which employed slaves and serfs. Inevitably, since the moral consciousness of these societies, being a reflection of the stages of economic development to which slavery and serfdom were respectively appropriate, could not do other than justify them. For this reason, appeals to right and justice by the exploited classes will never obtain a hearing, since the moral standards to which they appeal are based on the assumption of the rightness of the very system against which they are appealing. There are no such things as abstract right or absolute justice ; there are only those standards of right, those conceptions of justice which reflect and justify a particular phase of economic development. Together with politics, law, religion, and art, morals, individual no less

QF

than social, form a superstructure founded upon circumstance and modelled to the shape of its foundation. Now circumstance is, as we have seen, constituted by men's relation to things and consequential relation to their fellow-men.

Why Change must be Violent.

Fifthly, in accordance with the teaching of the Hegelian Dialectic, each phase of society is conceived as carrying within its matrix the seed of its own dissolution. " The means of getting rid of the incongruities that have been brought to light must," Marx says, " also be present, in a more or less developed condition, within the changed modes of production themselves." " The means " are in effect the next phase of social development which, potentially present from the first in the womb of its predecessor, is brought to birth by its predecessor's triumphant maturity. Thus slavery is superseded by feudalism for which it had prepared the way, and feudalism gives way to the Capitalism which it itself had fostered. Similarly the contradictions inherent in Capitalism, to which we have already referred, must eventually bring about its own overthrow through the agency of that very class, the exploited proletariat, which Capitalism has brought into being.

The changes involved are, however, not gradual, but violent, for the reason that the political, legal, and moral systems which grow upon the foundation of an economic substructure, generate a life of their own which gives them the vitality to persist, even when their economic substructure is crumbling away. Every political system embodies the authority of a governing class which has a vested interest in the maintenance of that system. This class clings to its privileges and refuses to abandon its authority without a struggle. Moreover, it uses the power over men's minds with which its command of the avenues of education and publicity invests it, to persuade them both of the social justice and the inevitable continuance of the system upon which it thrives. Thus, while change in the economic structure of society consequent upon the invention of new techniques of production is gradual and continuous, changes in the political system are discontinuous and violent. The need for political change accumulates in face of increasing resistance, and it is only the logic of economic circumstance that eventually invests the exploited class with the power necessary to break down this resistance. There is thus a time-lag before a community establishes the political, legal and moral systems appropriate to its continually changing economic substructure. It is because of this time-lag that political change when it comes is violent and revolutionary.

The Freedom of the Human Mind. One point which is often overlooked or misrepresented must be introduced to complete this outline sketch of the materialist or, as it is sometimes called, the realist conception of history. The question was raised above whether the dialectical process, which Marx adopted and adapted from Hegel, entailed a complete Determinism, and reasons were given for answering this question in the negative. The same question presents itself in relation to the materialist conception of history, and again the answer is a qualified negative. That the general tenor of men's beliefs about religion, morals, law, justice and politics is coloured, is even determined, by a particular phase of economic development, and that to this extent mental occurrences are the products of non-mental occurrences which condition them, is true. But the systems of men's beliefs possess, as we have seen, a life of their own which reacts upon the economic structure of society, and so causes changes in material things which would otherwise not have occurred. Marx's activist theory of knowledge, which was sketched in outline[1] above, has an important bearing upon his conception of the historical process, for it enables him to represent man's relation to events not as that of a passive spectator, but as that of an active moulder. " Man," says Marx, " is himself the agent

[1] See above, pp. 474-476.

of material production as of any other activity that he performs. Therefore, all conditions which affect man as a subject of production, modify more or less all his functions and activities, including those which he performs as creator of material wealth or commodities. In this respect it can be shown that all human functions and conditions, how and whenever they may appear, exercise a more or less decisive influence on material production."

Even if the roots of a political system are in the economic order, political systems outrun the economic orders which give them birth, and, outrunning them, affect and modify them. Thus a system of government, by virtue of the desires and ideals which it generates in men's minds, is enabled to influence the passage of events, including those events which constitute the process of economic development. There is, therefore, a continuous two-way process between matter and mind. Matter in the shape of the raw materials of the earth,—its minerals, its water, its climate— and the methods which are adopted to transform these raw materials into the commodities which satisfy human needs,—the mines and the machinery which are operated by workers and technicians—determine the ideological superstructure of society and so condition men's minds. But the ideological superstructure, by virtue of the systems of thought and desire which it generates in the minds of individuals, reacts in its turn upon matter, as human inventions alter the way in which matter is worked up into usable commodities, and human tastes and desires determine the way in which these commodities will be used. Again and again Marx insists that man is in this sense free. "Man," he says, "makes his own history : he does not make it out of conditions chosen by himself, but out of such as he finds close at hand." Material conditions, in other words, constitute the framework within the limits of which man's freedom operates.

But from the framework itself there is no escape. Although the process whereby matter influences mind and mind influences matter is a two-way process, the ultimate determiner is matter. Economic forces make society what it is and men what they are, and, although the institutions of society and the minds of men then proceed to generate a vitality of their own in virtue of which they enjoy a quasi-independence which gives them the power to modify economic forces, this influence is only a secondary and derivative cause of historical events. Human beings, in other words, affect circumstances by reason of their ideas, desires and wishes, which, on the basis of the activist view—that knowledge is not passive contemplation but is essentially bound up with action—produce effects upon matter. But these ideas, desires, and wishes are not spontaneous, the products of independent thinking and desiring by freely functioning minds. They are the outcome of the legal and moral systems under which the individual lives, and the institutional and educational training which he has received. They are, in a word, such as an individual, living in a community in such and such a stage of social development, must inevitably have. Now legal and moral systems, political institutions and education are, as we have seen, themselves related to and conditioned by the particular phase of economic technique which at any given time happens to prevail. Thus the economic structure of society which is the result of the way in which men satisfy their material needs is, in the long run, the factor which determines all the others.

Marx and Plato.

The distinctive character of Marx's view with regard to the nature of this determining factor may be clearly seen by a comparison between it and that of Plato. For Plato, what ultimately determines the structure and character of a society is the nature of men's wants. These, he held, are not invariable. They change from man to man and from age to age. Apart from the fact that one man wants different things at different times, one kind of man will want things which are on the whole and predominantly different from what another wants for most of the time. Some want wealth, some power, some knowledge. According to the type of man which predominates and holds power in the State, so, Plato maintained, will be the nature of the State. Where power-loving men predominate, you will have a tyrannical State, where wealth-loving, a democracy or a plutocracy, where honour-loving, an aristocracy.

Now, while Marx's activist theory of knowledge entailed the view that human beings are continuously changing, when he comes to treat them historically he conceives of them as being to all intents and purposes uniform, and represents the broad effect of their wants upon society as a constant effect. Treating human beings as more or less uniform and human wants as being broadly constant, Marx attributes the differences between forms of society not to differences between human wants, but to differences between the ways in which human beings satisfy what remain predominantly the same wants. If wants remain fundamentally uniform, they cannot, it is obvious, be the factor which determines differences between societies. Nevertheless, there may be great differences between the way in which raw materials are treated and between the relative efficiencies of different treatments, between, in other words, " the means and capacities of production."

Thus, while for Plato the ultimate factor in society is human wants, for Marx it is the mode of supplying human wants. It is characteristic of his outlook that the only wants which Marx considers in this connection should be wants for material things, for food and warmth, shelter and clothing, while the wants upon which Plato lays stress as ultimate are only partially material. Marx thinks of the satisfaction of bodily needs, Plato of the satisfaction of what he calls the soul.

IV. COMMENT AND CRITICISM

As I have already warned the reader, the above in no sense constitutes an account of Marx's thought, but only of its philosophical foundations. Criticism both of the foundations and of the structure of political and social ideas which Marx raised upon it, would be out of place in a book of this kind. A few words may, however, be added with regard to the question of the adequacy of the foundation in respect of the superstructure. How far, it may be asked, does the Hegelian Dialectic constitute a necessary or even a suitable background for the materialist conception of history and economic determinism. The answer to this question would appear to be that the Dialectic is in the main irrelevant both to the materialist interpretation of history and to the doctrine of the economic determination of events, and that it tends to be unsuitable when it is not actually irrelevant.

1. IRRELEVANCE OF METAPHYSICS. First, as regards the charge of irrelevance, many philosophers hold that questions of metaphysics are by their very nature precluded from having any bearing on practical affairs. Men of science, for example, have professed every kind of metaphysical opinion—Subjective Idealism, Objective Idealism, Materialism, Dualism, even Solipsism. But this has made no difference to their physics or their chemistry. Men of business have professed every kind of religion—Catholicism and Protestantism, Methodism, Calvinism and Quakerism, Mohammedanism and Confucianism. But their religion has never impaired their conduct of their business. Similarly, there seems to be no necessary reason why men's views about the ultimate nature of things should have any bearing either upon the interpretation which they give to the process of events which we call history, or to the process interpreted. What is more, in the opinion of many thinkers, it does not and cannot.

This, of course, would be denied, and rightly, by those who go all the way with Hegel, and hold that, since the distinction between thought and the world is ultimately invalid, thought literally constitutes the world. On this assumption, what men think about the universe will profoundly affect their interpretation of events, and their interpretation of events will alter the events interpreted. But Marx very definitely does not go all the way with Hegel in this respect. On the contrary, he explicitly disavows the view that thought is the ultimate reality, and substitutes the forces of production for ideas, as the prime movers of the dialectical process. He has, therefore, no right to assume that metaphysics, which is the product of abstract thought, has any bearing upon the passage of events, or that what happens can be fruitfully interpreted in terms of metaphysical notions derived from a study not of material, but of logical processes.

Marx would, no doubt, endeavour to meet this criticism by the distinction which he drew between metaphysics in general and Dialectical Materialism in particular. Metaphysics, by which Marx meant the speculations as to the nature of reality indulged in by other philosophers, particularly idealist philosophers, he regarded as a barren pursuit having no relation to fact. Marx, as we have seen,[1] stressed the essential unity of theory and practice, holding that thought has always a practical reference, since it is always undertaken in the light of possible actions, and that, in knowing the world, we also act upon it. It is on this ground that he is careful to distinguish Dialectical Materialism from all other metaphysical views, and even goes so far as to deny that the title " metaphysical " may properly be ascribed to it. For while metaphysics, as traditionally conceived, is a *mere* knowing of reality, Marx's doctrine maintained that the knowing of reality was also the changing of it. If this activist theory of knowledge is right, the criticism that metaphysics is irrelevant to history and practice would fall to the ground, or rather, the criticism would fail to touch the particular kind of metaphysical view embodied by Dialectical Materialism.

2. VARIETY OF FACTORS IN HISTORICAL CAUSATION. Secondly, as to the question of suitability, it is, I think,

[1] See pp. 474, 475 above.

clear that the ideas of the Dialectic are in Marx's hands at best a clumsy tool, and are frequently quite inadequate to the task which he requires them to perform.

In general it may be said that the rigorous application of logic to life is apt to result in an interpretation of events which is too final, too sharply cut, and too clearly defined. What actually happens in history is determined not only by the working out of fundamental principles and discernible underlying trends, but by a thousand and one irrelevant and disturbing factors whose genesis escapes detection and whose operations evade analysis. A thousand cross-currents deflect the stream, a thousand side-winds blow athwart the course of history ; personal intrigues, sexual jealousy and desire, love of power, thwarted ambition, slighted vanities and injured prides, religious enthusiasm, reforming zeal, party strife, even the disinterested desire for the public good, all these on occasion play a part in determining events. Nor is the influence of the exceptionally gifted individual to be ignored ; great men may be the mouthpieces of movements, but the movements are such as only *they* have made inevitable. To seek to confine all these factors, as various as human nature is various, within the Procrustean bed of a single formula, to derive them all from the working out of a dialectical process conceived in terms of material forces brought into operation by different techniques of production, is to do violence to the complexity of fact in the interests of theory. Human affairs are not cut and dried, as logic is cut and dried ; they are not painted in colours of black and white, but deepen and fade through innumerable shades of intermediate grey, and, as a result, their outcome is not predictable in the sense in which, if the application of the Dialectic were valid, they should be predictable. Human history hangs upon the threads of a thousand chances ; let but one of these be different, and the tale of history would have to be retold. The force and appositeness of illustration of the following quotation from Bertrand Russell's *Freedom and Organisation* justify its inclusion here as a better summary of the preceding point of view, than I could hope to give.

"Admitting that the great forces are generated by economic causes, it often," says Russell, "depends upon quite trivial and fortuitous events which of the great forces gets the victory. In reading Trotsky's account of the Russian Revolution, it is difficult to believe that Lenin made no difference, but it was touch and go whether the German Government allowed him to get to Russia. If the minister concerned had happened to be suffering from dyspepsia on a certain morning, he might have said ' No ' when in fact he said ' Yes,' and I do not think it can be rationally maintained that without Lenin the Russian Revolution would have achieved what it did. To take another instance : if the Prussians had happened to have a good General at the battle of Valmy, they might have wiped out the French Revolution. To take an even more fantastic example, it may be maintained quite plausibly that if Henry VIII had not fallen in love with Anne Boleyn, the United States would not now exist. For it was owing to this event that England broke with the Papacy, and therefore did not acknowledge the Pope's gift of the Americas to Spain and Portugal. If England had remained Catholic, it is probable that what is now the United States would have been part of Spanish America."

3. INAPPLICABILITY OF DIALECTICAL FORMULA. Moreover, the formula of the Dialectic seems at times singularly inapplicable to the facts of recorded history. Broadly this formula asserts that the development of events occurs through the synthesis of contraries. The synthesis itself is more developed than the contraries upon whose opposition it supervenes, and whose different tendencies it reconciles and embraces. This view is perilously like the doctrine of the inevitability of progress. Yet nothing of the kind is suggested by a reading of history. In innumerable cases the outcome of conflicts has not been the

establishment of a more developed system, but the complete destruction of one of the opposed forces. To quote Bertrand Russell again :

" The barbarian invasion of Rome did not give rise to more developed economic forms, nor did the expulsion of the Moors from Spain, or the destruction of the Albigenses in the South of France. Before the time of Homer the Mycenæan civilisation had been destroyed, and it was many centuries before a developed civilisation again emerged in Greece. The examples of decay and retrogression are at least as numerous and as important in history as the examples of development. The opposite view, which appears in the works of Marx and Engels, is nothing but nineteenth-century optimism."

The issue, as Russell goes on to point out, has practical importance to-day. The fundamental conflict in modern civilisation, according to the Marxist analysis, is that between Communism and Capitalism. In the Communist Manifesto, published in 1848, Marx envisages the possibility of chaos resulting from this conflict, but his usual view, which pervades his later writings, is that the conflict, after some partial victories for Capitalism, will end in the victory of the proletariat. This result is in strict accordance with the dialectical theory, which teaches that the one partial opposed tendency, namely, Capitalism, will lead to the triumph of its contrary, namely, Communism, which will also embody all that is good in Capitalism. In actual fact, however, it may quite possibly lead to a series of wars in which, under modern conditions, there is a substantial chance that the whole of civilisation, as we know it, will be destroyed. Hence not Communism, but barbarism, may well be the next stage in the development of human history.

Marx did not envisage this possibility, partly because of an optimism (whether innate in the man or the age must remain uncertain), that led him to think that the workings of the dialectical process in history must be progressive, partly because he did not foresee, or if he did, did not make allowance for, the enormous increase in men's powers of destruction.

But even when it is applied to the actual conceptions in terms of which Marx's thought moved, the Dialectic does not yield very satisfactory results. Marx cited, as an illustration of the Dialectic in action, the process whereby slave-owning societies gave way to Feudalism and Feudalism to Capitalism. By virtue of the same process, Capitalism, he held, would in due course give way to Communism. But (a) if development is by the opposition of contraries, it is pertinent to point out that, even if Capitalism is in some sense the contrary of Communism, Feudalism is not the contrary of Capitalism, but its undeveloped form. Moreover, slave-owning societies are not the contraries of feudal ones. (b) Each phase in the development of the Dialectic is in the nature of a synthesis, gathering up into itself, while it transcends, all that is valuable in the preceding thesis. But is there any significant sense in which Capitalism can be said to be a synthesis of what is *valuable* in the feudalistic and slave-owning phases that preceded it ?

4. THE FUTURE OF THE DIALECTICAL PROCESS IN HISTORY. The application of the dialectical process to the interpretation of history leads to highly embarrassing results in its bearing upon the next stage of social development, which Marx identifies with Communism. The Dialectic, as we have seen, is envisaged as a process of social development, at once endless and inevitable, expressing itself in history in a series of revolutions which arise from the failure of political institutions and legal systems to transform themselves *pari passu* with the continuous process of economic change which is going on at the basis of society. The process envisaged is, or rather should be, endless. The Dialectic suggests, in fact, that there can be no resting-place for human society, which will be continuously driven forward by the stresses which the dialectical process develops. Revolutions are caused by the

uprising of a class which, according to the formula of the Dialectic, is brought into existence by the triumph of the very class which it is to supersede. Thus Feudalism created the bourgeoisie whose industry and commerce prepared the way for its own supersession, and Capitalism brings into existence the mass of expropriated workers whom it drives to organise for its overthrow.

But though Marx writes at length of the revolution which will result in the establishment of Communism, he says " it is only in an order of things in which there will no longer be classes or class antagonism that *social evolutions* will cease to be *political revolutions*." (My italics.) The reason he gives for this prophecy is that, while all previous revolutions have resulted in the supersession of class by class, this one alone will bring with it the emancipation of humanity. Once it has been successfully carried through, there will be no more suppressed classes whose struggles will lead to further revolutions. What, then, of the dialectical process? Apparently, once Communism is established, it ceases. If it be held that it will continue, but will manifest itself in the milder form of " social evolutions," we are entitled to ask how even the "social evolutions" can occur without the motive force of class antagonisms to generate them. Indeed, it is difficult to see how, on Marx's premises, political and social evolution can continue at all, once the division between the classes has disappeared. Technological changes will, no doubt, continue to produce some social changes, but it is difficult to see how these, if they occur, can be fitted into the framework of the dialectical process, according to which social evolution takes place through the opposition of contraries.

Marx's Materialism in Relation to Materialism Proper.
The peculiar form of activist Materialism outlined above, according to which changes in the physical world are in some sense a product of the activity of minds' knowledge of the world, is more akin to Pragmatism than to Materialism, as Materialism is commonly maintained

to-day. Marx is not consistent in his application of this doctrine, and his writing frequently assumes that a proposition can be true in a sense other than the pragmatic one of changing reality in such a way as to serve our purposes.[1] Truth, in fact, appears in his political and economic writings as that which corresponds with external fact, while the function of thought is represented rather as the discovery of what the facts are, than as their modification. Materialism as a philosophy owes its strength to science rather than to history or to politics, and of Scientific Materialism there is little trace in Marx. It is to this Scientific Materialism, which has been developed into a comprehensive world view embracing logic, psychology and metaphysics, that we must now turn.

MARX, K.   Eleven Theses on Feuerbach.

MARX, K.   Critique of Political Economy (especially the Preface).

MARX, K., and ENGELS, F.   The Communist Manifesto.

ENGELS, F.   Socialism, Utopian and Scientific (especially the introduction to the 1892 edition).

Lenin's *Materialism and Empirio-Criticism* contains an exposition of Dialectical Materialism on the philosophical side. The number of books dealing with Marxist philosophy is very large. The following may be recommended :

COLE, G. D. H.   What Marx Really Meant.

MACMURRAY, J.   The Philosophy of Communism.

HOOK, F.   Towards the understanding of Karl Marx.

HECKER, J.   Moscow Dialogues.

PLEKHANOV.   Fundamental Problems.

BUKHARIN.   Historical Materialism.

ADORATSKI.   Dialectical Materialism.

[1] See Chapter XV, p. 452–454, for an account of the pragmatic theory of truth.

Chapter XVIII : PHILOSOPHIES OF MODERN SCIENCE

1. Scientific Materialism : The Mind-Body Problem

I. NATURE OF MATERIALISM

Materialism Congenial to Science. Unlike the metaphysical theories hitherto considered, Materialism, in contradistinction to Dialectical Materialism, has not been maintained by any philosopher of the first rank. Haeckel (1834–1919) was a materialist, and his book *The Riddle of the Universe*, published in England in 1901, had a very considerable contemporary influence. But he is not generally regarded as a philosopher of the first rank, and although Karl Marx is undoubtedly entitled to that description, his Dialectical Materialism has very little in common with Scientific Materialism or Materialism proper. Indeed, it can scarcely be said that a philosophy of Materialism, if the expression be taken to denote a coherent and comprehensive body of doctrine to which all those who are disposed to adopt materialist views would subscribe, exists.

This is partly because Materialism has historically been professed by amateur philosophers rather than by professionals. While professional philosophers have on the whole tended to be idealists, Materialism is, as we shall shortly see, the natural, indeed it is the inevitable, creed of men of science. Scientists, that is to say, in so far as they confine themselves to the assertion of those conclusions and only those conclusions which science justifies, inevitably adopt a materialist outlook. One of the tenets of Materialism is that every event must have as its cause a preceding event or set of events, such that a complete knowledge of the latter would enable an observer with absolute certainty to predict the former. This belief is, it is obvious, a necessary presupposition of scientific method. The laboratory worker, if he is to adopt the method of experiment and verification, must assume not only that every event has its cause, but that like causes will produce like effects. He must, that is to say, proceed experimentally as if Materialism is true, at any rate in the particular department of research with which he is concerned. Not only do most scientists take materialist views in their own departments, but they are apt to extend their application into spheres such as ethics, æsthetics and psychology,[1] whose subject matter does not easily lend itself to materialist interpretation.

Definition of Materialism.   But just because it is a scientific predisposition rather than an official philosophy, the doctrine of Materialism tends to lack precise content. This vagueness of content makes it difficult to define. Mr. Chapman Cohen whose short book, *Materialism Restated*, contains one of the best modern accounts of Materialism with which I am acquainted, distinguishes three doctrines as characteristic of and essential to Materialism. First, on the negative side, Materialism may be defined as the denial of Supernaturalism. It holds, therefore, that what happens in the world is never the result of the agency of independent spiritual or mental powers, but is always explicable even when, owing to the lack of sufficient knowledge, it cannot at the time be explained " as a consequent of the composition of natural forces."

Secondly, Materialism makes a positive assertion as to the way in which things happen. It involves, in Mr. Cohen's words, " the belief that the state of the world, or of any portion of it, at any given time, is the exact consequence of the distribution and conjunction of forces preceding that moment." It involves, further, the view that no new force or new factor arises or has at any time arisen in the universe ;

[1] This generalisation must be qualified by a reservation in regard to the views advanced by some of the leading English physicists during the last dozen years.

nor has any such force or factor been introduced into the universe as it were from ·outside. Hence "every new phenomenon is the equivalent of a new arrangement of existing forces." Materialism, in so far as it makes this second assertion or set of assertions, is usually known as Determinism or Mechanism, or as Mechanist Determinism.

Thirdly, while Materialism insists that whatever exists in the universe is ultimately of the same sort as matter, it is committed to no particular theory of matter. The conceptions of matter current at different periods vary with and depend upon the state of physical science at different periods. Now whatever the ultimate analysis of matter may be—whether matter is fundamentally wave-like or projectile-like, whether it consists of charges of positive and negative electricity, of homogeneous atomic units, of electronic "mushes," or of "humps in space-time"—this too must, if Materialism is maintained, be accepted as the ultimate analysis of whatever exists.

On the basis of the above assertions we may provisionally give the following definition or definitions of Materialism. First, there is a definition in terms of substance :—everything which exists in the universe is ultimately of the same sort as those things which are called material. Secondly, there is a definition in terms of law :—all the happenings in the universe are subject to those laws which are recognised as governing the happenings of the things which are called material. This second definition emphasises that aspect of Materialism which is commonly known as Mechanism. Materialism so defined assumes the character of a philosophy. It is, that is to say, an affirmation both as to the nature of what exists and as to the way in which events take place. The former, it affirms, is material, the latter mechanical. This philosophy, held in an embryonic form by some of the early Greek thinkers—Leucippus (early fifth-century B.C.) and Democritus (born 470 B.C.) were materialists, as also was the Roman poet-philosopher, Lucretius (98–55 B.C.)—achieved prominence as the result of the scientific discoveries of the nineteenth century. While it received a backing from all the contemporary sciences, it derived its chief strength from psychology and biology. To the philosophical implications of these sciences we must now turn.

II. THE MIND-BODY PROBLEM

Commonsense View of Relation of Mind to Body. Common sense holds that a human being is not exclusively a body. He has a body, but he is, it would normally be said, more than his body ; and he is more, in virtue of the existence of an immaterial principle which, whether it be called mind, soul, consciousness or personality, constitutes the reality of his being. This immaterial principle, most people hold, is in some way associated with the body—it is frequently said to reside *in* it—and animates and controls it.

It is on some such lines as these that the plain man would, I think, be inclined to describe the make-up of the human being. He would describe the human organism, that is to say, as a duality. In the view of the present writer this commonsense account, which discerns in a human being the presence of two radically different principles, the one material and the other immaterial, is nearer to the truth than any other of the alternatives in the field. Nevertheless, it is difficult to maintain,—in the light of the knowledge accumulated by the sciences of psychology and physiology as to the actual mode of working of the living organism, it becomes increasingly difficult—and it is precisely the difficulties to which it is exposed which constitute the most important of the psychological arguments for Materialism.

The Mind and the Brain.   The great difficulty of the commonsense view is that of conceiving the mode of interaction between the two principles which common sense postulates. Let us assume for a moment that common sense is right in thinking that there is such a thing as a mind, and that the mind, though intimately related to the body, is different from the body. It is, therefore, different from the brain. If we were to open a man's skull and to look inside, we should see tiers and layers of cells constituting a covering of whitish grey matter known as the cortex. These cells and cortex constitute the brain, and their constitution and movements are studied by physiologists. Now, although it may be true that the brain is modified whenever a man thinks or feels, the fact that these modifications take place is not *the whole* of what we mean to assert when we say of anyone that he is thinking and feeling. Thinking and feeling are, we should affirm, at least in part, *mental* occurrences. As such, they cannot be discerned by any of the senses ; they can be neither seen, touched, smelled, tasted, nor heard ; they can only be experienced by the consciousness in which they occur. They may have cerebral accompaniments, which would of course be perceptible to the senses, but they do not themselves consist merely of cerebral movements.

The mind, then, assuming for the moment that common sense is right in holding that there is such an entity, is immaterial and is other than the brain.

Interaction between Mind and Body.
But though different from the body and brain, the mind is not in-different to them. On the contrary, the relations between it and them are very close. Mind and body continually interact in an infinite number of different ways ; in fact, mind influences body and body mind at every moment of waking life. If I am drunk, I see two lamp-posts instead of one ; if I fail to digest my supper, I have a nightmare and see blue devils ; if I smoke opium or inhale nitrous oxide gas, I experience celestial visions, pass into a state of beatitude and discourse with the Almighty and His angels. These are instances of the influence of the body upon the mind. If I see a ghost, my hair stands on end ; if I am moved to anger, my face becomes red ; if I receive a sudden shock, I turn pale ; if I am in dread of a coming ordeal, my mouth becomes dry and the palms of my hands moist. These are instances of the influence of the mind upon the body. The examples just quoted are only extreme and rather obvious cases of what is going on all the time. Many

psychologists, indeed, assert that there can be no event in the mind which is not accompanied by some corresponding event in the body and vice versa, although the corresponding event in the body may be too small to be perceptible by such recording instruments as we at present possess. The apparent interaction between mind and body is, at any rate, a fact beyond dispute.

Difficulty of Conceiving Interaction.

Yet, when we come to reflect upon the manner of this interaction, it is exceedingly difficult to see how it can occur. Mind, we are provisionally assuming, is immaterial ; if it were material, it would be part of the body. If it is immaterial, it has no substance and does not occupy space. The contents of, or the events which happen in, the mind, that is to say, wishes, desires, thoughts, aspirations, hopes, and acts of will which constitute what we call the stream of consciousness, are also immaterial. The body, on the other hand, is matter and possesses the usual qualities of matter such as shape, size, weight, density, inertia, occupancy of space and so forth. Its contents, blood, nerves, brain and flesh, are also material. They can be analysed into compounds and elements by chemists, and further analysed into atoms and electrons by physicists.

Now, if we waive for a moment the difficulties inherent in the conception of causation which we considered in Chapter VIII, we shall find no insuperable obstacle to the understanding of how one material thing can influence another. Each possesses the same attributes of size, shape, and weight, in virtue of which each can, as it were, communicate with or " get at " the other. Thus a paving-stone can crush an egg because the egg belongs to the same order of being as the stone. But how can the paving-stone crush a wish, or be affected by a thought ? Material force and mass have no power over ideas ; ideas do not exert force, nor do they yield to mass. How, then, can that which has neither size, weight, nor shape, which cannot be seen, heard, or touched, and which does not occupy space, come into contact with that which has these properties? You can measure and weigh a piece of matter; but how can you measure or weigh the inspiration which went to the production of Beethoven's Fifth Symphony?

Mind and matter seem, in fact, to belong to two different worlds, to partake of two different orders of being, and the problem of their interaction is the problem of the whale and the elephant raised to the nth degree.

Summing-up the foregoing, we may state the mind-body problem as follows: if mind and body are, as they appear to be, radically different, if thoughts and wishes are of a different order of being from bones and blood, how are we to explain their interaction?

Descartes's Solution.

The problem was first brought into prominence by the philosophy of Descartes (1596–1650). Descartes began his philosophising with a process of thoroughgoing doubt, his plan being to doubt all that he reasonably could, with a view to finding out what certainties remained. The process ended in his famous conclusion, "I think, therefore I am" (*cogito ergo sum*), a conclusion which purported to assert the one fact which Descartes regarded himself as knowing with complete certainty; that he did know it, appeared to him to be axiomatic. Among the implications of Descartes's axiom is the suggestion that mind knows its own processes, for example, the process of its own thinking, more easily than it knows the objects of those processes, that is to say, what is thought about. Hence Descartes was led to maintain a sharp distinction between mind and what was not mind, a distinction which brought in its train a complete separation of mind from body. The sciences of dynamics and mechanics were rapidly developing in Descartes's time, and seemed to show that, given certain data, the motions of matter could be calculated mathematically; if this were so, the motions of matter were mechanical and determined. Now, the body was a collection of material particles; therefore, the motions of the body were mechanical and determined, and, if the

mind were part of or continuous with the body, this conclusion would be true also of the mind. This result was
distasteful to philosophers, who wished to believe that their
minds were free, and taken in conjunction with the original
axiom, "I think, therefore I am," with its implication that the
primary objects of mind's knowledge are its own states and
not objects external to itself, led Descartes to maintain that
the mind was completely independent of bodily influences.

The Supreme Substance, namely God, had, he held, created two substances, mind and matter ; the essence of mind
is thought, the essence of matter extension or occupancy of
space. So different are these two substances that they cannot
possibly interact, and there cannot, therefore, be any effect
of mind upon body or of body upon mind. Mind and body,
according to this view, proceed on two parallel lines, circumstances being so arranged that an event in the one is always
accompanied by an event in the other. On this view—originally known as "Occasionalism," and in its later nineteenth-
century form as Psycho-physical Parallelism—the fact that
my body assumes a horizontal position when I *will* to lie
down, does not mean that there is any causal connection
between my willing and the movements of my body. Why,
then, does the one accompany the other? Because, Descartes
held, of the active and benevolent intervention of God,
who has provided for a continuous and miraculous syn-
chronisation between mental and bodily events, without
which human beings would be unable to survive. The
knowledge of God's benevolent intervention in the affairs
of the world is, Descartes believed, given *a priori*.[1]

Difficulties of Descartes's View.   The gulf which
Descartes established between mind and body has had
disastrous results for psychology. The living organism
is obviously in some sense a unity, and psychologists
have been engaged ever since in a more or less un-
successful attempt to piece together the fragments of the
unity which Descartes destroyed. The difficulties of

[1] See Chapter IV, pp. 113–115, for an account of *a priori* knowledge.

bringing together the two substances so sharply divided by Descartes are, indeed, almost insurmountable. For what precisely does Descartes's position involve? If mind and body are radically different, we cannot, he agreed, explain their interaction. Therefore, they do not interact, but keep time like two perfectly synchronised clocks.[1] There is no causal connection between the clocks; nevertheless, they keep time. Why do they keep time? Because they were wound and set together, and as a result every tick in the one is accompanied by a corresponding tick in the other. And just as nobody maintains that the ticking of the one *causes* the ticking of the other, so on Descartes's view, the perfect harmony between mind and body is evidence, not of their causal interaction but of their creation by God, who wound and set them together, with the result that, for so long as they are associated thereafter, they keep time.

The invocation of divine assistance, always a stumbling-block to the acceptance of a theory, proved particularly distasteful to nineteenth-century science. Was there no other way out of the *impasse*? Obviously there was. The whole difficulty had, it was asserted, arisen from the initial assumption that the mind and body are radically different. But why should this assumption be made? Other possibilities suggest themselves and should at least be explored. Two at any rate are obvious: if mind and body are not radically different, either mind is the same as and part of the body, or body is in some sense a product of or a part of the mind, being either a series of ideas and impressions in the mind, or a mode of perception by the mind. The second alternative leads to philosophical Idealism; the first was adopted by many nineteenth-century psychologists, and became an integral part of the philosophy of Materialism.

Supplementary Difficulties Occasioned by Free Will.

Before I proceed to outline the materialist development of this suggestion, it will be convenient to consider a further objection to the commonsense view of the human

[1] The analogy of the two clocks was suggested by Leibnitz.

organism as a dualism of mind and body which is constituted by the apparent fact of free will, a difficulty which,
like the difficulty of conceiving mind-body interaction,
constitutes a strong reinforcement of the materialist position.
Proceeding on the basis of the commonsense assumption
that we are minds, or at any rate have minds which
animate our bodies, let us now make the further commonsense assumption that our minds are " free." The " free "
mind expresses itself most naturally in the act of willing.
I think we may take it for granted that most people do
normally assume that they possess a free will, and that in
virtue of this freedom they can to some extent control
the movements of their bodies.

Let us see what this assumption involves. It is obvious, in
the first place, that some of the movements of our bodies take
place independently of our wills. My heart beats, my blood
circulates, my digestive processes occur, my hair and nails
grow, without the intervention of my will, and, if I am lucky,
without the knowledge of my consciousness. In the causation
of these bodily movements, then, my will plays no part. Moreover, if my body and a wax effigy of my body of equal weight
are tipped over the edge of a precipice, both will fall in the
same way and at the same speed, reach the bottom at the
same moment and exhibit the same sort of behaviour when
they get there, in spite of the fact that my body is animated
by a free, willing mind and the wax effigy is not.

Two Categories of Bodily Movement. On the assumption,
then, that I have a free will, the movements of my body
are divided into two sharply differentiated categories—those
which are caused by the immaterial agency of my will, and
those which take place in accordance with the laws of mechanics and dynamics which are ultimately resolvable into the
laws of physics, some of these latter movements being to all
intents and purposes identical with those which would be
performed by any other piece of matter of the same weight,
shape and size which was exposed to the same conditions.

But the two categories of movements extend far beyond

the confines of my body. Let us consider those movements of my body which fall within the first category. They are themselves the causes of other movements in the world outside my body. If, for example, the movements are those of my hand, signing a general mobilisation order, or of my finger pressing a button that explodes a mine beneath a battle-ship, the train of consequences set going by my movements is incalculable. Yet all these consequences and all the further physical movements which the consequences entail, must be assigned to the first category of movements, since, if it had not been for the intervention of my free act of will to cause the movements made by my fingers in signing the document or in pressing the button, they might not, they probably would not, have occurred. Thus the material movements that occur in the universe fall into two classes. Some, for example, movements on the other side of the moon, are, as far as we can tell, completely subject to mechanical causation ; that is to say, the laws of physics adequately account both for them and for all the preceding movements in the causal·chain which ends in them. Other movements cannot be completely accounted for on these lines.

Interruption of Causal Sequence. This supposition, involving as it does a bifurcation of the material happenings in the universe into two radically distinct classes, seems sufficiently improbable. But further improbabilities are involved. For instance, the same| action may belong to either of the two categories. Let us suppose, for example, that I cross my legs and *will* slightly to lift my upper foot. We will suppose that as a result my foot rises two or three inches in the air. Now let us suppose that, the foot having returned to its original position, somebody touches a nerve by tapping my crossed leg with the side of the hand just below the knee-cap. Again my foot will rise two or three inches in the air, the movement being known as a reflex. The two movements, the willed and the reflex, may be quite indistinguishable. Indeed, so far as their intrinsic characteristics are concerned, they are indistinguishable.

Yet one is caused by a material event, the application of a stimulus to a nerve, the other by a mental event, an act of will. Now we are accustomed to hold—indeed, in science we must hold—that the same effects are produced by the same causes. Yet in this case two radically different causes work to produce identical effects. Moreover, since the two movements, of which the one takes place as the result of a free act of the will, the other according to the accepted laws of mechanical causation, are indistinguishable, we are forced to the conclusion that, for all we know to the contrary, *any* movement may be a movement belonging to the first class, since there are no intrinsic marks by reference to which it can be decisively placed in the second. Thus science can never feel certain in respect of any movement on the part of a piece of matter, that its total causation does not include some incalculable factor. It can never feel certain, that is to say, that the rule of mechanical law which it seeks to establish is in fact universally operative.

A further difficulty is occasioned by the sudden and arbitrary break in the causal chain of material happenings which the hypothesis of free will entails. Let us consider the movements involved in deliberately withdrawing one's body from the course of a stampeding crowd. The stimuli by reason of which we become aware of the spectacle of the oncoming crowd are, as we have seen in the first chapter, conveyed by purely physical processes to the brain. For example, light rays strike the retina of the eye, as a result of which messages in the shape of nervous impulses travel along the optic cord and produce disturbances in the cells composing the cortex of the brain. So far, the sciences of physics and physiology between them can give an adequate account of all that has taken place : so far, in other words, the mechanical law of cause and effect has adequately explained the events that have occurred. Now, however, as a result of the disturbances occurring in the cells of the brain, an effect is produced in consciousness. What does this mean ? That when the impulses which travel along the optic cord have reached the brain, they produce an event of an entirely different order, that is to say, an event in the mind, which is a conscious event. How this transference from brain to mind takes place, we do not know. Presumably, however, it does take place and as a result we have the sensation of seeing the crowd, a sensation which is a purely mental event not explicable in bodily terms. Upon this sensation there ensues another mental event, an act of will, which is a decision to take action in respect of that which has been sensed, by instructing the nervous system to get to work to remove the body from the course of the oncoming crowd. As a result of this instruction, the machinery of the body, including the nervous system, again comes into action, and the laws of physics and physiology begin again to apply. But they do so after a break in the course of which events of an entirely different order have taken place. The position is, then, apparently, that physical science applies, in the sense of giving a complete account of what happens, up to a point. At this point there is a break during which it ceases to apply, and that then it begins to apply again, exactly as if the break had not occurred. For, as we shall see in a moment, the break and all that it implies are, if Materialism is right, completely unnecessary. We can, say the materialists, explain what happens perfectly well without assuming it ; and in view of the foregoing, it seems reasonable to agree with them that to devise an explanation which does not assume it, is extremely important.

Here, then, is a further set of improbabilities which the commonsense conception of a mind animating and controlling a body entails.

Summary of the Above. Our indictment of the commonsense account of the mind-body relation may be summed up as follows. The commonsense account involves two difficulties each of which is, so Materialism maintains, insoluble. There is, first, the difficulty of understanding how any material happening can cause to occur a happening of an entirely different order, namely, a mental happening, and *vice versa*. There is, secondly, the difficulty of understanding how the law of cause and effect which operates universally in the orderly arrangements of nature, can be suddenly and arbitrarily suspended by the intrusion of an immaterial agency, acting capriciously or in accordance with unknown principles of its own, which is completely unlike anything else discoverable in the universe, namely, the human will.

III. THE MATERIALIST SOLUTION

In order that the reader may be in a position to understand the way in which the materialist endeavours to solve these difficulties, it will be necessary to say a few words about the machinery of the nervous system.

Machinery of the Nervous System.   Let us suppose that I place my hand upon the poker, feel a sensation of violent heat, and quickly withdraw my hand. What exactly is it that has happened ? The heat of the poker stimulates the terminals of the nerve cells in my fingers. These nerve cells or neurones are in contact with other nerve cells, and a stimulus applied to any one of them is accordingly passed on to the next. The machinery of transference is as follows :—each nerve cell has a number of filaments attached to and extending from it. These filaments are known as dendrites. One filament which is considerably longer and finer than the others, is known as the axon, and it is through the axon that the stimulus is passed on to the next neurone or nerve cell in the chain. The points of contact between the axons, known as synapses, act like valves, that is to say, they let the stimulus or impulse pass in one direction only ; it is not allowed to return on its track. The central part of the nervous system, forming a sort of highway along which all impulses pass, is the spinal cord. Travelling by this road the heat stimulus which was applied to the nerve cells in my fingers reaches the brain. Here it enters a complicated system of tiers and layers of neurones. These tiers or layers act as the clearing-house of the nervous system, sorting out the different messages received from all parts of the body, and determining which of them shall be passed on for the purposes of action. Passing on a stimulus for the purposes of action means transferring it to another system of neurones, known as the effector nerves or motor nervous system, which govern the movements we make, as opposed to the receptor nerves or sensory nervous system, which receive and transmit the sensations we feel. Assuming that the brain has decided to take action in respect of the stimulus from the poker, it lets the stimulus pass through to the neurones composing the motor nervous system ; these in their turn pass on the stimulus received from the brain down the arm to the fingers, and as a result the latter are withdrawn from the poker. The whole procedure may be likened to sending a message from the fingers to the brain in response to which another message is sent back to the fingers.

Now the processes involved in the sending of these messages, complicated as they appear, seem, nevertheless, when we look at them from the point of view of the body, to be purely automatic. What takes place is exactly as if one were to put a penny into a slot-machine and take out a box of matches. Nor does it appear to be necessary to introduce a mind or consciousness at any stage of the process to explain what it is that happens or why it happens. It may be true that we *feel* the heat of the poker, and that the feeling is a psychological or mental, as opposed to a physiological or bodily event; but, so far as the observer can tell, this feeling has nothing to do with the withdrawal of the fingers, which is a purely automatic effect of the applied stimulus.

I have deliberately taken the simplest possible case and one in which the action of the body is, *on any view* of the mind-body relationship, as nearly automatic as it is possible for it to be. But, if we can explain some of our actions, even if they are very simple ones without postulating the mysterious intervention of mind, may it not be possible that *the same sort of explanation*, enormously complicated of course, but still confining itself purely to physical terms, might be invoked to account for all our actions. On this assumption, the passage of an impulse round the nervous system, a passage which can be completely described at every stage in physiological terms, is sufficient in itself to explain what happens, whenever the organism feels and acts. The actions of the body could, if this view turned out to be the right one, appropriately be conceived on the analogy of the movements of water in a full reservoir. One pipe leads into the reservoir, another out of it ; whenever, therefore, fresh water comes in through the first pipe, it will cause an overflow of water which will be drained off through the second. All the processes involved are purely automatic and take place in accordance with physical laws, so that whenever a stimulus is applied at one end of the chain, the appropriate reaction is bound to occur at the other. And if an explanation on these lines is, in the present state of our knowledge, difficult to sustain, and fails to account for *all* our actions, should we not, says the materialist, in the interests of science leave no stone unturned in order to make it do so, hoping that an increase in our knowledge of the body will gradually dispose of the many difficulties which at present beset the attempt to explain not only action but also thought exclusively in bodily terms ?

Extension of Materialist Interpretation to Include Consciousness. Let us suppose that we make the attempt. How, then, are we to explain in bodily terms the *conscious experience* of being hurt which we undoubtedly have, when we burn our fingers ? How, in fact, are we to explain consciousness at all ? The materialist answer to this question is that the conception of a mind or a consciousness, as a separate entity, functioning independently of the brain, is a figment. Consciousness is merely a function of or emanation from the brain, continuous with it and in all respects determined by it. It is in fact nothing more than an aspect of the brain's reaction to the events occurring in the body.

Consciousness, on the materialist view, may be metaphorically represented as a sort of glow like the halo round the head of a saint, the function of which is to light up the

events which occur in the brain. When the glow lights up
an event, we are said to become conscious of it. But the glow
cannot, it is obvious, light up what is not there, and it
is a matter of indifference to the event whether the glow
lights it up or not ; the event would occur just the same.
Our consciousness of the event is, in other words, merely
incidental. Two conclusions follow. First, nothing can
occur in the mind, unless its cerebral counterpart has first
occurred in the brain. Secondly, nothing which occurs in
the mind can possibly affect anything which occurs in
the body. The first conclusion denies free will—it denies,
that is to say, that the mind can function independently of
bodily causation ; the second denies interactionism—it
denies, that is to say, that the mind can have any influence
upon a physical happening, although it agrees that a
physical happening may affect a mind.

Epiphenomenalism.

These two conclusions taken to-
gether constitute what is known as the epiphenomenal
theory of mind. This is a widely-held theory which may be
regarded as an offshoot or variant of Materialism. It is
not Materialism proper, because it admits the existence of a
mind or consciousness which it shows no disposition to
analyse into chemical constituents, or completely to subject
in respect of its working to the laws of physics. On the
other hand, its philosophical significance is not widely
different from that of Materialism, since, although it
admits a mind, it denies that the mind has any causative
influence upon events ; it does not, therefore, influence
the body. Thus, although the theory is not strictly
materialist, it remains, so far as its view of causation is
concerned, strictly mechanist, with one important exception. All the movements of matter, it affirms, are determined by other and prior movements of matter. They are,
that is to say, subject to the law of cause and effect. It is
also the case that *some* mental events those, namely, which
are the reflections or registerings of brain events, are
completely determined by the movements of matter in

accordance with the same law. But it does not, therefore, follow that *all* the events which occur in the universe are subject to the law of cause and effect, in the sense in which this law governs the movements of matter. For, although some mental events are determined by the prior movements of matter which they reflect or register, it does not follow that all mental events are so determined. It is this second category of mental events which constitutes the exception just referred to. It is just possible, some epiphenomenalists would admit, that, once the mental events which are determined by the movements of matter they register have taken place, these mental events may generate other mental events without the occurrence of any accompanying bodily events. The mind, in other words, once it has been called into activity by the brain, may, they admit, have a life of its own. Images, for example, as opposed to sensations, might be regarded as constituting part of this independent mental life, and it may be the case, these epiphenomenalists would say, that images occur independently of any movements of matter. This does not mean that images are necessarily uncaused. But, it would be said, their cause may be the occurrence of a preceding mental and not of a preceding bodily event, and the mode of causation which operates between mental events may be something quite unlike the mechanical causation which we recognise in the material world. For these reasons, some epiphenomenalists are prepared to concede that there may be some events in the universe, namely, those which occur in minds, which, though they are caused events, are caused quite differently from the way in which the movements of matter are caused.

But what no epiphenomenalist would concede is that these mental events can possibly have bodily effects. Mental events, they hold, are caused either directly or indirectly[1] by movements in the body and brain ; but they

---

[1] A mental event caused indirectly by movements in the body and brain would be a mental event which was generated by a mental event which was itself caused by movements in the body and brain.

cannot cause movements in the body and brain. Thus no act of thought or act of will, no feeling and no emotion can possibly affect our actions.

On the epiphenomenal view, then, the mind is affected by, but does not affect, the body. For the apparent two-way process of interaction between body and mind, which common sense assumes, Epiphenomenalism substitutes a one-way process of action by body upon mind, and, if it be objected that a mind so conceived plays so little part in the universe that it is hardly worth the trouble of conception, most of those who belong to this school of thought would be disposed to agree. They have, they would say, only been willing to entertain Epiphenomenalism as a concession to the amiable weakness of the plain man, who cannot bring himself to give up his mind altogether ; but they would, they declare, be only too glad to discard it and adopt a thoroughgoing Materialism which denies the existence of mind altogether. Before we proceed to consider how such a view can in practice be maintained, let us anticipate one or two objections.

Materialist Explanation of Apparent Freedom. The first objection may be very briefly stated. According to the view which has just been outlined, we are the slaves of our bodily stimuli, by which the contents of our consciousness are entirely determined.[1] Our status is that of slot machines which, when the penny is inserted, work because they must. Now I certainly *appear* to be endowed with a power of choice, in virtue of which I can decide whether or no I shall obey the stimuli I receive, and, if I do, in what way. If, for example, I am hanging on to the edge of a precipice with one arm and a wasp stings my hand, I shall probably not withdraw the hand, in spite of the stimulus which it has received. Facts of this sort are, it may be said, difficult to explain without introducing mind. For in this case, it would be urged, there is what amounts to an active refusal on the part of my body to

[1] This statement would have to be qualified in the case of some forms of Epiphenomenalism by the reservation made on p. 512.

respond to the stimuli it is receiving. It is behaving not like an automatic machine but like an instrument of a will. How would the materialist deal with such cases?

It is, he would say, obvious that there must be *some* restraining influence which prevents the fingers from relaxing their hold, and that this influence, since it operates in the fingers which are physical things, must take the form of a series of physical events. It must, in fact, be a series of neural impulses. We may suppose, then, that another set of impulses stimulating the fingers to retain a tight hold of the precipice edge is already in command of the effector nerves leading to the arms ; that these nerves cannot, therefore, be utilised by the withdrawing impulses, unless the holding-on impulses are first ousted ; that two sets of impulses are, therefore, in competition for the use of the effector nerves, and that the nervous centres in the clearing house of the brain determine which of the two sets shall employ the effector nerves, by getting control of what is known as the " final common path." Now this determining process in the clearing house of the brain is a purely automatic one, depending on the relative strengths of the two sets of impulses. If it be objected that this explanation does not sound very convincing, the reply would be made that it, or something like it, is the only alternative to postulating the control of the body by the mind, with the corollary of interaction between two completely disparate substances, the difficulties and anomalies of which have already been exposed.

Difficulty for Materialism Constituted by Richness of Mental Life.

The second objection seems at first sight more serious. It is an objection suggested by the extraordinary richness and variety of our mental life. The possibilities of imagination, to cite only one aspect of conscious experience, appear to be infinite. Is it, then, really conceivable that every event in the mind, including everything which I choose to imagine, is really only a psychological counterpart of some material event in the body? Is the body, in other words, really complicated enough for the task assigned to it. Materialists point to the enormous complexity of the nervous system and the brain, emphasise the fact that our knowledge of the mode of their working is still in its infancy, and express the view that future research will exhibit connections between neural stimuli and mental responses which at present seem totally unrelated. But when every allowance is made for these considerations, the theory that we are asked to accept of the ultimate determination of *all* mental activities by bodily stimuli still seems to stretch our powers of credence to the full. Not only is our mental life incredibly rich and varied, it is also apparently exceedingly irrelevant —irrelevant, that is to say, to the physical stimuli which, on the view we are considering, would be said to have evoked it.

The difficulty here involved may be put in the form of the following question. Why, if all mental activities are ultimately to be regarded as bodily movements, and all bodily movements are to be interpreted as responses to stimuli, should comparatively simple stimuli be capable of producing such a bewildering variety and complexity of so-called mental effects ? A concrete example will help to throw the difficulty into relief. Let us suppose that I am sitting dozing in an armchair after dinner. My mind wanders, my attention is relaxed. Presently, however, I begin to think about a lecture I am to deliver next week. The occasion is one that I dread, and the ordeal fills me with nervous apprehension ; so much so, that I become restless, leave my chair, and begin to pace the room. Here, one would normally say, is an example of spontaneous mental activity, namely, expectation tinged with dread, producing certain physiological occurrences. The mind here is cause, and the bodily movements effect. But the normal explanation being ruled out by the epiphenomenalist theory of causation as proceeding always from the body to the mind, some other must be found.

In some way my apprehension of next week's lecture must be explained in terms of responses to bodily stimuli. What, then, are the stimuli to which my body is exposed ?

They are roughly of two kinds, external and internal. The external stimuli are constituted by the warmth of the fire upon my face and the pressure of the sides and seat of the chair against my back and legs. The internal stimuli are constituted by the activity of my bodily organs which accompanies digestion.

The latter are of two kinds, immediate and delayed. The immediate internal stimuli are provided by the actual processes of digestion ; the delayed internal stimuli are the result of similar processes stretching back into the remote past. For example, a certain condition of the liver consequent upon eating curries in India for thirty years, may result in present ill temper, indigestion and a tendency to swear at the servants. Thus the events in my body which determine present ill temper, are the results of curry stimuli applied in the past whose total effect is only now making itself felt.

Now the assertion that these combined stimuli, external and internal, cause responses in my body of such a kind that what by courtesy I call my mind is induced by them to en-visage a lecture which does not yet exist, while not capable of logical disproof, stands in need of considerable justification.

Importance of the Conditioned Reflex.

The difficulty is in part met by the theory of the conditioned reflex. Attention was first drawn to the conditioning of reflexes by the experiments of the psychologist Pavlov. Pavlov tied up a dog in a cabinet, in which the dog was screened, so far as possible, from all distracting outside influences. Food is put before the dog, and his mouth begins to water ; the stimulus of the food causes, in other words, a response which takes the form of an automatic secretion of the salivary glands. This is called an unconditioned response to an unconditioned stimulus. The next time that food is put before the dog, a particular note is sounded on a gong ; and this is done on each of a number of succeeding occasions, the food always being accompanied by the sounding of the note. After a time the note is sounded alone, whereupon it is found to cause the salivation which, in the first instance, was excited by the food. In other words, the salivation response is now produced by a new stimulus which has come to be associated with the original stimulus through constantly accompanying it. Salivation in response to the note alone is called a conditioned response or a conditioned reflex. Practically any stimulus which is applied sufficiently often in conjunction with the food stimulus is capable of conditioning the response appropriate to food. This is true even of a painful stimulus. Let us suppose that the dog is pricked on a number of occasions when food is put before him, and is later pricked in the same place without the food; instead of causing symptoms of pains and fright, the prick will now merely produce abundant salivation.

The subject is too technical, and would take us too far beyond the scope of the present enquiry, to pursue here. But its bearing upon the difficulty which we have raised above is sufficiently plain. The response which a particular stimulus will evoke may depend, and, as we grow older, does in large measure, in fact, depend, upon the stimulus or set of stimuli with which the stimulus has been associated on past occasions. Now there is apparently no limit to the extent and variety of the conditioning of our responses. If X be the unconditioned response to stimulus A, then, if A has been associated sufficiently often with B, X will become the response to B ; if B with C, to C ; if C with D, to D ; and so on.

Similarly, if X is the unconditioned response to stimulus A, Y to stimulus B, and Z to stimulus D, then by suitable conditioning we can evoke response Y or response Z by applying stimulus A.

Behaviourism. A famous school of psychology, the school of Behaviourism, makes great play with this principle in its attempt to explain the variety of mental life without introducing the conception of mind. Dr. Watson, the leading behaviourist, professes to have established by experiments on babies that the human infant at birth exhibits only three forms of unconditioned response which are capable of being subsequently conditioned. These are the love, the fear, and the rage responses which are evoked respectively by stroking and tickling (love), sudden loud noises and the feeling of sudden loss of support (fear), and hampering of bodily movements (rage). Thus when the young infant smiles at the sight of his mother, we are not to infer that he feels a sentiment of love which proceeds to express itself in the facial movements involved in smiling. The inference which Behaviourism suggests is that the pink round shape which is seen, the soft warm surface which is touched, are stimuli which in the past have been associated with gentle stroking and tickling, and come, therefore, to evoke as a conditioned response the unconditioned response which was originally evoked by stroking and tickling. Other unconditioned modes of behaviour appear from time to time as the infant develops. But, according to the principle of the conditioned reflex, all the movements which the human adult's body performs are either conditioned or unconditioned responses to stimuli, the term stimulus being interpreted in a very wide sense. The principle, in fact, purports to be all-embracing.

Talking and Thinking. This is not the place for a detailed description of Behaviourism which belongs rather to psychology than to philosophy. But mention must be made of the account which behaviourists give of such *prima facie* mental activities as thinking and such *prima facie* mentally caused movements as the movements of the larynx involved in talking.

Thinking, for the Behaviourist, *is* talking—talking, that is to say, under one's breath. When one thinks, certain muscles in the larynx are said to be in movement and subconsciously to form the words by means of which one's thought, if one were to speak it, would be expressed. This movement of the muscles in the larynx together with other incipient movements in the hands, in the viscera and, indeed, all over the body, is held by the behaviourist to accompany the act of thinking. More accurately, these movements constitute thinking; for thinking, on the behaviourist view, simply *is* the occurrence of those bodily activities which would normally be said to accompany it.

Thinking, therefore, may be regarded like all other psychological occurrences, in the light of a response to a stimulus. Look, says Dr. Watson at a child playing with its toys on the nursery floor ; you will find that he talks to them and to himself. If he sees you, he will as likely as not stop talking openly and begin mumbling to himself, not wishing you to hear him. Sooner or later his mumbling will probably be stopped by grown-ups, and he will subside into silence. But this silence does not mean that he is not still talking. He is ; but he is now doing it silently. This silent talking is what we call thinking. The great advantage of thinking as a mode of behaviour over talking is that there are no external signs of thinking in our *observable* behaviour. Thinking, in fact, cannot be observed ; therefore, we can think what we please, when we please. But the circumstance that we do it unobserved should not blind us to the fact that thinking is still essentially a bodily response to the stimulus of a certain situation, its development being derivable by traceable steps from the muttering of the child to its toys.

Because of the other bodily movements which accompany, or rather which *are*, thinking, thinking does not always or necessarily consist of words. Animals, for example, think without words. In ourselves, however, verbal thinking is usually dominant. The great advantage of verbal thinking is that it enables us to deal with objects in their absence, the word for the object coming by association to stand for and to take the place of the object. This substitution of word for object is an example of conditioning. Indeed, the whole use of language to convey meanings relating to things and persons not visibly present depends upon the establishment of conditioned responses. If we see a burglar in the room, we take our revolver from under the pillow, call for the police, or hand over our loose cash, according to our temperaments. If we are *told* that a burglar is in the next room, although there is as yet no visible stimulus, we may, nevertheless, react in the same way. The word " burglar " in fact causes us to make the same responses as the object " burglar." A child acquires an understanding of words, as he acquires any other form of conditioned reflex. If you say bottle whenever you give the child his bottle, he presently begins to react to the word bottle as he does to the object bottle, that is to say, his mouth waters. When he responds in this way, we say that he understands the word bottle.

When we react in the same way to a word as we would react to that for which the word stands, we are said to know the meaning of the word. Thus, according to the behaviourist theory, a person may be said to know the meaning of the word X, if the associative effects of X, when he hears it, are similar to those of the thing which the word X is used to describe. This account of talking and thinking constitutes a strong reinforcement from the side of psychology of the materialist account of the cosmos.

Behaviourist Position Summarised.

On some such lines as the above behaviourists implement their undertaking to explain the whole of human behaviour on the assumption that, even if people have minds, these play no part in determining their actions. As between extreme Materialism and Epiphenomenalism, Behaviourism does not find it necessary to decide. Its basic contention may be stated as follows : It is, indeed, possible that people have minds. As to this possibility we are not in a position to make a statement, since we cannot affirm or deny anything that we do not observe, and what we observe are not minds, but the movements of bodies—that is to say, behaviour. Now what we are prepared to try and show is that all behaviour is explicable on mechanist lines, that is to say, that it exemplifies the working of the law of cause and effect and is, in fact, nothing more nor less than a series of reflexes.

On our view, the movements in the bodies of human beings are always determined by preceding movements in their bodies, these in their turn by preceding movements, and so on through a continuous chain of bodily movements, which ends with the stimuli brought to bear on the body by the outside world to which the first movement in the chain is a response. Thus the law of cause and effect which operates universally in the outside world operates also within human bodies ; if there are minds attached to human bodies, they do not affect what these bodies do. Therefore, the hypothesis that there are such things as minds does not disturb the operation of causal laws or call for any substantial modification in the mechanist account of the causation of events, when we come to consider the case of living human organisms.

IV. THE MATERIALIST COSMOLOGY

The Origin of Variations. I noted at the outset that the main support for the scientific Materialism of the nineteenth century was derived from psychology and biology. With the contribution from psychology I have dealt. It remains to indicate the nature of the support derived from biology. This, as it lies outside the scope of philosophical enquiry proper, must be summarised very briefly. The crux of biological theory for those who were interested in the root cause of the evolutionary process was the origin of variations. Once these had occurred, then the Darwinian postulates of natural selection and the survival of the fittest afforded a reasonably adequate explanation of what happened to them, explaining whether they survived and prospered or were eliminated in the struggle for existence. But how did they occur ? Over the answer to this question there was and still is considerable controversy.

Darwin's answer was in effect that of a prudent agnosticism. He could not tell how or why the variations occurred ; what he could do, and did, was to emphasise the factors, struggle for existence, survival of the fittest and so forth, whereby the gradual accumulation of minute variations led to the appearance of new species. But, even if the origin of variations remained undetected or must be attributed to chance, it was generally agreed that their appearance had no relation either to the history of the parent or to their value to the offspring, since Weismann was believed to have shown that the germinal material in which they arise is virtually independent of developments in the organism which acts as its host.

De Vries's substitution of sudden and abrupt mutations for the gradual accumulation of small variations as the primary factors in the formation of new species, does not seriously affect the position. Where the origin of both is unknown, a marked variation is no more mysterious than a minute one ; if a materialist explanation is adequate for the latter, an explanation of the same kind will no doubt be forthcoming sooner or later for the former. If, on the other hand, we do not know what the materialist explanation of a mutation may be, it will avail us little to find one for the minute variation.

The only other theory in the field ascribed variations to the influence of the external environment. As the environment changes owing to climatic or other changes, it produces an effect upon the organisms living within it. This effect may be interpreted as the organism's response to a stimulus, the stimulus, namely, constituted by the change in the environment. If the response of the organism is such as to adapt it to the circumstances of the changed environment, it survives and prospers ; if not, it dies out. In the former event the variation in respect of which it survives is perpetuated.

Both views have one important feature in common ; in accounting for the formation of new species they both reject the intervention of mind and disclaim the notion of purpose. The appearance of life upon the earth, the evolution of life through an infinite variety of forms, the whole of the process which begins with the amoeba

and ends with man is explained not in terms of the operation of some purposive force or spirit, but as the result
of the action of purely haphazard external agencies;
the *deus ex machina*, in fact, is either chance, or the influence
of a physical environment.

It follows that changes which occur in living organisms
never spring from within, but are always imposed from without. In order to account for them we need postulate no spiritual force or purposive will, whether operating within the
organism or directing it from outside; assuming that we
are not prepared to rest content with the notion of chance,
it is necessary simply to specify the factors in the material
situation to which the organism is exposed, and which
cause it to react by varying in the way in which it does.

Evidence from Modern Genetics.

Modern genetics rein-
forces the same conclusion from a different angle. Biologists
seem now to be fairly generally agreed that the substances
passed from parent to offspring, which constitute the
individual's inheritance, are numbers of separate packets
of diverse chemicals embedded in a less diversified mass
of material. These packets of chemicals, the genes, are
strung like beads along the line of the chromosomes:
the chromosomes exist in pairs, so that for each packet
on one chromosome there is a corresponding packet on
another. When the organism becomes a parent, it distri-
butes to its offspring one packet only from each of its
pairs, the corresponding second packet of the pair being
supplied by the other parent.

The genes, therefore, constitute the raw material of
inheritance. Nor is this inheritance confined to bodily
characteristics. There are gene combinations for bad temper
and sadism, just as there are for red hair and pink eyes,
or in theory there ought to be. But whether in any individual a particular combination will or will not become
operative depends upon the environment the environment,
being taken to include not only the external circumstances
of the organism, but also the constitution of and conditions

prevailing in the rest of the body. It is not true that because one inherits certain characteristics, one will exhibit them. What is true, is that one inherits an immense number of potential " innate " characteristics, but that which of them one will in fact display depends upon the environment in which one is placed. Hence, the characteristics that appear under training are as much inherited as those that appear at birth ; the only difference is that the former set require the application of certain conditions over a period of time to " bring them out." The distinction between heredity and environment, between innate characteristics and acquired is, therefore, a false one. Strictly what one inherits are not characteristics at all, but certain material which, given certain conditions, will produce certain characteristics.

The scheme, it is obvious, is a purely deterministic one. It is not deterministic in the sense that what the individual will become is preordained by the supply of genes which he gets from his parents ; it is deterministic in the sense that what he will become is the result of a complex constituted by this initial supply and the environment in which he develops, for neither of which can he be considered responsible.

Mechanical Causation Universal.   Thus the characteristics of the organism are determined by the germinal material which he inherits. The nature of this material is determined by the characteristics of the parents. The characteristics of the parents depend in the last resort upon those of the species to which they belong, and those of the species to which they belong are determined by the influence of the external material environment, supplemented, if we take the Darwinian view, by the intrusion of chance in the shape of variations. Though many links have still to be inserted, the chain of mechanical causation is thus conceived to be in theory complete, and at no point is there an opening for freedom or a loophole for the intrusion of non-material factors. Professor Tyndal, predicting at the Belfast meeting of the British Association in 1874, that the future of science would enable us to survey the "ultimately purely natural and inevitable march of evolution from the atoms of the primeval nebula to the proceedings of the British Association for the Advancement of Science" gives at once the clearest and the most comprehensive expression to the resulting world view.

Statement of Materialist Cosmology.

In a universe so conceived, life is of profound unimportance. Among the infinite permutations and combinations through which matter has passed, one has supervened in which matter has achieved consciousness. This consciousness by matter of itself is life. Life, then, is a chance product of material forces and substances, evolved under certain conditions, and doomed to disappear when those conditions no longer obtain. As the sterner materialists were fond of saying, life is a "mere eddy in the primeval slime."

This general conception was in the nineteenth century reinforced by contemporary geology and astronomy. Geology had enormously increased the age of the world, astronomy the size and spread of space. It was known that for countless ages the earth had been lifeless ; through the limitless tracts of space ours was the only planet upon which life was known to exist. Thus in the vast immensities of geological time and astronomical space life seemed like a tiny glow, flickering uncertainly for a brief period before its ultimate and certain extinction. Once the earth had been too hot and too moist to maintain life ; in course of time it would become too cold and too dry. When this condition was reached, life would finish its pointless journey with as little significance as, in the person of the amoeba, it began it. The existence of spirit was not, therefore, a fact of cosmic significance, a signpost pointing in the fundamental character of the universe to something friendly and vital which underlay its apparent chaos and deadness and with which spirit was continuous ; spirit was a chance passenger across a fundamentally hostile environment, in which the alien and the brutal conditioned and determined at every point the mental and the vital.

As for the universe, it was like the works of a gigantic clock. Some one or something unspecified at some time unknown (materialists have often been inclined to pride themselves upon their candid admission of inability to account for a first cause) wound the clock up ; thenceforward, it has proceeded to function automatically through the interaction of its parts. One day, we may suppose, if the phenomenon of radio-activity may be accepted at its face value, the world process will come to an end. All the uranium in the world is breaking down, and we know of no source from which new uranium can come ; what is true of uranium, is true also of all the more complex atoms. The material universe is, therefore, visibly degenerating ; the clock, to revert to our metaphor, is running down. Since the method of winding up new universes is not known, we must suppose that in course of time the material universe will dissolve itself into a cool glow of radiation uniformly diffused through space, unless some force of a kind unknown to science intervenes to infuse it with new energy. In any event, life and mind will have disappeared with the disappearance of the material conditions which have produced them.

Comment on the Preceding Argument.

The view of the universe just outlined is derived from composite material. To provide this material I have drawn upon the arguments and conclusions of materialist thinkers of many different schools, some of the twentieth century, others of the nineteenth. From these arguments and conclusions I have selected what appeared to me to be at once the strongest and the most typical, and tried to combine them into a coherent whole. As I noted at the outset, a difficulty which besets the exposition of Materialism is the absence of any comprehensive and agreed statement of what precisely the materialist view of the universe entails. There is, in other words, no single materialist cosmology in the sense in which there is, for example, a single Hegelian cosmology. For this reason, although most materialists would be prepared to subscribe to most of the foregoing, it is possible that no single materialist would be prepared to accept it all. Nevertheless, it does, I hope, fairly represent the main conclusions which Materialism seeks to establish, and the arguments which have influenced many reputable thinkers in reaching these conclusions.

V. COMMENTARY AND CRITICISM

How far Scientists are Still Materialist.   I do not propose to comment at any length upon the world picture whose outlines I have briefly sketched. The observations which follow may, however, serve to give a philosophical orientation to Materialism and to indicate the status which it holds among modern philosophies. Unlike most of the philosophies with which we have hitherto been concerned, Materialism is based upon considerations which are not themselves exclusively or even mainly philosophical. Is it possible to explain the facts of human behaviour without introducing mind as a causal agent ? Is it the case that every event in the mind is preceded and determined by a prior event in the brain ? Is it a fact that variations in species are purely fortuitous, or are they the effects of preceding changes in the environment of the species to which they are adaptations ? These questions are, at least in theory, capable of determination by factual evidence. When we know enough about the ways in which the body works and species originate, we shall presumably be able to answer them. They are, therefore, in essence scientific questions determinable by empirical evidence and as such fall outside the scope of this book.

It is, however, a matter of common knowledge that science which, twenty-five years ago, was held to suggest, indeed to necessitate the materialist answer to these questions, is no longer exclusively materialist. This comparative weakening of the scientific backing for Materialism is not due to any revolutionary change in the sciences of psychology and biology with which in this chapter we have been mainly concerned. In psychology the attitude adopted by the behaviourists is still widely favoured and in some quarters is gaining ground. The endeavour to trace connections between mental events and neural and cerebral causes has in recent years been attended by considerable success, while the full implications of the principle of the conditioned reflex have still to be explored.

In biology the predisposition of all laboratory and field workers is still very largely materialist. The experimental worker in biology has to proceed, *as if* Materialism were true, since the admission of the intrusion into the evolutionary process of a free vital activity, whose urge to express itself constitutes the driving force of the process studied, is fatal to that certitude of calculable prediction which is the condition of successful experimental work. If we postulate the presence of some creative impulsion which expresses itself in living organisms, and concede that because of the drive of this impulsion the organism may at any moment develop in an entirely new and unforeseeable manner, the sequence of cause and effect, the assumption of which is necessary to scientific work, can no longer be relied upon. Thus psychology and biology still remain largely materialist in outlook and mechanist in method.

Developments of Physics.   It is from the side of physics that the foundations of Materialism have been most seriously undermined. The nineteenth century conception of matter as ultimately analysable into an assemblage of solid homogeneous atoms extended in space, formed at once an admirable basis for the convictions of the commonsense man and a satisfactory framework for the researches of chemical and physical science.

To-day that conception has been largely superseded. As we saw in Chapter XIII, modern matter has become infinitely mysterious and infinitely attenuated. So little, indeed, is known of its fundamental nature that the modern preference for explanations in terms of mind rather than of matter, is little more than a preference for working in terms of the less unknown rather than of the more. We know too much about the physical world to-day, to feel that we know anything for certain. Certainly we do not know enough about it to justify us in asserting that it possesses those characteristics which it must possess, if it is to act as a foundation for the imposing superstructure of a materialist universe. To quote from Sir Arthur Eddington : " If to-day you ask a physicist what he has finally made out the ether or the electron to be, the answer will not be a description in terms of billiard balls or fly-wheels or anything concrete ; he will point instead to a number of symbols and a set of mathematical equations which they satisfy. What do the symbols stand for ? The mysterious reply is given that physics is indifferent to that ; it has no means of probing beneath the symbolism." Modern science is, therefore, in a somewhat paradoxical position. While psychology, the science of mind, is doubtful of the existence of mind, and exhibits a marked preference for explanations of so-called mental phenomena in terms of physical causes, physics, the science of matter, professes agnosticism as to the nature of matter, and, when its implications are developed by eminent physicists like Sir Arthur Eddington and Sir James Jeans, is considered to point to a Kantian view of mind as the main artificer of the observed characteristics of the material world. As I pointed out in Chapter XIV, Kant is the philosopher whose view of the universe is most congenial to the modern physicist, and Kant is very far from affording any countenance to Mechanist Materialism. It is largely for this reason that Materialism as a philosophy does not to-day enjoy the vogue even among men of science that it enjoyed twenty-five years ago.

THE APPROACHES OF SCIENCE AND PHILOSOPHY CONTRASTED

(1) THE STANDPOINT OF SCIENCE. But, while Materialism as a philosophy may no longer be congenial to men of science, it is still their invariable method ; or, to be precise,

Mechanism is still the universal assumption of their method. The experiments of science are, in other words, conducted on the assumption that the universe, or at any rate that aspect of it which science studies, is like a gigantic piece of machinery in which each event is the cause of its necessary and predictable result. The assumptions of Mechanism are, indeed, as has already been hinted, necessary to the whole procedure of science. If *any* compound could result from a particular combination of elements, if the same compound did not always *in fact* result from that combination, if a possible effect of placing a kettle upon the fire were the freezing not the boiling of its contents, then science as an organised body of knowledge would be impossible.

Nor can science abandon these assumptions when it tackles the problems of life and mind. In so far as it seeks to give an account of a living organism, it must treat the organism *as if* it worked like a machine. It cannot allow the possibility that some arbitrary non-mechanical principle of life may at any moment intrude itself to upset the causal chain of stimulus and response which biology seeks to establish. Thus it is no accident that field and laboratory workers in biology are strongly mechanist in sympathy and outlook. As with biology, so with psychology. In so far as science is successful in bringing human beings within its ambit, its success depends upon its ability to treat them as highly complex mechanisms whose workings are subject to the same laws as those which are observed to hold in the rest of the world. It is the purpose of science to describe this world. Now of this world human beings are themselves a part, and the laws which science reveals as governing the events which occur in it must, if the scientific standpoint is to be maintained, be exemplified in the lives and histories of the men and women who are items in its contents. If we cannot as yet show this exemplification in detail, that, science insists, is only because of the lack of adequate scientific knowledge. Men, in other words, must be studied as mechanisms responding to stimuli, and the mind, in so far as its existence is conceded, must be studied as objectively in the speech and actions which are commonly said to spring from it, as the growth of a plant or the movements of a planet. Inevitably, then, Behaviourism is the appropriate psychology for the scientist. " The behaviourist," says Professor Watson, " puts the human organism in front of him and says, What can it do? When does it start to do these things ? If it doesn't do these things by reason of its original nature, what can it be taught to do ? "

Thus the human being is treated as a laboratory specimen who is under observation. Given a particular object or situation, how, the behaviourist asks, will the specimen behave when confronted with it, and, conversely, when we see the specimen behaving in a certain way, what, we ask ourselves, is the object or situation which causes it so to behave ? These are strictly scientific questions. Unquestioningly, they postulate the universal applicability of the law of cause and effect. They assume that an account of behaviour in terms of that law is adequate and ultimate, and they refuse to admit the existence of any intrusive immaterial element such as consciousness or mind. If such exists, it plays no part in determining what occurs.

Now these, it must again be insisted, are the only lines along which science can proceed. And in so far as science aspires to give an account of a human being, it is within the framework of these assumptions that the account must fall. To deny the applicability of the method or the adequacy of its results, is to deny the competence of science in certain spheres. It is to say in effect : "When it comes to a question of mind and soul, the scientific method is no longer fruitful ; at any rate its fruitfulness is limited."

(2) THE PHILOSOPHIC STANDPOINT. Now that there is this necessary limitation upon the value of scientific method, is precisely what philosophy has always maintained. Philosophy does not *necessarily* deny that the assumptions of Mechanism may work satisfactorily in the material world. The degree of a philosopher's willingness to concede that they do in fact work, would depend upon

the nature of his philosophy. It would depend, for example, upon whether he considered that there was a material world, such as common sense affirms and science purports to explore. For a Hegelian, for example, or a Berkeleyan idealist, there is no such world, and the question whether the theory of mechanical causation adequately describes its working would not arise. Broadly speaking, only a dualist, who holds that the sum-total of what exists is divided into at least two categories, the category of material entities and the category of mental entities, would find it easy to concede that the postulates of Mechanism might hold completely and universally in the material world, and he, as we have hinted above,[1] would find his course beset with serious difficulties, so soon as he began to reflect upon the case of material existences such as human bodies which are apparently animated and controlled by mental ones. But almost all philosophers would agree that the concepts of Mechanism cannot be applied to the workings of the mind, and, in so far as they affirm the existence of mind, they are bound to exclude it from the realm in which Mechanism reigns. Now the existence of mind, its freedom and its ability to think, are presuppositions of philosophy. That ethics, for example, presupposes human freedom is obvious. Unless ethics is to be dismissed as nonsense, a man must be free to do his duty, for, if he were not, it would, as Kant pointed out, be nonsense to say that it was his duty. The validity of ethics also implies that we may justly blame a man for doing wrong and praise him for doing right. Now the behaviourist theory of mind and the milder form of Materialism known as Epiphenomenalism are inconsistent with the freedom of men's actions in any of the senses in which they have been held to be free. But if men's wills are not free, praise is as irrelevant as blame is impertinent, and *tout comprendre est tout pardonner* is the beginning and end of ethics.

Again if the Self can in no sense be regarded as a unity—and it cannot, if it is correctly describable as a series of

[1] See discussion of Free Will, pp. 503–507 above.

psychological accompaniments to bodily responses—then that moral responsibility for action and character which ethics demands is a figment, for it is not just to demand of one isolated psychological state that it should accept responsibility for something willed or desired by another psychological state with which it owns no continuity. As with ethics, so with aesthetics. If matter is all, then to give a complete account of the material constituents of a picture, is to give a complete account of the picture. For there is nothing in the picture save the matter of which it is composed, there is neither beauty nor expression. Hence all that aesthetics can do is to catalogue the psychological accompaniments to those cerebral events, which are the automatic responses of the brain to the impact upon the retinas of light rays of certain specified rates and frequencies proceeding from the place in which the picture is situated.

As with ethics and aesthetics, so with logic. Just as the validity of ethics entails that men can act freely, so the validity of logic entails that they can think freely. For, if men's thoughts are not free, we may take leave to doubt if there is any sense in which they can be said to be true. I shall, however, return to this point in a moment.[1]

It follows that if Materialism be true in all that it asserts, philosophy must be abandoned. It is not, therefore, matter for surprise that few philosophers should have been materialists. To ascribe their inability to accept Materialism to men's natural disinclination to acquiesce in the elimination of a pursuit which supplies them at once with a livelihood and a *raison d'être*, would be unfair. For, apart from detailed objections which may be urged against any particular materialist assertion, philosophers have advanced two considerations of a general character which, if they can be established, undermine the basis of the materialist position. These considerations, since they would be urged in common by philosophers of almost every school, may properly find a place in these pages.

[1] See below, pp. 534-537.

Criticism of Materialism. (*a*) THE DIFFICULTY OF CAUSA-
TION. We have noted the difficulty which modern physicists have found in accepting the simple and straightforward
conception of matter which Materialism has been thought,
whether rightly or wrongly, to demand. Philosophers have
asked whether we can accept the simple and straightforward conception of the law of cause and effect which
Mechanism seems to demand. And as we saw in Chapter
VIII, in answer to their own question, they have insisted
that we cannot. Ever since Hume's criticism of the law of
cause and effect,[1] it has been reasonably certain that the
commonsense conception of causation which represents one
event as exerting a compulsive influence upon another
event, from which it is separated in space or time, is at best
ambiguous and at worst totally inadequate. Are we ever
entitled to affirm more than correlation between certain
sets of events ? Can we ever discover in what common
sense regards as necessary connection anything more than
regularity of sequence ? Unless these questions can be
answered in the simple affirmative which Mechanism seems
to require, while Mechanism will remain pragmatically
useful as a hypothesis to guide the investigations of experi-
menters, the materialist philosophy which is built upon it
must be pronounced unacceptable as a theory of the cosmos.
Now it seems fairly plain that these questions cannot be
so answered. There may be more in what is called necessary
connection than regularity of sequence ; there may even be
some kind of necessity, but what more there is or what kind
of necessity, we are not in a position to say. Philosophies
such as Idealism may be constructed which meet the difficulty by the simple process of not raising it ; but, while the
difficulty remains, Materialism as a philosophy is without
any sure foundation.

(*b*) MATERIALISM SELF-CONTRADICTORY. A no less
serious difficulty is suggested by logic. If Materialism is
true in all that it asserts, mental events are reflections of

[1] See Chapter VIII, pp. 207–213.

preceding bodily and cerebral events which determine their occurrence. Thoughts are mental events. A thought, then, occurs because certain events in the body and the brain have occurred, because, in a word, the body is in a certain condition. How does this conclusion bear upon the question of the truth of the thought? Ideas are normally advanced because they purport to be true. Waiving for the moment the question of the precise meaning of truth which we discussed in Chapter XVI, we may say provisionally that an idea is true because it squares with the facts, or accurately represents the facts, or asserts what is the case : that, in short, an idea is true because it corresponds with reality. If there are four people in a room and I think that there are, my thought would normally be called true because of the existence of a fact external to the thought which it correctly reports. Whatever be the ultimate philosophical meaning of truth, it must include this common-sense meaning of truth, according to which the truth of a thought depends upon its reference to something other than itself, namely, a so-called external fact which it purports to assert or report or describe.

Now let us return to the materialist position. Thoughts, the materialist asserts, occur, as bodily events occur, because of certain predisposing causes. These predisposing causes are internal to the body. A thought, then, so far as its causation is concerned, is on the same footing as a bodily event. Now it would be meaningless to ask whether a bodily event, for example, the state of my blood pressure or the temperature of my skin, was true. These are things which occur and are real ; they are facts. But they are not and cannot be true, because they do not assert anything other than themselves. It is, then, on this basis equally meaningless to say of a thought that it is true ; we can say only that it occurs. In so far as it indicates or is evidence for anything, it indicates or is evidence for a condition of the brain which produced it. The assertions of materialists do not, then, constitute evidence in favour of that which the assertions assert. Nor do their thoughts refer to a reality outside themselves. Their assertions are assertions to the effect that, their thoughts are evidence for the fact that, the bodies and brains of the materialists in question are in a certain condition, and they are evidence for nothing else.

Now Materialism itself is a set of ideas—a set of ideas which purports among other things to tell us what sort of universe this is in which we are living. But, if Materialism is correct, what the ideas do in fact tell us about is the conditions prevailing in the bodies and brains of those who advance them. If, in short, Materialism is true in all that it asserts, then Materialism tells us about that part of the world which is the body and brain of a particular individual, and only about that part. It follows that Materialism, in so far as it purports to give an account of the world as a whole cannot be true, or, more precisely, it is meaningless to say of it that it is either true or false, since it turns out that it does not tell us anything about the world at all. Thus in so far as it establishes its conclusion, Materialism destroys its case. Even if what Materialism says were by some odd coincidence to be correct, it could adduce no grounds for supposing it to be correct.

The Nemesis of Behaviourism.

I have so far considered this difficulty as it bears upon the less extreme form of Materialism, the form which concedes an epiphenomenal mind which, though it is dependent on events in the brain, is nevertheless really a mind. But, it is obvious, the more extreme forms of Materialism are logically still less defensible. That this is so, can be seen by considering the case of Behaviourism. If thought, as the behaviourist asserts, *is* movements in the larynx and other parts of the body, such movements are *all* that it is. Now the movements of the body may be necessary and determined, but they can no more be true, than a quadratic equation can be purple or a musical chord can be covetous. It is, of course, the case that I may feel convinced that my thought relates to the outside world and correctly asserts what happens there. But this conviction of mine is only another thought, and, therefore, another set of laryngeal movements, which, as I pointed out above, cannot of their very nature refer to anything outside themselves.

It is also the case, if Behaviourism is correct, that these arguments of mine are themselves no more than movements in my larynx and nervous system which are causally linked to other movements in my hand, as I write, and my face, as I talk. Therefore, they do not, presumably, refer to Behaviourism at all. The reader's view of them is another set of movements in his larynx, and the belief that this is the correct description both of the arguments and of the reader's view of them is another set. It is impossible on these lines to find any basis from which thought can operate, for there are no common premises, no common presumptions, and no common conclusions of thought. On the basis of a thorough-going Materialism, every so-called thinker is boxed up within the circle of his own experiences in a prison far more rigorous than that constructed by idealistic Solipsism.[1] For, while idealistic Solipsism enclosed the mind within the circle of its own ideas, yet conceded that the mind might be creative to the extent of producing its ideas, the materialist locks up the mind—if, indeed, he admits a mind at all—in a cell whose walls are the neural and cerebral movements of his own body, which movements he plays no part in initiating. And, since nothing which mind experiences can reach it from outside these walls, so nothing that it thinks can refer to anything outside them. Materialism, then, which purports to be thought about the universe, turns out to be unable to tell us anything about the universe. It can only tell us about what is happening in the bodies and brains of materialists.

Professor Broad's Logical Argument.

I cannot forbear to add the following argument against Materialism which emanates from Professor Broad, partly because it affords so admirable an example of the logician's art, partly because it shows how formidable a weapon logic can be, when it is

[1] See Chapter II, p. 56.

used to demolish the arguments of those who have paid more attention to science than to straight thinking. The argument is as follows : " However completely the behaviour of an external body answers to the behaviouristic tests for intelligence, it always remains a perfectly sensible question to ask : ' Has it really got a mind or is it merely an automaton ? ' It is quite true that we have no available means of answering such questions conclusively. It is also true that the more nearly a body answers to the behaviouristic tests for intelligence, the harder it is for us in practice to contemplate the possibility of its having no mind. Still the question ' Has it a mind ? ' is never silly in the sense that it is meaningless. At worst, it is silly only in the sense that it does not generally express a real doubt, and that we have no means of answering it. It may be like asking whether the moon may not be made of green cheese ; but it is not like asking whether a rich man may have no wealth. Now on the behaviouristic theory to have a mind means just to behave in certain ways, and to ask whether a thing which admittedly does behave in these ways has a mind would be like asking whether Jones, who is admittedly a rich man, has much wealth. Since the question can be raised, and is evidently not tautologous or self-contradictory, it is clear that when we ascribe a mind or a mental process to an external body we do not mean simply that it behaves in certain characteristic ways."

Summary. The above are some of the reasons why Materialism, although it has been frequently adopted as a working creed by scientists, has never been widely accepted by philosophers. The reader may find it convenient to have them in summary form.

1. The scientific picture of the world displays an assemblage of material things arranged in space, whose movements are determined by necessary laws. But if this picture is extended to include human beings, it is found to conflict with much else that we take to be true, for example, with ethical experience and with aesthetic.

2. For this reason, the assumptions upon which the scientific picture rests must be carefully scrutinised. The scrutiny reveals that matter as conceived by contemporary physics is extremely mysterious and most inadequately known. It also reveals that the so-called law of cause and effect is very far from being the simple thing that we had supposed. For this reason, mechanical causation, which Materialism takes for granted, cannot be unquestioningly accepted as a fact, even in the material world. Purposive or teleological causation[1] is certainly not less intelligible than mechanical, and it is something of which we have direct experience in our own minds.

3. Inconsistent with ethics and æsthetics and owning an inadequate basis in physics, Materialism is indefensible in logic. More precisely, in so far as it establishes the conclusions which it asserts, it robs those conclusions of any possibility of being true.

Books on Materialism :
LANGE, F. A.   The History of Materialism.
    The standard work.
COHEN, CHAPMAN.   Materialism Restated.
    A good brief modern statement.
Books on Behaviourism :
WATSON, J. B.   Behaviourism.
        A Study of Behaviour
Books on the Mind-Body Problem :
BROAD, C. D.   The Mind and its Place in Nature (Section A).
WISDOM, JOHN.   Problems of Mind and Matter (Part I).
STOUT, G. F.   Mind and Matter.
Books dealing with the issue between Vitalism and Mechanism :
HOGBEN, L.   The Nature of Living Matter.
    From the materialist standpoint.
HALDANE, J. S.   The Philosophical Basis of Biology.
    From the idealist standpoint.
THOMSON, SIR J. ARTHUR.   Purpose in Evolution.
    From the teleogical standpoint.
    Joseph Needham's *The Sceptical Biologist* contains a good popular discussion of the issues involved.

[1] See Chapter VII, pp. 185, 186.

Chapter XIX : PHILOSOPHIES OF MODERN SCIENCE

2. Outline of Bergson's Philosophy

Introductory. The philosophy which, as we saw in the last chapter, it was natural for the nineteenth century scientist to adopt, was materialist. But twentieth century science affords in some ways an uncongenial background for materialist views. This, broadly speaking, is true of the sciences both of physics and of biology. Modern physics makes it difficult to suppose that matter is simple and lumpy and that the laws which govern its workings are simple and mechanistic. Modern biologists find increasing difficulty in giving a satisfactory account of the behaviour of living organisms in terms of the concepts appropriate to the workings of a machine. Changes in the background of science have been reflected in philosophy. While modern physicists turn increasingly to philosophy, and find in some form of Idealism, whether of the Subjective[1] or of the Kantian[2] type, a solution of the difficulties raised by the contemporary analysis of matter, modern philosophers have given increasing attention to the problems raised by the scientists, and have elaborated metaphysical systems designed to provide the world of science with a cosmic background compatible with its present state of development.

It would be impossible within the limits of a single chapter to indicate, however briefly, the variety of metaphysical suggestions and hypotheses for which the conclusions of modern science have been either directly or indirectly responsible. I have, accordingly, selected for fairly detailed presentation two modern metaphysical systems, that of Bergson and that of Whitehead, which originated in the need for revising our notions of the nature of the universe on lines which the developments of modern

[1] See Chapter II, p. 38.
[2] See Chapter XIV, pp. 362, 363, and Chapter XII, p. 321.

science have seemed to these philosophers to necessitate.

In the years immediately preceding the war, when Bergson[1] was at the height of his reputation in Paris, biology was the science whose results chiefly struck the popular imagination, and seemed to stand in most urgent need of metaphysical interpretation. The considerations with which Bergson concerns himself are, therefore, largely biological in character, and his philosophy may be regarded in the light of a sustained attempt to make sense of the modern notions of change and evolution. Since the war, physics has taken pride of place, and Whitehead's philosophy may be regarded in the light of an attempt to make metaphysical sense of the modern notions of space, time, and matter. Both philosophies have attained a very considerable contemporary reputation. I shall in this chapter endeavour to give a brief outline of some of the leading ideas of Bergson's philosophy ; in the next, I shall describe those of Whitehead.

Bergson's Central Thesis. In an earlier chapter, I pointed out[2] that one of the possible alternatives to the commonsense notion of a world composed of changing things which, nevertheless, somehow endure through change, is the view that change alone is real, that reality, in fact, is a flux of change. This is the central principle of Bergson's philosophy. The view that the universe is nothing but a stream of perpetual change, was, as I mentioned in Chapter VII, first advanced by the Greek philosopher Heracleitus.[3] Heracleitus's conclusion is also Bergson's. In the universe as Bergson conceives it there is nothing which changes, since a something which changes—which remains, that is to say, in some sense the same through the changes that occur to it, so that we can say of it " *This* is the thing which was so-and-so and is now something else," can never be found.

Modern physics show that every apparently solid material thing resolves itself into an enormous quantity of elementary movements. Whether we represent these

---

[1] Born 1859. [2] See Chapter VII, pp. 178, 179.
[3] See Chapter VII, p. 178.

movements as vibrations, or as ether waves, or as electrons, or as event particles, it seems impossible to arrive at something which is sufficiently stable to be spoken of as that *in* which the changes, or movements take place. For if at any stage such an apparent something were reached, and you were to affirm of it that *this* is the *thing* that changes or in which the changes take place, further examination would always be found to show that the alleged thing is itself composed of changes, which are other than and additional to the changes which you predicated of it when you said "Here is something to which changes occur, but which is itself other than change."

What follows ? That, if Bergson is right, the universe must be conceived as one continuous flow, which is alive, evolution being the mere movement of the flow. Bergson visualises the process of evolution as though there is somewhere a centre from which worlds and life and matter are thrown off like fireworks in a vast illumination. But even this centre is not a concrete thing : if it were, it would be something other than ceaseless change, and would, therefore, contradict the view that nothing but ceaseless change can exist. The centre is, therefore, described as a " continuity of outflow," a metaphorical expression to suggest that the vital surge, which is the universe, has neither beginning nor end, completeness nor finality. This description is inherent in the general conception ; for, if the vital surge had a beginning or an end, there would be something before or after the vital surge which was not the vital surge, that is to say, there would be something other than mere change. The world, then, is the embodiment of an immanent principle of living change, which, as it comes into existence, progressively creates the evolving universe. This principle is Bergson's celebrated *élan vital*.

But Bergson does not rely for this conclusion solely upon the critical philosophical considerations adduced in Chapter VII. His philosophy is, as I have mentioned, largely biological in inspiration, and he adduces in support of his position a variety of considerations derived from the study

of living organisms and more particularly from the nature
of consciousness in living organisms. These considerations
constitute by implication a criticism of Materialism, and
Bergson's philosophy may, therefore, be regarded in the
light of an alternative reading of the facts upon which
Scientific Materialism is based. From this point of view it is
strictly relevant to the theme of the last chapter.

Classical Theories of Evolution.

The facts of evolution,
as I mentioned in the last chapter, have been broadly
attributed to the operation of one or the other of two
principles. According to Darwin, chance variations in
species fortuitously occur. Of these variations those which
are most suited to their environment tend to survive and
to reproduce themselves. The process whereby variations
arise is a purely chance one ; they are in no sense the outcome of purpose, nor are they manifestations of some
motivating force. The other principle is that of adaptation
to environment. Adaptation was originally conceived by
Lamarck as a purposive process. As the environment
changes, species develop new characteristics in order to
adapt themselves to it : those which are the more successful
in compassing the necessary adaptations tend to survive ; the
others tend to die out. But with a few exceptions, of whom the
most notable was Samuel Butler, nineteenth century biologists conceived of adaptation as a mechanical process, whereby the organism automatically responded to changes in the
stimuli reaching it from outside. Thus what may be called the
classical theories of evolution are, as we saw in the last chapter, in essential agreement on one cardinal point : they all
conceive the process of evolution on mechanical lines ; they
all find it unnecessary to postulate the existence of mind or
purpose to explain how and why the process takes place.

Bergson's Criticism.

It is this mechanist conception of
evolution that Bergson questions. He catalogues a long
list of phenomena taken from insect, animal and vegetable
life which, it is asserted, are inexplicable on mechanistic

principles. For example, the factors classically regarded as those which determine the course of evolution, such as adaptation to environment and chance survival of the fittest, totally fail, in his opinion, to explain what is known as transformism, that is to say, the occurrence of those small variations whose accumulation, on Darwin's view, results in the gradual evolution of new species ; they fail no less to account for the abrupt variations known as mutations.[1] They are also unable to explain such phenomena as the metamorphoses undergone by the insect.

Postulation of Evolutionary Driving Force.

Why, Bergson asks, if the determining factor in evolution is adaptation to environment, did not evolution cease thousands of years ago. " A very inferior organism," he says, " is as well adapted as ours to the conditions of existence, judged by its success in maintaining its life : why, then, does life, which has succeeded in adapting itself, go on complicating itself and complicating itself more and more dangerously ? . . . Why did it not stop wherever it was possible ? Why has it gone on ? Why—unless it be that there is an impulse driving it to take ever greater and greater risks towards its goal of an ever higher and higher efficiency ? "

This impulse he conceives as an immanent principle which pervades, which drives, which, indeed, *is* whatever is life. It is in fact the celebrated *élan vital*. The *élan vital* is the thrusting force behind evolution, and, Bergson holds, unless it is postulated, it is impossible to explain how and why the movement of evolution occurs. The factors emphasised by the classical theories of evolution no doubt play their part in determining the direction of evolution at any given moment, but they are incapable of explaining why evolution should take place at all. " The truth is," says

[1] Many biologists now hold that at least one of the causes of the development of new species is the manifestation simultaneously by a number of members of an existing species of abrupt, radically different variations which are not the final stage in a series of gradual developments, but occur spontaneously without any corresponding change in the environment of the species. These sudden variations, in so far as they breed true, are called mutations.

Bergson, "that adaptation explains the inner windings of evolutionary progress, but not the general direction of the movement, still less the movement itself."

The conclusion is that biology supplies us with a series of facts which can only be explained on the assumption that the universe is the creation and expression of a vital force or impulse, whose function it is continually to change and to evolve.

Consideration of the Evidence from Psychology.

The facts of psychology point to a similar conclusion. As we saw in the last chapter, mechanist theories of evolution have their counterpart in the so-called parallelist theory of psychology. This theory it will be remembered[1] asserts that whatever changes occur in the body are accompanied by corresponding changes in consciousness. There is, in fact, a complete parallelism between the mind and the body, all psychological events being attended by physiological modifications as their necessary accompaniments.

The more extreme views of Materialism proper tend, as we have seen,[2] completely to eliminate the notion of an independent, freely functioning mind. Mind they regard either as the sum total of the nerve cells which constitute the brain, or as a highly attenuated material substance surrounding the brain, or as an immaterial function of |or emanation from the brain. On any of these views, whatever happens in the mind is the result of something that has first happened in the brain, and the material always and in all respects determines and conditions the mental. The mind, in fact, is but the pale attendant of the brain.

Bergson brings against this conclusion a further series of facts with which it is alleged to be incompatible. Experiments have shown that the excision of large portions of the brain, and of those very portions which were considered essential for the causation of mental activity, have been succeeded by no psychological disturbances; whereas, if mental is the result of cerebral activity, modifications in

[1] For an account of psycho-physical parallelism see Chapter XVIII, pp. 501, 502. [2] See Chapter XVIII, pp. 517-520.

SP

psychology should inevitably have followed. The phenomena of abnormal psychology, and especially of dual personality, are independent of any corresponding physiological changes. Subconscious mental activity is also inexplicable on the parallelist hypothesis. Bergson infers that mental activity conditions cerebral activity and overflows it. The brain is not consciousness, nor does it contain the cause of conscious processes : it is simply the organ of consciousness, the point at which consciousness enters into matter ; and, as we shall shortly see, it has been evolved by consciousness for certain specific purposes which are bound up with the necessity for action.

Bergson is famous for the similes and illustrations by means of which he illustrates his exposition and helps to convey his meaning. A particularly happy simile is invoked to illuminate his view of the relation of consciousness to the brain.

The Brain as the Organ of Pantomime.

An actor in a play of Shakespeare not only speaks words, but makes gestures, so that, if a man were completely deaf, he would still be able to infer something of what the play was about from seeing the gestures. It is obvious, however, that there is much more in the play than the pantomime of the players. There are, for example, the words, the characters, the plot, and the poetry. Now the brain, says Bergson, is the organ of pantomime. If you were to observe a man's brain, you would know just as much of his thoughts as found vent in gestures. You would know, in other words, all that his thoughts imply in the way of actions or the beginnings of actions,[1] but the thoughts themselves would escape you, just as the words and meaning of the play would escape the deaf spectator. This is what is meant by saying that the mind overflows the brain. If our knowledge of both psychology and physiology were perfect, we should, Bergson maintains, be able to describe the movements of the brain without observing it, provided we had complete understanding

[1] Among the beginnings of actions may be mentioned those movements of the larynx which are involved in talking. (See Chapter XVIII, pp. 518, 519.)

of a man's state of mind ; but we should not from the most minute and thorough inspection of the brain be able to tell what the man was thinking, since, just as one gesture of the actor may stand for many different thoughts, so one state of the brain may represent any one of a host of states of mind. If mental activity is fundamental and cerebral activity incidental, if consciousness is independent of the brain and only employs the brain for certain special purposes, how is consciousness to be defined ?

Definition of Consciousness and Transition to Treatment of Time.

The answer is that consciousness is simply that stream of change or becoming with which, as we have seen, Bergson identifies reality. The arguments for this view of consciousness have already been given in Chapter VII,[1] and it is not necessary to repeat them here. Consciousness, they purport to show, can be conceived only as a flux of change. Now, if reality is change and nothing but change, and consciousness is change and nothing but change, consciousness is reality and all reality is of the same sort as consciousness.

But the world does not appear to us as a flux of change ; on the contrary, it seems to consist of a series of more or less static objects occupying space. How comes it, then, that in ordinary life we so consistently misconceive its real nature ? Bergson's answer to this question involves his celebrated distinction between the intellect and intuition. Briefly, Bergson holds that we arrive at metaphysical truth not by exercising the intellect, but by paying heed to the deliverances of a faculty which he calls " Intuition," and it is through " Intuition " and not through intellectual apprehension that we realise our own participation in the vital surge of change.

The distinction between intellect and Intuition may be most conveniently introduced by means of an account of Bergson's treatment of time. Bergson's theory of time constitutes an important feature of his philosophy, time being for him the very core and essence of reality. In Bergsonian

[1] See pp. 178-180.

language, time is identified with an aspect of the *élan vital* which has not yet been stressed, the aspect of it which Bergson calls " Duration."

Throughout the history of philosophy the nature of time has occupied the attention of philosophers. The questions which time raises are among the most difficult in philosophy, and two thousand years of more or less unintermittent speculation have produced little or no agreement as to what time is. Some have held that time is real ; others, like Kant, that it is only a form imposed upon reality by the nature of our own understandings, reality itself being timeless. This lack of agreement is only to be expected since theories of the nature of time are, to a very large extent, determined by a philosopher's general metaphysical position, of which, indeed, they form an integral part. The difficulty of the questions and the technical character of the discussions involved must serve as my excuse for not devoting a special chapter to the consideration of philosophical theories of time, although the problem has, to some extent, been touched upon by implication in connection with our discussion of change in Chapter VII.[1] Bergson's contribution to the problem is, however, so instructive and so closely bound up with his doctrine of " Intuition," that a brief summary of his treatment is essential to the understanding of his philosophy.

Mathematical Time.   Bergson begins by drawing an important distinction between two different conceptions which are included in the meaning of the word " time." In the first place, there is what he calls mathematical or scientific time. This time does not form part of the reality of the so-called external world of material things : it is simply a relation which we interpose between material things. If we consider any material thing which passes through two successive states, and then double the rapidity of succession between the two states, the operation of doubling the rapidity of succession will in no way affect the reality or the nature of the states, nor of the material thing

[1] See pp. 177, 178.

which passes through the states. If, further, we imagine the rapidity of the succession of states to be infinitely increased, so that the whole of existence were presented instantaneously to the contemplation of an omnipotent being, the relations between the objects presented would remain constant, and the reality of the objects would therefore remain unaffected. Time, then, as science conceives it, is not part of the material world. We think of time as a relation between things, because our intellect requires us to conceive of things as succeeding one another in time. Mathematical time is, therefore, a form which appears to be necessary for the understanding of reality by the intellect.

Duration and Intuition.   There is, however, another kind of time which Bergson calls "Duration"; and Duration is nothing but the *élan vital* itself. As we have seen, change is the reality of the existence of a living being ; our actual experience, the one thing of which we are completely sure, is a constant flow ; it is this flow which Bergson calls Duration. Now Duration is not a mere succession of instants ; it is, in Bergson's words, "the continuous progress of the past which gnaws into the future." In virtue of the fact that we ourselves are living beings, we belong to the stream of Duration, and, if we attend sufficiently closely to our own experience, we can become conscious of the pulsing of Duration within us. But our attention must not be an attention of the intellect ; it must rather be of an instinctive character. It is through instinct that we feel ourselves to be one with reality ; it is through instinct that we appear to ourselves to enter into the flow of life and to live it. Now Bergson gives a distinctive name to instinct, or rather to that aspect of the instinctive side of our natures through which we become directly conscious of the Duration in which we participate. It is instinct in this relationship that he calls "Intuition." "Instinct," says Bergson, "is sympathy. If this sympathy could extend its object and also reflect upon itself, it would give us the key to vital operations." Thus Intuition is simply instinct conscious of itself : it is instinct that has become disinterested, self-conscious, capable of reflecting upon its object and of enlarging it indefinitely. Can we further define this intuitive knowledge of things?

Character of Intuitive Knowledge.   Let us revert for a moment to the distinction between wholes and aggregates emphasised in the chapter on Hegel's philosophy.[1] I illustrated this distinction by means of the difference between a symphony and an aggregate of notes, and pointed out the sense in which the symphony could be regarded as more than the sum of its notes. From the point of view of physical science the symphony was, I pointed out, simply the sum-total of its constituent parts. In other words, it *was* all the vibrations in the atmosphere which were set in motion by the instruments of the players. From the point of view of aesthetics, however, the symphony is a whole which cannot be analysed into its constituent parts without falsification.

There would appear, then, to be two separate and distinct ways in which we may regard a symphony. Adopting the first, we shall think of it merely as an aggregate or accumulation of the various notes of which it is composed, just as we may think of a picture as the sum total of the various paints and colours which the artist places upon his canvas. But, as we saw in Chapter XV,[2] there is another way. We may regard the symphony not as aggregate but as a whole, that is to say, as something which is brought into existence by the coming together of its parts, but which is, nevertheless, a new and complete entity over and above the sum of those parts. Now whether or not it is the case, as Hegelians would maintain, that this is the *only* point of view from which a symphony may be *truly* regarded, it is certainly the case that it is a perfectly legitimate point of view. There is, that is to say, a very important sense in which the reality of the symphony may be said to consist not of the isolated and separate notes of which it is composed, but of the indivisible and complete whole which, as we say, *is* the symphony considered as an object of aesthetic valuation. Now the view

[1] See Chapter XV, pp. 415, 416.   [2] See Chapter XV, p. 416-418.

which Intuition gives us of reality is like the second way of regarding the symphony. It is by Intuition that we enter into and appreciate the nature and meaning of the symphony as an indivisible whole : it is by Intuition that we enter into and grasp the nature and meaning of reality as an indivisible whole. But if Intuition is involved in the appreciation of a picture or a symphony, it is involved still more directly in their creation. The great artist creates by penetrating through the superficial appearance presented by his subject to the reality beneath : it is, in fact, his vision of this reality that constitutes his greatness as an artist. This vision he places upon the canvas, and it is, as we have seen,[1] in the quality of this vision and not in the paint, the colours, the form, the technique, or the faithful portrayal of the subject that the value of the picture lies. And just as it is only by entering through sympathy into the life and meaning of his subject that the artist succeeds in grasping it, so it is through the sympathy which is Intuition that we are enabled to enter into the ceaseless flow of the changing reality, which is also the reality of our life, and to grasp its nature.

Thus, the Intuition we have of the real nature of our living experience as a flux of ceaseless change is knowledge of reality itself, and all beliefs about the nature of reality other than those arrived at by Intuition are misleading.

The Intellect as a Practical Faculty.

The presentation of reality as a continuous flux of change, in which we ourselves participate by virtue of our enjoyment of the intuitive faculty, raises in a new form the distinction between reality and appearance which we have already considered in our treatment of Objective Idealism. For, it cannot be too often repeated, reality, as it appears, is very far from being a flux of continuous change. Reality, as it appears, is a collection of solid and comparative static objects extended in space. How, then, and why does it so appear ? Bergson's answer to this question brings us back to the distinction between

[1] See Chapter XIII, p. 355.

Intuition and the intellect, and introduces us to one of the most distinctive features of his philosophy, namely, his conception of the intellect.

The intellect, according to Bergson, is a special faculty evolved for the purposes of action. Life in a world of ceaseless flow and change would present difficulties from the point of view of effective action which the intellect is designed to overcome. The intellect, therefore, makes cuts across the living flow of reality, and carves out of it solid objects which we call material objects, and separate states of consciousness which persist until they are succeeded by other states. But the distinct outlines we see in an object are not really there in the flux of reality. They are only the design that we have imposed on reality to suit our own purposes. The edges and surfaces, the shapes and forms of things, are, as it were, the representation of the actions that we desire to take with regard to these things : this representation which emanates from ourselves is reflected back upon ourselves by reality as by a mirror, so that we falsely believe reality to possess in its own right the modifications and features that proceed from us.

In the case of motion this manipulation by the intellect of reality produces contradictions which are so surprising, that even in ordinary life they sometimes thrust themselves upon the attention. Philosophers have devoted much attention to these contradictions to which the conception of motion foisted upon us by the intellect gives rise. In an earlier chapter I considered some of these contradictions, instancing Zeno's problem of the arrow and the difficulties half seriously propounded by William James in connection with the lapse of a period of time.[1] I pointed out also how the difficulties to which these problems give rise have led many philosophers to believe that change and motion are unreal.

The Intellect as Cinematographic.   Now Bergson, as we have seen, holds that motion, change and time are—or rather " is," since each is only the *élan vital* considered

[1] See Chapter VII, pp. 172–174.

under a special aspect—the sole reality, and he proceeds, therefore, to attribute the difficulties which Zeno and William James propounded to the cutting-up operations of the intellect. The intellect takes the flow of motion and cuts it up into moments and points : it takes the lapse of time and cuts it up into hours and half-hours. But these divisions imposed by the intellect, these stops inserted in the continuous flow of reality, are unreal and give rise to unreal results. It is not motion and time that the intellect grasps, but points in motion and intervals of time. The intellect, in fact, is cinematographic.

One of the most ingenious of Bergson's similes in illustration of the operations of the intellect is his comparison of the intellect to the cinematograph.[1] The cinematograph takes snapshot views of something which is moving, say a regiment of soldiers, each of which represents the regiment in a fixed and stable attitude. You may lay these snapshot photographs side by side and multiply them indefinitely, but you will not have recreated the movement of the original ; you will be presented only with an infinite number of static pictures. In order, then, that your pictures may become animated, you must introduce movement somewhere ; and it is not until you unroll your film on the operator's apparatus, that you substitute for a series of static pictures a moving representation of the moving original.

The pictures of reality presented to us by the intellect are like the series of static snapshots before they are placed upon the apparatus, and they substitute, in a similar way a succession of objects extended in space for the ceaseless flow and change of the original. Thus the intellect presents us with a false view of reality, because, in order to further the purposes of action, that is to say, the ends which we desire to achieve, it represents reality as composed of points upon which we may rest. " If matter," says Bergson, " appeared to us as a perpetual flowing, we should assign no termination to any of our actions. . . . In order that our activity may

---

[1] We have already made use of it in connection with the notion of change. See Chapter VII, pp. 205, 206.

leap from an act to an act, it is necessary that matter should pass from a state to a state."

Hence the intellect seeks always to present to us the results of motions and the ends of action, just because it is not interested in the fact of motion and the reality of action. To sum up, the intellect introduces stops or articulations into the ceaseless flow of reality ; and it is these stops or articulations, which the intellect has inserted for us, that provide the groundwork for the commonsense notion of reality as composed of solid objects which are separated from each other by real distinctions.

The Intellect and Matter. At this point, however, it is necessary to make a reservation ; for, in cutting up the flow of the universe into a world of material objects, the intellect is not acting *quite* arbitrarily. Matter is not a *mere* creation of the intellect ; it exists in reality in its own right ; at least, *something* exists other than the direct flow of life, which is the aspect of the *élan vital* hitherto considered, and to this " something " intellect is specifically related. The intellect and matter are, in Bergson's view, relative to each other : they were cut simultaneously by an identical process from the *élan vital* which contained and contains them both.

But when we put the question, " What is the real nature of this aspect of the *élan vital*, which the intellect works up for us into a world of solid matter ? " the answer is not so clear as we could wish.

The *élan vital* is a creative impulsion of endless duration : but its continual movement does not proceed without interruption. At a certain point the flow is interrupted and, like the recoil of a spring, turns back upon itself. This inverse movement is matter. Everything is still ceaseless change and flow, but matter is a flow in a direction opposite to that of the vital surge itself. In order to illustrate this conception of matter, Bergson again has recourse to metaphor. Life is likened to a rocket whose extinguished remains fall to the ground as matter ; and again, life is like a fountain, which, expanding as it rises, partially arrests or delays the drops which fall back : the jet of the fountain is vital activity in its highest form, the drops which fall back are the creative movement dissipated : in short, they are matter.

The Ground for Free Will.

Bergson's view of the intellect as a tool which has been fashioned in the course of evolution for the purposes of life enables him to approach the vexed question of free will from a new angle. Bergson admits the contention of the determinists that, if we consider any single action in isolation, it is possible to prove by irrefutable reasoning that it is entirely determined by what has preceded it. This contention, he says, is true, whether with the materialists we attribute the causation of the action to the influence of physical environment, and see in every case of ill temper another instance of faulty digestion, or whether, with the psycho-analysts and self-determinists, we locate it in the psychology of the individual, and pointing to the obvious fact that he is responsible neither for his motives nor his desires, demonstrate that his action is determined by the strongest motive or desire at the moment.

But, says Bergson, this interpretation is only true of the action taken in isolation. And the action taken in isolation is a false intellectual abstraction. It is the intellect which, as we have seen, represents our life as divided into states of consciousness which remain static until replaced by other states, and actions which proceed from these states ; and having made this abstraction, the intellect proceeds to reason about the actions so abstracted, as if they were isolated and self-contained entities springing from and entirely conditioned by the preceding states.

But, as we have seen, the life of the individual is not to be regarded as a succession of changing states ; the life of the individual is a continuous and indivisible flow, and it is precisely when taken as such that it is seen to be free and undetermined. Divide the individual's life into parts, consider the individual's actions separately, and you will find that each part and each action is determined by its predecessors. But, as we have seen,[1] the sum of the parts is not the same as the whole personality. And what is true of the parts is not, therefore, true of the personality. It is the nature of life to be creative, and the individual taken as whole is necessarily creative from the mere fact that he is alive. But if his life is creative, and creative in each moment of it, it is clear that it is not completely determined by what went before. If it were so determined, it would only be an expression of the old, and not a creation of the new.

Free will, then, is creative action ; while determinism is a belief imposed upon us by our intellectual view of reality, which reasons so convincingly, not about our lives as a whole, but about a false abstraction from our lives which it calls individual actions. But do we after all really believe in determinism ? Our reason may, indeed, be convinced, but our instinctive belief persisting in the teeth of reason is that we are free. Why ? Because this instinctive belief is a quality of Intuition, whose function it is to comprehend our life as a whole. In so doing, it realises that, as a whole, life is a creative activity, and insists, therefore, on its freedom to create the future.

Criticism. Bergson's philosophy, despite its obvious attractiveness, contains difficulties which expose it to damaging criticisms. These criticisms do not, however, form part of any general philosophical tradition, nor do they constitute the starting point for a new school. I have, therefore, in accordance with the policy stated in the Introduction decided to omit them. The reader who is interested will find them summarised in my *Introduction to Modern Philosophy*, Chapter V.

BERGSON, HENRI   Time and Free Will.
BERGSON, HENRI   Creative Evolution.
BERGSON, HENRI   The Two Sources of Religion and Morality.
GUNN, J. A.   Bergson and his Philosophy.
LEROY, EDOUARD   A New Philosophy by Henri Bergson.
CARR, H. WILDON   The Philosophy of Change.

[1] See Chapter IX, pp. 248-250.

3. Outline of Whitehead's Philosophy

I. CRITICISM OF MATERIALIST
SCIENCE

Imaginative Effort Involved in the Understanding of Whitehead. In the case of Whitehead's[1] philosophy the ordinary difficulties of exposition are enhanced by others of a quite special kind. In the first place, Whitehead's ideas are intrinsically difficult to grasp. They involve a total reconstruction of our imaginative picture of the universe, and, even when the intellect is convinced, the imagination refuses to implement the conviction. It is said that the men of the Renaissance, who had been convinced by Galileo and Copernicus that the earth was small, the sun large, and that the former rotated round the latter, were, nevertheless, incapable of the imaginative astronomical reconstruction of the heavens to which their acceptance of the new views committed them. They still thought of the sun as a little yellow ball going round the earth every night and turning up in the east in the morning. Similarly, many of those who in our own day have sought to grasp the general theory of relativity, and succeeded to the extent of an intellectual realisation of the modifications in the Newtonian conceptions of gravitation and force which the theory entails, are completely unable to picture to themselves the kind of universe which the theory of relativity apparently describes. A similar difficulty besets those who would understand Whitehead's philosophy. The acceptance of it requires us to abandon the notions not only of things but of place and time, and

[1] Born 1861.

to substitute the conception of the universe as a process which, while neither physical nor mental, is more analogous to a process of feeling than to anything else in our experience. This process, which is the universe, we are bidden to think of as going on everywhere all the time.

Most of us, I fear, are incapable of the imaginative effort required. The imagination does not necessarily outstrip the intellect. It often follows in its train. Hence, just as we may expect our grandchildren to take Einstein's conceptions imaginatively for granted with as much readiness as we take the world picture of Copernicus and Newton, so it is possible that Whitehead's philosophy will by subsequent generations be more readily comprehensible than it is by ours. Many other philosophies, those of Kant and Hegel for example, involve an equally radical departure from the imaginative picture of the world conceived by common sense ; but, although nobody has yet succeeded in visualising the Absolute as a fact, it is, I think, already less difficult to envisage the sort of world that Hegel's philosophy affirms, than it is to picture the world to which Whitehead introduces us.

In the second place, Professor Whitehead's views have themselves undergone a more or less continuous process of modification. Nor is it by any means certain that the process is yet complete. His two most important metaphysical works, *Science and the Modern World* and *Process and Reality*, present substantial points of difference, while both depart in important respects from the comparatively simple standpoint of his earlier book, *The Concept of Nature*. Professor Whitehead's earlier work is largely critical in character, his chief concern being to suggest far reaching doubts as to the adequacy of the accepted scientific view of the physical world. In his later work he has attempted to construct on the foundations laid by his criticism an all-embracing metaphysical system, a system which has grown continuously more elaborate, as it has grown more comprehensive. An account of Professor Whitehead's views at any particular stage of their development would, therefore, fail to do justice either to the earlier writings or to the later.

Obscurity of Whitehead's Writing.

In the third place, Professor Whitehead's mode of writing is exceedingly obscure. Nor is it always clear that this obscurity is due to the nature of the subject matter. There are, as I hinted in the Introduction, two kinds of obscurity—the expression of obscurity and obscurity of expression. The first is pardonable, perhaps inevitable. There is, as I pointed out, no *a priori* reason why the universe should be such as to be readily intelligible to a twentieth century mind, or why a man of average intelligence should be able to grasp the profounder thoughts of a philosopher of original insight. But obscurity of expression is simply another name for bad craftsmanship. A writer should study to make himself understood, and, the more difficult his subject, the more paramount is the obligation of clarity. It is by no means certain that Professor Whitehead has always recognised this obligation.

Indeed, so obscure is his writing, that few contemporary philosophers have any assurance that they have fully grasped its import. In the absence of this assurance the interpretation of Whitehead's meaning by one philosopher will be found to vary markedly from that of another. " What does Professor Whitehead mean by that ? " There is no question which is so frequently asked by contemporary philosophers ; none which it is more difficult to answer. That Whitehead's views are of first-rate importance is almost universally agreed. But there is no sort of agreement as to what they are.

Not the least of the difficulties by which the reader of Whitehead is confronted is his habit of using familiar words in new senses. He has also introduced a number of entirely new terms into philosophy. It is at least doubtful whether the traditional philosophical terms would not have conveyed his meaning as well as these new ones, and, while the doubt remains, a critic may always plausibly suggest that the apparent originality, no less than the difficulty, of Whitehead's philosophy is due to his use of unfamiliar terms and of familiar terms in novel senses. There is little doubt that this factor of obscurity militates strongly against the acceptance of Whitehead's views. So far as the imaginative difficulty referred to above is concerned, Whitehead is at little or no disadvantage compared with Bergson. Each has constructed a metaphysic whose fundamental tenets are remote from common sense ; each asks us to accept a cosmos which it outruns the ability of our imaginations to picture. Nevertheless, there is far less difficulty in understanding Bergson's philosophy for the reason that Bergson takes great pains to be clear and to be understood. Bergson is a master of exposition ; even the reader who fails to comprehend his thought is delighted with his style. But the reader of Whitehead, although his attention is often quickened by remarks of astonishing insight, his comprehension assisted by some illuminating phrase and his spirit elevated by passages of noble eloquence, is only too often baffled and irritated by the prevailing obscurity. In the face of these difficulties the most that I can hope to do is to outline a number of Whitehead's leading conceptions, devoting special attention to those which bear critically upon the materialist scheme of the universe, which is also the traditional scientific scheme of the universe, outlined in the last chapter. It is, then, as a criticism of scientific assumptions, methods and results rather than as a complete sketch of a comprehensive metaphysical system, that the following pages should be read.[1]

[1] On reading through the foregoing, I am conscious that I may have done disservice to Whitehead by frightening away possible readers from his books. Such an outcome would be very far from my intention, and would mean serious loss to those, if any, who had been deterred.

The restriction of the scope of this book to metaphysics, precludes me from giving any account of Whitehead's ethical, religious, political and historical writings. This restriction is in Whitehead's case unfortunate, since his views on morals, politics and history are directly derivable from his metaphysical position ; indeed, they are quite deliberately introduced as applications of it. Apart from their metaphysical significance, they

The World-Picture of Seventeenth-Century Science.

Whitehead's starting point is, for our present purpose, to be found in his demonstration of the disastrous results for science of Hume's criticism of causation. Science presupposes a world consisting of separate pieces of matter located in space. " What is the world made of ? ", asked the scientist-philosophers of ancient Greece. " A succession of instantaneous configurations of matter, or of material, if you wish to include stuff more subtle than ordinary matter, the ether for example," is Whitehead's summary of the answer given by the seventeenth-century originators of modern science. These configurations of matter were, he points out, thought of as possessing only primary qualities.[1] Matter possessing primary qualities impinges, so runs the scientific account, upon the sense organs, and, as a consequence, neural impulses are conveyed to the brain. Consciousness is brought into play, with the result that there occurs a sensation, a sensation, namely, of the particular material configuration which stimulated the sense organs. The story should by now be sufficiently familiar to the reader, and there is no need to enlarge on the details.[2] But, according to the seventeenth century scientists, the sensation did not merely represent the configuration ; it endowed it with secondary qualities, imparting to it warmth, colour, and texture, imputing also beauty and holiness. These almost instinctive

are highly important in themselves. Not only are they illuminated with flashes of penetrative insight, but they are instinct throughout with a humane and cultivated liberalism, in that sense of " liberalism " in which the word stands for all that most separates our species from the animal creation, for all that our modern civilisation most desperately needs. For these reasons, I would recommend those who are approaching Whitehead for the first time to start their reading with the nontechnical chapters in the first half of *Science and the Modern World* and with *Adventures of Ideas*, in which history and religion, art and morals are interpreted in the light of Whitehead's fundamental metaphysical notions. *Adventures of Ideas*, Whitehead's most substantial, recent book, consists entirely of these interpretations.

[1] See Chapter II, p. 40, for the use of the term primary qualities in Locke's philosophy.
[2] See Chapter I, pp. 31–34, for a fuller version.

assumptions of the scientists were, as Whitehead points out, adequately embodied in Locke's Representationalism.[1] Although every configuration of matter was separate and distinct from every other, it was held to be causally related to it. Seventeenth century science presupposed, in other words, an orderly scheme of nature, and the order of nature was in the last resort based upon causation. The belief in the orderliness of the world was expressed in the universally accepted maxim, " Same cause, same effect."

Its Difficulties. 1. CAUSATION AND INDUCTION. The

notion of causation so conceived was, as we saw in Chapter VIII, subjected to damaging criticism by Hume, and—Whitehead is particularly insistent upon the point—the criticism has never been satisfactorily met. What is more, no scientist ever seemed to realise how damaging it was ; nobody ever noticed that, in Whitehead's words, it made "nonsense of the scientists' scheme." For, as Whitehead shows, unless it can be established that there is some connecting tie or bond linking cause and effect, the notion of causation must be abandoned for mere regularity of. sequence, which, since it is in no sense necessary regularity, may at any moment cease to operate. But to introduce a connecting tie or bond, is to give up the scientific presupposition that nature consists of distinct " configurations of matter " separated by space.

Not only does Hume's criticism make " nonsense of the scientists' scheme " of the world ; it is equally destructive of our belief in induction. For the " scientists' scheme " envisages an external world composed of separate pieces of matter no one of which contains within itself " inherent reference " to any other. In this scheme each piece of matter just *is*, and *is* completely itself. Now the belief in induction[2] presupposes that the state of nature at one time justifies the human mind in entertaining a certain expectation in regard to the state of nature at some other

[1] See Chapter II, pp. 41, 42.
[2] See Chapter V, pp. 130–132, for an account of Induction.

time. From one state of things, in fact, the mind is held to be justified in inferring another. But this expectation and the inferences which are based upon it are only legitimate, if nature at one time does in fact refer to nature at another. Yet such reference presupposes in its turn, some underlying connection between one state of nature and another, a bridge, as it were, over which the mind can pass as it " infers " what will be or what was from what is now. If, however, science is right in supposing that nature consists of separate pieces of matter extended in space, owning neither tie nor bond to join them together, the belief in induction is not based upon anything that can be observed in nature. The belief in induction is not, then, justified by anything in the "scientists' scheme." Yet we are convinced that our belief in induction is valid, just as certainly as we are convinced that causation is a fact.

Its Difficulties. 2. DUALISM OF MIND AND MATTER.

The difficulties in which the "scientists' scheme" is involved by the so-called duality of mind and matter are no less than those presented by causation and induction. In the last chapter, I described the problems to which the apparent fact of mind-body interaction gives rise, and showed how Materialism arose in part as the result of the attempt to solve these problems by eliminating the conception of a free and causally independent mind. To Materialism regarded as a philosophy there are, as I tried to show, serious objections. Yet, if we reject it, the problem for which it sought to provide a solution remains. Now this problem, Whitehead insists, is insoluble, so long as we think of mind and matter as two different substances initially separate from each other, but brought together in some incomprehensible relation within the living organism.

The starting point of the traditional scientific Dualism is, he points out, " from independently existing substances, matter and mind." Each of these independent substances is qualified by its own appropriate features and functions, and each is affected by the presence of the other. Matter, as Whitehead puts it, " suffers modification of its external relation of locomotion and the mind suffers modification of its contemplated objects." But how, Whitehead asks, can two such independent substances be brought together? How can they modify each other? Interaction between two completely different substances separated by a gulf of real otherness is as inconceivable as causal connection between two material substances separated by a gulf of real space.

Its Difficulties. 3. SUBSTANCE AND QUALITIES. The notion of substance and its qualities fits in no better with the scientific scheme than the notion of mind and body. The problems raised by the nature of substance were dealt with at length in Chapter VI, and will by now be fairly familiar to the reader. Common sense presupposes the existence of a continuous enduring stuff which is the foundation for the qualities which belong to it. Yet (a) no such stuff can be discovered, (b) even if it could, we cannot tell what is its relation to the qualities. In Chapter VI, I indicated some of the solutions which philosophers have propounded for the problems which the notion of substance raises. That none of them is altogether satisfactory, most philosophers would, I think, agree. The solution most commonly adopted has been that of Idealism, which assigns the qualities of substance to the agency of the knowing mind which projects them upon the substances it knows. And this, says Whitehead, is in effect the only course open to us, if the scientists' picture of the world is correct. For science, as we saw in Chapter XII,[1] eviscerates the world of all secondary qualities. If the scientists are right, " there is," to quote Whitehead, " no light or colour as a fact in external nature. There is merely motion of material. Again, when the light enters your eyes and falls on the retina, there is merely motion of material. Then your nerves are affected and your brain is affected, and again

[1] See Chapter XII, pp. 314, 315.

this is merely motion of material. The same line of arguments holds for sound, substituting waves in the air for waves in the ether, and ears for eyes." Into such a world mind projects the secondary qualities which we know in sense experience. Substance being thus stripped of all its qualities, what is really " out there " in the world ? The answer apparently is electrical charges. To quote again the celebrated passage in which Whitehead sums up the implications of Locke's philosophy : " Thus nature gets credit which should in truth be reserved for ourselves : the rose for its scent : the nightingale for his song : and the sun for his radiance. The poets are entirely mistaken. They should address their lyrics to themselves, and should turn them into odes of self-congratulation on the excellency of the human mind. Nature is a dull affair, soundless, scentless, colourless ; merely, the hurrying of material, endlessly, meaninglessly."

Apart from the philosophical difficulties entailed by this view, at some of which we have already glanced,[1] it is, Whitehead points out, frankly incredible. Nobody believes that the face of a loved person consists merely of electrical charges or of arrangements of mathematically conceived point events which *he* has endowed with its warmth, its contours, its colours and its softness.

The Scientific World without Value.

Not only is the scientific world eviscerated of sense qualities ; it is also without values. It is neither good, nor beautiful, nor holy, nor just. There is thus nothing in nature which justifies or answers to our ethical, aesthetic and religious aspirations, which are the merest will-o'-the-wisps of our consciousness, self-spun fancies which the mind seeks to invest with a baseless objectivity, and projects for its comfort and assurance upon the empty canvas of a valueless universe. But a world which is without value, Whitehead points out, is also a world without meaning. If the world has no meaning, there cannot be any explanation of the world which a mind can grasp. The world just is ; it cannot be explained.

[1] See Chapters II and VI.

But the scientific world has meaning ; it does explain itself. Indeed, it was on the assumption that it obeyed certain laws, laws which, taken together, constituted what is known as the order of nature, that man succeeded in putting together the fabric of modern science. In addition, then, to the facts which science maps, there must, says Whitehead, be something in the universe to account for the facts being as they are. Yet this something is entirely omitted from science's account of the facts. To put the point in another way, in order that science may be possible, there must be more in the world than science admits to occur. This " more " is an element of meaning which Whitehead often seems to equate with value. The argument may be continued in Whitehead's own words. The world of modern physics consists, as we have seen, entirely of matter in movement : " Locomotion of matter involves change in spatial relationship." But, Whitehead insists, " it involves nothing more than that. Matter involves nothing more than spatiality, and the passive support of qualifications. It can be qualified, and it must be qualified. But qualification is a bare fact, which is just itself. This is the grand doctrine of Nature as a self-sufficient, meaningless complex of facts." But such a world does not even contain the ground for the forces and stresses which are found to operate in it. The following quotation from *Nature and Life*, a little book published in 1934, which contains a summary statement of Whitehead's philosophy, will bring this line of thought to its conclusion.

" Newton's methodology for physics was an overwhelming success. But the forces which he introduced left Nature still without meaning or value. In the essence of a material body—in its mass, motion, and shape—there was no reason for the law of gravitation. Even if the particular forces could be conceived as the accidents of a cosmic epoch, there was no reason in the Newtonian concepts of mass and motion why material bodies should be connected by any stress between them. Yet the notion of stresses, as essential connections between bodies, was a fundamental factor in the Newtonian concept of Nature. What Newton left for empirical investigation was the determination of the particular stresses now existing. In this determination he made a magnificent beginning by isolating the stresses indicated by his law of gravitation. But he left no hint why, in the nature of things, there should be any stresses at all. The arbitrary motions of the bodies were thus explained by the arbitrary stresses between material bodies, conjoined with their spatiality, their mass, and their initial states of motion. By introducing stresses—in particular the law of gravitation—instead of the welter of detailed transformations of motion, he greatly increased the systematic aspect of Nature. But he left all the factors of the system—more particularly, mass and stress—in the position of detached facts devoid of any reason for their compresence. He thus illustrated a great philosophic truth, that a dead Nature can give no reasons. *All ultimate reasons are in terms of aim at value.*" (My italics.)

What Humanism Entails. The world of science, then, Whitehead is pointing out, is a world from which value has been completely eliminated. Yet poetry and music and art, no less than ethics and religion, testify to the recognition which value obtains from the human soul. The supposition that they are merely subjective flights of the human spirit, owning no counterpart, finding no guarantee in the universe, reduces them to figments. Yet, if the scientific picture of the universe is true, this precisely is the status which we must assign to them.

No philosopher has written more forcibly than Whitehead of the significance of religion and art in the life of man ; no writer has stressed more emphatically " the divorce of science from the affirmations of our aesthetic and ethical experience." Because of this divorce, religion assumes the character of a collective delusion and mysticism of an individual madness. " Thus the science of Nature stands opposed to the presuppositions of humanism." For, Whitehead insists, the intimations of the ethical and religious consciousness have as much right to be treated as objectively valid as the perceptions of the external world upon which science is based. " The presuppositions of humanism " are as universal and as deserving of respect as those of science. If, then, we must choose between the two— and it is precisely this choice that science forces upon us— it is science that we must reject, in so far as science purports to give a complete and exhaustive account of the universe, to tell us what the world is really like. For nobody, after all, really believes in it. It contradicts too many of our basic convictions. Nobody really believes that there is no ground for causation and inference ; that the qualities of things do not in fact belong to them ; that the faces of those we love consist exclusively of electrical charges ; that the world is meaningless and offers no basis for religion or justification for ethics. Nobody, in fact, believes that " matter in motion is all."

The Scientific World as an Abstraction.

But if the scientific concept of the world, " is," as Whitehead insists, " quite unbelievable," how did it come to be formed ? By abstracting certain aspects of reality and completely neglecting all others. This " conception of the universe is," he says, " surely framed in terms of high abstractions, and the paradox only arises because we have mistaken our abstractions for concrete realities." Of the many abstractions involved in the formation of the scientific picture of the world, the abstraction of objects from their relations to other objects, and of substance from its qualities are the two upon which Whitehead chiefly insists.

The first abstraction we have already met in our discussion of causation under the name " Simple Location."[1] This, it will be remembered is the view that a thing is at a place at a particular time. Whitehead writes of it as follows : " The Ionian philosophers asked, What is nature made of ? The answer is couched in terms of stuff, or matter, or material—the particular name chosen is indifferent—which

[1] See Chapter VIII, p. 217.

has the property of simple location in space and time, or, if you adopt the more modern ideas, in space-time. What I mean by matter, or material, is anything which has this property of *simple location*. . . . The characteristic common both to space and time is that material can be said to be *here* in space and *here* in time, or *here* in space-time, in a perfectly definite sense which does not require for its explanation any reference to other regions of space-time." It is this notion that, as we have seen, lies at the root of the difficulties which causation and induction create for science. Implying, as it does, that a real gulf of spatial otherness separates things from each other, and a real gulf of temporal difference divides the state of the world at one time from the state of the world at another, it cuts away the basis from any interpretation whether scientific or philosophical of the universe which presupposes that events are somehow linked together and somehow refer to each other, that the universe in other words is a system. Yet this supposition is what causation and induction entail.

Misplaced Concreteness.

Now " abstraction is nothing else than omission of part of the truth." Therefore, the view that " occupation of space is the final real fact, without reference to any other instant, or to any other piece of matter, or to any other region of space," and that " instantaneous material configurations " are, therefore, " simply located " is regarded by Whitehead as a fallacy. More precisely it is an example of what he calls the " Fallacy of Misplaced Concreteness," that is to say, the taking as real of something, whether a physical thing or scientific conception, that has been abstracted from reality for special purposes by thought. The notion of substance and its qualities, is, Whitehead holds, another example of this fallacy.

Whitehead's arguments for the rejection of the common-sense notion of the spatially separate thing on the ground that it is an abstraction, are not markedly different from those adduced in the chapter on Hegel's philosophy in support of the Axiom of Internal Relations. Their conclusion is that to separate a thing from its environment and its context, and then to give an account of it so separated, is to give an account of it as it is not. It is, in other words, to describe an abstraction, and a world which, like that of modern science, is supposed to consist exclusively of these isolated separated things, is itself an abstraction.

While Hegel's reasons for this conclusion are mainly of a logical order, Whitehead adduces additional considerations derived from modern science, and points out that for physics itself the concepts of Simple Location and of Misplaced Concreteness are presenting great and increasing difficulties. They are, in fact, becoming unworkable. Modern science is no longer able to retain the notion of *the thing* whose boundaries are clear and fixed. " The environment," as Whitehead puts it, " with its peculiarities seeps into the group-agitation which we term matter, and the group-agitations extend their character to the environment." What, then, are we to say of the abstracting and departmentalising procedure of the scientists, which, ignoring the fact that " boundaries " are becoming increasingly untenable, pins down certain things for examination and ignores others, and ignores the relations of the things pinned down to others ? In one of Whitehead's striking phrases, any interpretation which, while including some activities excludes others, " severs the patterns of process which extend beyond all boundaries."

Criticism of Bifurcation. This leads us to the concept of " Bifurcation." Science, Whitehead declares, in another famous phrase, " Bifurcates the universe," that is to say, it draws an arbitrary line between what it is prepared to take account of as important and what it proposes to ignore. Thus it accepts some activities as relevant to its interpretation, such as, for example, those which are denoted by the concepts of energy, electricity, and force, and rejects as irrelevant all that is implied by the creative activity of the artist and the religious experience of the mystic. There is

" bifurcation " again in the distinctions between substance and qualities, cause and effect, thing and environment. Above all there is " bifurcation " between mind and body, life and matter, spirit and nature. There, spread out in space is nature, and here, inserting itself into the bits of nature, which we call bodies, is life, producing effects upon bodies which are other than those which the laws of physics will enable us to predict, and introducing an element of arbitrary caprice which we call free will into the apparently orderly scheme of nature.

Such, says Whitehead in effect, is the conventional pattern of the universe which the scientist takes for granted. Unable within its borders to find room for moral and aesthetic experience, for creativity and free will, science has had to leave them outside the pattern. Yet in actual concrete experience, they refuse to remain outside ; they insist on being taken into account. How, then, remodel the scheme of things so as to admit them ? Whitehead's answer is, in effect, by rejecting the principle of bifurcation in all its applications, that is to say, by refusing to separate substance from quality, thing from environment, cause from effect, life from matter, or mind from body, since all these things, taken in and by themselves, are only abstractions.

The Success of Science. For certain special purposes the scientific scheme works well enough. " As a system of concepts for the organisation of scientific research," its success, he concedes, has been astonishing. " In this respect, it is fully worthy of the genius of the century " (the seventeenth) " which produced it. It has held its own as the guiding principle of scientific studies ever since. It is still reigning. Every university in the world organises itself in accordance with it. No alternative system of organising the pursuit of scientific truth has been suggested. It is not only reigning, but it is without rival." And yet, as Whitehead has already insisted, as an account of things as they really are, " it is quite unbelievable."

The success of science has been won by " dividing the

seamless coat of the universe." But the division is proving increasingly unsatisfactory even within the boundaries of science. Modern physics no longer finds materialistic concepts adequate ; the theory of relativity has banished the notion of isolated things subjected to the influence of separately operative forces ; psychology is unable to maintain the duality of mind and body. But, even if they worked for science whose concern is primarily practical, philosophy, which has no such practical purpose to serve, can tolerate no such arbitrary distinctions. Philosophy cannot afford to deal in abstractions. It must try to give an account of the universe which faithfully renders what *is* ; it must try, in other words, to describe concrete reality. That it itself in common with all thought is an abstraction, is, of course, true. But that which is concrete may yet be describable in abstract terms. It is precisely this task, the task of rendering the concrete in terms of the abstract, that Whitehead lays upon philosophy. Its performance brings us to Whitehead's positive contribution to the understanding of the universe.

II. THE PHILOSOPHY OF ORGANISM

General Statement.   The fundamental principles of Whitehead's philosophy derive naturally enough from the foregoing criticism of science. Let us suppose that we divest ourselves of the notion of things existing in space at particular moments of time ; that we agree that there are " no instants, conceived as simple primary entities, there is no Nature at an instant," and that " matter, involving spatiality and the passive support of qualifications " together with " every single item in this general doctrine " has been jettisoned. What are we to substitute ? The notion of " process conceived as a complex activity with internal relations[1] between its various factors." Everything in the universe—if I may be permitted to invoke temporarily and for purposes of exposition only the improper conception

[1] See Chapter XV, pp. 413–415, for an account of "internal relations."

of " thinghood "—is in fact suffused by, and everything suffuses everything else, and the relations of things to other things, to their environment, for instance, to their past, to their future, and to the minds that know them, literally constitute part of the being or essence of the thing. The cosmos, therefore, is a unity ; it is a " patterned process " of events, and the method of abstracting certain aspects of the unity and considering them in and by themselves, which is the method of science, useful no doubt for practical purposes, cannot but give a false picture of the nature of reality, since in the very act of abstracting it falsifies the nature of that which is abstracted. These are the funda- mental presuppositions which constitute the framework within which Whitehead's process of world-building is to take place. What are the leading ideas which inform the process ?

The Mutual " Sensitiveness " of Bodies.

Let us start from the notion of the interdependence of things, a notion which is essential to the general " mix-up-edness " of Whitehead's universe. Whitehead attaches great import- ance to a passage from the philosopher, Sir Francis Bacon,[1] which he quotes on more than one occasion. The passage begins as follows :

" It is certain that all bodies whatsoever, though they have no sense, yet they have perception : for when one body is applied to another, there is a kind of election to embrace that which is agreeable, and to exclude or expel that which is ingrate ; and whether the body be alterant or altered, evermore a perception precedeth operation ; for else all bodies would be alike one to another. And sometimes this perception, in some kind of bodies, is far more subtile than sense ; so that sense is but a dull thing in comparison of it : we see a weatherglass will find the least difference of the weather in heat or cold, when we find it not. And this perception is sometimes at a distance, as well as upon the touch ; as when the loadstone draweth iron ; or flame naphtha of Babylon, a great distance off. It is therefore a

[1] 1561-1626.

subject of a very noble enquiry, to enquire of the more subtle perceptions ; for it is another key to open nature, as well as the sense ; and sometimes better."

Whitehead particularly stresses the conception of bodies " perceiving " or " taking account of " each other. The significance of this lies, he points out, in the suggestion it conveys that everything in the universe is sensitive to the presence of everything else. But the passage, in his view, errs in further suggesting that there is a distinction between " perception " or " taking account of " on the one hand and " sense " or " cognitive experience " on the other. This distinction drives a wedge between matter and the way in which it experiences things, and mind and the way in which it experiences things. It leads, therefore, to the bifurcation between mind and matter against which we have already been warned, and the arbitrary insertion of minds into a physical universe which is complete without them.

Feeling as the Fundamental Nature of the Process which is Reality.

Whitehead regards the mode of experience proper to a mind as fundamental to and therefore present in all experience, provided that we conceive of this mode of experience in terms of what we know as feeling rather than as intellectual thinking. The insistence on feeling is important. The highly developed consciousness which characterises our own minds is, Whitehead holds, a comparatively rare and very late stage of a far more elementary but infinitely pervasive form of experience. The original nature of a mind, its native character, he seems to suggest, is to be unconscious. The statement that the fundamental process which is the universe is, or is characterised by, the mode of experience proper to a mind is, therefore, misleading, if by " mind " is meant a mind like our minds. It is, rather, an unconscious mind that Whitehead is asking us to envisage, and the mode of experience proper to an unconscious mind is, presumably, feeling. The concept of " feeling " acts as a bridge to link the modes of reaction of the so-called animate and those of the so-called inanimate world. When Whitehead says that everything in the universe takes note of everything else, he is prepared to add that " the taking note of " is a feeling of or for the presence of everything else. " The key notion," he says, " from which such construction " [i.e. of the universe] " should start, is that the energetic activity considered in physics is the emotional intensity entertained in life." Whitehead is, I am afraid, more than usually obscure on this point. There seems, however, little doubt that, in the words of Miss Emmet, to whose interpretation of Whitehead's philosophy I am much indebted,[1] Whitehead envisages the " organic connections between things in terms of something like feeling." There is a celebrated passage in Whitehead's most elaborate work, *Process and Reality*, which seeks to show how the forms of energy postulated by physical science, wavelengths and vibrations and atomic particles, are merely scientific abstractions from what in ourselves we know as types of emotion. Thus the fundamental activity of process, which Whitehead believes to be the reality of the universe, may be most adequately described as " pure feeling," while a thing is, to quote Miss Emmet, " simply the becoming or growth of a new way of feeling the rest of the world."

The Flux and the Eternal Objects. Can we further differentiate and describe this fundamental process of feeling ? In *Science and the Modern World*, Whitehead makes an important distinction between the spatio-temporal flux of events and what he calls "eternal objects," a distinction which is strongly reminiscent of Plato's distinction between the world of becoming and the Forms. In terms of this distinction, the process of the world is conceived as a flux of events which own in their own right only spatio-temporal characteristics, all their other characteristics being due to " the ingression," into the flux of eternal objects. The eternal objects are envisaged by Whitehead as constituting what he calls " the realm of possibility." Like the subsistent

[1] *Whitehead's Philosophy of Organism*, by Dorothy Emmet (Macmillan).

objects described in Chapter XI, they are the realm of everything that can be thought about. But this realm of what can be thought about is not for Whitehead, as it was for Plato, a world of ultimate reality. On the contrary, he insists that, divorced from the flux of events, it is an abstract world. The eternal objects become concrete, and, therefore, real, only in so far as they are " ingredient " in the world of events. When an eternal object ingresses into the spatio-temporal flux, the result is a concrete occurrence. The actual world consists, then, of concrete occurrences. Thus the actual world is a selection ; it is one among an infinite number of worlds all of which are, as it were, latent in the realm of possibility. What makes it actual is the ingression of a certain selection of the eternal objects, the relations between which are a certain selection from all possible relations, into the flux of becoming.

Activity of God.   What determines the selection of the eternal objects which shall ingress into the spatio-temporal flux ? Whitehead's answer is that God determines this selection. God, then, is the principle of actuality who is also the principle of limitation, since it is by virtue of the limitation which He places upon the infinite number of possible worlds, any one of which might have been, that one world and only one, actually is. Whitehead puts this as follows : " We conceive actuality as in essential relation to an unfathomable possibility. Eternal objects inform actual occasions with hierarchic patterns, included and excluded in every variety of discrimination. Another view of the same truth is that every actual occasion is a limitation imposed on possibility, and that by virtue of this limitation the particular value of that shaped togetherness of things emerges." He then proceeds to show that the principle of limitation must itself stand outside the world that results from its application. It cannot, then, be located within the flux of process which constitutes the world ; nor can reasons be found for it, since from it all reasons flow. Thus " God is the ultimate limitation, and His existence is the ultimate irrationality. For no reason can be given for just that limitation which it stands in His nature to impose. God is not concrete, but He is the ground for concrete actuality. No reason can be given for the nature of God, because that nature is the ground of rationality." The argument is a difficult one and Whitehead's language is, unfortunately, far from clear. Let me try to summarise what I conceive to be its main stages : (1) The universe cannot be made up of mere possibilities; it must contain an element of actuality. (2) In order that a thing may be actual, there must be some limitation upon possibilities, since, by virtue of becoming *that* thing, a thing excludes all the other infinitely numerous possible things which it might have been and isn't. (3) The principle of limitation which, as it were, carves the actual world out of the realm of infinite possibilities, is God. (4) God is also the " Principle of Concretion," since it is through Him that unrealised possibilities become actual, that is to say, " concrete," those possibilities, namely, which are brought into concretion by the operation of the principle of limitation. (5) The limitation is irrational ; no reason, that is to say, can be given why just these possibilities should have been realised and not those. Therefore, God is the " Ultimate Irrationality."

The theological and religious implications of this doctrine are difficult to determine. One of them would seem to be that, since God's function is to determine the actualisation of one of an infinite number of worlds that might have been, rather than to *create* the world that actually is, He is exonerated from the reproach of being the origin of the world's evil, as well as of its good, and this is, I think, Whitehead's view. The reader is, however, referred to Whitehead's book *Religion in the Making*, a study of which will, I hope, not only confirm the implication I have drawn but reveal others with which I cannot here deal.

Prehension. Hitherto I have spoken, as if the eternal objects were in some sense distinct from the flux of events into which they " ingress " and upon which, as a result of their ingression, they impose characteristics. This conception must now be modified. The universe for Whitehead is a whole, the word " whole " being used with the technical significance which was explained in the course of the exposition of Hegel's philosophy in Chapter XV.[1] This is not to say that Whitehead's universe is a whole of the same kind as Hegel's. Hegel's universe is a completed whole, and, because it is completed, static. Whitehead's is dynamic and creative. It is, in other words, more like a living organism, or rather like a plurality of connected organisms in unison of development, or, still more accurately, like the process which is or contains this plurality, than like a work of art, for a living organism also may be regarded as a whole, in the sense that it is not only more than the sum of its parts but that its parts reciprocally determine one another's natures. But though the " whole " of Hegel's and the " whole " of Whitehead's philosophy are different, Whitehead's universe, no less than Hegel's, so imposes its character upon its parts, that their full nature can only be understood, because their full nature is only realised, in the context of the whole to which they belong. To consider them in isolation from the whole is, as we have seen in connection with Whitehead's criticism of science, to falsify them. The corollary is that the eternal objects which form the world of possibility are not in the last resort separate and distinct from the flux of events, even when they do not happen to be directly informing the flux in the sense of conferring properties upon it, as described above. They still affect it (and it them), even if their influence upon it is negative. In order to explain the significance of the expression " negative influence," it is necessary, first, to say something about Whitehead's doctrine of " prehension." Here, again, reference may appropriately be made to Hegel, for the doctrine of prehension is simply the doctrine of internal relations[2] in a developed form. The doctrine is, indeed, the key to that " mix-up-edness " of Whitehead's universe to which I have already drawn attention. But just as Whitehead's whole is

[1] See Chapter XV, pp. 415–417.   [2] See Chapter XV, pp. 413, 414.

living and creative, whereas Hegel's is static and complete, so his development of the doctrine of internal relations includes an element of activity, an active *taking into relation* instead of a passive *being in relation*, which differentiates it from Hegel's. For this active " taking into relation " Whitehead uses the term " prehension." A prehension is a grasping or taking hold of one thing by another, the word being used by Whitehead to denote what Miss Emmet calls " the grasping by one actual entity of some aspect or part of other actual entities, and appropriating them in the formation of its own nature." An actual entity thus comes to be described by Whitehead as a " prehensive occasion," an expression by which he seeks to bring out the fact that an entity is nothing more nor less than a synthesis of its relations to all the events which it prehends. Now every entity is related to all other entities. It enters, that is to say, into some relation, however remote, with everything else in the universe. It follows that the context of a thing, a context which literally forms part of the thing's being, is the whole world, what Whitehead calls " Nature " being analysable into a network of events, each one of which is conditioned by its relation to all the others. Every event, in fact, only is what it is because the others are what they are. So far little has been said which would differentiate Whitehead's doctrine from the Axiom of Internal Relations described in Chapter XV. Three points of difference may, however, be mentioned.

1. NEGATIVE PREHENSION

The conception of " interrelated prehensiveness " is pushed to its full logical conclusion. Events past as well as present, possible as well as actual, all these have *some* relation to a given event, and are, therefore, prehended in it. But the relation of prehension may be a negative one. This conception of negative prehension is one of the most distinctive features of Whitehead's philosophy. Let us consider the case of a square box. The box is not circular ;

therefore, in terms of Whitehead's formula, the eternal object, which is circularity, is not ingressing into the process of events which is the ultimate reality of the square box. At any rate the ingression is not direct. Nevertheless, the eternal object circularity does own some relation to the square box. It is related to it by the mere fact of its exclusion from it, and, since it is related, it is prehended, the particular kind of prehension involved being described as negative. Now everything, by virtue of the fact that it is *that* thing and not another thing, represents a selection. It represents, indeed it is, a selection, in respect of the attributes which it does have from all the attributes which it might have had, but does not have. Whitehead puts this by saying that it "negatively prehends" all the potential aspects of itself that it might have had, but does not have— that is to say, all the eternal objects whose ingression into the concrete occasion, which is the event, would have bestowed upon it the attributes which it does not in fact possess. Thus, while a positive prehension is a feeling—the significance of this expression will be explained below—an admission by the prehending entity of some element as being relevant to and, therefore, affecting its own nature, a negative prehension is said to "eliminate from feeling." Thus, all prehension involves abstraction, since a thing is, in respect of the attributes which it has, an abstraction from all the attributes which it might have. There are, for Whitehead, various grades of abstraction depending on the degrees of relevance of the relationships which different eternal objects have to a particular thing. At one end of the scale of relevance there is direct ingression, at the other absolute exclusion. But within the grades of position prehension, certain of the prehensions which constitute the being of a thing, may stand out, as it were in high relief, while others may be subordinated to a position of relative unimportance.[1]

---

[1] This conception is reminiscent of St. Thomas Aquinas's postulation of a "substantial form" to constitute the *real being* of a thing. See Chapter XI, p. 308.

2. Prehension as an Active Process

The fundamental stuff of the world, which we have identified with feeling, is a creative and changing process, and prehension is, therefore, conceived in terms of active process. It is described as the " underlying activity of the world." It is this conception which more than any other constitutes Whitehead's world a dynamic world. The prehensive event is, not, for him, a permanent or enduring thing ; it is a temporary selection from the underlying activity of process, which has been congealed into actuality by virtue of the prehensions which it prehends. To quote Whitehead : " Thus, concrete fact is process. Its primary analysis is into underlying activity of prehension, and into realised prehensive events. Each event is an individual matter of fact issuing from an individualisation of the substrate activity."

3. Attack on Dualism

Thirdly, as has already been pointed out, the essential nature of the underlying process of prehension is feeling, or is, at least, analogous to feeling. As we have already seen, the sensitivity in virtue of which one physical entity takes note of the presence of another by reacting to it is, for Whitehead, not fundamentally different from the way in which sentient beings " feel " the presence of one another. No formal reasons are given for this view, which follows more or less inevitably from the refusal to bifurcate the universe by the postulation of the two separate principles, life and matter, a bifurcation which entails the introduction of life into a non-living world and the resultant impossiblity of conceiving the mode of interaction between life and matter. Whitehead regards the dualism of life and matter as the most disastrous of all the bifurcations wherewith science has " divided the seamless coat of the universe." He speaks, for instance, of the vicious divorce between life and matter introduced by Descartes,[1] a divorce which has

[1] See Chapter XVIII, pp. 501–503.

" poisoned all subsequent philosophy." Descartes left a world in which matter was just matter, life just life ; the two obviously interacted, but it was impossible either for Descartes or anybody else to see how on this radically dualistic basis the gulf between them could be bridged.

Whitehead approaches the problem armed with his doctrine of prehension. Life and matter, he insists, are not two distinct things which have somehow to be brought together ; they are two interwoven threads in the pattern of active process which is the universe, threads which, distinguishable by commonsense and scientific thought, are, nevertheless, not separable in fact. Conceiving it to be the primary business of philosophical insight to restore the unity which science has shattered by its incurable departmentalism, Whitehead insists that neither matter nor life can be understood in isolation. They must first be " fused." He puts this as follows : " The doctrine that I am maintaining is that neither physical Nature nor life can be understood unless we fuse them together as essential factors in the composition of 'really real' things whose interconnections and individual characters constitute the universe."

The Universe as a Harmonious Process of Developing Organisms. There is, on this view, no fundamental difference between the study of life and the study of matter. The apparent difference is one of degree only, biology being defined as " the study of the larger organisms, whereas Physics is the study of the smaller organisms." Let us at this point recall two positions which have already been established. First, we have already emphasised the importance which Whitehead attaches to the conception introduced in the quotation from Bacon, that events in the so-called physical world take note of each other. Given that life and matter are not ultimately different, it is inevitable that this " taking note of " should be conceived after the model of our conscious experience, when we take note of those whose presence we "feel." This mode of experience may, then, be supposed to belong to all living things. Secondly, we have seen that Whitehead conceives of the universe not as a collection of individual things existing in separation, but as an active process in which each event appropriates or " prehends " into itself all the other aspects of the universe which are relevant to it. Given again that life and matter are not ultimately different, and the conclusion follows that the process which is the universe may be legitimately regarded as living. The universe is, thus, a living universe. It is living not in the sense of being a single organism which is alive, but living in the sense in which the process of the harmonious development of innumerable mutually prehending organisms may be said to be alive.

We may now proceed to apply this identification with "livingness" of the active process which is the universe to the further elucidation of the term event. An event is, as we have seen, something which, by virtue of its prehensions, is congealed out of the spatio-temporal flux which is the stuff of the universe. We have hitherto spoken of events as if they were neutral, neutral, that is to say, as between mind and matter. But in terms of the identification between living process and the universe just reached, we may now proceed further to specify them as " occasions of experience," these occasions of experience constituting, for Whitehead, the actual stuff of reality. " I hold," says Whitehead, " that these unities of existence, these occasions of experience, are the really real things which in their collective unity compose the evolving universe, ever plunging into the creative advance."

Introduction of Purpose.

One further feature must be introduced to complete the outline sketch of this very difficult philosophy. This is the conception of what Whitehead calls " Subjective Aim." This conception supplies the principle which determines the varying degrees of acceptance with which one entity, or perhaps, as we should now say, one " occasion of experience," will positively prehend others ; it also determines the negative prehensions of the entity. Since an occasion's positive and negative prehensions determine its characteristics, we may say that Subjective Aim is that which determines why an occasion is what it is.

In Chapter VII I drew a distinction between teleology and mechanism[1] and explained the significance of the term " teleological causation." Whitehead adopts Aristotle's conception of the end or telos as exerting a directive or determining influence on growth, but with a characteristic reservation. For Aristotle the end was something given and fixed, standing as it were outside the thing and determining the thing's growth towards it. For Whitehead the end is literally contained in, or, as he would say, immanent in, the thing.[2] It is, as it were, the thing's inner urge to become itself. Initially potential,[3] as the thing develops, it becomes, in Aristotelian language, increasingly actual. Now it is this immanent end which Whitehead calls the thing's " Subjective Aim." The Subjective Aim determines what prehensions a thing will incorporate into itself in the continuous process of its own self-formation. While everything in the universe is to some extent relevant to the realisation of a thing's Subjective Aim, different things will be relevant in different degrees. A thing will, therefore, prehend other things with different degrees of emphasis as the result of the determining influence of its immanent Subjective Aim.

This principle of determination constitutes the essential core of the thing's individuality ; it is the unity of the thing. The question might be raised why a thing or entity is not simply the sum-total, or at any rate the meeting place of all the other entities which it prehends. What, it may be asked, is the essential " it " which gives unity to and determines the pattern of other entities which " it " gathers up into itself ? Whitehead's answer is that this essential " it," which constitutes a thing's unity, is " its " Subjective Aim. It is this which gives definiteness and concreteness to the

[1] See Chapter VII, pp. 185–187.
[2] I use the more familiar word " thing " for the sake of simplicity, but it should be remembered throughout that by " thing " or " entity " Whitehead means an " occasion of experience."
[3] See Chapter VII, pp. 181–182.

entity by reason of the selection which it exercises over the other entities which are prehended into it. It is, therefore, in Whitehead's language, a " Principle of Concrescence," since, by virtue of the discrimination which it exercises over the other entities which constitute the universe, it determines with what degree of relevance each shall be prehended into the unity which is the thing. Thus Whitehead sometimes speaks of an actual occasion as a " concrescence."

It is an essential part of Whitehead's indictment of the scientific picture of the world as an abstraction that, while science gives an account of the entities which, in Whitehead's language, are prehended into the unity of a thing, it leaves out of account the prehending activity which is informed by the thing's Subjective Aim. In an earlier chapter,[1] I cited as an illustration of the abstractive tendencies of science the various analyses which the different sciences might offer of a human being, and pointed out that, however complete they might be made, they would nevertheless fail to include an account of his personality. The illustration is, I venture to think, one which Whitehead might regard as apposite to his own view. A man's personality is, he would say, the unifying activity which prehends the separate departmental aspects of which the different sciences take account, gluing them together, as it were, into a whole and unifying them. To catalogue the aspects as science does, is legitimate, but to omit the principle of which they are the aspects is completely to falsify the thing under consideration. The personality of a human being would, from this point of view, be a special case of what Whitehead calls a thing's Subjective Aim.

Whitehead's way of putting this is that science, which describes the pattern of a thing, omits its " real internal constitution." The real internal constitution of a thing is its Subjective Aim, or, alternatively, its " feeling for " its Subjective Aim. The presence of this feeling can only be perceived by means of a faculty which Whitehead describes in terms strongly reminiscent of Bergson's Intuition. In the

[1] See Chapter IX, pp. 248–249.

final analysis, then, a thing *is* its prehensions, in various degrees of relevance, of the rest of the universe, plus its " real internal constitution " which determines what prehensions it will make.

Comment. The above constitutes a brief exposition of some of the leading ideas of Professor Whitehead's philosophy. It is in no sense an account of the philosophy as a whole. From the more ambitious task of attempting to give to Whitehead's philosophical views an interpretation which purported to achieve the same degree of fullness as that accorded to those of Plato, of Kant or of Hegel, I have refrained for two reasons. In the first place, I am far from having any assurance that I do in fact understand Whitehead. For the reasons given at the beginning of this chapter, Whitehead's philosophy offers difficulties of a quite special kind to the expositor, and it is only the assurance of complete understanding which would give any ground for the hope that these difficulties had been satisfactorily overcome. It may well be doubted whether any contemporary philosopher possesses this assurance. Miss Dorothy Emmet, however, probably understands Whitehead better than most, and for a treatment of his work which is at once understanding and sympathetic, the reader is referred to her book, *Whitehead's Philosophy of Organism*.

In the second place, Whitehead's ideas are so difficult that a fuller exposition would have taken me beyond the limits of intelligibility within which I have endeavoured to keep. I stated in the Introduction that throughout the writing of this book, certain conditions would be kept continuously in mind. Of these, the one most strongly emphasised was that whatever appeared in its pages should be comprehensible to any reader of a normally sound intelligence who possessed no previous acquaintance with philosophy, provided, of course, that he was prepared to bring to his reading the requisite patience and good will. I cannot, I feel, proceed further with Whitehead's philosophy without transgressing this condition. I am, indeed, all too conscious that I may have transgressed it already.

This chapter on Whitehead's philosophy is, I am afraid, the least satisfactory in the book. I cannot avoid the suspicion that I have said either too much or too little, too little for adequate interpretation, too much for adequate comprehension. If the length of the course, the difficulties in the way, and the accident of Whitehead, the stiffest hurdle, being also the last, may be adduced as mitigating circumstances, I hope the reader will give me what benefit of them he can.

———

WHITEHEAD, A. N.   The Concept of Nature.
          ,,   Science and the Modern World.
          ,,   Process and Reality.
          ,,   Nature and Life.
          ,,   Adventures of Ideas.

Process and Reality is a most difficult work, and should not be attempted until the others have been read. *Adventures of Ideas* contains illuminating applications of Whitehead's general philosophy in non-philosophical spheres. Dorothy Emmet's *Whitehead's Philosophy of Organism* is a sympathetic interpretation of Whitehead's philosophy.

GENERAL BIBLIOGRAPHY

A LIST OF BOOKS relating to the topics discussed in each chapter is appended at the end of the chapter. For general reading the following are recommended :

Introductory :
RUSSELL, BERTRAND   The Problems of Philosophy.

Histories :
WINDELBAND, W.   History of Philosophy.
BURNET, JOHN   Greek Philosophy.
HOFFDING, H.   History of Modern Philosophy (2 vols.).
ADAMSON, R.   Development of Modern Philosophy (2 vols.).

Expository :
CALKINS, M. W.   The Persistent Problems of Philosophy.
    A scholarly summary of what the philosophers actually said.

INDEX